ELECTRONIC COMMERCE AND INTERNATIONAL PRIVATE LAW

Markets and the Law

Series Editor:
Geraint Howells, Lancaster University, UK

Markets and the Law is concerned with the way the law interacts with the market through regulation, self-regulation and the impact of private law regimes. It looks at the impact of regional and international organizations (e.g. EC and WTO) and many of the works adopt a comparative approach and/or appeal to an international audience. Examples of subjects covered include trade laws, intellectual property, sales law, insurance, consumer law, banking, financial markets, labour law, environmental law and social regulation affecting the market as well as competition law. The series includes texts covering a broad area, monographs on focused issues, and collections of essays dealing with particular themes.

Other titles in the series

Global Perspectives on E-Commerce Taxation Law
Subhajit Basu
ISBN 978 0 7546 4731 7

The Yearbook of Consumer Law 2008
Edited by Christian Twigg-Flesner, Deborah Parry,
Geraint Howells, and Annette Nordhausen
ISBN 978 0 7546 7152 7

International Insolvency Law
Themes and Perspectives
Edited by Paul J. Omar
ISBN 978 0 7546 2427 1

For more information on this series, visit www.ashgate.com

Electronic Commerce and International Private Law

A Study of Electronic Consumer Contracts

LORNA E. GILLIES
University of Leicester, UK

ASHGATE

Published by
Ashgate Publishing Limited
Gower House
Croft Road
Aldershot
Hampshire GU11 3HR
England

Ashgate Publishing Company
Suite 420
101 Cherry Street
Burlington, VT 05401-4405
USA

www.ashgate.com

British Library Cataloguing in Publication Data
Gillies, Lorna E.
Electronic commerce and international private law : a study of electronic consumer contracts. - (Markets and the law)
1. Electronic contracts 2. Contracts (International law)
3. Electronic commerce - Law and legislation
I. Title
346'.02'0285

Library of Congress Cataloging-in-Publication Data
Gillies, Lorna E.
Electronic commerce and international private law : a study of electronic consumer contracts / by Lorna E. Gillies.
p. cm.
Includes index.
ISBN 978-0-7546-4855-0
1. Electronic contracts. 2. Consumer protection--Law and legislation. 3. Electronic commerce--Law and legislation. 4. Conflict of laws--Contracts. I. Title.

K845.F6G55 2008
343.07'1--dc22

2008015378

ISBN 978-0-7546-4855-0

Mixed Sources
Product group from well-managed forests and other controlled sources
www.fsc.org Cert no. SGS-COC-2482
© 1996 Forest Stewardship Council
FSC

Printed and bound in Great Britain by
TJ International Ltd, Padstow, Cornwall

Contents

Table of Cases

United Kingdom

Bank of Scotland v Seitz 1990 SLT 584
BJ Mann (Advertising) Ltd v Ace Welding & Fabrications Ltd 1994 SCLR 763
Dallas & Co v McArdle 1949 SLT 349
Harada Ltd (t/a Chequepoint UK Ltd) v Turner, EAT, 2 November 1999 [2000] I.L.Pr. 574 (Westlaw, 1999 WL 1019545)
Latchin (t/a Dinkha Latchin Associates) v General Mediterranean Holdings SA [2002] C.L.C. 330 (Westlaw 2001 WL 1612708)
Owners of Cargo Lately Laden on Board the Rewia v Caribbean Liners (Caribtainer) Ltd (The Rewia) Also known as: Owners of the Cargo Lately Laden on Board the Rewia v Caribbean Liners (Caribtainer) Ltd The Rewia [1991] 1 Lloyd's Rep. 69
Picardi v Mr. and Mrs. Cuniberti, 19 December 2002 (Westlaw 2002 WL 31947416)
Prostar Management Ltd v Twaddle 2003 S.L.T. (Sh Ct) 11
A. Rayner v R. Davies [2003] 1 All ER (Comm) 394 (CA)
Russell McCarthy v Abowall (Trading) Ltd 1992 SLT (Sh Ct) 65
Semple Fraser WS v Ian Quayle 2002 SLT (Sh Ct) 33
Standard Bank London Ltd v Dimitrios and Styliani Apostolakis (No 1) [2000] IL Pr 766
Standard Bank v Apostolakis (No.2) [2001] Lloyd's Law Reports 240

European Court of Justice

Francesco Benincasa v Dentalkit Srl [1997] ECR I-3767
(150/77) *Bertrand v Ott* [1978] ECR 1431
(C-318/93) *Brenner and Peter Noller v Dean Witter Reynolds* [1994] ECR I-4275
(C-541/99) *Cape SNC v Idealservice Srl* [2001] ECR I-9049
22/70 *Commission v Council (ERTA)* [1971] ECR 263
C-96/00 *R. Gabriel v Schlanck & Schick GmbH* [2002] ECR I-6367
Peter Klomps v Karl Michel [1981] ECR 1593
LTU Lufttransportunternehmen GmbH & Co KG v Eurocontrol (29/76) [1976] ECR 1541
C-99/96 *Hans-Hermann Mietz v Intership Yachting Sneek BV* [1999] ECR I-2277

Pronuptia 161/84 [1986] ECR 353
Oceano Grupo Editorial SA v Quintero and Others [2000] ECR I-4941
R v Re Jurisdiction in A Consumer Contract [2002] I.L.Pr. 14
C-89/91 *Shearson Lehman Hutton v TVB* [1993] ECR I-139
Tessilli v Dunlop AG [1976] E.C.R. 1473

United States

Accuweather Inc. v Total Weather Inc. M.D Pa. No.4:DV-02-0006 2 October 2002
Advanced Software Inc. v Datapharm Inc. C.D Cal. No. CV 98-5943 DDP 3 March 1998
Agar v Multi-Fluid Inc., DC Texas Civil Action No. 95-5105
Allen v James 381 F.Supp.2d 495 (E.D.Va., 29 July 2005)(NO. 2:05CV297)
ALS Scan Inc. v Digital Service Consultants Inc, 293 F.3d 707 (4th Circuit 2002)
Amazon.com v Webovation, W.D.Wash., C00-1173C 2 November 2000
Amberson Holdings LLC v Westside Story Newspaper, D.N.J, Civil Action No.00-1108 (NHP), 22 August 2000
America Online Inc. v Huang, E.D. Va 00-290-A 13 July 2000
America Online Inc. v Superior Court [Mendoza] No A 092813 Cal 1st Appeal District Division 2 21 June 2001
American Eyewear Inc. v Peepers, CV-1657-D 16 May 2000
American Homecare Federation Inc v Paragon Scientific Corporation et al Case No CV-893 (WWE) 1998 US Dist Lexis 17962 (D.Conn 26 October 1998)
American Hondo Motor Co Inc. v Rinkied Inc., C.D.Cal., CV 98-7315 DDP (RZx) 3 March 1999
American Information Corporation v American Informetrics Inc., No. CIV JFM-00-3288, 139 F. Supp. 2d 696, 12 April 2001
American Network Inc. v Access America / Connect Atlanta Inc., DC SNY 96 Civ 6823 13 August 1997
Asahi Metal Industry Co. v Superior Court, 480 US 102, 109, 107 S.Ct. 1026, 1033 94 L.Ed.2d 92 (1987)
Atlantech Distribution Inc. v Credit General Ins. Co., 30 F.Supp 2d 534 D.Md., 10 November 2003
Audi AG v Izumi, E.D Mich No.01-CV-74520-DT, 23 May 2002
Audi AG and Volkswagen of America, Inc. v D'Amato 341 F.Supp.2d 734, E.D.Mich., 19 October 2004 at p.744.
Bancroft & Masters Inc. v Augusta National Inc., No.99-15099 223 F.3d 1082
Barrett v Catacombs Press E.D Pa. Civ. No. 99-736 12 April 1999
Bates v Starnes No. Civ.JFM-04-1956. 2005 WL 705345 (D.Md.) 24 March 2005
Bensusan Restaurant Corp. v King, 937 F. Supp 295 (S.D.N.Y 1996)

Beyond Systems, Inc. v Realtime Gaming Holding Co., LLC, 388 Md. 1, 878, A.2d 567 (Md., 22 June 2005)(NO. 119 SEPT.TERM 2004)

Blumenthal v Drudge 992 F. Supp. 44 (D.D.C. 1998)

Blackburn v Walker Oriental Rug Galleries ED. Pa. No.97 – CV – 5704 7 April 1998

Bochan v LaFontaine et al No.98-CV-1749 (ED. Va 26 May 1999)

Bremen v Zapata Off-Shore Co., 407 US 1, 12, 92 s.Ct., 1907, 1914, 32 L.Ed.2d. 513 (1972)

Bridgeport Music, Inc. v Still N The Water Publ'g 327 F.3d 472, 483 (6th Cir.2003) (per curiam).

Bunn-O-Matic Corp. v Bunn Coffee Serv., CD Ill. No.97-3259 1 April 1998

Burger King Corp. v Rudewicz 471 US 462, 105 S.Ct. 2174, L.Ed.2d.528 (1985).

Cable News Network v Go SMS.com Inc., SDNY No. 00 CIV 4812 (LMM) 6 November 2000.

Calder v Jones, 465 US 783, 788, 104, S.Ct. 1482, 1486, 79 L.Ed.2d. 804 (1984)

Carefirst of Maryland Inc. d/b/a Carefirst Blue Cross/Blue Shield v Carefirst Pregnancy Centers Inc., d/b/a Carefirst and Netimpact Inc. (CA-01-1578-CCB) 2 July 2003

Carnival Cruise Lines, Inc. v Shute, 499 US 585, 111 S.Ct. 1522, 113 L.Ed. 622 (1991)

Carrott Bunch Co, d/b/a Carrott Ink Cartridges v Computer Friends Inc. d/b/a Printer Ink Cartridges Inc., N.D Tex. No. 3:01-CV-1229-R, 14 August 2002

CFOS 2 GO Inc v CFO 2 GO Inc., No C97-4676, 1998 US Dist Lexis 8886 (ND Cal 5 June 1998).

Christian Science Board 259 F3d 209 (4th Cir.2001)

City of New York v Cyco.Net, Inc., Slip Copy, 2005 WL 174482, RICO Bus.Disp. Guide 10,824, S.D.N.Y., 27 January 2005

Clipp Designs v Tag Bags 996 F. Supp. 766 (N.D. Ill. 1998).

Coastal Video Communications v Staywell Corp., 1999 U.S. Dist. LEXIS 11827 (E.D. Va. 1999)

Compuserve v Paterson 89f. 3D 1257 (6th Circuit 1996)

Computeruser.com Inc. v Technology Publications LLC, D.Minn., Civil File No. 02-832 (MJD/JGL) 20 July 2002

Conseco Inc. v Hickerson 698 N.E.2d 816 (Ct. App. Ind., 1998)

CoolSavings.com Inc. v IQ Commerce Corp., SD Ill No.98 7750 10 June 1999.

Core Vent Corp v Nobel Industries AB 11 F.3d 1482, 1486 (9th Cir.1993)

Cybersell v Cybersell, F.3d (1997 WL 739021 9th Cir.) and 130f.3d 414 (9th Cir. 1997)

Dagesse v Plant Hotel NV DNH No. CV-98-713-B 5 January 2000

Decker v Circus Circus Hotel D NJ Civ 97-1848 (WHW) 12 May 1999

Desktop Technologies Inc. v Colorworks Reproduction and Design Inc. Civ Act No 98-5029, 1999 US Dist Lexis 1934 (D.Pa. February 24, 1999) 1999 WL 98572 (ED Pa.)

Digital Control v Boretronics Inc., WD Wash No.C01-0074L 6 September 2001

Digital Equipment Corporation v Alta Vista Technology Inc., Civil Action No.96-12192NG 13 March 1997

Drucker Cornell v Assicurazioni General SpA Consolidates SDNY No.98–CIV 9186 16 March 2000

Robert and Lauren Efford t/a Goldhope Farm v The Jockey Club, No.1621 EDA 2001 Superior Court of Pennsylvania, http://www.courts.state.pa.us/opPosting/Superior/OUT/s04004_02.pdf (obtained 22 April 2002)

Electronic Broking Services Ltd v E-Business Solutions & Services, 285 F. Supp.2d 686 U.S.P.Q.2d 1531, D.Md, 30 September 2003 (Westlaw).

Enterprise Rent-A-Car v Stowell Ed.Mo. No.4:00CV0555 TCM 5 April 2001

Ecotecture Inc. v Wenz, F Supp 2d. 2000 W760961 D.Me 16 May 2000.

Envirotech Pumpsystems Inc. v Sterling Fund Systems AG (No. 2:99CV814K 2000 US Dist. LEXIS 16942 (D. Utah 16 November 2000))

*ESAB Group Inc. v Centricut Inc. (*4th Circuit) 126 F.3d 6 17, C.A 4 (SC), 1997, 17 October 1997

Euromarket Designs Inc. v Crate & Barrel Ltd., 96 F. Supp. 2d 824, 837 (N.D.Ill 2000)

Fix My P.C. LLC d/b/a/ Fixx My PC v N.F.N. Associates, Inc. d/b/a Pure Logic Computers, 48 F.Supp. 2d 640 (N.D. Tex. 1999)

Gateway Gaming, L.L.C. v Custom Game Design, Inc. Slip Copy, 2006 WL 2781043 D.S.C. 2006., 25 September 2006

Gator com Corp., v L.L. Bean Inc., No. 02-15035 2001 WL 1528393 2 September 2003

Gorman d/b/a Cashbackrealty.com v Ameritrade Holding Corp., D.C. Cir. No. 01–7085 14 June 2002

Graduate Management Admission Council v Raju, E.D.Va No. 02-581-A 23 January 2003

John G. Green et al v William Manson & Co et al (1998 US Dist Lexis 331, 996 f. Supp.394 (D.N.J 5 March 1998)

GTE New Media Servs., Inc. v Bell South Corp., 199 F.3d 1343 (D.D.C. 2000).

Hall v LaRonde, Calif Ct App, 2nd District, Civil No. B107423, 7 August 1997

Hanson v Denckla, 357 US 235 (1958)

Hasbro, Inc. v Clue Computing, Inc., 994 F. Supp. 34 (D. Mass. 1997)

Harcourt v Hogue, Florida District 5th Court of Appeal 5D 01-683 7 June 2002

Hartoy Inc. v Thompson d/b/a Truckin' Little Co., S.D. Fla No.02-80454-CIV-Middlebrooks 29 January 2003

Hearst Corporation v Goldberger, 96 Civ. 3620(PKL) (AJP), 1997 WL 97097 S.D.N.Y 26 February 1997

Heathgrades.com v Northwest Healthcare Alliance US 02-1250

Helicopteros Nationales de Colombia, S.A v Hall 466 US 408, 414–416, 104 S.Ct 1868, 1872–73, 80 L.Ed.2d 404 (1984)

Heroes, Inc. v Heroes Foundation, 958 F. Supp. 1 (D.D.C. 1996)

Heroes v Heroes Foundation 958 F. Supp. 1

Hurley v Cancun Playa E.D. Pa 99–574 31 August 1999

Hy Cite Corp. v Badbusinessbureau.Com, LLC F Supp 2d. 2004 WL 42641 W.D. Wis., 8 January 2004 (Westlaw)
IAcess Inc v Webcard Technologies Inc, 182 F. Supp.2d 1183, 24 January 2002
Inset System, Inc. v Instruction Set 937 F.Supp. 161 164 (D.Conn. 1996)
Intercon v Bell Atlantic Internet Solutions Inc., 205 F.2d 1415, 1417 (10th Cir.1998)
International Shoe v State of Washington, 326 US 310, 316, 66, S.Ct. 154, 158, 90, L.Ed. 95 (1945)
International Star Registry v Bowman-Haight Ventures, Inc., 1999 U.S. Dist. LEXIS 7009 (N.D. Ill. 1999)
Jacobson v Mailboxes, Etc USA., Inc., 419 Mass. 572 (1995)
Jennings v AC Hydraulic No. 03-2157 383 F.3d 546, Prod.Liab.Rep. (CCH) P 17,084 2 September 2004
Jewish Defense Org., v Superior Court of Los Angeles Cal Ct App B129319 8 June 1999, California Court of Appeal, Second District
Johnson v King Media Inc., E.D. Pa. Civil Action No.01-2311, 24 June 2002
Lofton v Turbine Design, F. Supp.2d (2000 WL 6364711 N.D., Miss., 2000)
Mar-Eco, Inc. v T&R and Sons Towing and Recovery Inc., A.2d 2003 WL 22718179, 2003 PA Super 444, Pa. Super, 19 November 2003 (Westlaw)
Maritz, Inc v Cybergold, Inc., 947 F. Supp. 1328 (E.D.Mo.1996)
Mashantucket Pequot Tribe v Redican, 309 F.Supp.2d 309, 70 U.S.P.Q.2d 1549, D.Conn., 18 March 2004
Med-Tec Iowa Inc. v Computerized Imaging Reference Systems Inc. (S.D.Iowa No.4-02-CV-90338 3 October 2002)
Metcalf v Lawson, 148 N.H. 35, 802 A.2d 1221 (25 June 2002).
Mieczkowski v Masco Corp., DC ETexas No.5:96cv286 18 March 1998
Millenium Enterprises Inc d/b/a Music Millenium et al v Millenium Music et al Civ No. 98-1058-AA (D.Or. Jan –1999) 33 F.Supp.2d. 907 (D.Or., 1999)
Mink v AAAA Development et al 190 F.3d 333 (5th Cir.1999)
Minnesota v Granite Gate Resorts Inc State of Minn Dist Crt., Ramsey County Court File No. c6-95-7227, 568 N.W.2d 715 (Dec.11 1996) aff'd No.C6-97-89, 576 N.W 2d 747 (Minn Ct App. 5 September 1997)
Molnlycke Healthcare AB v Dumex Medical Surgical Procedures No. CIV. A. 99-1725 64 F.Supp.2d 448 7 September 1999
Multi Tech Systems Inc. v Net 2 Phone Inc., Case 00-346 ADM/RLE
McDonagh v Fallon McElligott Inc 1996 US Dist Lexis 15139 (S.D. Cal 5 August 1996)
McGhee v International Life Ins. Co., 355 US 220, 23, 78 S.Ct. 199, 291, 2 L.Ed. 2d. 223 (1957)
Nam Tai Electronic Inc. v Titzer California Court of Appeal 2d Dist. No. B149382 26 November 2001
Newspaper Association of America Inc., v Mancusi, E.D.Va No. 01-1635-A 8 May 2002
Neogen Corp. v Neo Gen Screening No.00–217

No Mayo--San Francisco v Memminger, 1998 U.S. Dist. LEXIS 13154 (N.D. Cal. 1998)
Northwest Healthcare Alliance v Healthgrades.com 2002 WL 31246123 (9th Circuit Washington)
Nowak v Tak How Investments Ltd., 94F.3d708712 (1st Circuit)
Online Partners.com Inc. v Atlanticnet Media Corp., 2000 U.S. Dist. LEXIS 783 (N.D. Cal. 2000)
Panavision Intl L P v Dennis Toeppen, 938 F. Supp. 616 (C.D. Cal., 1996), aff'd 141 F.3d 1316 (9th Cir. 1998)
People Solutions Inc. v People Solutions Inc., No.Civ.A. 399-CV-2339-L. 2000 WL 1030619 (N.D.Tex)
Pennoyer v Neff, 95 US 714, 24 L.Ed. 565, 95 Otto 714 (1878) Peridyne Technology Solutions LLC v Matheson Fast Freight Inc., N.D Ga., Civ A.1:00CV1587VCAP 16 October 2000
Quokka Sports v Cup Int'l. Ltd., 1999 U.S. Dist. LEXIS 21000 (N.D. Cal. 1999)
Rainy Day Books v Rainy Day Books and Café LLC, 186 F. Supp. 2d. 1158 (D.Kan.2002)
Rannoch, Inc. v Rannoch Corp., 52 F. Supp. 2d 681 (E.D. Va. 1999)
Reliance Steel Prod. Co., v Watson, Ess, Marshall and Engass, 657 F.2d 587, 589 (3rd Cir.1982)
Response Reward Systems LC v Meijer Inc., MD. Fla Case 8:01-CV-2271-T-17 EAJ 31 January 2002
Resuscitation Technologies Inc v Continental Health Care Corp IP 96-1457 –C-M/S, 1997 US Dist Lexis 3523 (So. Dist. Indiana March 24, 1997) 1997 WL 148567 (s.d Ind 24 March 1997)
Revell v Lidov et al 317 F.3d 467, 463 (5th Cir.2000)
Robbins v Yutopian Enterprises Inc., D.Md., Civil No. CCB-01-3096 15 May 2002
Roche v Worldwide Media, Roche v Worldwide Media ED Va. No.99-1534-A 27 March 2000
Rubbercraft Corp. of California v Rubbercraft Inc., CV97-4070-WDK 17 December 1997
Ruston Gas Turbines Inc. v Donaldson Company Inc., 9 F.3d 415, 418 (5th Cir.1993)
Sage Realty Corp. v Barhart Interests Ltd., SDNY No.02 Civ.0725 (LAK) 18 April 2002
School Stuff Inc. v School Stuff Inc., N.D.Ill No.00 C 5593 Ct
Schweers v Hovaton, D NM No. Civ 99-162 MV/DJS 31 August 1997
SF Hotel Co. L.P. v Energy Investments, Inc., 985 F. Supp. 1032 (D.Kan. 1997)
Snyder v Dolphin Encounters Ltd., E.D. Pa. No.02-CV-1264 10 December 2002
Soma Medical International v Standard Chartered Bank, 196 F.3d 1292, 1295 (10th Cir.1999)
Standard Knitting Ltd v Outside Design Inc., unreported, E.D Pa., 2000, 23 June 2000

Starmedia Network Inc. v Star Media Inc., SDNY case No.00 CIV 4647 23 April 2001
State by Humprey v Granite Gate Resorts N.W.2d, 1997 WL 557670 (Ct. App., Minn.) and 568 N.W. 2d 715 (Ct App., Minn., 1997)
Stephen C. Edberg et al v Neogen Corporation 17 F.Supp.2d 104 (D.Conn. 1998)
Stomp Inc. v NeatO LLC, 61 F.Supp.2d 1074, 1078, n.7 (C.D.Cal.1999)
Sulton v Ashley SDNY No. 01 Civ 8179 (JSM) 22 January 2002
Swarovski Optik North America Ltd v Euro Optics Inc., 2003 WL 22014581, D.R.W., 25 August 2003 (Westlaw)
Systems Designs Inc. v New Customware Co., No.2-01-CV-00770PGC, 5 March 2003
Telco Communications v An-Apple-A-Day, 977 F. Supp. 404 (E.D.Va. 1997)
Telebyte Inc., v Kendaco Inc. d/b/a Telebyte Northwest and Telebyte NW, EDNY 99-CV-3866 (ADS) 24 July 2000
The Lyme Timber Co. v DSF Investors LLC, 150 N.H. 557, 842 A.2d 115, N.H., 17 February 2004
Thomas Publishing Co. v Industrial Quick Search Inc., SDNY No.02-3307(RO) 18 December 2002
Toys "R" Us Inc et al v Step Two SA et al SA 3rd Cir. No. 01-3390 27 January 2003
Transcraft Corp. v Doonan Trailer Corp., DC Nill No 97C 4943 12 November 1997
Ex P. Troncalli Chrysler Plymouth Dodge, Inc In re David J. Case v Alexander Dodge Chrysler Plymouth, Inc., 876 So.2d 459, Ala., 12 September 2003
Ty Inc., Ty Inc. v Sullivan d/b/a Ebeanies Online ND Ill No 01 1604 12 March 2002
Uncle Sams Safari Outfitters Inc v Uncle Sams Army Navy Outfitters Manhattan Inc. E.D.Mo CV 1633 DDN 13 April 2000
United Cutlery Corp. v NFZ Inc., 2003 WL 22851946, 2003 Copr. L. Dec P. 28,709, D.,Md., 1 December 2003 (Westlaw)
Verizon Online Services Inc. v Ralsky (Ed. Va Civil Action No. 07-432 –A 7 June 2002
V'soske Inc. v Vsoske.com SDNY No.00 CIV 6099 (DC) 23 May 2001
Weber v Jolly Hotels 977 F.Supp 327, 330 (D.N.J. 1997)
Westcode Inc v RBE Electronics Inc., 2000 WL 124566 (E.D.Pa. 1 February 2000)
Wildfire Communication Inc. v Grapevine Inc., D.Mass No. 00-CV-12004 28 October 2001
Williams v Reynolds, Slip Copy, 2006 WL 3007347 (W.D.Va., 20 October 2006)(NO. 4:06CV00020)
Winfield Collection v McCauley, 105 F. Supp 2d 746, 750 (E.D.Mich., 2000)
Wise, et al., v Lindamood, et al., 89 F. Supp. 2d. 1187 (D. Col. 1999)
World Wide Volkswagen v Woodson, 444 US 286, 100 S.Ct. 559 (1980)

Yahoo! Inc v La Ligue contre le racisme et l'antisemitisme Case No.C-00-21275 US N.D Cal 7 November 2001
Young v New Haven Advocate US No 02-1394
Zippo Manufacturing v Zippo Dot Com, Inc. 952 F.Supp, 1119

Table of Statutes

United Kingdom

Acts

Civil Jurisdiction and Judgments Act 1982
Civil Jurisdiction and Judgments Order 2001/3929
Civil Procedure Rules 1998/3132
Consumer Protection Act 1974
Contract (Applicable Law) Act 1990
Electronic Commerce (EC Directive) Regulations 2002/2013
Sheriff Court (Scotland) Act 1907
Unfair Contract Terms Act 1977
Unfair Terms in Consumer Contract Regulations 1999/2083

European Union

Article 6, 'European Parliament legislative resolution of 29 November 2007 on the proposal for a regulation of the European Parliament and of the Council on the law applicable to contractual obligations' (Rome I) (COM(2005) 0650 – C6-0441/2005 – 2005/0261(COD)
'Commission adopts draft Regulation on Jurisdiction, Recognition and Enforcement of Judgments in Civil and Commercial Matters,' Document IP/99/510, 14/07/1999
'Committee on Legal Affairs and the Internal Market, Preliminary Draft Report for a Council Regulation' (EC) (COM (1999) 348 final – C5-0619/1999 – 99/0154 (CNS)
'Committee of the Regions The Need for Strengthened International Coordination,' COM (98) 50
'Competence Judiciaire, Reconnaissance et Execution des Decisions Civiles et Commerciales – Version Provisoire Communication a la Presse 2314ème session du Conseil – Justice, Affaires Interieures et Protection Civile', Version Provisoire - Brussels, 30 November / 1 December 2000. Article 76, 2001 OJ L12/1
Convention on Jurisdiction and Recognition and Enforcement of Judgments in Civil and Commercial Matters, 1978 OJ L304

Convention on the Law Applicable to Contractual Obligations (80/934/EEC), 1980 OJ L266

'Council Decision on the signing, on behalf of the Community, of the Convention on jurisdiction and the recognition and enforcement of judgments in civil and commercial matters,' Brussels, 10 September 2007, 12247/07 JUSTCIV 218

Council of the European Union, 'Conclusions concerning work in The Hague, with a view to preparing a draft Convention on international Jurisdiction and the Effects of Foreign judgments in civil and commercial matters,' 25-30 October 1999, JUSTCIV 139 11751/99, 11 October 1999

Council Regulation (EC) No 44/2001 of 22 December 2000 on jurisdiction and the recognition and enforcement of judgments in civil and commercial matters,' 2001 OJ L12/1

'Council Report on the Convention on the law applicable to contractual obligations, by Professors Mario Giuliano and Paul Lagarde,' 1980 OJ C282

Directive 93/13/EC on Unfair Terms in Consumer Contracts, 1993 OJ L95/29

Directive 97/7/EC of the European Parliament and of the Council of 20 May 1997 on the Protection of Consumers in respect of Distance Contracts (Directive on Distance Selling), 1997 OJ L0007

Directive 98/34/EC (as amended by Directive 98/48EC) laying down a procedure for the provision of information in the field of technical standards and regulations

Directive 2000/31/EC on certain legal aspects of information society services, in particular electronic commerce, in the Internal Market' (Directive on electronic commerce), 2000 OJ L178

Directive concerning unfair business-to-consumer commercial practices in the internal market (Unfair Commercial Practices Directive) COM(2003) 17/06/2003, 2005 OJ L149/22

Directive on Certain Aspects of Mediation in Civil and Commercial Matters, COM 2004/0718 final, 2004/0251 (COD)

Draft Directive 2002/65/EC of the European Parliament and of the Council concerning the Distance Marketing of Consumer Financial Services and Amending Council Directives 90/619/EEC, 97/7/EEC and 98/27/EEC, 23 September 2002

'Draft Hague Convention on Jurisdiction and the recognition and enforcement of foreign judgments,' JUSTCIV 172, 13225/99, 22nd November 1999

Economic and Social Committee, 'Opinion of the European Economic and Social Committee on the Proposal for a Regulation of the European Parliament and of the Council on the law applicable to contractual obligations (Rome I),' COM(2005) 650 final – 2005/0261 (COD), 13 September 2006

European Commission, 'Assessment of the Tampere Programme and Future Orientations' (COM (2004) 0401 final), 2 June 2004.

European Commission, 'Communication From the Commission to the European Parliament, The Council, The Economic and Social Committee and The

Committee of the Regions, Consumer Policy Strategy 2002–2006' (Tampere Council), Brussels COM (2002) 208

European Commission, Directorate – General XIII, Telecommunications, Information Market and Exploitation of Research, 'Communication from the Commission to the European Parliament, The Council, The Economic and Social Committee and The Committee of the Regions The Need for Strengthened International Coordination,' COM (98) 50

European Commission, 'eEurope 2005: An information society for all,' 21/22 June 2002, COM(2002) 263, and 'i2010 - A European Information Society for growth and employment,' COM (2005) 229 final

European Commission, 'Green Paper on the conversion of the Rome Convention of 1980 on the law applicable to contractual obligations into a Community instrument and its modernization,' COM(2002) 654 final, 14th January 2003

European Commission, Justice and Home Affairs DG, 'Statement on Articles 15 and 73,' JUSTCIV 1413900 14/12/00

European Commission, "Opinion of the Economic and Social Committee on the Proposal for a Council Regulation (EC) on jurisdiction and enforcement of judgments in civil and commercial matters," (COM (1999) 348 final - 99/0154 - (CNS)) and C117 26 April 2000 006

European Commission, 'Proposal for a Council Regulation (EC) on jurisdiction and the recognition and enforcement of judgments in civil and commercial matters,' COM (1999) 348 FINAL 99/0154(CNS), Brussels 14th July 1999

EU Commission, 'Proposal for a Regulation of the European Parliament and the Council on the law applicable to contractual obligations (Rome 1),' COM (2005) 650 final, 2005/0261 (COD), 15th December 2005, OJ

EU Commission, 'Regulation establishing a European Small Claims Procedure,' COM 2005 87 final, 2005/0220 (COD), 15 March 2005

European Parliament, Legislative Observatory, 'Consumer Disputes: creation of a european extra-judicial network,' INS/2000/040

European Parliament, Legislative Observatory, 'Out-of-court settlement of consumer disputes (recommendation 98/257/EC, Tampere European Council Conclusions),' INI/2000/2209

'Guidelines for Vertical Restraints' (on EC Competition Rules), 2000 C291/1

'Proposal for a Decision establishing a programme of Community action in the field of Health and Consumer Protection 2007-2013' (COM(2005) 115 final 2005/0042 (COD))

Regulation (EC) No 593/2008 of the European Parliament and of the Council of 17 June 2008 on the law applicable to contractual obligations (Rome I) OJ L177 6

'Report by Mr. P. Jenard on the Convention of 27 September 1968 on jurisdiction and the enforcement of judgments in civil and commercial matters, 3 June 1971,' 1979 OJ C59/1

'Report by Professor Dr Peter Schlosser on the Convention of 9 October 1978 on the Association of the Kingdom of Denmark, Ireland and the United Kingdom of Great Britain and Northern Ireland to the Convention on jurisdiction and the enforcement of judgments in civil and commercial matters and to the Protocol on its interpretation by the Court of Justice,' 1979 OJ C59/71

'Second protocol conferring on the Court of Justice powers to interpret the 1980 convention (Consolidated version),' OJ C334, 30.12.2005

United States

Clinton and Gore, *A Framework for Electronic Commerce*, The White House, 1997

Federal Civil Rules of Procedure

Uniform Commercial Code

Uniform Computer Information Transactions Act (UCITA)

Uniform Electronic Transactions Act (UETA)

International

Hague Conference on Private International Law

Hague Conference on Private International Law, Convention on the Recognition and Enforcement of Foreign Judgments in Civil and Commercial Matters 1 February 1971

Hague Conference on Private International Law, Draft Convention on International Jurisdiction and Foreign Judgments in Civil and Commercial Matters, October 1999

Preliminary Document No.7, 'International Jurisdiction and Foreign Judgments in Civil and Commercial Matters,' report drawn up by Catherine Kessedjian, revised translation October 1997

Preliminary Document No.8, 'Synthesis of the Work of the Special Commission of June 1997 on International Jurisdiction and the Effects of Foreign Judgments in Civil and Commercial Matters,' drawn up by Catherine Kessedjian, November 1997

Preliminary Document No.9, 'Synthesis of the Work of the Special Commission of March 1998 on international jurisdiction and the effects of foreign judgments in civil and commercial matters,' drawn up by Catherine Kessedjian, March 1998

Preliminary Document No.11, 'The Future Hague Convention on International Jurisdiction and the Effects of Judgments in Civil and Commercial Matters,' Report of the Special Commission by Peter Nygh and Fausto Pocar, August 2000

Preliminary Document No. 12, 'Electronic Commerce and International Jurisdiction,' summary of discussions prepared by Catherine Kessedjian, Ottawa, 28 February to 1 March 2000, August 2000

Preliminary Document No. 17, Avril Haines, 'The Impact of the Internet on the Judgments Project: Thoughts for the Future,' Hague Conference on Private International Law, February 2002

OECD

'Consumers in the Online Marketplace: The OECD Guidelines Three Years Later,' Report by the Committee on Consumer Policy on the Guidelines for Consumer Protection in the Context of Electronic Commerce,' DSTI/CP(2002)4/FINAL, 3 February 2003

'Ministerial Declaration on Consumer Protection in the Context of Electronic Commerce,' Ottawa 7–9 October 1998, DSTI/CP(98)12/FINAL, 'Consumer Protection in the Electronic Marketplace,' DSTI/CP98(13)/FINAL, 22 December 1998

'Ministerial Declaration on Consumer Protection in the Context of Electronic Commerce,' Ottawa 7-9 October 1998, DSTI/CP(98)12/FINAL

Acknowledgements

I would like to thank my family, my husband Stephen and our daughters Eilidh and Emma, parents Hilda and Ian Calderwood and Una and Andrew Gillies for all their help, support and encouragement in helping me complete this book.

This book largely originates from a thesis awarded by the University of Strathclyde and from various publications. In particular I would like to thank The Clark Foundation for Legal Education and the University of Strathclyde Scholarship Fund which both provided financial support for the period of PhD study and to my supervisor Professor Barry J. Rodger. I would also like to give special thanks to Catherine Colston, Maura McCaw, Liz McCallum, Isobel McGregor, Professor Jenny Hamilton, Professor Ian Lloyd and Dr Rowena Murray.

I would also like to thank The Society of Legal Scholars who provided financial assistance for me to be able to present a paper on revision of the Rome Convention at the Tenth International Consumer Law Conference, Peru in 2005. I would also like to thank the University of Leicester for providing a period of academic study leave and for the friendship and support of my colleagues at the University of Leicester, in particular, Professor Trevor Buck (now at De Montfort University, Leicester), Professor David Bonner, Professor Chris Clarkson, Professor Sarah Dromgoole (now at the University of Nottingham), Professor Cosmo Graham and Professor Robin White. Finally, I would also like to thank Alison Kirk and Carolyn Court, Elaine Couper and Aimée Feenan at Ashgate for their assistance.

Lorna E. Gillies
Leicester
July 2008

For Stephen, Eilidh and Emma

List of Abbreviations

B2B	Business-to-Business
B2C	Business-to-Consumer
CPR	Civil Procedure Rules
ECJ	European Court of Justice
EESC	European Economic and Social Committee
EFTA	European Free Trade Association
EU	European Union
FTC	Federal Trade Commission
ISP	Internet Service Provider
OECD	Organisation for Economic Cooperation and Development
SME	Small-to-Medium Sized Enterprise
UNCITRAL	United Nations Commission on International Trade Law
WWW	World Wide Web

Introduction

International Private Law and the Dematerialisation of Electronic Consumer Contracts

This book is concerned with international private law rules for electronic consumer contracts. Since the advent of commercial activity via the World Wide Web, there has been a need to regulate electronic commercial activities and disputes by implementing model laws, frameworks or conventions on electronic commerce (as exemplified by UNCITRAL, the OECD and the United States) and introducing or amending specific national legislation on particular legal aspects of electronic commerce (as exemplified by the EU Directive on Electronic Commerce). In the context of consumer protection these model laws, frameworks and statutes contain specific rules to regulate commercial activity between businesses and consumers in different jurisdictions in order to provide an extension of consumer protection policy by ensuring that the consumer who takes advantage of contracting with a foreign business via a web site can still rely on the level of protection provided by his own law. The extension of substantive consumer protection to the electronic environment is necessary due to the 'inequality of bargaining power'[1] experienced by consumers when contracting by electronic means with business sellers in foreign jurisdictions. In the context of electronic commerce, consumers experience inequality of bargaining power as a result of the particular risks associated with contracting with foreign sellers, compounded by electronic commerce as follows; the lack of prior contact with the foreign seller, the consumer's reliance on the information contained in the seller's web site regarding the seller's identity, location and information on the goods / services on offer, the inability of the consumer to view or inspect the goods prior to contracting with the seller, the requirement for the consumer to reveal personal information and pay for goods or services prior to receiving them and the potential risk of interception of the consumer's personal (including financial) data by third parties.[2] Examples of the extension of such protection to the consumer who buy goods or services online include the right

1 I. Ramsay (ed), *Consumer Protection, Texts and Materials* (London, 1989), at p.57.

2 Directive 2000/31/EC on certain legal aspects of information society services, in particular electronic commerce, in the Internal Market (Directive on electronic commerce), 2000 OJ L178 (hereafter 'the Electronic Commerce Directive').

to particular information regarding the seller,[3] the goods or services and costs,[4] the right to view standard contractual terms[5] in advance of making payment and in particular cases the right of limited withdrawal.[6] If a consumer subsequently has a dispute with a foreign seller and seeks redress, the need arises for effective juridical protection of the consumer. Aside from any agreement on jurisdiction and applicable law in the parties' contract, the identity of the parties and the place where they are located are the most significant connecting factors in determining which jurisdiction and law applies to the parties' dispute.[7]

The existence, operation and effect of traditional connecting factors to electronic consumer contract disputes raises two important theoretical and practical questions – first, in which jurisdiction should consumers who buy goods online from foreign sellers seek redress and second, what law should the court apply? Since electronic commerce is simply a means of instantaneous communication,[8] the answer to these questions should theoretically be no different than if the consumer used a fax machine or a mail order catalogue to contract with the seller, i.e. the consumer ought to be provided with protection via his own forum and law. However, the challenge posed by electronic commerce is that it dematerialises the parties' location and the place where their contractual activities occur, rendering location and commercial activities difficult to determine in a certain and predictable manner.

When parties in different jurisdictions contract by means of electronic commerce, it is difficult for either party to know the other's identity or location with certainty. As a result, it is correspondingly difficult to determine the most appropriate substantive and juridical protection that ought to be provided to consumers. The combination of the risks consumers experience and the dematerialised nature of electronic commerce have increased the need for effective juridical protection for consumers and the improvement of consumer confidence in the electronic marketplace.

Maximising Consumer Protection via the Consumer's Jurisdiction and Law

The theme of this book is three-fold. The first aspect to this book's theme is that consumers should be provided with the substantive and juridical protection of

3 Ibid.

4 Ibid.

5 Ibid.

6 Ibid.

7 A. Nordhausen, 'Distance Marketing in the European Union,' in L. Edwards (ed), *The New Legal Framework for E-Commerce in Europe* (Oxford, 2005).

8 A.D. Murray, 'Entering Into Contracts Electronically: The Real WWW', in L. Edwards, and C. Waelde (eds), *Law and the Internet A Framework for Electronic Commerce*, 2nd ed (Oxford, 2000).

their own law in a contractual dispute with the seller i.e. international private law rules should provide juridical protection for consumers by ensuring any dispute with a foreign seller can be heard in the consumer's jurisdiction and the law of the consumer's domicile applies, thereby facilitating maximal consumer protection. International private law rules already provide juridical protection for consumers via special rules of jurisdiction, choice of law and the recognition and enforcement of judgments. The aim of international private law is premised on a 'desire to do justice'[9] to the parties involved in a cross-border dispute. This aim is particularly significant with regard to the role of international private law vis-à-vis the legal regulation of cross-border electronic consumer contract disputes. As the author of this book has written elsewhere,

> [W]hen a consumer contract is entered into between parties across borders by electronic means and a dispute arises between the parties, the effective application of certain and predictable jurisdiction and choice of law rules to determine which jurisdiction will hear the dispute and what law will apply is crucial.

Consumers require the same, i.e at least a minimum, level of juridical protection irrespective of the means by which they contract with foreign sellers. Consumers who contract online with foreign sellers must be afforded a maximum level of harmonised consumer protection via both substantive consumer protection law and international private laws, ergo rather than relying on soft law approaches to juridical protection for consumers. Furthermore, consumers require more than a minimum level of substantive protection due to the lack of the identity and location of the parties, the dematerialised nature of electronic commerce and the risks associated with electronic commerce mentioned previously.

The Limitations of Current Connecting Factors for Electronic Consumer Contracts

The second element of this book's theme proposes that a new connecting factor should be used to improve the certainty, fairness and effectiveness of juridical protection for consumers who contract with foreign sellers by electronic means. International private law rules do not currently provide sufficient juridical protection for consumers who contract electronically with foreign sellers. At the heart of jurisdiction and choice of law rules are the limited application (and effect) of current connecting factors. Both jurisdiction and applicable law rules apply restrictively as they do not apply to all consumer contracts. In the case of jurisdiction rules, different rules operate depending on the defendant's domicile (whether situated in a part of the UK, in an EU Member State or a third state) whilst with choice of law rules, certain requirements must be satisfied for the law

9 A.E. Anton, *Private International Law*, 2nd ed (Edinburgh, 1990), at p.1.

of the consumer's domicile to apply. At the time of writing, as far as proposals to replace Article 5 of the Rome Convention were concerned, a partial improvement had been, in the recently approved Regulation, to restrict party autonomy but the connecting factor proposed is still not sufficiently predictable to apply to electronic consumer contracts.

Theoretical Approaches in International Private Law to the Regulation of Electronic Consumer Contracts

It is recognised that different models have been proposed for the reform of international private law rules for commercial contracts conducted by electronic means. With regard to commercial contracts between businesses, Fawcett, Harris and Bridge have proposed that:

> Three models [...] could be applied for the reform and development of the law of jurisdiction in cases of electronic commerce [...] first, apply the normal rules on jurisdiction, leaving it to the courts to develop the law; second, reform the law by modifying the normal rules on jurisdiction; third, reform the law by introducing a special regime of rules of jurisdiction for cases of electronic commerce.[10]

The first and third models are, to a greater extent, inappropriate for electronic consumer contracts. Consumer protection is a specialist area, regulated throughout the EU at Treaty level via general and specific primary and secondary legislation.[11] Indeed, reform of international private law rules for consumer contracts cannot be left solely to the courts. For example, analysis of US case law demonstrates the difficulties in leaving reform and development of jurisdiction rules to the courts. A special or completely separate set of rules are not as inherently necessary since electronic commerce is simply another, more sophisticated and faster means of cross-border communication. The theme of this book alludes that the second 'model' – reform of existing jurisdiction and choice of law rules[12] – is the most appropriate, necessary and effective means of regulating cross-border electronic consumer contract disputes.

The third strand of this book's theme seeks to conclude that existing jurisdiction and choice of law rules for electronic consumer contracts should be amended further to provide a harmonised basis for the consumer to sue in his own jurisdiction and for the law of the consumer's domicile to apply. In particular, the

10 J. Fawcett, J. Harris and M. Bridge, *International Sale of Goods in the Conflict of Laws* (Oxford, 2005) at p.529. Words removed for syntax.

11 <http://ec.europa.eu/consumers/overview/cons_policy/index_en.htm>; G. Howells and S. Wetherill, *Consumer Protection and Law* (Aldershot, 2005).

12 Indeed Fawcett, Harris and Bridge would appear to be arguing this for choice of law from the commercial contract perspective.

consumer should be provided with such protection when a foreign business has intentionally targeted the consumer via its active or interactive web site.

Intentional Targeting: A New Connecting Factor for Electronic Consumer Contracts

The effective application of jurisdiction and choice of law rules for electronic consumer contracts relies on the operation of two key factors. First, there needs to be a restriction on party autonomy to select the forum and law in an electronic consumer contract. Second, a more appropriate connecting factor needs to be applied to establish that the foreign business targeted the consumer via its web site and that a contract resulted from such activity. There are sufficient policy reasons why such a connecting factor that can be applied to both jurisdiction and choice of law rules. Firstly, it would ensure consistency in approach. Secondly, it would prevent 'fortuitous locations of connecting factors.'[13] Thirdly, it would provide the maximal consumer protection desired for electronic consumer contracts and fourthly from the businesses perspective a clear, effective connecting factor to determine both jurisdiction and choice of law would not thwart or restrict businesses from utilising electronic commerce to target foreign markets.

The connecting factor used to establish the jurisdiction and law of an electronic consumer contract needs to be precise and effective in establishing the jurisdiction and law of an electronic consumer contract. This book will demonstrate that existing connecting factors contained in EU laws and US case law are not currently as precise and effective as they should be. For example, the term 'directing such activities' was integrated into the Brussels 1 Regulation and copied in the non-EU rules in the UK and is now being proposed vis-à-vis choice of law. There are chapters on jurisdiction and choice of law which will demonstrate that the term 'directing such activities' is inappropriate to determine the jurisdiction and law an electronic consumer contract. These chapters will also demonstrate that the level and extent of web site activity needs to be refined as a more precise test premised on intentional targeting. A new connecting factor premised on targeting would address the ambiguities in determining the jurisdiction and applicable law of an electronic consumer contract.

---

13 R. Schu, 'The Applicable Law to Consumer Contracts Made Over the Internet: Consumer Protection Through Private International Law?' (1997) 5:2 *Int J Law and Tech* 192 at p.225 *et seq*.

Harmonising International Private Law Rules for Electronic Consumer Contracts

Underlying the theme of this book is the proposal that international private law rules for electronic consumer contracts should be harmonised. The preference for harmonisation of international private law rules is premised on the need to prevent a 'race to the bottom' when foreign sellers try to invoke a jurisdiction or choice of law clause in their online contracts favourable to their own interests. Such an approach could also facilitate those countries developing electronic commerce regulations to adopt the same approach to protecting their consumers.

Method

As electronic commerce is not restricted to consumers and businesses situated in one jurisdiction, the ways in which other countries have sought to adapt their international private law rules for such contracts are worthy of consideration.[14] The book focuses on how jurisdiction and choice of law rules have been developed in throughout the United Kingdom and in the United States. Both countries' economies have continued to maintain high levels of participation in electronic commerce,[15] which, in the United States, can be attributed to the historical development of the World Wide Web and, in the case of both countries, the political will to develop and sustain electronic commerce as, inter alia, an advertising medium, a legitimate commercial activity and educational tool.[16] Furthermore, as stated earlier, these countries have actively adapted or introduced substantive laws to regulate electronic commerce in their own jurisdictions in support of regional and political objectives. These countries have also adapted existing jurisdiction rules for consumer contracts. The courts of the United States have adapted their existing rules of personal jurisdiction in an attempt to ensnare the online activities of a foreign defendant. The United Kingdom has implemented an EU Regulation which modified the jurisdiction rule for consumer contracts. Both countries are participating in processes to amend or introduce choice of law rules for electronic consumer contracts. The countries are broadly similar in that they comprise separate, internal jurisdictions (Scotland and England, Wales and Northern Ireland in the UK and the fifty states of the United States). However, for the parties to

14 T.M. De Boer, 'The Evolution of Postwar Private International Law', in T.M. De Boer (ed), *Forty Years On: The Evolution of Post War Private International Law in Europe, Symposium in Celebration of the 40th Anniversary of the Centre of Foreign Law and Private International Law, University of Amsterdam, on 27 October 1989* (Kluwer, Deventer, 1990) at p.10 and Schu, at p.198.

15 OECD, 'Measuring the Information Economy', Chapter IV, Electronic Commerce, <http://www.oecd.org/dataoecd/34/35/2771139.pdf>. Copyright OECD.

16 Chapters 4, 5 and 6.

know with certainty or predict the effect of a particular jurisdiction or choice of law rule when contracting online and for electronic commerce to continue to flourish, jurisdiction and choice of law rules for electronic consumer contracts must be applied consistently via the operation of a clear, effective, connecting factor which operates in favour of the consumer's jurisdiction and law.

Summary

The remaining chapters of this book will now examine the existing rules of jurisdiction and choice of law for electronic consumer contracts in the United Kingdom (with reference to European Union policy and developments) and in the United States. Despite recent adaptation, rules of jurisdiction and choice of law for such consumer contracts do not ensure certainty and predictability of result and thereby conflicts justice. It will be considered, with reference to the Hague Conference's Judgments Convention project, that existing rules should be further amended and harmonised to provide an automatic rule in favour of the consumer's jurisdiction and applicable law. Given the commercial significance of electronic commerce, governmental and non-governmental organisations, businesses, consumers and their representatives have a vested interest in how international private law rules operate. International private law rules must facilitate 'global access to [conflicts] justice'[17] by enabling a consumer who has entered into an electronic consumer contract after being targeted by the business' active or interactive web site to sue a business in his own jurisdiction and rely on the application of the law of his domicile. Such a global, harmonised approach[18] of jurisdiction and choice of law rules for electronic consumer contracts will be required for legal certainty and predictability to be achieved in the on-line environment.

17 L.E. Gillies, 'Adapting International Private Law Rules for Electronic Consumer Contracts', in C.E.F. Rickett, and T.G.W. Telfer (eds), *International Perspectives on Consumers' Access to Justice* (Cambridge, 2003) at p.361. Word in brackets added.

18 As with other areas of international private law; H. Van Loon, 'Globalisation and The Hague Conference on Private International Law' (2000) 2 *International Law Forum du droit international* 230; C.T. Poggi, 'Electronic Commerce Legislation: An Analysis of European and American Approaches to Contract Formation' (2000) 41 *Va J Int'l L* 224 at p.277.

Chapter 1
Electronic Consumer Contracts and International Private Law

The Aim and Scope of International Private Law

> In a democracy, the law may be deemed to reflect the values and beliefs of the society that lives by it. This explains some of the differences between national laws … (O)ther differences can be traced to the geographical, demographic, economic or social conditions prevailing in each state.[1]

International private law provides rules of jurisdiction, choice of law and recognition and enforcement of foreign judgments for cases where the existence of a foreign element is present in the facts of the dispute.[2] The importance of choice of law rules to the regulation of cross-border disputes is undoubted. According to Jaffey '… the aim of the choice of law rule must be to select the appropriate governing law on criteria of justice and convenience for the parties.'[3] The purpose of Article 5 of the Rome Convention on the Law Applicable to Contractual Obligations is to ensure certainty and predictability of result by applying the mandatory rules of the consumer's habitual residence. The reason for this approach, as Jaffey confirms, is that the consumer has the 'convenience in consulting [his] law,' rather than being entitled to rely on whatever law is more favourable to him, whether the law of his domicile or a foreign law.[4] Jurisdiction rules are a 'manifestation of state sovereignty,'[5] since their purpose is to determine whether the state and its

1 T.M. De Boer, 'The Relation between Uniform Substantive Law and Private International Law', in A.S. Hartkamp, M.W. Hesselink, E.H. Hondius, C.E. Du Perron, J.B.M. Vranken (eds), *Towards a European Civil Code* (Martinus Nijhoff Publishers/ Kluwer Academic Publishers Group, 1994) at p.21.

2 A.E. Anton, *Private International Law*, 2nd Edition. (Edinburgh, 1990) at p.1; P.M. North and J.J. Fawcett, *Cheshire and North's Private International Law*, 13th ed (London, 1999) at p.5.

3 A.E. Jaffey, *Topics in Choice of Law* (London, 1996) at p.49 and 51.

4 Jaffey, ibid at p.540, words in brackets added.

5 D.W. Bowett, 'Jurisdiction: Changing Patterns of Authority over Activities and Resources,' in R.St.J. MacDonald, and D.M. Johnston, *The Structure and Process of International Law* (Dordrecht, 1986) at p.555 and R.St.J. MacDonald and D.M. Johnston, 'International Legal Theory: New Frontiers of the Discipline,' in R.St J. MacDonald and D M. Johnston, ibid at p.1.

courts can adjudicate over cases with a foreign element.[6] Once the jurisdiction of a cross-border dispute has been determined, the *lex fori*'s choice of law rules will be applied. The effective operation of 'judicial'[7] or 'juridical'[8] jurisdiction rules relies upon locating the parties or their activities in a particular jurisdiction.[9] Byassee has succinctly commented on the significance of physical presence in determining jurisdiction as follows,

> (T)he fundamental jurisdictional premise of the common law is physical presence, either actual or constructive within the jurisdiction attempting to assert authority over an individual. The body of the individual action may be located in the jurisdiction, the individual may perform an action that has physical effects within the jurisdiction or the individual boundaries of the jurisdiction itself are defined in physical geographical terms.[10]

The operation of international private law rules are premised on connecting factors which are used to determine whether parties are physically present or their activities are associated with certain jurisdictions and laws in a material way. Domicile is an important connecting factor most often used to determine whether parties are physically located in a jurisdiction. For example, a party is domiciled in England if he can demonstrate both residence and an intention to remain in England.[11] The place where the parties' commercial activities occur also connects the parties to a particular jurisdiction and applicable law. Once the parties know where each other is geographically located, or where their activities have taken place, they will be able to determine which jurisdiction will hear their dispute and what law(s) will apply. Connecting factors are a means of ensuring that the closest,[12] and thereby the most appropriate, jurisdiction of a dispute can be foreseen[13] or determined with

---

6 Michael Akehurst, 'Jurisdiction in International Law' (1972–73) 46 BYBIL 145

7 Akehurst, ibid.

8 L.E. Gillies, 'Choice of Law Rules for Electronic Consumer Contracts: Replacement of the Rome Convention by the Rome 1 Regulation' (2007) 4 *Journal of Private International Law*: 89 at p.91.

9 Anton, *Private International Law*, at p.6; North and Fawcett, *Cheshire and North's Private International Law*.

10 W.S. Byassee, 'Jurisdiction of Cyberspace: Applying Real World Precedent to the Virtual Community' (1995) 30 *Wake Forrest L Rev* 197.

11 North and Fawcett, *Cheshire and North's Private International Law* at p.137 *et seq*.

12 A.P. M.J. Vonken, 'Balancing Processes in International Family Law, On the determination and weighing of interests in the conflicts of laws and the "openness" of the choice of law system,' in T.M. De Boer, *Forty Years On: The Evolution of Post War Private International Law in Europe, Symposium in Celebration of the 40th Anniversary of the Centre of Foreign Law and Private International Law*, University of Amsterdam, on 27 October 1989 (Deventer, 1990) at p.171 and 173.

13 P. Hay, O. Lando, and R.D. Rotunda, 'Conflict of Laws as a Technique for Legal Integration,' in M. Capelletti, M. Seccombe and J. Weiler (eds), *Integration Through Law*,

a degree of certainty and predictability.[14] Once the parties know or have anticipated what jurisdiction will hear any dispute between them, they will then be able to determine whether the *lex fori* will apply its own laws, the law that the parties have agreed in their contract or another law to govern the dispute. As international private law rules are to provide justice for the parties – and moreover justice for a particular class of claimants such as consumers – determining the jurisdiction with the closest geographical connection or interest to a dispute with a foreign element is of crucial significance.[15] Since international private law rules seek to ensure justice to the parties in a cross-border dispute, an important consideration is the meaning of 'justice' in this context and in the context of disputes between consumers and foreign sellers who have contracted by electronic means.

International Private Law Rules and the Pursuit of 'Conflicts Justice'

Clarkson and Hill identify a number of aspects that underpin conflicts justice, namely 'giving effect to the parties' intentions ... giving effect to the parties' legitimate expectations ... certainty and predictability ... balancing public interests and principles of conflicts justice.'[16] The two aspects of justice that interplay in cross-border electronic consumer contract disputes are conflicts justice and the material justice enshrined in substantive consumer protection laws. The Oxford English Dictionary defines justice, inter alia, as 'the administration of law in a fair and reasonable way.'[17] The Collins English Dictionary defines justice, inter alia, as 'the moral principle that determines the fairness of actions.' It also defines justice more specifically as 'the administration of law according to prescribed and accepted principles.'[18] In international private law cases the pursuit of conflicts justice is sought as the parties are from different jurisdictions with different expectations of their legal rights and remedies. International private law rules seek to provide certainty and predictability of result[19] to facilitate 'conflicts justice.'[20] In particular, the aim of jurisdiction rules is two-fold. The first aim is to provide the parties with legal certainty by providing rules that direct their dispute to the most appropriate jurisdiction[21] whether a choice of forum has been agreed or not. Vonken

Volume 1, Book 2 (New York, 1986) at p.192.

14 Vonken, 'Balancing Processes in International Family Law,' at p.176.

15 Vonken, 'Balancing Processes in International Family Law,' at p.174 and 180.

16 C.M.V. Clarkson and J. Hill, *The Conflict of Laws* (Oxford, 2006), at pp.573–577.

17 *Compact Oxford Dictionary, Thesaurus and Wordpower Guide* (Oxford, 2002).

18 *Collins Dictionary and Thesaurus* (Glasgow, 1991).

19 Vonken, 'Balancing Processes in International Family Law,' at p.176.

20 Vonken ibid and Hay, Lando and Rotunda, 'Conflict of Laws as a Technique for Legal Integration,' at p.190 citing Kegel.

21 S.C. Symeonides (ed), *Private International Law at the End of the 20th Century: Progress or Regress?* (London, 2000) at pp.44–45.

has described this as the 'parties' conflicts interests.'[22] Each party may reasonably expect the dispute to be heard in the jurisdiction where they are located, where their activities take place or the jurisdiction specified in the contract.[23] Furthermore each party may reasonably expect the substantive laws of those jurisdictions to apply.[24] The aim of contractual choice of law rules is to give effect to the parties' choice of applicable law(s), determine the applicable law in the absence of choice and where necessary or appropriate restrict or limit their choice of law in favour of the operation of mandatory rules or laws to protect public policy. Choice of forum and applicable law clauses are prima facie evidence that the parties have agreed what jurisdiction will hear any dispute between them and what law will apply to their contractual obligations. Nevertheless, international private law rules must provide a clear basis to determine whether or not the parties can agree a choice of forum or applicable law clause and what effect such choices have on the resolution of their dispute. International private law rules must also determine whether a purported choice of forum or law clause, for example in a standard form or a click-wrap agreement[25] on a web site, enables one or either parties to override the forum or law specified in the contract.

The purpose of international private law rules is not therefore to determine the final outcome of a dispute between the parties. There is the potential for more than one jurisdiction and law to apply in a cross-border dispute. The second aim of international private law rules is to facilitate predictability of result.[26] The content and scope of both jurisdiction and applicable law rules must be clear for a jurisdiction to be established and a particular law to be applied. By determining the place where a consumer can sue a business, both parties can foresee what procedural rules and substantive law(s) will apply to their cross-border dispute.[27] As Jaffey affirms,

> ... a party in an international dispute cannot complain of injustice if the justice given to him or her is that of his or her own country. The difficulty, of course, is that the parties will often belong to different countries, *whose standards of justice differ*.[28]

In addition the use of connecting factors, the 'litigational convenience of [...] the parties [and their] witnesses'[29] and the legal regulation of cross-border activities are

22 Vonken, 'Balancing Processes in International Family Law,' at p.178.

23 Vonken, ibid.

24 Vonken, ibid.

25 See Chapter 2.

26 Vonken, 'Balancing Processes in International Family Law,' at p.176.

27 North and Fawcett, *Cheshire and North's Private International Law* at p.5 and 32.

28 Jaffey, *Topics in Choice of Law*, at p.18. Words italicised for emphasis.

29 J. Fawcett, 'The Interrelationships of Jurisdiction and Choice of Law in Private International Law' (1991) 44 *Current Legal Problems* 39 at p.52.

significant 'wider considerations'[30] in establishing jurisdiction in the consumer's domicile. There are legal, practical and economic benefits to the consumer when a dispute is heard in his jurisdiction. As Vonken confirms, '(T)he parties cannot be expected to have a detailed knowledge of substantive law provisions. Rather it must be assumed that they have a general perception of the essential principles of justice embodied in 'their' law.'[31] A consumer is more likely to know the procedural or substantive consumer protection rules of his jurisdiction and will want to take advantage of the protection provided by those rules. Jurisdiction rules therefore provide the 'means [for] observance of [consumer's] rights.'[32] Establishing jurisdiction is therefore a crucial 'first' step in determining where the dispute will be heard to enable the applicable law to be applied to that dispute. The inextricable purpose and link between jurisdiction and choice of law rules for consumer contracts is evident since both seek to facilitate conflicts' justice for consumers in one jurisdiction who contract with sellers in foreign jurisdictions. As Fawcett has explained, whilst questions of choice of law often arise when jurisdiction is being determined,[33] the function (i.e. purpose) of jurisdiction and choice of law rules is different[34] and therefore requires separate treatment.[35] As stated earlier, it is the purpose of jurisdiction rules to establish the most appropriate jurisdiction by means of connecting factors. The function of contractual choice of law rules is to determine the applicable law to be applied to the parties' contract and dispute. This might be the *lex fori*, or another law in accordance with the particular choice of law rule in question. A jurisdiction rule requiring the consumer to sue a business in the business' jurisdiction would, as Halfmeier has argued, be costly to the consumer and have a prohibitive effect on consumer-led litigation.[36] Consumers would also be prevented, or at least discouraged, from contracting with foreign sellers by electronic means if they could not rely on the same level of protection available via their own forum and law. Nevertheless, the notion of predictability is as important to a business. A business should have regard to the legal implications of contracting with foreign consumers when planning, marketing and undertaking its cross-border activities towards consumers in foreign jurisdictions. In particular, businesses must be able to foresee which jurisdiction could hear the dispute and

30 Fawcett, ibid.

31 Vonken, 'Balancing Processes in International Family Law,' at p.178.

32 T. Janssens, 'The Shearson judgment of the European Court of Justice: Problems raised by the "Europeanisation" and "Communitisation" of the Term "Consumer" in the Brussels Jurisdiction and Judgments Convention' (1995) 4 *ERPL* 605 at p.606. Words in brackets added for syntax.

33 Fawcett, 'The Interrelationships of Jurisdiction and Choice of Law in Private International Law,'at pp.50–51.

34 Fawcett, ibid at p.40.

35 Fawcett, ibid.

36 A. Halfmeier 'Waving Goodbye to Conflicts of Laws? Recent Developments in European Union Consumer Law,' in C.E.F. Rickett, and T.G.W. Telfer (eds), *International Perspectives on Consumers' Access to Justice* (Cambridge, 2003) at p.386.

crucially what law would govern contracts with consumers and any disputes that occur. Businesses want and need to know the legal and commercial effect of rules that confer jurisdiction in the consumer's domicile and the effect of applicable law rules on the contract. As Hay et al confirm '(I)n international trade, predictability can be achieved only if the courts of all countries strive to establish conflicts of law rules which ensure uniform results.'[37] By ensuring that jurisdiction and choice of law rules apply in a certain and predictable fashion, conflicts justice contributes significantly towards the just resolution of a cross-border dispute.

The Operation of Connecting Factors in Determining Jurisdiction and the Applicable Law

Jurisdiction and applicable law rules seek to achieve conflicts justice by using connecting factors to establish that the parties are associated with a particular jurisdiction and law in a material way. The parties' physical presence or activities in a particular jurisdiction are used as 'connecting factors' for this purpose.[38] For example, the *actor sequitur forum rei* principle (hereafter the '*actor sequitur* principle') ensures the defendant is sued in the jurisdiction wherever he is domiciled.[39] The *actor sequitur* principle also ensures that if a party domiciled in one jurisdiction takes legal proceedings against a defendant domiciled in another jurisdiction, it is appropriate that a dispute should be heard in the jurisdiction where the defendant is situated. Otherwise, the defendant may be prejudiced by not having reasonable notice of the dispute and it may be more difficult for him[40] to obtain legal representation and defend himself in another jurisdiction. The interests of the defendant are enshrined in both rules of jurisdiction for civil and commercial matters in the EU Brussels 1 Regulation[41] and the US constitutional requirement for 'minimum contacts' in asserting personal jurisdiction. As Zaphiriou[42] confirms '(T)he dominant [US] constitutional concern as to the

37 Hay, Lando and Rotunda, 'Conflict of Laws as a Technique for Legal Integration,' at p.167.

38 Hay, Lando and Rotunda, 'Conflict of Laws as a Technique for Legal Integration,' at p.192.

39 'Report by Mr. P. Jenard on the Convention of 27 September 1968 on jurisdiction and the enforcement of judgments in civil and commercial matters, 3 June 1971,' 1979 OJ C59/1 (hereafter 'the Jenard Report'), at p.13, 18 *et seq*. I.F. Fletcher, *Conflict of Laws and European Community Law* (Amsterdam, 1982). M. Chissick and A. Kelman, *Electronic Commerce Law and Practice*, 3rd ed (London, 2002) at p.116.

40 For the purposes of brevity, references to the masculine throughout the book also imply reference to the feminine gender.

41 In the Brussels Convention and Brussels 1 Regulation respectively. Chissick and Kelman, *Electronic Commerce Law and Practice*, at pp.117, 118 *et seq*.

42 G.A. Zaphiriou, 'Basis of the Conflict of Laws: Fairness and Effectiveness' (1988) 10 *Geo Mason UL Rev* 301 at pp.303, 304 and 310. Word in square brackets added.

exercise of jurisdiction is fairness to the defendant. It matters not that the manner in which the defendant's interests are considered in terms of "constitutional [...] or jurisprudential objectives."'[43]

Achieving Conflicts Justice for Consumers: A Definition of Consumer

In certain situations it has become necessary, for example to protect a certain class or group of persons such as consumers, that jurisdiction and choice of law rules for particular disputes facilitate conflicts justice and depart from the *actor sequitur* principle or restrict the parties' freedom to choose the applicable law by imposing another applicable law respectively. Stuyck confirms that '(A) central issue in consumer law literature is the notion of the consumer [...] for many subjects of consumer law it doesn't matter whether a broad or restrictive concept is chosen.'[44] It is crucial that the 'concept of 'consumer''[45] is defined when establishing juridical protection for consumers vis-à-vis international private law rules for cross-border electronic consumer contracts. The consumer must know whether he will be provided with juridical protection via the courts of his domicile and from his own substantive law. The foreign business must be able to predict with certainty if and in what circumstances the consumer can rely on such protection. As Stuyck continues, '(T)he definition of consumer however does matter when rules govern contractual matters in order to protect the weaker "consuming" party against the supposedly more powerful (professional) "supplying" party.'[46]

Section 3(1) of both the United Kingdom's Unfair Terms in Consumer Contract Regulations 1999[47] and the Consumer Protection (Distance Selling) Regulations 2000[48] both define a consumer as a 'natural person ... acting for purposes which are outside his trade, business or profession.'[49] Whilst a consumer has been defined as the "non-specialist" party to a consumer contract,[50] the Unfair Commercial Practices Directive, which came into force in December 2007, now defines the 'average consumer' as a consumer 'who is reasonably well informed,

43 Zaphiriou, ibid at p.305.

44 J. Stuyck, 'European Consumer Law After The Treaty of Amsterdam: Consumer Policy In Or Beyond The Internal Market?' (2000) 37 *CMLR* 367 at p.376.

45 Stuyck, ibid.

46 Stuyck, ibid.

47 Incorporating the EU Directive on Unfair Terms in Consumer Contracts, 1993 OJ L95/29.

48 Incorporating the EU Directive on the protection of consumers in relation to distance contracts, 1997 OJ L144/16.

49 Unfair Terms in Consumer Contracts Regulations 1999 SI/2083 incorporating the Unfair Terms in Consumer Contracts Directive 93/13/EC, 1993 OJ L95/29 and the Consumer Protection (Distance Selling) Regulations 2000 SI/2334 incorporating the Distance Selling Directive 97/7/EC 1997 OJ L144.

50 Chissick and Kelman, *Electronic Commerce Law and Practice*, at p.32.

and reasonably observant and circumspect, taking into account social, cultural and linguistic factors, as interpreted by the Court of Justice, but also contains provisions aimed at preventing the exploitation of consumers whose characteristics make them particularly vulnerable to unfair commercial practices.'[51] Even if consumers have been re-defined as average consumers, all consumers experience the same risks when contracting with foreign sellers by electronic means.

This book regards consumers as 'natural persons, acting outside their trade or profession.'[52] If a consumer in one jurisdiction enters into a contract with a foreign seller by electronic means and a dispute – essentially a 'true conflict' – arises between the parties, the crucial questions that must be determined are can the consumer sue the seller in his own jurisdiction and should the law of his domicile apply? As Howells and Weatherill acknowledge, '(T)hese cross-border transactions inevitably give rise to consumer complaints, which are even more difficult to resolve than domestic disputes.'[53] In order to provide certainty and predictability for consumers who enter into consumer contracts, subject to certain conditions,[54] the consumer should be able to raise proceedings in his own jurisdiction and rely on the application of his own law. It is necessary to establish that the parties are a consumer and a seller selling in the course of a business in which jurisdictions those parties are domiciled or have a place of business respectively. As the theme of this book seeks to demonstrate, it is necessary to determine whether the foreign business intended to contract with consumers from particular jurisdictions as a result of their online marketing or commercial activities. The ability of consumers to contract with businesses via web sites has challenged the effective operation of jurisdiction and choice of law rules for consumer contracts. Whilst the aim of international private law rules is to ensure that conflicts justice is achieved, the pursuit of material justice should also be facilitated. To that end, the relationship

51 Directive 2005/29/EC of the European Parliament and of the Council of 11 May 2005 concerning unfair business-to-consumer commercial practices in the internal market and amending Council Directive 84/450/EEC, Directives 97/7/EC, 98/27/EC and 2002/65/EC of the European Parliament and of the Council and Regulation (EC) No 2006/2004 of the European Parliament and of the Council ('Unfair Commercial Practices Directive'), Recital 18.

52 In accordance with Article 5 of the 'Rome Convention on Contractual Obligations Council Convention on the Law Applicable to Contractual Obligations,' Rome, 19 June 1980 (80/934/EEC), 1980 OJ L266 (hereafter referred to as the 'Rome Convention'); the United Kingdom Unfair Terms in Consumer Contract Regulations 1999, Implementing Directive 93/13 EEC, 1993 OJ L95/29. 1997 OJ L144/16; the Organisation for Economic Cooperation and Development's (OECD) Guidelines on Consumer Protection in Electronic Commerce 1999; Article 2(e) of the Directive on the Legal Aspects of Electronic Commerce, OJ 2000 L178 (hereafter the 'Electronic Commerce Directive'); Article 15 of the Brussels 1 Regulation,

53 Howells and Weatherill, *Consumer Protection and Law* (Aldershot, 2005) at p.651.

54 Considered later in Chapters 5 and 8.

between international private laws and substantive consumer protection laws must therefore be explored.

The Relationship Between Conflicts Justice and the Material Justice of Consumer Protection Law

International private law rules are not concerned with implementing substantive consumer protection policies as such.[55] Instead, the purpose of international private law is to provide rules that will determine the particular jurisdiction and choice of law of a cross-border dispute in a fair and just manner. Jurisdiction and applicable law rules seek to compliment 'material justice' in substantive consumer protection laws. Symeonides has described material justice as 'the same type and quality of justice as is pursued in fully domesticated situations.'[56] The starting point for substantive consumer protection law is to provide material justice to consumers in recognition of the inequality of bargaining power between the parties.[57] In his seminal text 'Consumer Protection,' Ramsay was somewhat critical of inequality of bargaining power as a rationale for consumer protection and maintained that it was an

> … umbrella concept for those market and private-law failures which cause consumers to suffer economic detriment. It is therefore necessary in a case of alleged unequal bargaining power to diagnose its particular source, for example, information failures, or the high transaction costs of redress or of consumer organization. [58]

Whilst electronic commerce facilitates increased choice and information on goods or services for consumers, it compounds the inequality of bargaining power many consumers face when goods do not arrive or are unsatisfactory. As a natural person, the consumer's bargaining position in a consumer contract is weaker in comparison to the economic position and negotiating power of a business.[59] The consumer is not expected to have the same specialist knowledge of the goods or services offered by the business and the legal, financial and operational implications of

---

55 V. Black, 'Consumer Protection in the Conflict of Laws: Canada, the United States and Europe,' in I. Ramsay (ed), *Consumer Law in the Global Economy, National and International Dimensions* (Dartmouth, 1997) at pp.195 and 199.

56 S.C. Symeonides, *Private International Law at the End of the 20th Century: Progress or Regress?* at p.45.

57 G. Howells and S. Wetherill, *Consumer Protection and Law*, at p.6 and 8; European Commission, Communication from the Commission to the European Parliament, the Council, the Economic and Social Committee and the Committee of the Regions, 'Consumer Policy Strategy 2002–2006,' COM 2002 (208) FINAL, 7 May 2002, pp.7–9, at <http://europa.eu.int/eur-lex/lex/LexUriServ/site/en/com/2002/com2002_0208en01.pdf>.

58 I. Ramsay, *Consumer Protection, Text and Materials* (London, 1989), at p.57.

59 Ibid.

contracting in particular jurisdictions. The pursuit of material justice for consumers in substantive consumer protection law is illustrated during various stages of the consumer contract.[60] At the contract formation stage, the consumer is protected by varied substantive consumer protection laws that may, inter alia, limit the seller's ability to impose unfair (standard) terms in contracts with consumers. For example in the United Kingdom, the Unfair Contract Terms Act 1977 and the Unfair Terms in Consumer Contracts Regulations 1999 limit the business' ability to impose unfair contractual terms. The consumer often has recourse to specific legislative protection when purchasing or financing the purchase of goods or services from a business. For example in the EU, consumer protection is premised on, inter alia, *ius poenitentiae*.[61] In the event of a contractual dispute between the consumer and the business, the consumer's jurisdiction provides the consumer with 'access to justice' in three main respects.[62] Firstly, the consumer can seek additional remedies when there has been a breach of the contract of sale by the seller. For example under the Sale of Goods Act 1979, as amended,[63] the consumer can[64] request additional remedies from the seller. Secondly, simplified procedural or evidential rules may be available to the consumer for him to initiate court proceedings such as Small Claims Rules.[65] Thirdly and most significantly for this book, international private law rules are influenced by and compliment substantive consumer protection laws[66] as they enable the consumer to bring proceedings against a business in his own jurisdiction and for the law of his domicile to apply. Articles 15-17 of the Brussels 1 Regulation have been described as 'an example of the vulnerable consumer being protected against those with actual or imaginary stronger bargaining power.'[67] A business has actual bargaining power since it can assess foreign markets in advance and determine in advance the conditions upon which it will contract with foreign consumers. The role of international private law

60 Gillies, 'Choice of Law Rules for Electronic Consumer Contracts.'

61 The other two aspects to EU consumer protection have been identified as 'information disclosure and juridical protection': S. Van Der Hof, 'European Conflict Rules Concerning International Online Consumer Contracts' (2003) 12:2 *Information and Telecommunications Law*, 165; Giusella Finocchiaro, 'European Law and Consumer Protection in the Information Age' (2003) 12:2 *Information and Communication Technology Law* 111; Gillies, ibid.

62 Gillies, ibid.

63 Unfair Terms in Consumer Contracts Regulations 1999 SI/2083 as amended by SI 2001/1186.

64 The additional remedies inserted into the 1979 Act for consumer cases came into force on 31st March 2003.

65 European Small Claims Procedure, COM 2005 87 final, 2005/0220 (COD), 15 March 2005, available at <http://europa.eu.int/comm/justice_home/fsj/civil/recognition/fsj_civil_recognition_general_en.htm>.

66 Jaffey, *Topics in Choice of Law*.

67 E.P. Mendes, 'The Troublesome Workings of the Judgments Convention of the European Economic Community' (1980) 13 *Vand J Transnat'l L* at p.96.

in providing 'juridical protection'[68] for consumers has been described as a ' [...] protective attitude [which] reflects the belief, more common in Europe than the United States, in the duty of the State to balance social or economic inequalities between its citizens or to make access to justice easier for those in particular need of it.'[69]

Whilst a protectionist policy towards consumers is not as generally evident in the United States as it is amongst European Union member states, jurisdiction rules for consumer contracts in the US remain well-established, 'entirely reasonable and in step with the emergence of consumer protection laws in Western Europe and in other industrialised nations.'[70] Specific jurisdiction rules and applicable law for electronic consumer contracts are therefore crucial if the consumer is to continue to be afforded juridical protection against a foreign seller.[71] When the parties to a consumer contract are situated in different jurisdictions, each party may understandably prefer the courts of their own jurisdiction to hear any dispute between them and their own laws to apply. The parties are more likely to know and understand how the rules of jurisdiction apply in their own domicile compared to foreign jurisdictions. The consumer is in a contractually weaker position than the seller no matter whether the consumer contracts with a business by electronic means or not. However, the nature of the online contract renders the consumer's already weaker contractual position more acute. The OECD reported that consumers continue to experience increased choice and risk as a result of electronic commerce activity via the World Wide Web.[72] The present author has previously observed that consumers regard 'data protection and security concerns, fraud, breach of privacy, jurisdiction and [applicable] law'[73] as risks that they have perceived or experienced when contracting electronically over the World Wide Web (WWW). Black has also argued that a consumer who contracts with a business online would

68 Van Der Hof, 'European Conflict Rules Concerning International Online Consumer Contracts,' and Gillies, 'Choice of Law Rules for Electronic Consumer Contracts.'

69 M. Reimann, *Conflict of Laws In Western Europe A Guide Through The Jungle* (New York, 1995) at p.82. Words in square brackets removed and modified respectively.

70 Mendes, 'The Troublesome Workings of the Judgments Convention of the European Economic Community,' at p.96.

71 Black, 'Consumer Protection in the Conflict of Laws: Canada, the United States and Europe,' at p.195.

72 OECD, 'Consumers in the Online Marketplace: The OECD Guidelines Three Years Later,' Report by the Committee on Consumer Policy on the Guidelines for Consumer Protection in the Context of Electronic Commerce, DSTI/CP(2002)4/FINAL, 3 February 2003, available at <http://www.oecd.org>. Hereafter referred to as the 'OECD 2003 Report.' Copyright OECD. L.E. Gillies, 'Legal Regulation of Risk in B2C Electronic Commerce – From Top-Down Regulation to Promoting Consumer Trust' in I. Ramsay, J. Salloum, N. Horrox, G. Mowatt (eds), *Risk and Choice in Consumer Society* (Ant. Sakkoulas: Athens, 2007).

73 Gillies, ibid. Word in brackets added.

be 'psychologically vulnerable and exposed'[74] if he had to raise proceedings in the 'foreign business' jurisdiction. The increase of online activities between consumers and businesses over the WWW has necessitated a reconsideration of jurisdiction and choice of law rules for consumer contracts. Puurunen has also argued that a consumer would have 'poor means of obtaining effective judicial relief'[75] if there was uncertainty about where he could sue a foreign business and by implication what laws would apply to his online activities. The consumer can obtain legal advice and representation to raise proceedings in his own jurisdiction far quicker and cheaper than if he had to do so in a foreign business' jurisdiction.[76]

If international private law rules are to facilitate consumer's access to justice, the 'individual consumer – individual business' paradigm must be taken into account. As Howells and Weatherhill state:

> legal reforms which continue to view consumer problems as individual problems are going to lead to a continuation of many of the present difficulties. [...] Unless the full range of consumer concerns are taken on board, consumer law will continue to be viewed as 'middle class' law, for it will only be worth litigating disputes involving high-cost goods and services ... [77]

The authors suggest class actions or consumer organisations being able to pursue legal remedies against sellers. Such an approach may also seek to reinforce access to justice for consumers who contract with foreign sellers by electronic means.

Summary

It was commented by Peterson that 'the goal of uniformity (or predictability) is inherent' in conflicts justice.[78] In recent years countries such as the United Kingdom and the United States have adapted their existing jurisdiction and choice of law rules for consumer contracts to apply to consumer contracts conducted electronically. However, it will also be demonstrated that the continued application of those jurisdiction and choice of law rules will create diverging results. For

74 Black, 'Consumer Protection in the Conflict of Laws: Canada, the United States and Europe,' at p.208.

75 T. Puurunen, 'The Legislative Jurisdiction of States Over Transactions in International Electronic Commerce' (2000) XVIII *John Marshall Journal of Computer and Information Law* 689 at p.696.

76 Black, 'Consumer Protection in the Conflict of Laws: Canada, the United States and Europe,' at pp.207–8.

77 Howells and Weatherill, *Consumer Protection Law*, at p.604–605.

78 C.H. Peterson, 'American Private International Law at the End of the 20th Century: Progress or Regress?' in Symeonides, *Private International Law at the End of the 20th Century: Progress or Regress?* at p.427.

example, the jurisdiction rule for consumer contracts amongst (the majority of) EU member states only permits the consumer to raise proceedings in his own jurisdiction if the defendant business is situated in or directs its commercial activities towards consumers in an EU Member State.[79] The courts in the United States can assert jurisdiction over a defendant who does business in a consumer's jurisdiction. However, the US courts have regard to and usually enforce the jurisdiction agreement in a consumer contract when determining which jurisdiction should hear the parties' dispute.[80] In order to ensure that the aims of certainty and predictability for conflicts justice are achieved,[81] this book seeks to demonstrate that the existing United Kingdom and United States jurisdiction and choice of law rules for electronic consumer contracts must be further amended. In addition it will also be argued that regardless of a purported choice of forum, jurisdiction and applicable law rules for electronic consumer contracts should be harmonised to enable the consumer in the event of a dispute with the foreign seller to by able to both raise proceedings against the business in his own jurisdiction and rely on the application of the law of his domicile irrespective of where the parties are domiciled.

---

79 See Chapter 5.

80 See Chapters 8 and 9.

81 Symeonides, *Private International Law at the End of the 20th Century: Progress or Regress?*

Chapter 2
The Internet, Electronic Commerce and Electronic Consumer Contracts

Introduction[1]

The Internet is a network of computers that enables users to communicate with each other[2] regardless of where those computers, or those that use them, are situated. The Internet was originally set up as a means of communication between defence experts in different countries through as system known as 'ARPANET.'[3] The reason for creating the link between these computers was that in the event of ordinary terrestrial telephone lines failing, the Internet still enabled different computers to communicate with each other.[4] It did this by enabling the messages to be divided up electronically into pieces or 'packets.' These packets would be sent via different telephone lines at different times, via different 'routes', to different computers in order to reach their end destination.[5] By 1984, the academic community also began to use a version of ARPANET known as NSFNet[6] and

1 Sections of this Chapter were recently published in L.E. Gillies, 'Addressing the "Cyberspace Fallacy": Targeting the Jurisdiction of an Electronic Consumer Contract' (2008) 2 *Int Journal Law and Inf Tech* 1.

2 M. Chissick and A. Kelman, *Electronic Commerce Law and Practice*, 3rd ed (London, 2002) at p.xxxix.

3 The Internet Society, 'All About the Internet,' <http://www.isoc.org/internet/history/> and 'A Brief History of the Internet,' <http://www.isoc.org/internet/history/brief.shtml>. I.G. Mahoney, 'United States' in D. Campbell (ed), *Law of International Online Business* (London, 1998), Chapter 17 at p.617; T.S. Trout-McIntyre, 'Personal Jurisdiction and the Internet: Does the Shoe Fit?' (1997) 21 *Hamline L Rev* 223 at p.249; R. Yagura, 'Does Cyberspace Expand the Boundaries of Personal Jurisdiction?' (1998) 38 IDEA 301 at p.302.

4 The Internet Society, ibid.

5 The transfer of messages in this way was known as 'packet switching' and still occurs today on the Internet, M.A. Froomkin, 'The Internet as a Source of Regulatory Arbitrage,' in B. Kahin and C. Nesson (eds), *Borders in Cyberspace Information Policy and the Global Information Infrastructure* (Cambridge, Massachusetts, 1997) at p.129; H. Kronke, 'Applicable Law in Torts and Contracts in Cyberspace,' in K. Boele-Woelki and C. Kessedjian (eds), *Internet Which Court Decides? Which Law Applies?* (The Hague, 1998) at p.66.

6 Yagura, 'Does Cyberspace Expand the Boundaries of Personal Jurisdiction?' at p.302, who refers to M.R. Burnstein, 'Conflicts on the Net: Choice of Law in Transnational

since 1995 the Internet opened out to businesses and consumers via the WWW.[7] The increasing use of the Internet led to the creation of other global computer networks of which the most well known and 'commercial' is the WWW. The WWW enables those with access to a computer with a suitable Internet browser,[8] telephone connection, modem and an account with an Internet Service Provider (or 'ISP') to view web pages of potentially millions of organisations around the globe, ranging from multi-national enterprises, through to small to medium sized businesses (or SMEs), academic institutions and governments. The ability of a consumer to communicate or contract with a seller online is dependant upon, inter alia, the accessible nature and level of activity of the seller's web site.

The World Wide Web and Electronic Commerce

The WWW is a communication tool,[9] enabling information to be viewed, shared, requested and retrieved between computer networks. The WWW also enables parties to enter into contracts with each other for goods and services[10] which is a key aspect to electronic commerce. Electronic commerce enables parties to use digital language on computers to communicate, negotiate and contract with each other.[11] Whilst a number of attempts have been made to define electronic commerce, no single definition has been universally applied.[12] Sookman has defined electronic commerce as 'any kind of transaction that is made using digital technology, including transactions over open networks such as the Internet, closed networks such as electronic data interchange (EDI) and debit and credit cards.'[13] The definitions of electronic commerce tend to be distinguishable in two key respects. Firstly, electronic commerce is often defined by reference to the accessibility of computer networks as communications media. In the past, electronic commerce activity took place over 'closed'[14] or restricted access computer networks.[15] Private (i.e.

Cyberspace' (1996) 29 *Vand J Transnat'l L* 75.

7 Yagura, ibid at p.303; Trout-McIntyre, 'Personal Jurisdiction and the Internet: Does the Shoe Fit?' at pp.225–226.

8 Now predominantly Microsoft Internet Explorer.

9 Yagura, 'Does Cyberspace Expand the Boundaries of Personal Jurisdiction?'

10 Chissick and Kelman, *Electronic Commerce Law and Practice*, at p.68 *et seq*.

11 J. Rothchild, 'Protecting the Digital Consumer: The Limits of Cyberspace Utopianism' (1999) 74 *Ind LJ* 893 at p.900; B.B. Sookman, 'Electronic Commerce, Internet and the Law – A Survey of the Legal Issues' (1999) *CTLR* 52.

12 Sookman, ibid at p.52.

13 Sookman, ibid at p.52. Chissick and Kelman defined electronic commerce as 'a broad term describing business activities with associated technical data that are conducted electronically,' *Electronic Commerce Law and Practice*, at p.xxxviii.

14 Sookman, ibid.

15 Sookman, ibid.

restricted) computer networks, such as EDI,[16] are not used by businesses in their contracts with consumers. In the last ten years, electronic commerce has taken place between businesses and consumers over open, unrestricted computer networks.[17] The Organisation for Economic Cooperation and Development (OECD), World Trade Organisation (WTO) and World Intellectual Property Organisation (WIPO) have each sought to define electronic commerce in the context of their various work programmes and activities on the legal regulation of electronic commerce. The OECD refers to electronic commerce as a 'global network.'[18] The WTO has defined electronic commerce as 'the production, distribution, marketing, sale, or delivery of goods and services by electronic means.'[19] The WIPO has defined the Internet (representing the network of computers that enable electronic commercial activity to take place) as 'allow(ing) communications and transactions to take place over an 'open network.'[20] Catchpole has similarly defined electronic commerce as 'a term that has become synonymous with commercial transactions involving both organisations and individuals, based upon the processing and transmission of digitised data […] transmitted over open networks such as the Internet.'[21] The definition of electronic commerce used in this book is the combination of the terms derived from the OECD and WIPO given to 'commercial transactions conducted over a digitised [open] global network.'[22] The most prominent open network on the Internet is the WWW. Consumers must be able to access the WWW as an open

---

16 Electronic Data Interchange ('EDI') is an example of a restricted form of electronic commerce used exclusively by businesses as an automated order and payment system; Chissick and Kelman, *Electronic Commerce Law and Practice*, at p.67.

17 WIPO, Primer on Electronic Commerce and Intellectual Property Issues.

18 OECD, 'Ministerial Declaration on Consumer Protection in the Context of Electronic Commerce,' Ottawa 7–9 October 1998, DSTI/CP(98)12/FINAL, 'Consumer Protection in the Electronic Marketplace,' DSTI/CP98(13)/FINAL, 22 December 1998, and 'Ministerial Declaration on Consumer Protection in the Context of Electronic Commerce,' Ottawa 7–9 October 1998, DSTI/CP(98)12/FINAL. Copyright OECD.

19 WTO, 'Work Programme on Electronic Commerce,' Adopted by the General Council, 25 September 1998, <http://www.wto.org/english/tratop_e/ecom_e/wkprog_e.htm>. This definition is preferred and used by B.J. Willingham, 'Electronic Commerce and the Free Trade Area of the Americas,' NAFTA: Law and Business Review of the Americas, Summer 2000, 483 at p.484.

20 WIPO, Primer on Electronic Commerce and Intellectual Property Issues.

21 J. Catchpole, 'The Regulation of Electronic Commerce: A Comparative Analysis of the Issues Surrounding the principles of Establishment' (2000) 1.9 *Int J Law and Info Tech* 1 at p.2.

22 OECD, 'Ministerial Declaration on Consumer Protection in the Context of Electronic Commerce,' Ottawa 7–9 October 1998, DSTI/CP(98)12/FINAL, 'Consumer Protection in the Electronic Marketplace,' DSTI/CP98(13)/FINAL, 22 December 1998, and 'Ministerial Declaration on Consumer Protection in the Context of Electronic Commerce,' Ottawa 7–9 October 1998, DSTI/CP(98)12/FINAL. Copyright OECD.

computer network to be able to view web sites and enter into contracts for goods and services with foreign businesses online via those web sites.

Secondly, the types of markets businesses pursue via electronic commerce can be used to distinguish the different definitions of electronic commerce. Two predominant business models have emerged from electronic commerce activity via the WWW.[23] In a 'business-to-business' or 'B2B' model, businesses use electronic commerce to contract directly with other businesses, often without the requirement for an intermediary or agent. Before the advent of the Internet and the WWW, these contracts were the only contracts to be entered via the use of computer networks. However over the last ten years businesses have adopted electronic commerce as a business model and communication tool to attract foreign consumers. The contracts that result from such activities are termed 'business-to-consumer' or 'B2C' contracts. The parties use open computer networks via the WWW to contract directly with each other, without the need for the business to operate via an agent, branch or representative in the consumer's jurisdiction.

Over the last fourteen years,[24] a global market of goods and services has become increasingly evident as businesses and consumers contract with each other electronically.[25] The international development of commerce and trade[26] and the resulting increase in disputes[27] arising between businesses and consumers in different jurisdictions have become, as North has affirmed, the 'seed-bed for international conflicts.'[28] In response to the increasing level of commercial activity conducted via the WWW, national governments introduced new laws or adapted existing substantive laws and policies. For example, the Member States of the European Union adopted the umbrella Electronic Commerce Directive to regulate the provision of Information Society Services in the coordinated field.[29] The

23 There are other types of business activities conducted by electronic means which are out with the scope of this book. These include, for example contracts between businesses and governments (B2G) and peer-to-peer contracts (P2P) such as those conducted between private individuals via an online auction web site such as Ebay <http://www.ebay.co.uk>.

24 M. Neligan, 'Ten Years of Selling in Cyberspace,' BBC News, 25 October 2004, <http://news.bbc.co.uk/1/hi/business/3945775.stm>.

25 OECD, 'Ministerial Declaration,' at p.3.

26 J. Basedow, 'The Effects of Globalization on Private International Law,' in J. Basedow and T. Kono (eds), *Legal Aspects of Globalization Conflict of Laws, Internet, Capital Markets and Insolvency in a Global Economy* (The Hague, 2000) at p.6.

27 D. Campbell (ed), *Law of International Online Business*, and J. Basedow and T. Kono (eds), *Legal Aspects of Globalization Conflict of Laws, Internet, Capital Markets and Insolvency in a Global Economy* (The Hague, 2000).

28 P.M. North, 'Preface' in S.C. Symeonides (ed), *Private International Law at the End of the 20th Century: Progress or Regress?* (London, 2000), at p.vii and Franz Mayer, 'Europe and the Internet: The Old World and the New Medium' (2000) 11 *EJIL* 149.

29 'Directive 2000/31/EC on certain legal aspects of information society services, in particular, electronic commerce in the Internal Market' (Directive on electronic commerce), 2000 OJ L178 (hereafter the 'Electronic Commerce Directive).

introduction of the Electronic Commerce Directive has led to further directives which regulate particular aspects of electronic commerce activities such as, inter alia, electronic signatures,[30] distance selling[31] and the distance marketing of consumer financial services.[32] The United States has introduced, inter alia, the Uniform Electronic Transactions Act (UETA) and the Uniform Computer Information Transactions Act (UCITA) to regulate electronic commerce activity. The courts in the United States have also sought to adapt the rules of personal jurisdiction to apply to the defendant's commercial activities conducted via electronic commerce in a particular state. Various international organisations such as the Hague Conference on Private International Law,[33] OECD,[34] WIPO[35] and UNCITRAL[36] have undertaken projects and written reports and guidelines that have directed a national, and an inherently particularist, approach to the legal regulation of contracts conducted by electronic commerce.

---

30 'Directive 1999/93/EC of the European Parliament and of the Council of 13 December 1999 on a Community framework for electronic signatures,' 2000 OJ L013. Hereafter the 'Electronic Signatures Directive.'

31 'Directive 97/7/EC of the European Parliament and of the Council of 20 May 1997 on the Protection of Consumers in respect of Distance Contracts' (Directive on Distance Selling),' 1997 OJ L0007 (hereafter the 'Distance Selling Directive).

32 'Directive 2002/65/EC of the European Parliament and of the Council concerning the Distance Marketing of Consumer Financial Services and Amending Council Directives 90/619/EEC,' 97/7/EEC and 98/27/EEC, 23 September 2002 (hereafter the 'Distance Marketing of Consumer Financial Services Directive).

33 Hague Conference on Private International Law, 'Round table on electronic commerce and the Internet in conjunction with the University of Geneva,' and Preliminary Documents No.7 of April 2000 and No.12 of August 2000 on 'Electronic Data Interchange, the Internet and Electronic Commerce.'

34 Note 1.

35 In 1999 and 2001, WIPO held conferences on 'Electronic Commerce and Intellectual Property Issues,' and a forum on Private International Law and Intellectual Property Issues (which included the following papers; H.J. Perritt, 'Electronic Commerce: Issues In Private International Law And The Role Of Alternative Dispute Resolution,' at <http://www.wipo.int/edocs/mdocs/mdocs/en/wipo_pil_01/wipo_pil_01_6.doc> and R.C. Dreyfuss, 'Draft Convention On Jurisdiction And Recognition Of Judgments In Intellectual Property Matters').

36 UNCITRAL, 'Model Law on E-Commerce' (1996) 37:3 *EDI Law Review* 275 and its Working Group IV on electronic commerce.

The Legal Nature of Web Site Activities

The commercial activities of web sites have been increasingly[37] distinguished as 'active', 'passive' or 'interactive.'[38] A web site that enables a consumer to conclude a contract by going through a series of steps or pages on that web site, such as <http://www.amazon.co.uk> or <http://www.easyjet.com>, are examples of 'active' web sites. Conversely when a web site is nothing more than an information source to potential consumers, it is a 'passive' web site. Furthermore, 'interactive'[39] web sites are web sites that provide a combination of information and communication with potential consumers such as information request options or, as is frequently offered, sign up facilities to receive information on goods, services or special promotional offers by e-mail. An interactive web site combines information and is a means whereby parties can communicate with each other to a greater or lesser extent. The level of web site activity is a crucial connecting factor in determining whether businesses intended to use their web sites to sell goods and advertise[40] to consumers in foreign jurisdictions.[41]

The Disintermediation of Consumer Contracts by Electronic Commerce

Electronic commerce enables businesses and consumers to enter into contracts with each other for the purchase of goods and services via computer networks whether or not the parties are situated in the same jurisdiction.[42] The use of the Internet (and the WWW) has raised important issues for the legal regulation of

37 Chapter 7 on the extent to which an active, passive or interactive web site plus additional activity establishes personal jurisdiction in the United States. The EU and the Hague have each endorsed the application of the 'Sliding Scale' of web site activity. A. Haines, 'The Impact of the Internet on the Judgments Project: Thoughts for the Future,' Hague Conference on Private International Law, Preliminary Document No.17, <http://www.hcch.net>.

38 Preliminary Draft Report for a Council Regulation (EC) (COM (1999) 348 final – C5-0619/1999–99/0154 (CNS)) by the Committee on Legal Affairs and the Internal Market at 'Explanatory Statement'. F. Debusseré, 'International Jurisdiction over E-Consumer Contracts in the European Union: Quid Novi Sub Sole?' (2002) 10 *IJLIT* 344 at p.357.

39 Debusseré, 'International Jurisdiction over E-Consumer Contracts in the European Union: Quid Novi Sub Sole?'

40 See the European Commission's comments on the interpretation of 'active' and 'passive' sales (derived from the application of Article 4(b) of the Block Exemption Regulation) in its 'Guidelines for Vertical Restraints' (on EC Competition Rules), 2000 C291/1; considered at pp. 90-91.

41 L.E. Gillies, 'Rules of Jurisdiction for Electronic Consumer Contracts – Scottish Perspectives' (2001) 2 *SLPQ* 124 at p.132.

42 Willingham, 'Electronic Commerce and the Free Trade Area of the Americas,' and Sookman, 'Electronic Commerce, Internet and the Law – A Survey of the Legal Issues.'

electronic commerce activity. In terms of protecting the consumer who enters into online transactions, Rothchild[43] highlights that the 'inherent[ly] international nature'[44] of electronic commerce presents both an opportunity and a 'challenge' to consumer protection policy as a result of 'disintermediation.'[45] Rather than the consumer contracting via a supplier in the same jurisdiction, disintermediation enables the consumer to contract directly with a seller located in another jurisdiction. The disintermediation of consumer contracts provides benefits and challenges to businesses and consumers alike. Reed has recently reiterated that the key commercial and financial benefits of electronic commerce to businesses are '(G)lobal equivalence … (T)he digital transmission of information … [and] … (A)utomated decision making.'[46] The most significant benefit to businesses that use electronic commerce via the WWW is the ability to seek out and target new consumer markets. As Reed recently affirmed, businesses using electronic commerce as a commercial medium can operate on a 'globally equivale[nt]'[47] scale with other businesses. Businesses of any size can therefore compete with other businesses for sales to consumers in the same (i.e. domestic) or foreign markets. The corresponding result of global equivalence for consumers is the increased choice of goods and services available to them on a 'take it or leave it' basis 'at the click of a mouse.'[48] A web site which is accessible in the consumer's jurisdiction may determine whether or not the seller's goods or services are available to the consumer in his jurisdiction. If not, both parties would have to use other means of communicating with each other, for example by telephone or in writing. As a last resort, the consumer could travel to the seller's jurisdictions to contract with the seller. These examples demonstrate how the ability to access 'digital information'[49] on the seller's web site on the WWW is an efficient way for the consumer to contract with a foreign seller. Furthermore, in addition to accessing (new) foreign markets, an additional advantage for the business contracting online is that the consumer makes payment when entering into the online click-wrap agreement. However, the consumers may either perceive or experience an increased risk when contracting with a foreign seller over the WWW than if they had contracted that seller by visiting the seller's shop.[50] Conversely, the foreign seller may not be

43 Rothchild was a member of the OECD Working Party on the Guidelines for Consumer Protection in E-Commerce.

44 J. Rothchild, 'Protecting the Digital Consumer,' at p.897. Word in bracket modified for syntax.

45 Rothchild, ibid at p.896 *et seq*.

46 Chris Reed, *Internet Law, Text and Materials*, 2nd ed (Cambridge, 2004) at p.5. Word in brackets added.

47 Reed, ibid at p.5. Word in brackets modified for syntax.

48 T. Puurunen, 'The Legislative Jurisdiction of States Over Transactions in International Electronic Commerce' (2000) XVIII *John Marshall Journal of Computer and Information Law* 688 at p.692.

49 C. Reed, *Internet Law, Text and Materials*, at p.5.

50 Rothchild, 'Protecting the Digital Consumer,' at p.896.

satisfied that the other party is a 'consumer'. Whilst 'automated decision making'[51] on the WWW has diminished the need for a local supplier or middleman in the consumer's jurisdiction, there has been a corresponding increase in the risks to the parties who contract online.

The Disintermediation of Electronic Consumer Contracts and the Operation of International Private Law's Connecting Factors

The traditional connecting factors of location of the parties and the location of business' activities are important to a consumer contract. For example, Zain reiterates Rothchild's 'disintermediation' point that in a 'traditional sale,'[52] the consumer must visit the seller's premises in order to contract with that seller. In that situation, the consumer is re-assured by factors such as the physical presence of the seller, the ability to inspect the goods and assess their suitability in advance of contracting with the seller and paying for the goods.[53] Alternatively, the consumer may contract with a seller who is located in another jurisdiction if that seller issued advertisements in the jurisdictions where that consumer is domiciled. However, as the present author has recently argued,

> the use of the Internet challenges how parties to an electronic consumer contract can be adequately identified so that they, and their activities, may be sufficiently connected with a particular jurisdiction. If the parties' presence or their activities are connected with a particular jurisdiction, then it can be foreseen both by the consumer and seller where their dispute is likely to be heard. Regardless of the method of communication used, the ability of the parties to foresee where each other is geographically located and where business activities are directed are 'decisive'[54] factors in determining which jurisdiction will hear their dispute.[55]

Furthermore,

> (W)hen the seller in one jurisdiction uses traditional media such as a catalogue, mail, newspaper, radio or television to seek business from potential consumers in other

51 C. Reed, *Internet Law, Text and Materials,* at p.5.

52 S. Zain, 'Regulation of E-Commerce: Is It Fair To Consumers?' (2000) 31 *UWLA Law Review* 163 at p.167 ; L.E. Gillies, 'Addressing the "Cyberspace Fallacy": Targeting the Jurisdiction of an Electronic Consumer Contract' (2008) 2 *Int Journal Law and Inf Tech* 1 at p.8.

53 Zain, ibid at p.167.

54 R. Fentiman, 'English Private International Law at the End of the 20th Century: Progress or Regress?' in S.C. Symeonides (ed), *Private International Law at the End of the 20th Century: Progress or Regress?* (London, 2000), at p.190; Rothchild, 'Protecting the Digital Consumer,' at p.915 referring to the Brussels Convention.

55 Gillies, 'Addressing the "Cyberspace Fallacy",' at p.4.

> jurisdictions, the seller is likely to know with certainty in which countries customers receiving the catalogues or viewing the advertisement are located. [56]

For example, a South African wine producer sells wine via mail order catalogues to addresses in England, or puts an advertisement in an English newspaper to attract custom and consumers in England, contracts with the seller for goods contained in the catalogue or newspaper advertisement. In that situation, the consumers' location is known to the seller. The consumer is also likely to be aware of the seller's location when following the instructions in the catalogue or advertisement for ordering goods. If the seller does not want to contract with consumers in particular jurisdictions for financial, legal or operational reasons, then it will not send catalogues or advertise to potential consumers in those jurisdictions. As an additional precaution, the seller can still refuse to contract with the consumer by filtering orders sent by consumers from particular jurisdictions. However, as the present author has recently argued,

> when the seller uses other forms of globally accessible [...] 'de-materialized,'[57] media such as electronic commerce to attract custom, it is difficult for either party to know or foresee where the other is physically located. [...] As Rice confirmed, foreseeability is a 'fundamental jurisdictional issue' raised by the Internet.[58]

Geist also premised his targeting test on the need for foreseeability.[59]

Furthermore,

> (T)he consumer must rely on information on the foreign business' web site if he wishes to contract with that foreign seller online. The online information of a foreign business can be confirmed or checked with information offline,[60] for example by newspaper advertisements or the business' address if it has a branch in the consumer's jurisdiction. The business contracting online with a consumer must rely on the delivery address and payment details provided by the consumer in the online contract.[61] This information is

---

56 Gillies, ibid at p.6.

57 Fentiman, 'English Private International Law at the End of the 20th Century: Progress or Regress?' at p.190.

58 Gillies, 'Addressing the "Cyberspace Fallacy",' at p.6; D.T. Rice, 'Jurisdiction in Cyberspace: Which Law and Forum Apply to Securities Transactions on the Internet?' (2001) 21:3 (Fall) *University of Pennsylvania Journal of International Economic Law* 585.

59 Michael Geist, 'Is There a There? Towards Greater Certainty for Internet Jurisdiction' (2001) 16 *Berkeley Tech Law Journal* 1345 available at <http://www.law.berkeley.edu/journals/btlj/articles/vol16/geist/geist.pdf>.

60 Offline activities are those activities not conducted via web sites, for example traditional advertising in newspapers, television or invitations by post.

61 Geist, 'Is There a There?' Geist's article refers to payment details providing either an indication or confirmation of the consumer's location.

> crucial as it determines whether the business is dealing with a consumer, if the contract is a consumer contract and what jurisdiction rule will be applied as a result. If the location of either party is uncertain or cannot be foreseen then it becomes more difficult to determine which jurisdiction will hear a dispute between the parties.[62]

There are three main options for businesses. Firstly businesses can try to either limit or, as Geist[63] and Svantesson[64] each suggest, 'de-target' the accessibility of their web sites in particular jurisdictions. Whilst, as Øren suggests, it is feasible for businesses to 'ring-fence'[65] the availability of their web sites, unscrupulous consumers could try to access the web site via Internet Service Providers (ISPs) in other jurisdictions. Furthermore, in order to provide greater certainty for consumers and predictability for businesses, the jurisdiction test should be premised on a positive act on behalf of the seller to engage in business activity in a particular jurisdiction. For example in determining the jurisdiction of a contract, Article 5 of the Brussels 1 Regulation focuses on the place of performance of the obligation in question. Article 5 of the Rome Convention on the Law Applicable to Contractual Obligations requires that the seller '... must have done certain acts such as advertising in the press, or on radio or television, or in the cinema or by catalogues aimed specifically at that country.'[66] The European Commission rejected ring-fencing as the criteria for determining how a business directs its commercial activities.[67] As Chapters Eight and Nine will consider, general or specific personal jurisdiction are established by the United States' courts either when a business is deemed to have 'continuous and systematic contacts with the forum'[68] or when the business has purposefully availed itself by doing business in the jurisdiction[69] respectively. Given the global, dematerialised nature of the WWW, any adaptation of current jurisdiction rules for electronic consumer contracts must continue to focus on the requirement that the business positively intended to target particular jurisdictions rather than a test on which jurisdictions the business wished to avoid. Secondly, businesses can, and should be encouraged, to specify on their web sites which jurisdictions their online commercial activities

---

62 Gillies, 'Addressing the "Cyberspace Fallacy",' at p.6.

63 Geist, ibid.

64 D. Svantesson, 'Jurisdiction Issue in Cyberspace What Should Article 7 – Consumer Contracts, of the Proposed Hague Convention, Aim to Accomplish in Relation to E-Commerce?' (2001) 5 *CLSR* 318 at p.323. Svantesson defines the term as 'dis-targeting.'

65 J.S.T. Øren, 'International Jurisdiction Over Consumer Contracts in e-Europe' (2003) 52 *ICLQ* 665, at p.682.

66 'Council Report on the Convention on the law applicable to contractual obligations, by Professors M. Giuliano and P.l Lagarde,' 1980 OJ C282 (hereafter the 'Giuliano and Lagarde Report') at p.24. Words italicised for emphasis.

67 Øren, 'International Jurisdiction Over Consumer Contracts in e-Europe,' at p.682.

68 *Bancroft & Masters Inc. v Augusta National Inc.*, No.99-15099 223 F.3d 1082.

69 *Helicopteros Nationales de Colombia, S.A v Hall* 466 US 408, 414–416, 104 S.Ct 1868, 1872–73, 80 L.Ed.2d 404 (1984).

are directed towards. Thirdly, businesses can limit the activities of their web sites by using a 'passive' web site. As Campbell has affirmed '(I)f electronic commerce is to realise its full potential, the parties doing business must know what rules will be applied to their activities.'[70] It is submitted that changes to the jurisdiction rules for consumer contracts in the United Kingdom and the United States will continue to provide inconsistent results. For those reasons, international private law rules must now provide a clear and consistent jurisdiction and choice of law rule when a consumer has contracted with a seller by electronic means over the WWW. In order to achieve that objective, jurisdiction rules for electronic consumer contracts must ensure certainty and predictability of result by enabling the consumer to raise proceedings in his own jurisdiction and for his own law to apply when the business has targeted him intentionally via an active or interactive web site.

Jurisdiction and Electronic Commerce: An Old Problem, a New Method of Communication

"The problem of establishing where parties are located or where their activities take place for the purposes of determining jurisdiction is not a new one."[71] Fixed[72] connecting factors of residence and activity have been used to facilitate conflicts justice in cross-border cases. However, the application of these connecting factors may not always lead to certain and predictable results. "On more than one occasion, the challenge of applying pre-Internet rules to activities on the WWW has been equated to '(O)ld wine in new bottles'."[73] The Internet is simply another means of communication. That said, when the parties use the WWW to contract with each other it may be difficult to determine[74] where either the consumer is domiciled or the place where the seller is situated or conducts its business. Mayer's comment sums up the central issue that, '(I)nternet regulation does not start from a clean

70 D. Campbell (ed), *Law of International Online Business*, at p.24.

71 A. Reed, 'Jurisdiction and Choice of Law in a borderless electronic environment,' in Y. Akdeniz, C. Walker and D. Wall (eds), *The Internet, Law and Society* (Harlow, 2000) at p.79 cited in Gillies, 'Addressing the "Cyberspace Fallacy",' at p.1.

72 A.P.M.J. Vonken, 'Balancing Processes in International Family Law, On the determination and weighing of interests in the conflicts of laws and the "openness" of the choice of law system,' in T.M. De Boer, *Forty Years On: The Evolution of Post War Private International Law in Europe, Symposium in Celebration of the 40th Anniversary of the Centre of Foreign Law and Private International Law, University of Amsterdam, on 27 October 1989* (Deventer, 1990) at p.176.

73 A. Reed, 'Jurisdiction and Choice of Law in a borderless electronic environment,' at p.80 and C. Reed, *Internet Law, Text and Materials,* at p.173, cited in Gillies, "Addressing the "Cyberspace Fallacy",' at p.7.

74 Gillies, 'Addressing the "Cyberspace Fallacy",' at p.1.

slate. Most legal problems related to Cyberspace already existed in the real world long before.'[75]

The emergence of electronic commerce as a new, global form of business activity questions the application of the existing international private law connecting factors of geography or location of the parties and their activities. As a result these connecting factors have, as Puurunen has indicated, been 'applied, modified, or abandoned to measure up to societal goals.'[76] Willingham has identified time and distance[77] as two of the most significant barriers to 'traditional' international trade. It is submitted that the use of the Internet as a commercial communication method has 'redefined the significance' of the time and distance between businesses and consumers who contract with each other.[78] When a consumer enters into a contract with a business via a web site, it is accepted that the contract is entered into instantaneously in the same way as if the parties had used a fax machine.[79] Electronic commerce via the WWW is a means or medium of communication[80] used by parties to contract with each other.[81] Docherty and Fletcher confirm that

75 Franz C. Mayer, 'Europe and the Internet: The Old World and the New Medium' (2000) 11 *EJIL* 149 at p.151 cited in Gillies, 'Addressing the "Cyberspace Fallacy",' at p.7.

76 Puurunen, 'The Legislative Jurisdiction of States Over Transactions in International Electronic Commerce.'

77 Willingham, 'Electronic Commerce and the Free Trade Area of the Americas,' at p.488.

78 Puurunen, 'The Legislative Jurisdiction of States Over Transactions in International Electronic Commerce,' at p.692; P. Stone, 'Internet Consumer Contracts and European Private International Law' (2000) 9:1 *Information and Communications Technology Law* 5 and Reed, *Internet Law, Text and Materials,* at p.173.

79 A.D. Murray, 'Entering Into Contracts Electronically: The Real WWW,' in L. Edwards and C. Waelde (eds), *Law and the Internet A Framework for Electronic Commerce*, 2nd ed (Oxford, 2000) at p.25.

80 S. Dutson, 'The Internet, the conflict of Laws, international litigation and intellectual property: the implications of the international scope of the Internet on intellectual property infringements' (1997) JBL 495 at p.496 and Stone, 'Internet Consumer Contracts and European Private International Law.'

81 Yagura, 'Does Cyberspace Expand the Boundaries of Personal Jurisdiction?' at p.302. See also S. Hayakawa, 'Private Law in the Era of the Internet,' in J. Basedow and T. Kono (eds), *Legal Aspects of Globalization Conflict of Laws, Internet, Capital Markets and Insolvency in a Global Economy* (The Hague, 2000), at pp.30–31; Murray 'Entering Into Contracts Electronically,' at p.18. Dutson, 'The Internet, the conflict of Laws, international litigation and intellectual property,' and H. Rowe, 'Electronic Commerce and Consumers' (1998) *IBL* 165 at p.170. In Focus, 'Defining E-Commerce,' I-Ways, First Quarter (2000) 32 at p.45 where reference is made to the paradigm that whilst a separate set of rules or cyber-laws are not necessary for consumer protection, a modification of the existing rules are necessary to 'accommodate electronic commerce.'

the Internet has 'revolution[ised]' commercial communications.[82] Consensus on that observation is found in Catchpole's assertion that the Internet is 'one of the most important commercial mediums to emerge in the latter years of the 20th century.'[83] Indeed, in his article on European jurisdiction rules for internet contracts, Stone acknowledges that electronic commerce is a communication method[84] that requires a harmonised approach to establishing jurisdiction in the consumers' domicile at international[85] level. Despite the parties being at a distance to one another, electronic commerce enables contracts between businesses and consumers to be concluded as fast as face-to-face[86] communication. It is the global, networked infrastructure of the WWW that Willingham and Chris Reed attribute to its popularity[87] and efficiency as an effective cross-border business tool.[88] However, the geographical distance between the parties is legally significant when a consumer contracts with a seller via a web site. Given that commercial activity between businesses and consumers has become increasingly 'globali[sed] ... and demateriali[sed]'[89] by electronic commerce, it has become correspondingly challenging to determine where the consumer or business is located and to which jurisdictions a foreign business directs its commercial or marketing activities. As stated earlier, the seller's physical location or place of commercial activities are connecting factors or 'signposts' that the consumer can rely on when contracting 'offline' (i.e. when the WWW is not used). However these connecting factors must be re-considered when the consumer contracts with a business online via a web site on the WWW. For these reasons it is imperative that consumer contract jurisdiction rules are applied with certainty if the consumer has contracted electronically with a business. In his paper on 'The Progress or Regress of English Private International Law,' Fentiman concludes, inter alia, that

> ... traditional assumptions of private international law may become inappropriate. In particular, the notions that acts and their consequences may be territorially located for the purposes of choice of law and jurisdiction, which lies at the heart of the subject,

82 M. Docherty and R. Fletcher, 'Responding to the legal problems of electronic commerce' (2000) 5 *Communications Law* 2.

83 Catchpole, 'The Regulation of Electronic Commerce,' at p.1.

84 P. Stone, 'The Treatment of Electronic Contracts and Torts in Private International Law under European Community Legislation' (2002) 11:2 *Info and Comm Tech Law* 121 at 122.

85 Stone, ibid at p.125.

86 Murray, 'Entering Into Contracts Electronically,' and Reed, *Internet Law, Text and Materials*, at p.173.

87 OECD, 'Consumers in the Online Marketplace: The OECD Guidelines Three Years Later.'

88 Willingham, 'Electronic Commerce and the Free Trade Area of the Americas,' at p.483; Reed, *Internet Law, Text and Materials*, at p.5.

89 Fentiman, 'English Private International Law at the End of the 20th Century: Progress or Regress?'. Words modified for syntax.

> may become irrelevant. At the very least it becomes necessary, if the notion of territorial connection is to be retained, first to identify the characteristic and (in conflicts terms) most significant events which occur in novel transactions or processes, and secondly to locate those events in a particular jurisdiction. Is transmission or reception the key moment in a satellite broadcast? What is (or what are) the decisive features of the use of the internet?[90]

The increasing number of cross-border consumer contracts has rendered the concern over establishing which jurisdiction should hear the dispute more acute.[91] When a business uses electronic commerce to contract with a consumer, it has the potential to attract consumers on a global scale. As stated earlier, the decisive features of the Internet are the ability to identify the parties, their geographical location and the place where their activities are directed towards or take place. The Internet facilitates anonymity[92] of the parties, coined in Steiner's cartoon punch-line '(O)n the internet, nobody knows you're a dog.'[93] For example, the seller's anonymity may be enhanced when its web site contains a top-level domain ending such as '.com' or multiple web site domain endings that appear to be directed towards consumers in those jurisdictions. The consumer's anonymity may also be facilitated by the ISP used. For example, the consumer may register and use an email address with more than one ISP in more than one country. The consumer can also use an entirely separate identity in their email address for example <pseudonym@AOL.com> or <nickname@yahoo.com>. In addition, either party could use cryptography to encrypt their email correspondence and preserve their anonymity.[94] The combined lack of physical contact between the parties and the technology used sustains the anonymity of parties to an electronic consumer contract. The anonymity of the parties to an electronic consumer contract is, according to Zain, an 'ambiguity' that legislators must protect consumers against.[95] However the opportunity for anonymity has implications for both parties. As Puurunen rightly asserts, the business may not know for certain whether a consumer is located in a particular country or not.[96] Businesses may not wish to

90 Fentiman, ibid at p.190, cited in Gillies, 'Addressing the "Cyberspace Fallacy",' at p.5.

91 L.E. Gillies, 'A Review of the New Jurisdiction Rules for Electronic Consumer Contracts within the European Union,' Commentary, 2001 (1) *The Journal of Information, Law and Technology* (JILT) <http://www2.warwick.ac.uk/fac/soc/law/elj/jilt/2001_1/gillies>

92 Reed, *Internet Law, Text and Materials*, at p.35.

93 P. Steiner, 'On the Internet, nobody knows you're a dog,' *The New Yorker*, 5 July 1993, <http://www.cartoonbank.com> and Reed, ibid at p.140. This well-known cartoon depicts a dog sitting at a workstation, talking to another dog.

94 Froomkin, 'The Internet as a Source of Regulatory Arbitrage,' at p.133 *et seq*.

95 Zain, 'Regulation of E-Commerce: Is It Fair To Consumers?' at p.166–168.

96 Puurunen, 'The Legislative Jurisdiction of States Over Transactions in International Electronic Commerce,' at p.690.

contract with consumers in particular jurisdictions for economic or legal reasons. For example, the business may only want to target specific markets and ship goods to certain countries or there may be a prohibition on selling certain goods, such as alcohol or pornographic material, to consumers in certain countries. Furthermore, the cost of having to defend claims made by, or litigate against, consumers in a foreign jurisdiction is a legitimate disincentive for businesses that have invested in technology or are contemplating whether to do so.[97] As stated earlier, both parties to an electronic consumer contract are reliant on each other, or third parties,[98] to provide information on their identity and location. The business may use technical measures (on its web site) or contractual devices (in an online click-wrap agreement) to encourage and restrict consumers from particular jurisdictions from being able to contract with the business via its web site. An example of a technical measure would be when the seller's web site requires the consumer to select his country from a 'drop-down list'[99] of countries on a web site to be able to access the web site, join a mail list[100] or proceed to order goods. Alternatively, as Johnson and Post suggest, the business could use different country domain name endings,[101] for example '.uk' (United Kingdom) or '.de' (Germany), to direct consumers to use the web sites with the domain name ending of their own country. However, whilst the domain name of a web site may indicate where the seller is located or seeks custom to an extent, if a business uses a '.com' domain ending, the ambiguity of the seller's location continues. A contractual measure may require the consumer to confirm his address during the contract formation stage. Furthermore, a business may impose a choice of forum clause in a contract in order to protect itself or limit its liability from claims by a consumer. Equally, in comparison to the earlier example of the catalogue or advertisement from the South African wine seller, the consumer who contracts with the business online may not know with certainty where that business is located. A consumer does not have the same ability to impose a technical measure on a web site or stipulate a choice of forum clause in a contract. For a consumer contract to proceed online via a web site, the consumer

---

97 Sookman, 'Electronic Commerce, Internet and the Law – A Survey of the Legal Issues,' at p.54.

98 Geist, 'Is There a There?'

99 For example, see <http://www.gucci.com>. By clicking on the country the person browsing the web site may be taken to the relevant 'country' page of that web site where country-specific information can be viewed.

100 For example, at the time of writing, the web site of a Spanish jewellery company <http://www.tous.es>, did not specify the United Kingdom and the United States from its drop-down list of countries for potential customers to be able to sign up for online information and news.

101 D.R. Johnson and D.G. Post, 'The Rise of Law on the Global Network,' in B. Kahin and C. Nesson (eds), *Borders in Cyberspace Information Policy and the Global Information Infrastructure* (Cambridge, Massachusetts, 1997) and affirmed by Puurunen, 'The Legislative Jurisdiction of States Over Transactions in International Electronic Commerce,' at p.690.

is usually required to confirm acceptance of the contractual terms. By clicking on an 'I accept' or 'I agree' icon on a web page the consumer is deemed to accept the contractual terms that, together with details of the consumer's order and confirmation of payment, creates the click-wrap or 'online'[102] agreement between the parties.[103] The click-wrap agreement has been regarded as an 'adaptation'[104] or an up to date version of a shrink-wrap agreement.[105] The click-wrap agreement therefore imposes standard terms and conditions that the consumer must accept for the online contract to be concluded, or find another seller. The click-wrap agreement will invariably include choice of forum and law clauses. The seller may also use one or more language or currency payment options on its web site. The method of payment may provide some indication of where the consumer is located, for example if a currency conversion is required from the consumer's currency to the currency required to pay for the contract goods. Whilst these options may be used to either facilitate or restrict consumers in certain jurisdictions from contracting with the seller online, they are not sufficiently consistent factors to determine the jurisdiction or applicable law of a cross-border dispute. Indeed, the European Union rejected language and currency as suitable connecting factors to determine where a business directs its activities via a web site.[106]

The present author recently remarked that

> (D)espite Burnstein's suggestion that 'place matters less on the Internet,'[107] it is submitted that the traditional connecting factors of location and activity must still operate to determine which jurisdiction will hear the parties' dispute and what law will apply. To ensure that their sovereignty is asserted over a cross-border dispute, states must ensure that parties are domiciled or their commercial activities take place within or are connected in a sufficient manner to the territorial boundaries of that state. The connection between the parties and their location or where their activities take place ensures that the state can assert jurisdiction over a dispute and, as Sookman affirms,[108] apply its own laws. To enable a state to assert its sovereignty over an electronic consumer contract dispute, substantive consumer protection rules must be complimented by a consistent, harmonised jurisdiction rule in favour of the consumer's jurisdiction. Since electronic commerce is a method of dematerialised cross-border

102 A. Gatt, 'Electronic Commerce – Click Wrap Agreements, The Enforceability of Click-Wrap Agreements' (2002) 18:6 *CLSR* 404.

103 Gatt, ibid at p.405.

104 Gatt, ibid.

105 M. Burnstein, 'A Global Network in a Compartmentalised Legal Environment,' in K. Boele-Woelki and C. Kessedjian (eds), *Internet Which Court Decides? Which Law Applies?* (The Hague, 1998) at p.31.

106 Chapter 5.

107 Burnstein, 'A Global Network in a Compartmentalised Legal Environment,' at p.24; Gillies, 'Addressing the "Cyberspace Fallacy",' at p.7.

108 Sookman, 'Electronic Commerce, Internet and the Law – A Survey of the Legal Issues,' at p.54.

> communication, the general consensus is that electronic consumer contracts ought to be regulated in the same manner as consumer contracts conducted offline.[109] Indeed, the ability to effectively regulate electronic consumer contracts illustrates a wider need for appropriate legal regulation of commercial activities conducted online. The certainty and predictability of the legal regulation of electronic commerce will be a significant influence on the continued use and popularity of electronic commerce as a commercial communication medium.[110]

As Docherty and Fletcher have remarked 'commercial interests [cannot be trusted] to protect the interests of consumers.'[111] Jurisdiction and choice of law rules for consumer contracts have been adapted in response to the adaptation of substantive consumer protection rules. Nevertheless, the following Chapters will demonstrate that the particularists' approach that has been used to adapt these[112] rules for electronic consumer contracts in the United Kingdom and the United States are not conducive to enable the consumer to sue the business in his own jurisdiction, thereby ensuring justice is achieved in such circumstances.

109 OECD, 'Ministerial Declaration on Consumer Protection in the Context of Electronic Commerce,' 'Consumer Protection in the Electronic Marketplace,' 'Ministerial Declaration on Consumer Protection in the Context of Electronic Commerce.' Copyright OECD. Froomkin, 'The Internet as a Source of Regulatory Arbitrage,' Catchpole, 'The Regulation of Electronic Commerce' at p.1. Although it would appear that, by referring to the perceived, separate nature of the physical and online worlds, Catchpole tends to endorse the view that they are indeed separate and are therefore different; D. Campbell (ed), *Law of International Online Business*, at p.24; Docherty and Fletcher, 'Responding to the legal problems of electronic commerce.'

110 Gillies, 'Addressing the "Cyberspace Fallacy",' at p.7 citing Catchpole, ibid at p.1.

111 Docherty and Fletcher, 'Responding to the legal problems of electronic commerce,' at p.3 cited in Gillies, 'Addressing the "Cyberspace Fallacy",' at p.8. Words in brackets added. The need for sovereign states to regulate electronic commercial activities and the disputes arising from them is a key argument against businesses or third parties operating Alternative Dispute Resolution (ADR) schemes, such as online arbitration or mediation, for resolving cross-border consumer contract disputes. Whilst a number of ADR schemes have operated, for example TrustUK and BBBOnline in the USA, these schemes should still remain complimentary to providing consumers with sufficient juridical protection via jurisdiction rules.

112 E.P. Mendes, 'The Troublesome Workings of the Judgments Convention of the European Economic Community' (1980) 13 *Vand J Transnat'l L* 75 at p.96 and Rothchild, 'Protecting the Digital Consumer,' on the matter of disintermediation of consumer protection policy.

Summary

Given the expansion in the globalisation of markets and finance combined with national regulations and initiatives to regulate electronic commercial activities, it has become increasingly necessary to refer to rules of international private law.[113] Whilst the level of cross-border consumer activity has increased,[114] the application of international private law rules to consumer contracts has not been entirely consistent. Before the WWW opened new markets to businesses and consumers, the number of cross-border consumer contracts was not significant. Vaughan Black's observation that 'international private law only required to be considered in one-off cases when cross-border matters ar[o]se'[115] is a historical indicator of the prevalence of cross-border disputes. However with the advent of electronic commerce, the requirement to determine the jurisdiction of a cross-border consumer dispute has now become a 'demonstrably significant'[116] issue. Indeed, the present author has also observed that '(R)ules and principles of international private law often need to be applied in many more cross-border disputes than before.'[117] The onset of electronic commerce by means of the WWW to advertise, promote and sell goods or services have contributed to the internationalisation or disintermediation of consumer contracts.[118] Consumers continue[119] to have

---

113 See J.H.A. Van Loon, 'The Increasing Significance of International Co-operation for the Unification of Private International Law,' in T.M. De Boer, *Forty Years On: The Evolution of Post War Private International Law in Europe, Symposium in Celebration of the 40th Anniversary of the Centre of Foreign Law and Private International Law, University of Amsterdam, on 27 October 1989* (Deventer, 1990) at p.102 and 122.

114 Puurunen, 'The Legislative Jurisdiction of States Over Transactions in International Electronic Commerce,' at p.696.

115 V. Black, 'Consumer Protection in the Conflict of Laws: Canada, the United States and Europe,' in Iain Ramsay (ed), *Consumer Law in the Global Economy, National and International Dimensions* (Aldershot, 1997) at p.210. L.E. Gillies, 'Adapting International Private Law Rules for Electronic Consumer Contracts,' in C.E.F. Rickett and T.G.W. Telfer (eds), *International Perspectives on Consumers' Access to Justice* (Cambridge, 2003). Word in bracket modified for syntax.

116 Black, 'Consumer Protection in the Conflict of Laws,' at p.208.

117 Gillies, 'Adapting International Private Law Rules for Electronic Consumer Contracts,' at p.360.

118 Gillies, ibid.

119 As reported by C. Gethin and S. Gribble, 'Cyber Rules for Consumer Protection Urgently Needed Says International Federation,' Consumers International Press Release, 6 September 1999. See also J. Whiteley, 'Understanding the Online Buyer' (2000) July/Aug *ADMAP* pp.14–16. OECD, 'Consumers in the Online Marketplace: The OECD Guidelines Three Years Later, Report by the Committee on Consumer Policy on the Guidelines for Consumer Protection in the Context of Electronic Commerce,' DSTI/CP(2002)4/FINAL, 3 February 2003. Copyright OECD.

concerns regarding the risk of 'fraudulent activity'[120] and the privacy and security of their online transactions. Consumers must also be assured that jurisdiction rules will alleviate the legal and financial risks of having to sue a foreign business in a foreign jurisdiction.[121] The risks associated with electronic commerce have necessitated governments to re-think and, as Rothchild affirms, re-assess both substantive consumer protection policy[122] and international private law rules.[123] Businesses and consumers have become more aware of which court should[124] hear any dispute resulting from an electronic consumer contract[125] and what law should apply. As consumers have accepted electronic commerce as a legitimate, convenient and efficient method of contracting with a foreign business, the content and implementation of appropriate international private law rules has become globally significant. The recommendations of the OECD Council are particularly indicative of the interaction between the national and international regulation of international commercial activity.

> Business-to-consumer cross-border transactions, whether carried out electronically or otherwise are subject to the existing framework on applicable law and jurisdiction. Electronic commerce poses challenges to this existing framework. Therefore, consideration should be given to whether the existing framework for applicable law and jurisdiction should be modified, or applied differently, to ensure effective and transparent consumer protection in the context of the continued growth of electronic commerce. In considering whether to modify the existing framework, governments should seek to ensure that the framework provides fairness to consumers and business, facilitates electronic commerce, results in consumers having a level of protection not less than afforded in other forums of commerce, and provides consumers with meaningful access to fair and timely dispute resolution and redress without undue cost or burden.[126]

---

120 Rothchild, 'Protecting the Digital Consumer,' at pp.898–899.

121 Gillies, 'Adapting International Private Law Rules for Electronic Consumer Contracts,' at p.359.

122 Rothchild, 'Protecting the Digital Consumer,' at p.899.

123 Rothchild, ibid at p.914 and 916.

124 OECD, 'Ministerial Declaration on Consumer Protection in the Context of Electronic Commerce,' at p.7. Copyright OECD.

125 In their comments on the October 1999 draft of the proposed Judgments Convention, contributors to the Consumer Project on Technology's page on the Hague Conference's proposed judgments convention pointed out that the issue was not simply an 'academic one' for businesses; <http://lists.essential.org/pipermail/hague-jur-commercial-law/>, 2–3 April 2001.

126 OECD, 'Recommendation of the OECD Council Concerning Guidelines for Consumer Protection in the Context of Electronic Commerce,' ILM 29 (2000): 504. Copyright OECD. See also Puurunen, 'The Legislative Jurisdiction of States Over Transactions in International Electronic Commerce,' at p.692. This section was repeated and acknowledged by the Hague Conference on Private International Law in their report 'Electronic Data Interchange, Internet and Electronic Commerce,' drawn up by Catherine Kessedjian, at p.9.

In the years since that recommendation, different jurisdictions have adapted jurisdiction rules for electronic consumer contracts in response to the disintermediation of consumer protection by electronic commerce.[127] The majority of European Member States,[128] including the United Kingdom,[129] have already adapted rules of jurisdiction for consumer contracts in the Brussels 1 Regulation and, Brussels 1 Regulation and the EU has recently adopted Regulation EC 593/2008 (the Rome 1 Regulation).[130] Mayer has acknowledged that whilst the EU has implemented legislation to address the legal aspects of electronic commerce, it has 'failed to shift the crucial issue of regulation of technical control over the Internet onto a truly international arena.'[131] For example, rules of jurisdiction for electronic consumer contracts in the Brussels 1 Regulation apply, inter alia, only when the consumer is domiciled and the defendant business is situated in an EU Member State. Meanwhile, the courts in the United States[132] have adapted their existing jurisdiction rules for the increasing number[133] of contracts that are entered into electronically. Despite adaptation by the courts, rules of personal jurisdiction are not consistent in establishing jurisdiction over a foreign business in the consumer's domicile. Chapter Seven will also explore the difficulties with the draft Rome 1 Regulation vis-à-vis electronic consumer contracts. As this chapter has indicated, electronic commerce activity is not restricted to parties domiciled in EU Member States. Mayer's comment highlights the challenge of regulating electronic commerce activity at global level. As the OECD reported above and

127 Docherty and Fletcher, 'Responding to the legal problems of electronic commerce,' at p.3 where they cite the United States, Australia and New Zealand as examples. See also R. Schu, 'The Applicable Law to Consumer Contracts Made Over the Internet: Consumer Protection Through Private International Law?' (1997) 5:2 *Int J Law and Tech* 192 at p.203.

128 Schu, ibid.

129 According to data obtained by IMRG, the long term growth in UK Internet sales is beginning to emerge; 'Internet Shopping Hits £3 Billion in November,' 14 December 2006, available at <http://www.imrg.org/ItemDetail.aspx?clg=News&cid=nws&pid=News_IMRG_Index&language=en-GB>. Out-law.com also quotes IMRG's forecast that 'UK e-retail would grow 36% in 2006,'; 'Christmas Figures Reveal Massive Rise in E-Commerce," 20 January 2006, <http://www.out-law.com/default.aspx?page=6554>.

130 In June 2008 Regulation EC 593/2008, the Rome 1 Regulation, OJ L177 6, was adopted. Despite debate on the matter, party autonomy to select the applicable law of a consumer contract was retained in Article 6.

131 Chapter 5 with regard to EU jurisidiction rules and Chapter 7 with regards to EU choice of law rules.

132 Schu, 'The Applicable Law to Consumer Contracts Made Over the Internet,' at p.228–29.

133 According to the Office of National Statistics, '(T)he value of Internet sales to households rose to £21.4 billion in 2005 from £16.5 billion in 2004, a rise of 29.7 per cent.' E-Commerce Survey by Businesses, 13 October 2006 <http://www.statistics.gov.uk/pdfdir/ecom1006.pdf>.

as Catchpole confirms, 'e-commerce should be embraced as an integral part of business and, therefore, regulated and controlled to afford consumers, and alike, the legislative protections that are available in the physical world.'[134]

Whilst jurisdiction rules for electronic consumer contracts have been adapted by national governments to an extent, divergences still exist in the content and application of jurisdiction and choice of law rules for electronic consumer contracts. The key divergences are as follows. Firstly, given the global, anonymous nature of electronic commerce, the scope of the consumer jurisdiction rules requires to be clarified. The definition of consumers as natural persons acting for their private use should be retained and should not be extended to enable sole traders and small enterprises to benefit from a protective jurisdiction rule intended for a party who is a non-specialist. Secondly, the use of jurisdiction agreements to direct a dispute to a jurisdiction other than the consumer's domicile must be resolved. If rules of jurisdiction for electronic consumer contracts are to provide certain and predictable results, they should not be thwarted by a jurisdiction agreement which directs the parties' dispute to the business' jurisdiction. Thirdly, it remains to be clarified exactly what level of web site activity will establish that the business directed (the term used in the United Kingdom rules) or targeted (the approach in the United States rules) its online activities towards the consumer's jurisdiction. If the level of web site activity required for the operation of those tests is appropriately determined, it will be clearer to both parties that the consumer jurisdiction rule will apply. 'Active' and 'interactive' web sites should be regarded as directing commercial activities or targeting consumers for the purposes of jurisdiction. Fourthly, if the directing activities/targeting tests are clarified and satisfied, jurisdiction must be established in the consumer's domicile no matter where the defendant is domiciled. Fifthly, the approach used in the draft (and subsequently adopted) Rome 1 Regulation which replicates the requirements for establishing jurisdiction of a consumer contract in Article 15(1)(c) of the Brussels 1 Regulation is inappropriate for ensuring the law of the consumer's domicile applies. These current divergences demonstrate how a particularist approach has prioritised national interests in the adaptation of international private law rules.[135]

The effect of these divergences is two-fold. Firstly, the practical effect of these divergences is that the parties continue to be unable to determine with certainty and predictability which jurisdiction and applicable law will apply to their dispute. Secondly, conflicts justice cannot be achieved if certainty and predictability of result are not assured even after jurisdiction and choice of law rules have been adapted. However, given the general importance of electronic commerce to world trade[136] and the specific incidence of electronic consumer contracts, cooperation between countries is now necessary to ensure that both conflicts justice is achieved

134 Catchpole, 'The Regulation of Electronic Commerce' at p.1.

135 P. Hay, O. Lando and R.D. Rotunda, 'Conflict of Laws as a Technique for Legal Integration,' at p.167.

136 Catchpole, 'The Regulation of Electronic Commerce' at p.3.

and confidence in electronic commerce as a commercial medium is maintained. Basedow has described such cooperation as contributing to a 'new world order'[137] in the international regulation of commercial activities. The use of electronic commerce as a communication medium has brought about the 'internationalisation of consumer issues.'[138] Harmonisation of jurisdiction rules to protect consumers and provide certainty for businesses contracting online[139] and, as Goldring suggests, limit forum shopping, is now necessary.[140] The existing rules of jurisdiction and choice of law for electronic consumer contracts are not consistent to enable the consumer to sue a business in his own jurisdiction.[141] A globally harmonised consumer contract jurisdiction and choice of law rule in favour of the consumer's jurisdiction and law respectively that requires the business to have intentionally targeted consumers via active or interactive web sites will ensure that conflicts justice is achieved no matter where either party is located.

137 J. Basedow, 'The Effects of Globalization on Private International Law,' in J. Basedow and T. Kono (eds), *Legal Aspects of Globalization Conflict of Laws, Internet, Capital Markets and Insolvency in a Global Economy* (The Hague, 2000) at p.5.

138 Puurunen, 'The Legislative Jurisdiction of States Over Transactions in International Electronic Commerce,' at p.690 and Rothchild, 'Protecting the Digital Consumer,' at p.896.

139 J. Goldring, 'Netting the Cybershark: Consumer Protection, Cyberspace, the Nation-State, and Democracy,' in B. Kahin and C. Nesson (eds), *Borders in Cyberspace Information Policy and the Global Information Infrastructure* (Cambridge, Massachusetts, 1997) at p.324 refers to the consumer as the weaker party i.e. that consumer protection law rather than general law and/or market forces should regulate.

140 Goldring, ibid at p.93 and 94.

141 Given that international private law is inherently 'national law,' Schu, 'The Applicable Law to Consumer Contracts Made Over the Internet,' at p.199, the harmonisation of such laws is worthy of consideration, a point considered by Steven Gallagher, 'Contracting in Cyberspace – A Minefield for the Unwary' (2000) 16 *CLSR* 101 at p.103 where he stresses that such are the 'limitations of the existing legal framework … some have been moved to call for a comprehensive overhaul of the existing legislation and have put forward proposals ranging from the international unification of choice of law rules to the creation of an independent Internet jurisdiction in its own right where disputes would be dealt with by a special court or arbitral body.'

Chapter 3
International Private Law Rules for Electronic Consumer Contracts: Theoretical Approaches

Introduction

The main approaches to the legal regulation of electronic commerce activity are individual state regulation, model laws and harmonisation.[1] Since the purpose of substantive consumer protection law is to protect consumers, consumers should be provided with juridical protection via international private law regardless of the method used by the parties to contract with each other. To attain that objective, governments have already adapted jurisdiction rules for electronic consumer contracts. As electronic commerce is not restricted to consumers and businesses situated in one jurisdiction, the ways in which other countries have sought to adapt their international private law rules for such contracts must be considered.[2] For that reason, this book will consider how jurisdiction and choice of law rules have been developed in the United Kingdom and the United States. Both countries' economies have continued to maintain high levels of participation in electronic commerce.[3] These levels of participation can be attributed to the historical development of the World Wide Web in the United States and, in the case of both countries, the political will to develop and sustain electronic commerce as, inter alia, a legitimate commercial activity and educational tool.[4] These countries have actively adapted or introduced substantive laws to regulate electronic commerce in their own jurisdictions in support of regional political objectives. These countries have also adapted existing jurisdiction rules for consumer contracts and are in

1 C.T. Poggi, 'Electronic Commerce Legislation: An Analysis of European and American Approaches to Contract Formation' (2000) 41 *Va J Int'l L* 224 at pp.227–228.

2 T.M. De Boer, 'The Evolution of Postwar Private International Law,' in T.M. De Boer, *Forty Years On: The Evolution of Post War Private International Law in Europe, Symposium in Celebration of the 40th Anniversary of the Centre of Foreign Law and Private International Law, University of Amsterdam, on 27 October 1989* (Deventer, 1990) at p.10 and R. Schu, 'The Applicable Law to Consumer Contracts Made Over the Internet: Consumer Protection Through Private International Law?' (1997) 5:2 *Int J Law and Tech* 192 at p.198.

3 OECD, 'Measuring the Information Economy,' Chapter IV, Electronic Commerce, <http://www.oecd.org/dataoecd/34/35/2771139.pdf>. Copyright OECD.

4 Chapter 8.

the process of modernising choice of law rules. The courts of the United States have adapted their existing rules of personal jurisdiction in an attempt to ensnare the online activities of a foreign defendant and the United States, as part of the Organisation of American States, is currently participating in negotiations for a convention on choice of law rules for consumer contracts.[5] The United Kingdom has implemented an EU Regulation which modified the jurisdiction rule for consumer contracts. The European Union has recently adopted a Regulation to replace the Rome Convention 1980. Fourthly, the countries are similar in that they comprise separate, internal jurisdictions (Scotland and England, Wales and Northern Ireland in the UK and the fifty states of the United States). However, for electronic commerce to continue to flourish and for the parties to know with certainty or predict the effect of a particular jurisdiction or choice of law rule when contracting online, jurisdiction and choice of law rules for electronic consumer contracts must be applied consistently and provide an automatic, harmonised rule in favour of the consumer's jurisdiction and law.

Theoretical Development of International Private Law

During the twentieth century there was a theoretical shift in the development of international private law. Since the 1960s in particular,[6] codification and harmonisation of international private law rules have become the predominant methods of developing international private law rules.[7] According to the Oxford Dictionary, the meaning of harmonisation is described as bringing something 'into consonance or accord,' and the verb 'unify,' a synonym of harmonisation, means 'to gather or combine parts or elements into a close mass or a coherent whole.'[8] The starting point to harmonisation of international private law rules can be summed up by reference to Storme's observation that '(A)ny unification project must meet

5 At the time of writing, proposals for a model law on choice of law to protect consumers is under consideration by the Organisation of American States' Seventh Inter-American Specialised Conference on Private International Law (CIDIP-VII); <http://www.oas.org/dil/Report_Session_January_18_2007.pdf> and <http://www.oas.org/dil/esp/Choice_of_Law_Rules_for_Consumer_Contracts%20_nov_2006.pdf>.

6 T.M. De Boer, 'The Evolution of Postwar Private International Law,' at p.3.

7 A.P.M.J. Vonken, 'Balancing Processes in International Family Law, On the determination and weighing of interests in the conflicts of laws and the 'openness' of the choice of law system,' in T. M. De Boer, *Forty Years On: The Evolution of Post War Private International Law in Europe, Symposium in Celebration of the 40th Anniversary of the Centre of Foreign Law and Private International Law, University of Amsterdam, on 27 October 1989* (Deventer, 1990) at p.171.

8 *Compact Oxford Dictionary, Thesaurus and Wordpower Guide* (Oxford University Press, Oxford, 2002).

a particular need and at the same time be feasible.'[9] As stated earlier, the need for harmonisation of jurisdiction and choice of law rules for electronic consumer contracts is to ensure that certainty and predictability of result are achieved. Conflicts justice can be achieved when a consistent rule for electronic consumer contracts is provided in favour of the consumer's jurisdiction and law. The need to harmonise such jurisdiction and choice of law rules is realistic given the economic significance of electronic commerce and the need to ensure that predictability of result is assured for the benefit of both parties. If it can be established that the business meant to contract with the consumer in a particular jurisdiction via the WWW, then as Stone affirms,[10] it is fair and just that the business ought to be subject to the jurisdiction of the consumer's domicile in the same way as if the business had directed its commercial activities via an advertisement in a newspaper or on television in the consumer's domicile.

Universalism and Particularism

According to Jeunger '(O)ne may wonder why it took so long to discern what should have been obvious from the start, namely that decisional harmony is in jeopardy as long as each state remains free to classify legal rules as it sees fit.'[11] During the last century, the theories of universalism[12] and particularism[13] were used to develop international private law rules. The purpose of a universalist approach is to ensure that international private law rules provide predictability of result. A universalist approach upholds international private law as 'primarily a coordinating task ... for uniformity of result and decisional harmony.'[14] The universalist approach,

9 M. Storme, 'Procedural Consequences for a Common Private Law for Europe,' in A.S. Hartkamp, M.W. Hesselink, E.H. Hondius, C.E. du Perron, and J.B.M. Vranken, *Towards a European Civil Code* (London, 1994) at p.86. J.H.A. Van Loon, 'The Increasing Significance of International Co-operation for the Unification of Private International Law,' in T.M. De Boer, *Forty Years On: The Evolution of Post War Private International Law in Europe, Symposium in Celebration of the 40th Anniversary of the Centre of Foreign Law and Private International Law, University of Amsterdam, on 27 October 1989* (Deventer, 1990) at pp.102 and 122.

10 P. Stone, 'The Treatment of Electronic Contracts and Torts in Private International Law under European Community Legislation' (2002) 11:2 *Information and Communications Technology Law* 121 at p.125.

11 F.K. Juenger, *Choice of Law and Multistate Justice* (Dordrecht, 1993) at p.71.

12 P. Hay, O. Lando, and R.D. Rotunda, 'Conflict of Laws as a Technique for Legal Integration,' in M. Capelletti, M. Seccombe, and J. Weiler (eds), *Integration Through Law*, Volume 1, Book 2 (New York, 1986) at pp.168–169.

13 Hay, Lando and Rotunda, ibid at p.172.

14 A.P.M.J. Vonken, 'Balancing Processes in International Family Law, On the determination and weighing of interests in the conflicts of laws and the 'openness' of the choice of law system,' at p.172.

as espoused by the EU in both the Brussels and Rome Conventions,[15] seeks to ensure that foreign judgments are given equal recognition and enforcement which, according to Hay et al facilitates the reduction in forum selection. By contrast, particularism centres on reflecting national interests in international private law rules. Particularism focuses on the development of international private law rules in tandem with the development of substantive laws of the forum state.[16] Hay et al suggest that despite the Restatement (Second) (Conflict of Laws), the US approach to international private law rules has traditionally tended to favour particularism.[17] As stated earlier, the regulation of electronic commerce activity via international private law rules raises two important points. Firstly, there is the need to ensure that jurisdiction and choice of law rules facilitate conflicts justice by ensuring that the parties to an electronic consumer contract can determine or predict with a degree of certainty which jurisdiction will hear a dispute between them. To that end, a business will be able to predict which jurisdiction and law will apply to a dispute with a foreign consumer. Secondly, as stated earlier, international private law rules should strive to compliment the objectives of substantive laws in order to reach a "just solution" to a cross-border dispute.[18] As Furrer has indicated 'all considerations regarding conflict of laws focus on national law and national interests. Even the opening of the national system of conflict of laws towards foreign legal systems is, fundamentally, directed by national interests.'[19]

Particularism questions the need for international private law to reflect societal influences[20] and substantive private law.[21] This is rightly so; since international private law is national law, it must not circumvent national law and national interests. To that extent, Vonken has suggested that particularism imposes a wider, perhaps regulatory, role in the development of suitable and effective

15 P. Hay, O. Lando, and R.D. Rotunda, 'Conflict of Laws as a Technique for Legal Integration,' at pp.167–168.

16 Ibid at p.172.

17 Ibid at pp.167–168.

18 Ibid at p.172. Word in brackets modified for syntax.

19 A. Furrer, 'European Law without Peak and Centre? Observations on the Europeanization Process in Private Law Towards a Supranational Multi-level System,' in C. Joerges and O. Gerstenberg (eds), 'Private governance, democratic constitutionalism and supranationalism,' Proceedings of the COST A7 Seminar, Florence, 22 to 24 May at p.181.

20 A.P.M.J. Vonken, 'Balancing Processes in International Family Law, On the determination and weighing of interests in the conflicts of laws and the "openness" of the choice of law system.'

21 A. Furrer, 'European Law without Peak and Centre? Observations on the Europeanization Process in Private Law Towards a Supranational Multi-level System'; I. Volkmer, 'Universalism and Particularism: The Problem of Cultural Sovereignty and Global Information Flow,' in B. Kahin and Charles Nesson (eds), *Borders in Cyberspace Information Policy and the Global Information Infrastructure* (Cambridge, Massachusetts, 1997).

international private law rules.[22] As stated earlier, disputes between consumers and businesses that have contracted electronically with each other will increase in a dematerialised, globally equivalent marketplace. The recent adaptation of existing jurisdiction and choice of law rules in the United Kingdom and the United States is indicative of a particularist response by those governments to secure juridical protection for consumers. When new forms of business activities and methods of communication require to be regulated, it is to be expected that states will adopt an approach that focuses on current national laws and interests. A particularist approach has been reflected by amendments to substantive consumer protection laws and the introduction of rules to regulate electronic commerce activities in the United Kingdom and the United States. National interests and the societal need to regulate new forms of commercial activities have directed such an approach. Whilst jurisdiction and choice of law rules for electronic consumer contracts have been adapted at national level in recent years, national interests are no longer confined to commercial activities within jurisdictional boundaries. Since the United Kingdom and the United States will continue to apply their own modified jurisdiction and choice of law rules to electronic consumer contract disputes, the possibility of diverging results will increase.[23] At this point, it is submitted that the two theories of particularism and universalism meet. At EU level there has been a concerted effort to harmonise national or 'horizontal' international private law rules of individual Member States with regional or 'vertical' 'post-war European'[24] international private law to meet the objectives of the Internal Market. By contrast, the courts in the United States still have regard to the internal United States constitutional requirement of 'Due Process' when determining whether jurisdiction can be asserted over a foreign or 'out of state' defendant. The influence of particularism in the adaptation of jurisdiction and choice of law rules for electronic consumer contracts renders those rules inefficient in the long term. As electronic commerce facilitates global commerce, it is therefore paramount that jurisdiction and choice of law rules for electronic consumer contracts provide certainty of application and predictability of result and ensure forum shopping is limited. Whilst it is conceded that international private law will continue to reflect particularists' interest in substantive law to an extent,[25] it must be noted

22 A.P.M.J. Vonken, 'Balancing Processes in International Family Law, On the determination and weighing of interests in the conflicts of laws and the 'openness' of the choice of law system.'

23 Indeed according to De Boer, ibid, '(D)iverging national laws have been attributed as signifying different national interests.'

24 T.M. De Boer, 'The Evolution of Postwar Private International Law,' at p.9. See Chapter 4.

25 A.P.M.J. Vonken, 'Balancing Processes in International Family Law, On the determination and weighing of interests in the conflicts of laws and the "openness" of the choice of law system,' note 7 supra.

that '(P)rivate international law is not itself international; but should certainly be drawn up in an international frame of mind.'[26]

The continued application of particularism as a theory to develop jurisdiction rules for electronic consumer contracts is now outmoded. According to Akehurst, unless international private law rules are developed by considering similar rules in other countries,[27] then such rules were likely to be unsatisfactory[28] and that their development would be 'along increasingly divergent lines.'[29] It is submitted that these points are crucial to the increasing number of consumer contracts being conducted across borders by electronic means and the rules of jurisdiction currently applicable to such contracts. It is the aim of this book to consider not only how jurisdiction and choice of law rules have been adapted in the United Kingdom and United States but how uncertainty of application and unpredictability of result are manifested by such rules. Such rules require further refinement either in tandem or harmoniously with other countries to ensure that conflicts justice and international[30] 'decisional harmony' [31]are achieved. Furthermore, it is submitted that as a theory for developing jurisdiction and choice of law rules for electronic consumer contracts, particularism has now been overtaken by the necessity for universally consistent jurisdiction and applicable law rules. The divergences that still exist in those jurisdiction and choice of law rules will continue to hinder the consumers' ability to sue the seller in his own jurisdiction.

Harmonisation: A Future Theoretical Approach

Kotting has questioned whether the theoretical development of international private law rules should be initiated 'on a national, interregional or international level.'[32] Since this book supports a universalist approach to the harmonisation of jurisdiction rules for electronic consumer contracts, it must therefore be considered

---

26 Akehurst 'Jurisdiction in International Law' (1972–73) 46 *BYBIL* 145 citing Wolff.

27 Indeed, according to Jeunger, since unilateralism and multilateralism 'geared as it is to the classification of legal rules, can achieve decisional harmony only if all legal systems classify their private law in the same manner'; F.K. Juenger, *Choice of Law and Multistate Justice*, at p.71.

28 Akehurst, ibid at p.231 explains that this is why the Hague Conference had an initial lack of success in achieving harmonisation by way of Conventions.

29 Akehurst, ibid.

30 A.P.M.J. Vonken, 'Balancing Processes in International Family Law, On the determination and weighing of interests in the conflicts of laws and the "openness" of the choice of law system,' at p.178.

31 Meijers, 'Gemeenschappeliijke toelichting op het Benelux-Verdrag houhende een Eenvormige Wet betreffende het Internationaal Privachrecht,' cited in T.M. De Boer, 'The Evolution of Postwar Private International Law,' at p.2.

32 R. Kotting, 'The Vicious Circle of Forum Law,' in T.M.De Boer, *Forty Years On: The Evolution of Post War Private International Law in Europe, Symposium in Celebration*

at what level such harmonisation has to take place to be truly effective? As Van Loon asserts,[33] there has been an increasing internationalisation of international private law rules that have developed not in a vacuum but in a context of growing internationalisation of daily life which presents many challenges to private international law and to the unification of private international law in part.' Over the last century, harmonisation of international private law has increased as a result of the efforts of regional (supranational) and international organisations. Indeed, as Symeonides aptly describes,

> (M)any nations, not least since the establishment of the United Nations, have seen the need to come together on the international plane to provide mechanisms not only for the resolution of disputes between States, but also to resolve some of the issues which arise from [the] globalization of our activities.[34]

The international treaty or convention has become the most prevalent instrument used to promote international cooperation between countries.[35] The European Community is the most prominent example of regional involvement in the development and implementation of international private law rules for the purposes of the Internal Market.[36] The Hague Conference on Private International Law is an international organisation that was set up for the purpose of harmonising international private laws amongst its member countries.[37] The Hague Conference has harmonised a range[38] of international private law topics by way of

---

of the 40th Anniversary of the Centre of Foreign Law and Private International Law, University of Amsterdam, on 27 October 1989 (Deventer, 1990) at p.xv.

33 J.H.A. Van Loon, 'The Increasing Significance of International Co-operation for the Unification of Private International Law,' in T.M.De Boer, *Forty Years On: The Evolution of Post War Private International Law in Europe, Symposium in Celebration of the 40th Anniversary of the Centre of Foreign Law and Private International Law, University of Amsterdam, on 27 October 1989* (Deventer, 1990) at p.102.

34 S.C. Symeonides (ed), *Private International Law at the End of the 20th Century: Progress or Regress?* (London, 2000) at Preface, vii (word in bracket substituted).

35 J.H.A. Van Loon, 'The Increasing Significance of International Co-operation for the Unification of Private International Law.'

36 The Brussels Convention and the Brussels 1 Regulation are the relevant European Community instruments for analysis in this Book and are considered in Chapters 4, 5 and 6. The proposals for the replacement of the Rome Convention to a Community Instrument are considered in Chapter 7, *cf* EC 593/2008 OJ L177 6.

37 The Hague Conference on Private International Law, <http://www.hcch.net>. Article 1 of 'Statute on the Hague Conference on Private International Law,' 15 July 1955, states that '(T)he purpose of the Hague Conference is to work for the progressive unification of the rules of private international law.' J.H.A. Van Loon, 'The Increasing Significance of International Co-operation for the Unification of Private International Law.'

38 Later commercial conventions included the Convention on the Service Abroad of Judicial and Extrajudicial Documents in Civil or Commercial Matters in 1965, the

international conventions.[39] By the end of the last century the Hague Conference aimed to harmonise rules on jurisdiction, recognition and enforcement in civil and commercial matters via a Jurisdiction and Judgments Convention, latterly a Convention on Choice of Court Agreements. The convention was regarded as one of the most ambitious and fraught projects that the Hague Conference had undertaken in recent years.[40] However the scope of the convention was substantially reduced to a convention on 'choice of court' rules only. The proposals in the earliest (1999 and 2001 draft) conventions are important to consider for the following reasons. Firstly, the proposed convention would have had, in its modified form, worldwide effect. Secondly, the present author has questioned[41] whether the initial and subsequent articles in those draft conventions could apply to electronic consumer contracts. The present author has previously concluded that the proposed convention should retain jurisdiction rules for consumer contracts and that Option B in the draft of Article 7 in the 2001 proposed convention was the most appropriate proposed jurisdiction rule for electronic consumer contracts.[42] Thirdly, the two drafts of the proposed convention continue to represent a unique and significant effort towards harmonisation of, inter alia, jurisdiction rules for electronic consumer contracts. Fourthly, it should be noted that, by its own admission, the Hague Conference's efforts may one day form the basis of a separate project for an international convention on either electronic commerce or electronic consumer contract jurisdiction.[43] A similar convention, such as the one currently under consideration by the Organisation for American States (OAS) could provide a basis for harmonised choice of law rules for future debate on electronic consumer contracts.

Summary

The need for a universalist approach to jurisdiction and choice of law rules for electronic consumer contracts is now evident and should be pursued. It is crucial that such a coordinated approach to international private law rules is applied in

---

Convention on Taking Evidence Abroad in Civil or Commercial Matters in 1970 and the Convention on the Law Applicable to Contracts for the International Sale of Goods in 1986.

39 S.C. Symeonides (ed), *Private International Law at the End of the 20th Century: Progress or Regress?* (London, 2000).

40 Chapter 9.

41 L.E. Gillies, 'The Impact of the Hague Conference's Proposed Judgments Convention for Electronic Commerce and Intellectual Property Disputes' (2002) 16:3 *Int Rev L Comps and Tech* 233.

42 Gillies, ibid at p.243.

43 A. Haines, 'The Impact of the Internet on the Judgments Project: Thoughts for the Future,' Hague Conference on Private International Law, Preliminary Document No.17, <http://www.hcch.net>.

order first to ensure that consumers are given sufficient juridical protection when contracting electronically with foreign sellers and second to facilitate commercial activity across borders via the WWW. Such an approach would go some way to ensure that in the event of a contractual dispute between the consumer and the business, the overarching desire towards predictability of result in determining the jurisdiction and law to be applied is achieved.

Chapter 4

The Development of European International Private Law Rules for Electronic Consumer Contracts

Introduction

Whilst consumer protection policy has developed in the EU since the 1970s,[1] the Treaties of Maastricht and Amsterdam have sought to further strengthen[2] the development of such policies to increase the level of protection afforded to consumers in the EU Member States. The Single European Act inserted Article 100a into the Treaty, which affirmed the extent of the European Commission's policy on consumer protection as follows:

> 3. The Commission, in its proposals envisaged in paragraph 1 concerning health, safety, environmental protection and consumer protection, will take as a base a high level of protection.[3]

The Maastricht Treaty sought to ensure that consumers received, in accordance with Article 129a(1) (re-numbered Article 153 by the Treaty of Amsterdam), a 'high level of consumer protection' in specific action either taken to pursue completion of the internal market or to '... protect the health, safety and economic interests of consumers.'[4] The Treaty of Amsterdam also imposed a duty on the European Community to ensure that consumers' rights are taken into account in the development and adoption of relevant measures. Article 153 also ensured that the Community achieved a high level of consumer protection when 'defining other Community policies and activities' and '... in the context of completion of the internal market.' For example, Article 153 enabled Member States to continue

1 Article 5(2) of the Treaty of Rome required the consumer to be protected; M. Lehmann, 'Electronic Commerce and Consumer Protection in Europe' (2000) 17 Comp High Tech Law Journal 101; J. Stuyck, 'European Consumer Law After The Treaty of Amsterdam: Consumer Policy In Or Beyond The Internal Market?' (2000) 37 *CMLR* 367 at p.377 *et seq*.

2 Article 3, EC Treaty; Stuyck, ibid at p.377.

3 Article 100a, EC.

4 Article 129a(1) EC; Stuyck, 'European Consumer Law After The Treaty of Amsterdam: Consumer Policy In Or Beyond The Internal Market?'

to implement their own consumer protection rules, even if those rules were more stringent than the provisions contained in European Community instruments.[5] However, in any event, national rules had to be compatible with the Treaty.[6]

The European Community has continued to develop its consumer protection policies post-Treaty of Amsterdam.[7] The Tampere Council sought to increase mutual cooperation between the civil laws of the EU Member States as follows,

> The main objective of co-operation in civil law is to establish better collaboration between Member States in order to encourage free movement of citizens. The European Council of Tampere (15 and 16 October 1999) established a map for the effective implementation, among others, of the civil co-operation provisions introduced by the Amsterdam Treaty. The three priorities in this field are better access to justice, mutual recognition of judicial decisions, and increased convergence in the field of procedural law.
>
> The Commission will pursue the targets set for the effective implementation of the civil cooperation provisions introduced by the Amsterdam Treaty and developed by the conclusions of the European Council of Tampere. The Commission will continue to update, at regular intervals, a 'Scoreboard', to monitor the progress in the adoption and implementation of the range of measures needed to meet these targets.
>
> The Commission will take into account the consumer's interest when Community rules on international private law are established.[8]

The European Community has developed a policy of ensuring that, as consumers, the citizens of Europe all have the same level of consumer protection afforded to them.[9] Van Def Hoff has defined the three 'pinnacles'[10] of EU consumer protection

5 Member States were also under an obligation to notify the Commission of such rules.

6 Article 153 TEU.

7 As illustrated by the most recent Health and Consumer Protection Programme (2007–2013) and the Green Paper on the Review of the consumer *acquis*; COM(2006) 744, 8 February 2007.

8 European Commission, 'Communication From the Commission to the European Parliament, The Council, The Economic and Social Committee and The Committee of the Regions, Consumer Policy Strategy 2002–2006,' Brussels COM (2002) 208, <http://ec.europa.eu/consumers/overview/cons_policy/doc/EN_99.pdf> and <http://europa.eu.int/comm/consumers/policy/intro/intro_en.html> at para.3.2.3.3.

9 Tampere Council Recommendations, ibid.

10 S. Van Der Hoff, 'European Conflict Rules Concerning International Online Consumer Contracts' (2003) 12:2 *Information and Telecommunications Law* 165.

as 'information disclosure, *ius poenitentae* and juridical protection.'[11] The basis of juridical protection for consumers is to provide the consumer with access to the jurisdiction and consumer protection rules of the consumer's domicile. Today, substantive consumer protection rules apply to a wide range of matters including, *inter alia*, product liability, consumer credit, rules governing contracts concluded at a distance ('distance selling')[12] including the distance marketing of consumer financial services[13] and the regulation of unfair commercial practices. Juridical protection for consumers is provided by jurisdiction and choice of law rules for consumer contracts in line with the Tampere Council's remit to improve security and justice across the Member States.[14] Such measures reflect also objectives that have evolved for consumer protection through amendments of the Treaty.[15]

Background to the Brussels 1 Regulation

According to the Commissioner for Justice and Home Affairs, the initial revision process to replace the Brussels Convention with a Community Regulation[16] was to allow for,

> improv(ing) access to justice within the EU. This will strengthen the rights of the citizen as a consumer as well as in other roles. It will also contribute to a more stable legal framework for industry, in particular small and medium sized companies, and thereby give a positive impetus to the further development of the internal market.[17]

The EU Commission recognised the need to ensure consumers receive adequate juridical protection when contracting with foreign sellers. The Commissioner for the Single Market, Mario Monti, reiterated the essence of the proposals which was

11 Van Der Hoff, ibid.

12 H.L. MacQueen and R. Azim-Khan, 'The Argos free TV debacle: two legal opinions' (1999) 1:9 *Electronic Business Law* 9.

13 Directive EC 2002/65 on the Distance Marketing of Consumer Financial Services OJ L271/16, 23 September 2002.

14 European Commission, 'Assessment of the Tampere Programme and Future Orientations' (COM (2004) 0401 final), 2 June 2004.

15 Unless otherwise stated, reference to the Treaty in this Book is the Treaty of Amsterdam as amended by the Treaty of Nice where appropriate.

16 Until July 2007, the Brussels Convention, as amended, applied between Denmark and the other Member States; Brussels Regulation, Recital 22. In June 2008, a Community Instrument – Regulation EC 593/2008, the Rome 1 Regulation, OJ L177 6 – was adopted to replace the Rome Convention 1980. See Chapter 7.

17 'Procedural law: The Commission advocates more efficiency in obtaining and enforcing judgments in the European Union,' in 'Update on the Single Market,' previously available at <http://www.europa.eu.int/comm/dg15/en/update/general/1038.html>.

to facilitate closer cooperation[18] between Member States in furtherance of Treaty objectives.[19]

Since the commencement of the proposals to replace the Brussels Convention with the Brussels 1 Regulation, the European Union recognised the need to provide certain and predictable jurisdiction rules for electronic commerce. In 1999 the European Commission adopted a draft Regulation on Jurisdiction, Recognition and Enforcement of Judgments in Civil and Commercial Matters to 'replace and update the 1968 Brussels Convention with a view to take into account of new forms of commerce which did not exist in 1968.'[20] The EU Commission acknowledged the need to regulate electronic commerce including consumer contracts entered into via the WWW. Indeed as Beaumont confirmed, the articles given priority in the revision process included the exclusive rules of jurisdiction for consumer contracts in Articles 13–15.[21] The basis for adopting the Brussels 1 Regulation was further explained by Beaumont as follows,

> The sound operation of the internal market creates a need to have clear rules on jurisdiction and speed up the recognition and enforcement of judgments in civil and commercial matters. To this end, rapid procedures and legal certainty are of the essence at a time when the increasing frequency of exchanges between persons and economic operators in different Member States leads to a growth in litigation.[22]

After much debate on the provisions of, inter alia, Articles 15–17, the European Union approved the Brussels 1 Regulation. On 1 March 2002,[23] it replaced the Brussels Convention with modified rules of jurisdiction for, inter alia, electronic consumer contracts.

18 H. Kortenberg, 'Closer Cooperation in the Treaty of Amsterdam' (1998) 35 *CMLR* 833 at p.845.

19 'Procedural law: The Commission advocates more efficiency in obtaining and enforcing judgments in the European Union.'

20 'Commission adopts draft Regulation on Jurisdiction, Recognition and Enforcement of Judgments in Civil and Commercial Matters,' Document IP/99/510, 14 July 1999.

21 P.R. Beaumont, 'A United Kingdom Perspectives on the Proposed Hague Judgments Convention' (1998) XXIV *Brook Int'l L* 75 at p.91.

22 Beaumont, ibid. Interestingly, the primary negotiations for the revision of the Brussels Convention appeared to proceed on the basis that the provisions would remain in the form of a Convention, not a Community Instrument.

23 'Compétence Judiciaire, Reconnaissance et Exécution des Décisions Civiles et Commerciales – Version Provisoire Communication à la Presse 2314ème session du Conseil – Justice, Affaires Interieures et Protection Civile', Version Provisoire – Brussels, 30 November/1 December 2000. Article 76, 2001 OJ L12/1, first confirmed by the European Council in Competence Judiciaire, Reconnaissance et Exécution des Décisions Civiles et Commerciales – Version Provisoire, 30 November/1 December 2000.

Judicial Cooperation in Civil and Commercial Matters and Juridical Protection for Consumers in the Brussels 1 Regulation

The Brussels 1 Regulation provides for the free movement of judgments in civil and commercial matters in terms of the European Union's 'acquis communautaire'.[24] The acquis extends to facilitating cooperation in civil and commercial matters throughout the European Union. The application of jurisdiction rules for consumer contracts in the Brussels 1 Regulation is restricted for the following reasons. Firstly, the legal basis of the Brussels 1 Regulation restricts the application of those rules since they only apply when the defendant is situated or has a branch or agency in an EU Member State. In cases involving a defendant situated in a non-Member State, Article 15 confirms that the national laws of the Member State (by virtue of Article 4) must be applied. As far as the United Kingdom is concerned, rules of jurisdiction for consumer contracts contained in Schedules 4 and 8 to the Civil Jurisdiction and Judgments Act 1982 and Paragraph 6.20(5) of the Rules of Civil Procedure ('CPR') must be amended to apply consistently to contracts conducted over the WWW. Secondly, the legal basis for adopting the Brussels 1 Regulation has implications for Member States amending or adopting future jurisdiction rules for defendants not domiciled in an EU Member State. The lack of a harmonised approach is not conducive for a certain and predictable jurisdiction rule in favour of the consumer's domicile. Until recently, with regard to matters relating to Denmark, a lack of coherence prevailed with the continued application of Articles 13–15 of the Brussels Convention. Fourthly, the specific provisions in Articles 15–17 of the Brussels 1 Regulation must be amended to clarify and ensure that the consumer can establish jurisdiction in his own domicile with greater consistency.

The revision of the Brussels Convention was based on Article 61(c) and Article 65, and implemented in terms of Article 67, of the EC Treaty. Article 65, as opposed to Article 95,[25] was the correct basis for implementing the Brussels 1 Regulation[26] since the free movement of persons must include measures for judicial cooperation in civil and commercial matters. Article 95 dealt with the free

24 Preamble of the Amended proposal for a Council Regulation on jurisdiction and the recognition and enforcement of judgments in civil and commercial matters (presented by the Commission pursuant to Article 250 (2) of the EC-Treaty), Recital 5. See also A. Wiener, 'The Embedded Acquis Communautaire: Transmission Belt and Prism of New Governance' (1998) 4:3 *ELJ* 294 at p.299 where the author describes the essence of the Community Acquis as 'represent(ing) the continually changing institutional terms which result from the constructive process of "integration through law".'

25 J. Israël, 'Conflicts of Law and the EC after Amsterdam. A Change for the Worse?' (2000) 7 *MJ* 81.

26 J. Basedow, 'The Communitarisation of The Conflict of Laws Under The Treaty of Amsterdam' (2000) 37 *CMLR* 687 at pp.698–699. O. Remien, 'European Private International Law, The European Community and its Emerging Area of Freedom, Security and Justice' (2001) 38 *CMLR* 53 at pp.74–75.

movement of services whereas Article 65 specifically referred to promoting the compatibility of conflicts of law and jurisdiction. This was the correct approach since consumers must be provided with effective juridical protection via personal jurisdiction rules when contracting with foreign businesses.

The revision of the Brussels Convention was regarded as assisting the mutual recognition of civil and commercial matters, being the 'cornerstone of judicial cooperation.'[27] As Beaumont[28] reported, the measures provided in Article 65 EC 'for the field of judicial cooperation in civil matters having cross-border implications…insofar as necessary for the proper functioning of the internal market' included,

a. improving and simplifying:
   … the recognition and enforcement of decisions in civil and commercial cases, including decisions in extra judicial cases;
b. promoting the compatibility of the rules applicable in the member States concerning the conflict of laws and jurisdiction;
   …[29]

The starting point for action under Article 65 was, as Basedow confirmed, for the benefit of "intra Community relations."[30] Remien supports Basedow assertion that Article 65 only provides a basis for Community competence in international private law in matters between the EU Member States.[31] Therefore the amendment of jurisdiction rules in the Brussels Convention was only for the benefit of the Internal Market. Furthermore, as Kotuby has observed, the effect of Community competence 'operates as a "blocking effect", precluding Member States action only insofar as that action may "affect Community rules" or "alter their scope".'[32]

Whilst Community competence enables the EU to implement international private law rules such as the Brussels 1 Regulation amongst Member States, protective jurisdiction rules still must be provided for consumers when they contract with businesses situated in non-Member States. Basedow, Kotuby and

27 EU Bulletin 10/99, 'VI. Mutual recognition of judicial decisions.'

28 P.R. Beaumont, 'European Court of Justice and Jurisdiction and Enforcement of Judgments in Civil and Commercial Matters' (1999) 48 *ICLQ* 223 at p.225.

29 1997 OJ C340/203. C.T. Kotuby Jr., 'External Competence of the European Community in the Hague Conference on Private International Law: Community Harmonization and Worldwide Unification' (2001) NILR 1 at pp.17–18 suggests that the 'mere existence' of this legislation is 'representative of the exercise of competence provided for in the Treaty.'

30 Basedow, 'The Communitarisation of The Conflict of Laws Under The Treaty of Amsterdam,' at p.702.

31 Remien, 'European Private International Law, The European Community and its Emerging Area of Freedom, Security and Justice,' at p.75.

32 Kotuby, 'External Competence of the European Community in the Hague Conference on Private International Law,' at p.20 and pp.11–12 and 17.

Remien have all suggested that the internal competence (*in foro interior*) provided by Article 65 implies that the European Union has external competence (*in foro exterior*)[33] to legislate in matters involving non-Member States.[34] Given the restrictive application of Articles 15–17 of the Brussels 1 Regulation, it is important to determine the extent to which Member States jurisdiction rules are consistent and predictable when the consumer contracts via the WWW with a business situated in a non-Member State. Indeed, the EU Commission has acknowledged the practical significance of EU competence vis-à-vis global electronic commerce when it said that a 'sound, predictable and *internationally co-ordinated* framework', was needed for the development of electronic commerce.[35] Nevertheless, despite the academic consensus, it has yet to be tested whether each Member State, the EU collectively, or both [36] have competence under EU law to implement such measures. The movement of particular[37] national competencies to the European Union by the process of parallelism[38] has resulted in the 'Communitisation' of policies and 'a new division of powers'[39] not previously within the European Union's explicit remit. In addition to parallelism, the European Union has sought to 'communitarise' or 'harmonise' substantive and procedural rules of its Member States in line with the Union's increased competencies post-Treaty of Amsterdam.[40] Five years after the introduction of the Treaty of Amsterdam matters involving the free movement of persons were transferred by way of Communitisation[41] to the 'exclusive'[42] remit

33 Beaumont, 'European Court of Justice and Jurisdiction and Enforcement of Judgments in Civil and Commercial Matters,' at p.228.

34 Kotuby, 'External Competence of the European Community in the Hague Conference on Private International Law,' at pp.3–4 *et seq* who asserts that Article 65 provides just that, an extension of community competence to matters not strictly limited to the proper functioning of the internal market.

35 European Commission, 'Opinion of the Economic and Social Committee on the Proposal for a Council Regulation (EC) on jurisdiction and enforcement of judgments in civil and commercial matters' (COM (1999) 348 final – 99/0154 – (CNS)) and C117 26 April 2000, 006, at para.4.2.2.

36 Beaumont, 'European Court of Justice and Jurisdiction and Enforcement of Judgments in Civil and Commercial Matters.' T. Tridimas and P. Eeckhaut, 'The External Competence of the Community and the case-law of the Court of Justice: Principle versus Pragmatism' (1994) 14 *YEL* 143.

37 O. Lando, '*Lex Fori* in *Foro Proprio*' (1995) 2 MJ 359 at p.366.

38 Lando, ibid.

39 J. Monar, 'Justice and Home Affairs in the Treaty of Amsterdam: Reform at the Price of Fragmentation' (1998) 23 *EL Rev* 320 at p.323.

40 Basedow, 'The Communitarisation of The Conflict of Laws Under The Treaty of Amsterdam.'

41 K. Nanz, 'The Schengen Agreement: Preparing The Free Movement of Persons in the European Union,' in R. Bieber and J. Monar (eds), *Justice and Home Affairs in the European Union The Development of the Third Pillar* (Brussels, 1995).

42 Monar, 'Justice and Home Affairs in the Treaty of Amsterdam: Reform at the Price of Fragmentation,' at p.329.

of the First Pillar. The effect of this transfer now has significant implications for disputes requiring reference to international private laws[43] such as consumer contracts entered into via the WWW with businesses not situated in an EU Member State. The ability of Member States and now the European Community itself to accede to the Hague Conference on Private International Law's Convention on Choice of Court Agreements is a significant example of the scope and effect of Community competence. Remien's theoretical approach suggests that measures under Article 65 could be taken by Member States regardless of whether the measures were for 'intra-European' disputes[44] or not. Remien's point is persuasive on the basis that individual Member States have previously been able to adopt international conventions and treaties on cross-border matters with non-Member States. It has been rightly observed that the communitarisation of jurisdiction rules in the Brussels 1 Regulation via Title IV equips the European Union with external competence in matters relating to the free movement of persons.[45] Beaumont also maintains that external competence is justified when the matter concerns the proper functioning or advancement of the Internal Market.[46] Since consumers can contract with businesses situated in Member and non-Member States, it is crucial that consumers are provided with certain and predictable jurisdiction rules regardless of where the business is domiciled. However, Beaumont qualified his assertion that external Treaties such as the Hague Conference's proposed Convention 'are likely to regulate things which go well beyond the proper functioning of the community's internal market.'[47] The objective of a predicable and harmonised jurisdiction rule for electronic consumer contracts is 'inextricably linked'[48] to both the aims of the Internal Market (the free movement of judgments between Member States) and the global regulation of electronic commerce via consistent jurisdiction rules. The assertions that a joint consensus from the EU Member States and the Community is required for the EU to have external competence in cross-border matters involving defendants situated in non-Member States[49] has now become evident given the

43 Beaumont, 'European Court of Justice and Jurisdiction and Enforcement of Judgments in Civil and Commercial Matters,' at pp.227–228.

44 Remien, 'European Private International Law, The European Community and its Emerging Area of Freedom, Security and Justice,' at p.74.

45 Israël, 'Conflicts of Law and the EC after Amsterdam. A Change for the Worse?' where she argues that the free movement of goods and services are unaffected by the Treaty of Amsterdam. Kotuby, 'External Competence of the European Community in the Hague Conference on Private International Law,' at p.22.

46 Beaumont, 'European Court of Justice and Jurisdiction and Enforcement of Judgments in Civil and Commercial Matters,' at p.228.

47 Ibid.

48 Kotuby, 'External Competence of the European Community in the Hague Conference on Private International Law,' at p.15.

49 Basedow, 'The Communitarisation of The Conflict of Laws Under The Treaty of Amsterdam,' at p.704 and Remien, 'European Private International Law, The European Community and its Emerging Area of Freedom, Security and Justice,' at p.76.

European Community's recent Membership of the Hague Conference on Private International Law. Kotuby also concludes his analysis by recommending such a 'flexible approach.'[50] Given the inextricable link between Articles 15–17 of the Brussels 1 Regulation, the global nature of electronic commerce and the need to provide consistent juridical protection for consumers regardless of where the defendant is domiciled, a consistent approach amongst EU Member States and non-Member States alike is desirable and necessary. Given the inherent restrictions of the Brussels 1 Regulation and the need for jurisdiction rules for consumer contracts to apply with certainty and predictability, the European Union and its Member States must reach joint consensus on a future global instrument which contains rules of jurisdiction for electronic consumer contracts over businesses situated in non Member States. Alternatively, if a future global instrument is not politically preferred, each Member States' internal jurisdiction rules must be amended to ensure that the consumer who contracts via the WWW with a business can establish jurisdiction in his domicile when the business has intentionally targeted him via an active or interactive web site.

The Brussels 1 Regulation and Denmark

The introduction of the Brussels 1 Regulation was an example of Community efforts towards completion of the Internal Market.[51] In particular, the Preamble to Brussels 1 Regulation reinforced the requirement for a 'Community legal instrument' to achieve the objective that rules of jurisdiction and enforcement of judgments would be dealt with consistently throughout the European Union.[52] However, up until 2005, Denmark continued to opt out of Title IV of the Treaty.[53] Until 1 July 2007 the Brussels Convention (hereafter BC) continued to apply in determining the jurisdiction of civil and commercial matters concerning Denmark.[54] It was remarked that Denmark's initial opt out represented '(T)he most serious negative aspect'[55] of the reorganisation of the Treaty Pillar structure. Until Denmark adopted Title IV, fragmentation[56] of judicial cooperation between the Member States occurred

50 Kotuby, 'External Competence of the European Community in the Hague Conference on Private International Law,' at p.29.

51 Article 65/95 TEU.

52 Ibid. In December 2009, the Rome Convention 1980 will be replaced by a Community Instrument for predominantly the same reasons as the replacement of the Brussels Convention by the Brussels 1 Regulation; Chapter 7.

53 Demark, Ireland and the United Kingdom initially opted out of Title IV and until 19 October 2005, Denmark remained the only Member State not to opt in to Title IV.

54 Brussels 1 Regulation, at Recital 22.

55 N. Fennelly, 'The Area of "Freedom, Security and Justice," and the European Court of Justice – A Personal View' (2000) 49 *ICLQ* 1 at p.3.

56 It has been suggested that the extent of external community competence depends on whether the matter falls within Title IV or VI of the Treaty; G. Gaja, 'How Flexible is Flexibility Under the Amsterdam Treaty?' (1998) 35 *CMLR* 855. Monar, 'Justice and

and consequently there was no harmonisation of regional (vertical) jurisdiction rules. The continued application of both the (unamended) Brussels Convention and Brussels 1 Regulation would have affected both the consumer's ability to establish jurisdiction in his own domicile and the EU's objective to improve the compatibility of international private laws. The lack of 'harmonisation'[57] resulted in an imbalance in the application of jurisdiction rules throughout the EU together with a corresponding impact in facilitating conflicts justice to parties domiciled in different EU Member States. The current fragmentation of jurisdiction rules also has implications for consumers seeking to establish jurisdiction against a business situated in a non-Member State.

For example, before Denmark adopted the Brussels 1 Regulation in July 2007, a consumer from Denmark and a consumer from England each enter into a contract with a Canadian business via that business' web site. Both consumers want to sue the Canadian business in their own jurisdiction. Unlike the English consumer, the Danish consumer had to rely on the rules in Articles 13–15 BC (subject to Articles 4 and 5(5)) to establish jurisdiction over the Canadian business in Denmark. The Danish consumer will have to establish that the Canadian business had a branch or agency in a Contracting State. The Danish consumer had to establish that the Canadian business' web site constituted a specific invitation or advertising to him in Denmark. In addition, the Danish consumer also had to demonstrate that the contract was concluded in Denmark. By contrast, the English consumer had to demonstrate that the Canadian business's branch directed its commercial activities towards English consumers via its web site and that his contract was concluded as a result of such commercial activity.

Had the application of jurisdiction rules continued in this fragmented fashion amongst the EU Member States, consumers throughout Europe would have had to use different jurisdiction rules in order to establish jurisdiction against a business domiciled in a non-Member State. From a practical perspective, both the English and the Danish consumer would have had difficulty in establishing jurisdiction under Articles 15(1)(c) of Brussels 1 Regulation or Article 13(3) BC respectively. The Canadian business will be unable to predict with certainty whether its online activities will constitute directed activity to the English consumer or a specific invitation or advertising to the Danish consumer. Furthermore the Danish consumer could only have relied upon Article 13(3) BC if he concluded the contract in Denmark. The adoption of the Brussels 1 Regulation by Denmark in July 2007

Home Affairs in the Treaty of Amsterdam: Reform at the Price of Fragmentation,' at p.327 suggests that this is largely dependant upon the '*legal personality of the Union* ' (emphasis added).

57 Kotuby argues that if Community legislation does not 'harmonise a particular field' this would not appear to affect the overriding effect of Community competence over national law *per se*, but that in any event, analysis is required to determine the extent of Community law over Member State action; at p.13.

will go some considerable way to addressing the fragmentation of jurisdiction rules amongst the Member States.

The Development of the Information Society in Europe

The European Union has a vested interest in the development and regulation of 'Information Society Services.'[58] 'Information Society Services' are defined as 'any service, normally provided for remuneration, at a distance, by electronic means and at the request of a recipient of services.'[59] The European Union acknowledged that in addition to technical and commercial solutions, legal measures were required to regulate the emerging electronic marketplace and the continued development of the Information Society. Technical measures and contractual devices are not sufficiently consistent and predictable connecting factors for determining the jurisdiction of an electronic consumer contract. However given the dematerialised, global nature of electronic commerce activities, the application of protective jurisdiction rules for consumers should not be confined to where the defendant is domiciled in an EU Member State.[60] The EU Commission acknowledged this point as follows, 'the need for strengthened *international coordination* in order to create an enabling framework for the global electronic marketplace … which is a fundamental element of the Information Society.'[61]

Nevertheless, in the last seven years the European Union has only introduced measures to regulate electronic commerce activity between parties situated in different Member States.[62] These measures were introduced largely in response to developments in the Information Society,[63] including the E-Europe Action

58 As exemplified by the i2010 Strategy launched in 2005 which seeks to, *inter alia*, 'create a Single European Information Space … [and] … achieve an inclusive Information Society'; <http://www.europa.eu/scadplus/leg/en/lvb/l24100.htm>. Word in brackets added.

59 Article 1(2) of the Directive 98/34/EC (as amended by Directive 98/48EC) laying down a procedure for the provision of information in the field of technical standards and regulations.

60 The i2010 Information Society Strategy has a range of themes and programmes on development of Information Society services.

61 European Commission, Directorate-General XIII, Telecommunications, Information Market and Exploitation of Research, 'Communication from the Commission to the European Parliament, The Council, The Economic and Social Committee and The Committee of the Regions The Need for Strengthened International Coordination,' COM (98) 50. Words italicised for emphasis.

62 J. Hörnle, 'The European Union Takes Initiative in the Field of E-Commerce,' Commentary 3 The Journal of Information, Law and Technology (JILT) (2000) <http://www2.warwick.ac.uk/fac/soc/law/elj/jilt/2000_3/hornle>.

63 COM (98) 50. The Commission's Communication highlighted the need for legal frameworks for the global electronic market place in response to increasing demand and scope of services; Figure 1 and para.2.4.

Plan and the i2010 Information Society Policy Initiatives[64] and the increase in the growth of online trading between businesses and consumers.[65] According to the EU Commission's Consumer Policy Strategy 2002–2006,

> In the context of the eEurope Action Plan adopted in 2000, the Commission has developed a strategy to build consumer confidence online, made up of four elements; high quality e-commerce codes, quality alternative dispute resolutions (ADRs); clear and consistent laws and effective enforcement.[66]

These initiatives have included, inter alia, the 'Directive on certain legal aspects of information society services, in particular electronic commerce, in the Internal Market' (hereafter the Electronic Commerce Directive), the 'Directive on the Protection of Consumers in respect of Distance Contracts'[67] and most recently the Directive on Unfair Commercial Practices.[68] The Electronic Commerce Directive was created to provide guidance and rules for the national regulation of electronic commerce activities.[69] However, Recital 23 of the Directive's Preamble specifies that it would 'not seek to make provision for rules of international private law nor affect existing rules.' The Electronic Commerce Directive allows for the regulation of Information Society Service Providers by subjecting them to their own state's regulatory regimes, where they exist. It is not for the consumer to enforce these. Information Society Service Providers are therefore subject to regulation of their

---

64 European Commission, 'eEurope 2005: An information society for all,' 21–22 June 2002, COM(2002) 263, and 'i2010 – A European Information Society for growth and employment,' COM (2005) 229 final.

65 John Goldring, 'Netting the Cybershark: Consumer Protection, Cyberspace, the Nation-State, and Democracy,' in B. Kahin and C. Nesson (eds), *Borders in Cyberspace Information Policy and the Global Information Infrastructure* (Cambridge, Massachusetts, 1997).

66 Consumer Policy Strategy 2002–2006 European Commission, 'Communication From the Commission to the European Parliament, The Council, The Economic and Social Committee and The Committee of the Regions, Consumer Policy Strategy 2002–2006,' Brussels COM (2002) 208, at para.3.1.4. The Commission has proposed a new Health and Consumer Protection Programme 2007–2013 (COM(2005) 115 final 2005/0042 (COD)).

67 Directive on electronic commerce, 2000 OJ L178, Directive on Distance Selling, 1997 OJ L0007. *Journal of the Law Society of Scotland*, 'Consumer Rights enhances by amendments to draft distance selling directive' (1999) 44 JLSS 37. Directive on the Distance Marketing of Consumer Financial Services; OJ L271/16, 23 September 2002.

68 Directive 2005/29 EC concerning unfair business-to-consumer commercial practices in the internal market (the Unfair Commercial Practices Directive) OJ L149, 11 May 2005.

69 G. Pearce and N. Platten, 'Promoting the Information Society: The EU Directive on Electronic Commerce' (2000) 4 *ELJ* 363; T. Smale and J. Upton, 'E-Commerce Untangling the International Web' (2000) 5 *EU Counsel* 6, 43.

online activities from their 'Country of Origin.'[70] At that time of revision of the Brussels Convention, concerns were expressed by the Confederation of British Industry (CBI) that the proposals for consumer contract jurisdiction rules in the Brussels 1 Regulation would clash with the 'Country of Origin' principle in the Electronic Commerce Directive.[71] Geist remarked that the Country of Destination approach reinforces the point that consumers must be provided with effective juridical protection when contracting with foreign businesses online.

> The origin versus destination debate has polarised [industry and consumer] groups, making it difficult to reach a compromise that recognizes that effective consumer protection does not depend solely on which law applies … that business must shoulder some of the risk arising from e-commerce transactions.[72]

Nevertheless, it is agreed that the basis of jurisdiction of the Directive and the Regulation are different.[73] The purpose of the Electronic Commerce Directive is to provide a framework for Members States to regulate Information Society Service providers. By contrast, the Brussels 1 Regulation provides jurisdiction rules for consumer contracts in favour of the consumer's jurisdiction. Articles 15–17 of the Brussels 1 Regulation exemplify the 'Country of Destination'[74] principle since any dispute is to be determined by the place where the business' online activities are directed towards, i.e the consumer's domicile. As Stone, Dutson and Øren[75] confirm the rationale for these two EU instruments, and the references to 'jurisdiction' contained within them, are different and therefore do not conflict with each other. These three authors correctly maintain that the Brussels 1 Regulation provides rules of personal jurisdiction whereas the Directive is premised on subject-matter jurisdiction. Moreover, the Electronic Commerce Directive is a public law measure which provides a framework for Member States to regulate the provision of information society services via Information Society Service providers situated in their jurisdiction. The Brussels 1 Regulation provides private, juridical rules for natural persons, such as consumers. Article 3 of the Electronic Commerce Directive confirms that it does not seek to limit or restrict international private

70 Will Roebuck, 'Jurisdiction and E-Commerce' (2002) *CTLR* 29.

71 Pearce and Platten, 'Promoting the Information Society,' at p.175; S. Dutson, 'E-Commerce – European Union Transnational E-Commerce' (2000) 16 *CLSR* 105 at p.106.

72 M. Geist, 'Is There a There? Towards Greater Certainty for Internet Jurisdiction' (2001) 16 *Berkeley Tech Law Journal* 1345. Words in brackets added.

73 Dutson, 'E-Commerce – European Union Transnational E-Commerce,' and P. Stone, 'Internet Consumer Contracts and European Private International Law' (2000) 9:1 *Information and Communications Technology Law* 5.

74 Pearce and Platten, 'Promoting the Information Society,' at pp.374–375.

75 J.S.T. Øren, 'International Jurisdiction Over Consumer Contracts in e-Europe' (2003) 52 *ICLQ* 665 at p.668.

law's provisions for consumer protection.[76] Therefore it is correct that the aims of the Electronic Commerce Directive and the Brussels 1 Regulation do not conflict since, as Turner and Traynor confirm, the Electronic Commerce Directive is 'silent'[77] on the matter of jurisdiction for cross-border disputes between consumers and businesses. As the present author has previously remarked, the European Union's preference for the 'Country of Origin' principle to regulate the activities of Internet Service providers within Member States' territories is maintained and therefore does not affect the juridical protection for consumer provided by the Brussels 1 Regulation.[78]

The Commission has proposed a new Health and Consumer Protection Programme 2007–2013 which seeks to

> realis[e] the potential for cross-border shopping by eliminating
>
> - remaining barriers to the completion of the retail dimension of the internal market.
> - the combined challenge of improving the application and enforcement of legislation, in particular across borders.[79]

Certain and predictable rules of jurisdiction[80] are required firstly for the protection of consumers who contract with foreign sellers via the WWW and secondly for businesses to predict the legal consequences of contracting with foreign consumers. According to Auf der Mar,

> (C)onsumer protection issues are particularly tricky for online merchants, since they routinely provide for jurisdiction of the courts at the consumer's domicile and for the application of his or her national law.[81]

76 Article 3, Electronic Commerce Directive; Stone, 'Internet Consumer Contracts and European Private International Law,' at p.12; Pearce and Platten, 'Promoting the Information Society,' at pp.374–378.

77 M. Turner and M. Traynor, 'Electronic Commerce (EC Directive) Regulations 2002 – Worth the Wait?' (2002) 18 *CLSR* 396 at p.399.

78 L.E. Gillies, 'A Review of the New Jurisdiction Rules for Electronic Consumer Contracts within the European Union,' Commentary, *The Journal of Information, Law and Technology* (JILT) 1 (2001) <http://www2.warwick.ac.uk/fac/soc/law/elj/jilt/2001_1/gillies>.

79 European Commission, 'Health and Consumer Protection Programme 2007–2013,' 2007–2013 (COM(2005) 115 final 2005/0042 (COD)) <http://europa.eu.int/comm/consumers/overview/programme_2007-2013_en.htm> at p.10.

80 In Europe the Rome Convention on Contractual Obligations will also be replaced in due course by a Community Instrument as part of the European Union's Framework for Judicial Cooperation in Civil and Commercial Matters.

81 R. Auf der Mar, 'Internet-Enabled Distribution Models,' IBL (1999) 264.

It was suggested that the changes to the Brussels Convention were 'uncontroversial'[82] and 'minor in nature.'[83] Nevertheless, one of the most contentious, controversial[84] and important set of rules to be replaced by the Regulation related to electronic consumer contracts.[85] Indeed the European Parliament acknowledged that the proposals for Articles 15–17 had 'given rise to a fierce debate.'[86] Until 2002, any consumer wishing to sue a foreign business in his jurisdiction would have had the difficulty in satisfying the requirements of Articles 13–15 of the Brussels Convention. During the negotiations to replace the Brussels Convention, it was necessary to consider the extent to which any changes to consumer contract jurisdiction rules had to encompass electronic commerce. Indeed the UK Government's (then) Department of Trade and Industry succinctly summarised the issue, '(T)he (Brussels) Convention pre-dates the Internet and in the absence of any case law it is not clear how Article 13 applies to electronic commerce and websites in particular.'[87]

The controversy[88] focused on the revision of key aspects of the jurisdiction rules for consumer contracts. Firstly, the restricted scope of the consumer contract jurisdiction rule had to be affirmed. In particular, the definitions of consumer and consumer contract also had to be reconfirmed, with particular regard to whether legal persons such as small and medium sized enterprises (SMEs) should benefit from juridical protection intended for traditional consumers. Secondly, and most importantly, the jurisdiction rules for consumer contracts had to be modified to apply to contracts conducted electronically via web sites on the WWW. The jurisdiction rules for consumer contracts had to incorporate a new connecting factor that established a sufficiently certain and predictable link between the level of activity on a business' web site and the business' intention to contract with consumers in specific jurisdictions. Thirdly, given the 'dematerialised' nature of electronic commerce via the WWW, the consumer jurisdiction rule had to stipulate whether or not the contract had to be concluded in the consumer's

82 European Parliament, 'Agreement on e-commerce jurisdiction,' 20 September 2000.

83 W. Kennett (ed), 'Current Developments: Private International Law' (1999) 48 *ICLQ* 465 and 966.

84 Wendy Kennett (ed), 'Current Developments: Private International Law The Brussels 1 Regulation' (2000) 50 *ICLQ* 725.

85 P. Stone, 'The Treatment of Electronic Contracts and Torts in Private International Law under European Community Legislation' (2002) 11:2 *ICTL* 121.

86 European Parliament, 'Agreement on e-commerce jurisdiction.'

87 United Kingdom Department of Trade and Industry Consultation Paper 'European Commission Proposals for Changes to Article 13 of the 1968 Brussels Convention,' Copyright Department of Trade and Industry, 12 April 2000. Word in brackets added.

88 Both internal between the different Commission DG's and external to those with a vested interest in the proposals; Kennett, 'Current Developments: Private International Law The Brussels 1 Regulation,' at p.735 and Stone, 'The Treatment of Electronic Contracts and Torts in Private International Law under European Community Legislation,' at p.122 and 124 *et seq*.

domicile. Lastly, the effect of jurisdiction agreements in an electronic consumer contract, for example in click-wrap agreements on business' web sites, also had to be reconsidered. Despite adaptation, the application of Articles 15–17 of the Brussels 1 Regulation will still generate inconsistent results in determining which jurisdiction should hear a dispute over an electronic consumer contract. Moreover, as the next chapter will suggest, the rules of jurisdiction in Schedules 4 and 8 to the Civil Jurisdiction and Judgments Act 1982 and CPR 6.20(5) must also be amended in order to provide certainty and predictability when a consumer wishes to sue a business situated in another part of the United Kingdom or a non-Member State.

Summary

In line with Treaty objectives, the European Union has led in the protection of 456 million consumers[89] within the (current) 27 Member States. The need for effective juridical protection of consumers via international private laws brings together EU objectives vis-à-vis consumer protection, judicial cooperation in civil and commercial matters and the regulation of the Information Society.

89 See Europa 'ScadPlus Consumers: Introduction' <http://europa.eu/scadplus/leg/en/lvb/l32000.htm>.

Chapter 5
Jurisdiction Rules for Electronic Consumer Contracts in the Brussels 1 Regulation

Introduction – A 'Lex Specialis' of the Brussels 1 Regulation – Jurisdiction Rules for Consumer Contracts[1]

One of the categories, 'sub-code(s)'[2] or '*lex specialis*'[3] of jurisdiction rules that has always been provided in the Brussels Convention was for 'certain consumer contracts.'[4] Initially, the original Brussels Convention contained limited provisions for consumer contracts. The special ground of jurisdiction in Articles 13–15 of the Brussels Convention was introduced to provide protection of the consumer as the contractually weaker party.[5] The Jenard Report acknowledged that special status ought to be afforded to consumer contracts under the Convention.[6] Furthermore, the special grounds of jurisdiction for consumer contracts are required to be interpreted independently based on the objectives of the Convention.[7] Article 13 determined how jurisdiction would be established for certain types of consumer contracts. Firstly, such contracts had to be for the 'sale of goods on instalment credit terms, or [for] loans expressly made to finance the sale of goods and repayable by instalments.'[8] The original version of the Brussels Convention therefore only

1 Sections of this Chapter were recently published in L.E. Gillies, 'Addressing the "Cyberspace Fallacy": Targeting the Jurisdiction of an Electronic Consumer Contract' (2008) 2 *Int Journal Law and Inf Tech* 1.

2 A. Briggs, 'The Brussels Convention' (1993) 13 *YEL* 511. Word modified for syntax.

3 C-96/00 *R. Gabriel v Schlanck & Schick GmbH* [2002] ECR I-6367.

4 The others being for insurance contracts and employment contracts, supra.

5 Reaffirming *Bertrand v Ott* [1978] ECR 1432, where the European Court stated that Article 13 could not be extended to cover the sale of goods between businesses by instalments. Indeed, Article 13 of the Brussels Convention was amended to take into account the issue of consumer protection together with the proposals for the Rome Convention on contractual obligations. A. Dashwood, R.J. Hacon, and R.C.A. White, *A Guide to the Civil Jurisdiction and Judgments Convention* (Deventer, 1987) at p.28.

6 'Report by Mr P. Jenard on the Convention of 27 September 1968 on jurisdiction and the enforcement of judgments in civil and commercial matters, 3 June 1971,' 1979 OJ C59/1 (hereafter 'the Jenard Report') at p.33.

7 C-89/91 *Shearson Lehman Hutton v TVB* [1993] ECR I-139.

8 Ibid, word in brackets substituted.

applied initially to these types of consumer contracts. The Brussels 1 Regulation now states that jurisdiction rules for consumer contracts will apply, *inter alia*,

> Article 15
>
> 1. In matters relating to a contract concluded by a person, the consumer, for a purpose which can be regarded as being outside his trade or profession, jurisdiction shall be determined by this Section, without prejudice to Article 4 and point 5 of Article 5, if:
>   (a) it is a contract for the sale of goods on instalment credit terms; or
>   (b) it is a contract for a loan repayable by instalments, or for any other form of credit, made to finance the sale of goods; or
>   (c) in all other cases, the contract has been concluded with a person who pursues commercial or professional activities in the Member State of the consumer's domicile or, by any means, directs such activities to that Member State or to several States including that Member State, and the contract falls within the scope of such activities.
> 2. Where a consumer enters into a contract with a party who is not domiciled in the Member State but has a branch, agency or other establishment in one of the Member States, that party shall, in disputes arising out of the operations of the branch, agency or other establishment, be deemed to be domiciled in that State.
> 3. […][9]

The ability of the consumer to raise proceedings in his domicile is premised on establishing that the contract is a 'protected'[10] consumer contract in accordance with Article 15(1). The Brussels 1 Regulation provides jurisdiction rules for three types of consumer contract. The first type of consumer contract is for the sale of goods on instalment credit terms (Article 15(1)(a)). The second type of consumer contract is for a loan to finance the sale of goods or for any other form of credit, made to finance the sale of goods (Article 15(1)(b)).[11] Thirdly, the remit of Article 15 extends to *any other* consumer contract for the supply of goods and services subject to the requirements of Article 15(1)(c).[12] It is this part of Article 15(1) that is most relevant to establishing the jurisdiction of an electronic consumer contract. The exclusive rule that consumers are entitled to sue businesses either in

9 The provision which excludes transport contracts, other than package holidays; Brussels 1 Regulation, at pp.6–7.

10 P. Stone, 'The Treatment of Electronic Contracts and Torts in Private International Law under European Community Legislation' (2002) 11:2 *Information and Communications Technology Law* 12, at p.123.

11 Brussels 1 Regulation. L.E. Gillies, 'Rules of Jurisdiction for Electronic Consumer Contracts – Scottish Perspectives' (2001) 2 *SLPQ* 124 at p.132.

12 Gillies, ibid; Frederic Debussere, 'International Jurisdiction over E-Consumer Contracts in the European Union: Quid Novi Sub Sole?' (2002) 10 *IJLIT* 344 at pp.356–357.

the business' or the consumers' jurisdiction is retained in Article 16 of the Brussels 1 Regulation. Article 16 provides:

> Article 16
>
> 1. A consumer may bring proceedings against the other party to a contract either in the courts of the Member State in which that party is domiciled or in the courts for the place where the consumer is domiciled.
> 2. Proceedings may be brought against a consumer by the other party to the contract only in the courts of the Member State in which the consumer is domiciled.
> 3. [...][13]

However, as the previous chapter explained, from a legal, practical and financial perspective, a consumer will want to take advantage of the ability to sue a foreign business in their own jurisdiction.

Retaining the Restricted Definitions of 'Consumer' and 'Consumer Contract' in the Brussels 1 Regulation

If the consumer wishes to rely on the provisions of Article 15(1), he must fall within the definition of a 'consumer' and his contract must be a 'consumer contract'. The original 1968 Convention did not define the precise meaning of a 'consumer contract.' Instead, guidance on the meaning of a consumer contract derived from the Official Reports to the Convention and subsequent Accession Conventions and the Protocol on Interpretation. In its explanation of the purpose of Section 4 of the original Brussels Convention, the Jenard Report stated:

> (T)his Section relates to the sale of goods where the price is payable in a series of instalments, and to the sale of goods where the sale is contractually linked to a loan (Abzhalungsgeschafte). The rules here adopted are similar to those applicable in the national law of the Member States and, like them, stem from a desire to protect certain categories of persons. Article 13 provides that this Section applies independently of the rest of the Convention, and like Article 7, without prejudice to the provisions of Articles 4 and 5(5).[14]

According to the Jenard Report, the protection of the buyer or borrower was regarded as paramount and consequently such individuals could only be sued where they were domiciled. According to Briggs, the original Brussels Convention

---

13 A right of counter-claim provision; Brussels 1 Regulation, at pp.6–7.

14 Jenard Report at p.33, also referred to in C-99/96 *Hans-Hermann Mietz v Intership Yachting Sneek BV* [1999] ECR I-2277.

provided an 'unusually wide'[15] basis for a consumer to sue a seller in his or her own jurisdiction. Nevertheless in *Bertrand v Ott*,[16] the first case to consider the exclusive rules of jurisdiction for consumer contracts in the original[17] Brussels Convention, the ECJ held the rules of jurisdiction provided in Article 14 (now Article 16) had to be 'strictly limited to the objectives proper to Section 4 of the said Convention.'[18] According to the ECJ, those 'objectives' were specifically 'inspired by a desire to protect certain categories of buyers.'[19] The ECJ confirmed that the categories of buyers to which Section 4 provided a 'jurisdictional advantage' were those buyers who were economically weaker

> … in comparison with sellers by reason of the fact that they are private financial consumers and are not engaged, when buying the product acquired on instalment credit terms, in trade or professional activities.[20]

The jurisdiction rules for consumer contracts were to be treated independently from the rest of the Convention and only applied to very specific categories of protected consumer contracts.[21] The philosophy of Articles 13–15 continues to operate on that basis. In *Bertrand*, the ECJ refused to consider whether a small business could be as economically disadvantaged as an individual private consumer when contracting with a company for the purchase of goods or services. The ECJ therefore ensured that only specific categories of buyers would be able to take advantage of the exclusive jurisdiction rules enshrined in Section 4 of the Convention. The consumer jurisdiction rules were therefore to be applied restrictively.

Article 13 of the 1978 Accession Convention provided a more precise, but still restricted,[22] meaning of the terms 'consumer' and 'consumer contract.' The 1978 Accession Convention provided two important clarifications on the scope of Articles 13–15. Firstly, Article 13 defined the meaning of consumer as 'a person who acted outside their trade or profession when concluding a contract with the other party. Secondly, the application of Article 13 of the Brussels Convention extended to *any other contract* for the supply of goods or services. In ruling that the agreement between the parties in *Hans-Hermann Mietz v Intership Yachting*

15 Briggs, 'The Brussels Convention'.

16 (150/77) *Bertrand v Ott* [1978] ECR 1431.

17 A. Briggs and P. Rees, *Civil Jurisdiction and Judgments*, 2nd ed (London, 1997) at p.61.

18 *Bertrand v Ott*, at p.1445.

19 Ibid.

20 Ibid at p.1446.

21 *Bertrand v Ott*.

22 Briggs and Rees, *Civil Jurisdiction and Judgments*, at p.60. The Schlosser Report refers to the term consumer as 'central' to Section 4, Schlosser Report, at p.118.

Sneek BV[23] was not a consumer contract, the ECJ referred to the earlier decision in *Benincasa* where it said,

> ... in order to determine whether a person has the capacity of consumer ... reference must be made to the position of the person concerned in a particular contract, having regard to the nature and aim of that contract, and not to the subjective situation of the person concerned.[24]

The court in *Mietz* confirmed that '(T)he status of consumer is thus not reserved only to those persons who are economically weak or disadvantaged.'[25] The definition of a consumer in Article 13 of the Brussels Convention was not strictly limited to its 'formal definition.'[26] The Schlosser report confirmed that natural persons acting as consumers were to be afforded protection under Section 4, as follows '... for future purposes that only *final* consumers *acting in a private capacity* should be given *special protection* and *not* those contracting in the course of their business to pay by instalments for goods and services used.'[27]

The decision of the ECJ in *Shearson Lehmann Hutton Inc. v TVB* exemplified the remit of Articles 13–15.[28] In that case the ECJ made it clear that not only did Article 13 'define the consumer as a person acting "for a purpose which can be regarded as being outside his trade, business or profession"'[29] Janssens maintains that since Article 13 did not specifically exclude legal persons from its remit, legal persons could rely on the protective provisions of Article 13. However, it is submitted that the ECJ in *Shearson*, and subsequently in *Benincasa v Dentalkit*,[30] correctly specified the types of contracts given juridical protection under Article 13.[31] The ECJ confirmed that the provisions contained in Article 13 could therefore only have applied in respect of "a private final consumer, not engaged in trade or

23 *Mietz v Intership Yachting Sneek BV.*

24 *Mietz*, ibid citing *Francesco Benincasa v Dentalkit Srl* [1997] ECR I-3767.

25 *Mietz*, ibid.

26 Briggs and Rees, *Civil Jurisdiction and Judgments*, at p.60.

27 Report by Professor Dr Peter Schlosser on the Convention of 9 October 1978 on the Association of the Kingdom of Denmark, Ireland and the United Kingdom of Great Britain and Northern Ireland to the Convention on jurisdiction and the enforcement of judgments in civil and commercial matters and to the Protocol on its interpretation by the Court of Justice,' 1979 OJ C59/71 (hereafter 'the Schlosser Report'). Emphasis added. Reference to this particular aspect of the Schlosser Report was recently affirmed in the ECJ's decision in *R. Gabriel v Schlanck & Schick GmbH* [2002] ECR I-6367.

28 *Shearson Lehman Hutton v TVB.*

29 Ibid at p.I-188. T. Janssens, 'The Shearson judgment of the European Court of Justice: Problems raised by the "Europeanisation" and "Communitisation" of the Term "Consumer" in the Brussels Jurisdiction and Judgments Convention' (1995) 4 *ERPL* 605.

30 *Benincasa v Dentalkit.*

31 Ibid.

professional activities … who is bound by one of the contracts listed in Article 13 and who is a party to the action, in accordance with Article 14.'[32]

Therefore, no matter the manner of communication used between the consumer and foreign seller, the consumer can rely on Articles 15–17 provided they enter into the contract as a private, final consumer for their own private use or consumption. More recently, it was held in *Standard Bank v Apostolakis (No.1)*[33] that a private investor who invested in foreign exchange contracts for the purposes of profit and not disposable income was a consumer for the purposes of Article 13 of the Brussels Convention. The respondents initially raised proceedings against the claimants in Greece as a result of serious losses on certain investments alleged to have been caused by the claimant's previous conduct. The claimants commenced their own proceedings against the respondents in the English courts to obtain an injunction restraining proceedings in Greece. At the first hearing, the respondents argued firstly that the contract was a consumer contract and that the provisions of Article 13 applied, and secondly that the exclusive jurisdiction agreements were unfair contract terms in accordance with the Unfair Contract Terms Regulations 1994 and 1999, thereby rendering the contract void. The respondents averred that the claimants had specifically invited them to enter into a contract.[34] The respondents maintained that under Regulation 5(1) of the 1999 Regulations, a limitation on their right to sue only in England caused 'a significant imbalance in the parties' rights and obligations.'[35] The court accepted that it was not in the parties' 'trade, business or profession'[36] to enter into exchange contracts. The court held that as the respondents sought to obtain a profit that was specifically for their own private use or consumption they were deemed to be consumers. In reaching that decision, the court had to consider the purpose of the contract itself and not simply the 'subjective situation of the person [i.e. the consumer] concerned.'[37] The courts are predominantly concerned with the *purpose* behind the contract and not the situation of the parties to the contract.[38] As stated earlier, for Article 13 to apply, a consumer who entered into an electronic consumer contract would therefore have had to ensure that he came within the definition of a 'consumer' in order to assert jurisdiction under Articles 13–15. Whilst the legitimate consumer would be able

32 Ibid. Article 13–15, as Briggs acknowledged that it did not therefore apply as between consumer and seller or supplier – not if the consumer has 'assigned his claim to a non-consumer'; 'The Brussels Convention' at p.512.

33 *Standard Bank London Ltd v Dimitrios and Styliani Apostolakis (No 1)* [2000] IL Pr 766.

34 A point that was confirmed in the second report of the case, *Standard Bank v Apostolakis (No.2)* [2001] Lloyd's Law Reports 240 at p.248.

35 Ibid at pp.249–250 and recently affirmed in *Picardi v Mr and Mrs Cuniberti* (2003) 19 Const, L.J. at p.350.

36 Ibid at p.248 affirming Longmore, J. in *Standard Bank (No.1)*.

37 *Standard Bank (No.1)*, per Longmore, J. at p.772, in accordance with the ECJ's decision in *Benincasa v Dentalkit*. Words in square brackets added.

38 *Mietz v Intership Yachting Sneek BV.*

to satisfy this requirement, businesses would have to be satisfied that the other party contracting via its web site was a consumer. A business can anticipate or foresee contracts with consumers in particular countries when it uses an active or interactive web site to specifically target those jurisdictions. As the second report of the *Standard Bank* case confirmed, the consumer has to satisfy the court that the 'threshold requirement of Article 13' has been met; that is, prior to conclusion of the contract, the consumer had been specifically targeted by the business in his own jurisdiction.[39]

The ECJ's 'policy of construing the various heads of special jurisdiction strictly, so that they apply only to the extent necessary to fulfill their objectives'[40] continued to restrict the operation of Articles 13–15 to private consumers. The decision *Francesco Benincasa v Dentalkit Srl*,[41] specifically confirmed that juridical protection in Article 13 did not apply to small and medium sized enterprises. The ECJ ruled that the contract was not a consumer contract as 'an agreement intended to establish a trade or profession must be deemed to have been concluded for the purpose of a trade or profession.'[42]

The Advocate General stressed the necessity for a Community interpretation of 'consumer contract.'[43] Indeed, the ECJ in *Bertrand* reiterated the Schlosser Report and ruled that Article 13 could only apply to private consumers and not for the purposes of a trade or profession.[44] Interestingly, Advocate General Colomer's Opinion pointed out that it was the *activity in question*, namely the purchasing of goods or services for private purposes, and not the *individual party to the agreement* that formed the basis of Article 13.[45] This is an important point for consumer contracts conducted by electronic commerce. Since the basis of Article 13 was to provide particular rules of jurisdiction for the purchase of goods or services for private purposes, Article 13 ought to have reflected the consumer's ability to contract by electronic commerce to ensure such juridical protection was preserved. The Advocate General concluded that Article 13 could not be extended to cover situations where *any party* in an economically weaker position than the other party to the contract could rely on asserting protective jurisdiction contained in Article 13.[46] In *Benincasa*, the ECJ sought to ensure that a restrictive interpretation applied to the meaning of a consumer contract.[47] The Advocate

39 *Standard Bank (No.2)* at p.248.

40 1994 ELRev 537 at p.538.

41 *Benincasa v Dentalkit.*

42 Ibid at p.I-3772.

43 Ibid, per AG Colomer. Reference was made to the previous Preliminary Ruling in *Shearson* that, in turn, referred to *Handte* in support of such an interpretation and *Bertrand* in respect of Article 13 in particular.

44 Ibid at p.I-3778.

45 Ibid at p.I-3781. Emphasis added.

46 Ibid, emphasis added.

47 In accordance with the Schlosser Report.

General's remarks clarified that Article 13 did not cover contracts entered into by legal persons such as small to medium sized enterprises.

Should Small to Medium Sized Enterprises be Regarded as 'Consumers'?

On more than one occasion during negotiations on the Brussels 1 Regulation, the argument was put forward by representatives of businesses and the e-lobby[48] that businesses, including small to medium sized enterprises (SMEs), should be provided with the same juridical protection as the traditional, less experienced consumer. The main reasons for the argument was that in comparison to the foreign business trading via a web site, SMEs were also in an economically weaker position and lacked knowledge of the foreign seller's jurisdiction and laws in the same way as the traditional consumer. However, earlier authority from the ECJ's judgment in *Benincasa* affirmed that the interpretation of the word 'consumer' 'must be strictly construed.'[49] The ECJ held that Article 13 could only apply to natural persons entering into private contracts with no link whatsoever to the person's trade or professional activities. If the proposals to replace Article 13 of the Brussels Convention had been extended to include legal persons such as SMEs then this would have been a shift in EU policy and by implication an extension of substantive and juridical protection for consumers.

Therefore, whilst the basis for determining who is deemed to be a consumer for the purposes of the Brussels 1 Regulation has not changed,[50] the types of contract deemed to be a 'consumer contract' have extended. It is right that the specific definition of consumer derived from the 1978 Accession Convention and ECJ decisions should still operate in the context of Article 15 of the Brussels 1 Regulation. The traditional consumer must be provided with juridical protection when contracting with a foreign business via the WWW. Equally, a foreign business should only be sued by a consumer in the consumer's jurisdiction provided that consumer was targeted by the business to contract for their own private use or consumption. If the provisions of Article 15 had been extended to legal persons, such as small and medium sized enterprises, then this would have been a disincentive to businesses investing in technology to target foreign markets. However, in the absence of specific guidance on the meaning of the connecting factor 'directing such activities,' the consistent application of Article 15 vis-à-vis electronic consumer contracts will continue to be hindered.

---

48 P. Stone, 'Internet Consumer Contracts and European Private International Law' (2000) 9:1 *Information and Communications Technology Law* 5 and A. Briggs, *The Conflict of Laws* (Oxford, 2002) at pp.67–68; Øren, see note 80.

49 *Benincasa v Dentalkit*, at p.I-3795.

50 And hence this decision at ECJ level has remained steadfast (*cf* the decision of the Scottish Sheriff Court in *BJ Mann Advertising*, see Chapter 6, regarding whether a small business could be deemed to be a consumer).

The New Connecting Factor: 'Directing its Activities' to Consumers in Other Jurisdictions

Article 13(3) of the 1978 Accession Convention established jurisdiction over any other consumer contract for the sale of goods or the provision of services. This jurisdiction rule was subject to two requirements which will now be considered. It will be demonstrated that both requirements would have hindered the operation of Article 13 vis-à-vis establishing jurisdiction of an electronic consumer contract in the consumer's jurisdiction. Firstly, the contract had to be preceded by a specific invitation or advertising to the consumer in his domicile. Secondly, the consumer had to take steps to conclude the contract in his domicile. Despite these requirements, it is clear that the overall application of Article 13 widened in comparison to analogous provisions in the original Brussels Convention. The Schlosser Report on the 1978 Accession Convention confirmed[51] that the difference between the 1968 and the 1978 Conventions was premised on the European Community's increasingly 'broader based' objective towards consumer protection. Indeed, the Jenard Report previously affirmed:

> (T)he rules here adopted are similar to those applicable in the national law of several of the Member States and, like them, stem from a desire to protect certain categories of persons. Article 13 provides that this Section applies independently of the rest of the Convention, and like Article 7, without prejudice to the provisions of Articles 4 and 5(5).[52]

This remark reiterates the hierarchy of juridical protection for consumers over the *actor sequitur* principle in the Brussels Convention. The Schlosser Report summed up the consequences of a failure to provide sufficient juridical protection for consumers to compliment consumer protection rules.

> (I)ntolerable tensions would be bound to develop between national legislation and the 1968 Convention in the long run if the Convention did not afford the consumer much the same protection in the case of transfrontier contracts as he received under national legislation.[53]

If the jurisdiction rules for consumer contracts had not been amended by the Brussels 1 Regulation, the additional requirements in Article 13(3) would have had to be satisfied in order to determine the jurisdiction of an electronic consumer

51 Schlosser Report, at p.117.

52 Jenard Report, at p.33.

53 Schlosser Report, at p.117.

contract.[54] Indeed, it has been commented on more than one occasion[55] that the requirements of Article 13 were 'intended to apply to cross-border marketing.'[56] The Giuliano and Lagarde report on the Rome Convention on Contractual Obligations made the following (oft cited) observations on the consumer provisions of the Rome Convention.

> Thus the trader must have done certain acts such as advertising in the press, or on radio or television, or in the cinema or by catalogues aimed specifically at that country, or he must have made business proposals individually through a middleman or by canvassing. If, for example a German makes a contract in response to an advertisement published by a French company in a German publication, the contract is covered by the special rule. If, on the other hand, the German replies to an advertisement in American publications, even if they are sold in Germany, the rule does not apply unless the advertisement appeared in special editions of the publication intended for European countries. In the latter case the seller will have made a special advertisement intended for the country of the purchaser.[57]

Specific Invitation or Advertising in the Consumer's Domicile

The two requirements of Article 13(3) would have had to be satisfied when determining the jurisdiction of an electronic consumer contract. First, before conclusion of the contract, the seller either had to send invitations addressed to consumers or advertise to consumers in their jurisdictions.[58] Secondly and significantly, the consumer was obliged to conclude the contract in his or her own jurisdiction. In any event, the two requirements of Article 13(3) would have been difficult to establish vis-à-vis an electronic consumer contract. The basis of juridical protection repeated twice in the previous quote from the Giuliano and Lagarde report required the business to have specifically advertised to a foreign consumer in that consumer's jurisdiction. Since there was no case law specifically on the application of Article 13(3) to electronic consumer contracts, it is necessary to consider previous decisions of the ECJ on Article 13 of the Convention in order to highlight the potential difficulties in establishing the requirements of both

54 Article 13(3)(a) and (b), 1978 Accession Convention, 1978 OJ L304 at p.5; Briggs and Rees, *Civil Jurisdiction and Judgments*, at p.61.

55 *Gabriel v Schlank and Schick.*

56 Briggs and Rees, *Civil Jurisdiction and Judgments* at p.61, who suggest that 'the nature of the advertising is a matter of degree'.

57 'Council Report on the Convention on the law applicable to contractual obligations, by Professors Mario Giuliano and Paul Lagarde,' 1980 OJ C282 (hereafter the 'Giuliano and Lagarde Report') at p.24, as referred to in the DTI Guidance Note. Considered in Chapter 7.

58 1978 Accession Convention, and Briggs and Rees, *Civil Jurisdiction and Judgments*.

Article 13(3) of the Convention or Article 15(1)(c) of the Brussels 1 Regulation to electronic consumer contracts.

The case law after the 1978 Accession Convention demonstrated that there had to be a *link* (albeit not a causal connection)[59] between the advertising and the inducement of the consumer to enter into the contract with the seller or supplier. In *Shearson Lehmann Hutton Inc. v TVB*,[60] the question before the ECJ was whether 'before conclusion of the contract the other party to the contract with the consumer advertised in newspapers in the State of the consumer's domicile,'[61] and if so, whether a *connection* with the advertising and conclusion of the contract was needed. The Commission took the view that for the purposes of Article 13, advertising had to be an activity '*targeted … in that State* by the provider of services.'[62] With regard to the link between the advertising and the consumer contract, the Commission regarded such a relationship as 'purely chronological in as much as the advertising [in the consumer's domicile] must precede the conclusion of the contract.'[63] From these remarks it is clear that the business' advertising or specific invitation had to be intended for particular consumers, take place within the consumer's jurisdiction and precede the contract between the parties. Briggs has expressed concern with AG Darmon's reasoning in *Shearson* that a consumer could establish jurisdiction under Article 13 without having necessarily seen the business' advertisement beforehand.[64] However in the interests of efficacy, if the business intended to use an advertisement for the purpose of obtaining business in the consumer's jurisdiction, it was only necessary that the business' advertisement (whether the consumer saw it or not) preceded the parties' contract. Since it is the purpose and nature of web sites to be available globally and simultaneously to consumers in different countries, web sites neither constitute advertising nor a specific invitation to consumers in one particular country. Essentially, there needs to be a more accurate connecting factor that can be applied to the dematerialised, global accessibility of the WWW and still precede the electronic consumer contract.

---

59 The *Hutton v TVB* case raised the issue of the relationship between the consumer contract and prior advertising. *Hutton* averred that in accordance with the Schlosser Report, it was necessary to establish a clear link or 'causal connection' (at p.I–145) between the consumer contract in dispute and the advertising which preceded it (a view that was also espoused by the German government (ibid at p.I–150)). *TVB*, on the other hand, maintained that there was no requirement for a causal link between any advertising and a consumer contract, arguing instead that a broad interpretation of subparagraph 3(a) of Article 13 was sufficient.

60 *Shearson Lehmann Hutton v TVB*.

61 Ibid at p.I–142.

62 *Shearson Lehman Hutton v TVB*, at p.I–154. Words italicised for emphasis.

63 Ibid. Words in brackets added for emphasis.

64 Briggs, 'The Brussels Convention,' at pp.514–515.

The requirement for a specific invitation in Article 13(3) culminated in the ECJ case *R. Gabriel v Schlank & Schick GmbH.*[65] In that case, the ECJ was requested to consider whether Gabriel could bring proceedings against Schlank & Schick, domiciled in Germany, for payment of money from a prize draw in the courts of his Austrian domicile. In order to claim his prize, Gabriel was required to order goods from Schlank & Schick. The ECJ observed that, in comparison to Articles 5(1) and 5(3) of the Convention, Article 13(3) was 'tailor-made for Mr. Gabriel's situation'[66] in seeking recovery of the prize money owed to him. Advocate General Jacobs confirmed that '(T)he purpose of the second and third cumulative conditions is to ensure a sufficiently strong connection between the contract and the country of domicile of the consumer.'[67] The Gabriel case confirmed that Article 13 was a '*lex specialis*' in relation to Article 5(1)[68] and that it only applied if Mr. Gabriel had entered into the contract with Schlank & Schick 'for a purpose outside his trade or profession.'[69] The ECJ held that Mr. Gabriel's contract satisfied this definition. Furthermore, the ECJ held that the two specific requirements i.e. prior advertising or invitation and conclusion of the consumer's contract in his domicile for Article 13(3) to operate referred to:

> ... all forms of advertising carried out in the Contracting State in which the consumer is domiciled, whether disseminated generally by the press, radio, television, cinema *or any other medium*, or addressed directly, for example by means of catalogues *sent specifically to that State*, as well as commercial offers made to the consumer in person, in particular by an agent or door-to-door salesman.[70]

The ECJ accordingly held that Mr. Gabriel had received a specific invitation by Schlank & Schick to purchase goods in order to receive his prize money and that he took all the steps necessary to conclude the contract in Austria. Had Mr. Gabriel received a personal invitation via email instead, the requirement of a specific invitation in the consumer's domicile would have been satisfied. By comparison, the requirement of specific invitation would not have been satisfied if business used a web site to seek out orders from consumers in other jurisdictions such as Mr. Gabriel. Web sites do not constitute a form of advertising addressed directly to consumers. Since web sites are inherently global, dematerialised and accessible in many jurisdictions simultaneously, they are not the equivalent of specific invitations, advertisements by newspaper, radio or television or the issuing of catalogues in the consumer's jurisdiction.

---

65 *Gabriel v Schlank and Schick.*

66 *Gabriel*, ibid in the Opinion of AG Jacobs at A32.

67 *Gabriel*, ibid.

68 In the sense that it must be considered prior to ascertaining whether the special rules of jurisdiction in Article 5(1) should be applied.

69 *Gabriel*, at p.6367.

70 *Gabriel*, at para.44 of Judgment. Words italicised for emphasis.

More recently, the English Court of Appeal ruled in *Rayner v Davies*[71] that the defendant had neither advertised in nor sent invitations specifically to the claimant's domicile to confer jurisdiction upon the English courts. The defendant was a marine surveyor domiciled in Italy who had been approached by Mr. Rayner for a survey of a yacht. Mr. Rayner then claimed breach of contract and negligence. The Court of Appeal upheld the decision at first instance that the contract was not a consumer contract for the purposes of asserting jurisdiction under Article 13 of the Brussels Convention. The court also upheld the ECJ decision in *Gabriel* that the first requirement of Article 13(3) required the seller to have actively sought business in the consumer's domicile by prior advertising or a specific invitation. The court confirmed that 'the Convention is looking for ... the solicitation of business'[72] in the consumer's jurisdiction. Furthermore, with regard to the requirement for a specific invitation, the court confirmed that Mr. Davies' (subsequent) fax to Mr. Rayner was not a specific invitation in accordance with Article 13(3) as Mr. Davies had already met Mr. Rayner in Italy to discuss and agree contractual terms. The court was therefore satisfied that Mr. Rayner had sought out Mr. Davies' services in Italy and therefore 'there had been no marketing of the defendant's service here and the offer letter cannot properly be described as such.'[73] This case is also particularly relevant as on appeal the claimant sought to introduce new information regarding the respondent's web site. The court remarked that whilst the claimant had 'examined' the web site, '(T)here was no suggestion of the web site being "interactive". There was no reliance on the web site itself either being "advertising" or being a "specific invitation".'[74]

In essence, for Article 13(3) to operate, the court confirmed that even if the claimant's business been sought by the defendant, the claimant would have to show that he took steps to conclude the contract which, the court said, amounted to 'writing or any action taken in consequence of an offer or advertisement.'[75] Furthermore, the court confirmed that Article 13(3) would only apply to consumer contracts when those requirements were satisfied, which reiterated the restrictive application of the provisions. Even though the court confirmed no evidence had been led that the respondent's web site was interactive in nature, it would still not have constituted a specific invitation or advertising.

The Steps Necessary to Conclude the Contract in the Consumer's Jurisdiction

The second requirement of Article 13(3) was that the consumer had to take the steps necessary to conclude the contract in his own jurisdiction. Whilst the ECJ did not make an explicit ruling in *Shearson Lehmann Hutton Inc. v TVB* on the

71 *A. Rayner v R. Davies*, [2003] 1 All ER (Comm) 394 (CA).

72 *Rayner*, ibid.

73 *Rayner*, ibid.

74 *Rayner*, ibid.

75 *Rayner*, ibid.

issue, the Commission did not think that there required to be a causal link between advertising and the ensuing consumer contract. The Commission maintained that proving such a causal link would be difficult and costly for consumers to establish. Briggs and Rees have suggested that it would not have been unduly onerous on the consumer to ascertain the necessary steps required by Article 13(3).[76] Those authors maintain that as long as the consumer did all that was necessary to conclude the contract in his or her own domicile, this would have been sufficient for the second requirement of Article 13(3) to apply.[77] However, it is submitted that the very nature of this requirement restricted the application of Article 13 to situations where the consumer concluded the contract in his own jurisdiction. In the absence of guidance from the ECJ, the consumer could not have relied upon Articles 13-15 when he took steps *elsewhere* to conclude the contract. Indeed, the European Commission confirmed that this requirement was a 'proved deficiency in the text of the old Article 13, namely that the consumer could not rely on this protective jurisdiction when he had been induced, at the co-contractor's instigation, to leave his home State to conclude the contract.'[78]

When the consumer contracts with a business via a web site, he could be deemed to be taking all the necessary steps to conclude the contract whilst in his domicile. However since web sites are accessible simultaneously in different countries, there would have been problems in establishing that the consumer was present in his domicile and not another country at the time the contract was concluded over the web. Furthermore, if the requirement was necessary then it would have been too onerous for a consumer to prove that he contracted with the seller via a web site whilst in his jurisdiction. For example, a consumer does not need to be situated in his own jurisdiction when he contracts with a business via that business' web site. For example, an English consumer accesses a French business' web site to browse the goods on offer whilst in his own jurisdiction. The consumer then travels to another jurisdiction (Spain) and whilst there accesses the business' web site to order and pay for goods. If the consumer had contracted in England (and the web site constituted a specific invitation or advertising) Article 13 would have applied. However, even if the business' web site constituted a specific invitation or advertising to consumers in Spain, the English consumer could still not rely on Article 13. First, since the consumer was not domiciled in Spain, the business could argue that by analogy with the observations in the Giuliano and Lagarde report, the web site was not intended for English consumers contracting in Spain. Second, if the web site was intended for consumers in England, Article 13 could not be used since the contract was not concluded by the consumer in England. The fact that the consumer took advantage of the global, dematerialised nature of

76 Briggs and Rees, *Civil Jurisdiction and Judgments*, at p.61.

77 Ibid.

78 European Commission, 'Proposal for a Council Regulation (EC) on jurisdiction and the recognition and enforcement of judgments in civil and commercial matters,' COM (1999) 348 FINAL 99/0154(CNS), Brussels 14 July 1999, at p.16.

electronic commerce to contract with the seller whilst present in Spain meant that he would not have been able to take advantage of the juridical protection provided by Article 13. The only way in which a consumer could argue that Article 13 could have applied in that situation was if the consumer had to travel to Spain in order to access the business' web site and entered into a contract. However, web sites are communication tools that enable businesses and consumers to contract with each other at a distance and regardless of location. A further example which reinforces the dematerialised nature of electronic commerce is the increasing availability of third generation, wireless technology in (predominantly laptop) personal computers and mobile telephones that enables the mobile consumer to access the WWW. Despite the consumer having the convenience of entering into a contract online whilst travelling on a boat or aeroplane between two jurisdictions, he would have not been afforded the protection of Article 13 since the contract was not concluded in his jurisdiction. To ensure that Articles 13–15 were applied with certainty and predictability, a business would require confirmation that the contract was concluded when the consumer was present in his domicile and not another country. The consumer could be expected to confirm his personal details such as his address by clicking on a drop-down list of countries or postcodes. However this would not necessarily satisfy the requirement that the consumer took the steps necessary to conclude the contract in his own domicile. Alternatively, the business could check the Internet Protocol (IP) address of the consumer's computer to identify the consumer's location when the contract was being concluded. Given the volume of online transactions, the cost and time associated with such investigations would outweigh the benefit of contracting with foreign consumers. Furthermore, Article 11(1) of the Electronic Commerce Directive requires Information Society Service Providers to provide confirmation of the consumer's order when that order is made by electronic means. Article 11 confirms that both the order and acknowledgement are deemed to be received 'when the party to whom they are addressed are able to access them.' Article 11 would therefore be satisfied if the consumer was able to access the order acknowledgement in another jurisdiction. In the above example Article 11 would be satisfied if the consumer received the order confirmation in either Spain, England or whilst travelling between different jurisdictions. It was therefore appropriate that the requirement for the consumer to conclude the contract in his own jurisdiction was not included in Article 15 of the Brussels 1 Regulation.

Therefore, in order to satisfy the requirements of Article 13 in establishing the jurisdiction of an electronic consumer contract, a consumer would have had to assert that a business' web site was either an advertisement intended for, or a specific invitation addressed to, him in his domicile. In addition, the consumer would have had to conclude the contract in his own jurisdiction. As stated earlier, since web sites are available globally on the WWW, a web site cannot constitute a specific individual invitation addressed to a particular consumer. One of the main purposes of a web site is to facilitate the search for information and the promotion of goods and services to consumers in different jurisdictions simultaneously. In comparison to a mail order catalogue, web sites are not addressed to or directed towards individual consumers in one jurisdiction. Therefore, it is doubtful given the comments cited on analogous provisions in the Rome Convention that a web site would have constituted advertising or a specific invitation for the purpose envisaged by Article 13.

The remarks quoted earlier tended to suggest advertising or an invitation directed to consumers *in a particular country*, a requirement which would not have adequately reflected the nature of business' 'globally equivalent,'[79] dematerialised marketing operations invested in their web sites. As the present author and Øren have previously affirmed, the requirements imposed by Article 13 were therefore outdated as far as electronic commerce is concerned.[80] It is therefore necessary to consider the extent to which the connecting factors in Article 15(1)(c) operate to establish jurisdiction of an electronic consumer contract.

Applying Article 15(1)(c) of the Brussels 1 Regulation to Electronic Consumer Contracts

Article 15(1)(c) makes Article 16 applicable for consumer contracts conducted by electronic means. As the present author and Øren have previously confirmed, Article 15(1)(c) is regarded as 'perhaps one of the most significant aspects of the new Regulation and … one that will cause continued legal debate and discussion.'[81] These provisions state that jurisdiction will be established firstly, in all other cases if, either the business pursues commercial activities in the Member State or by 'any means directs its professional or commercial activities' to the Member State of the consumer's domicile or to other States including 'individual Member States' and secondly that the consumer contract falls within the scope of such activities. Each of these requirements will be considered in turn. The reference to 'all other cases' is important. From the consumers' perspective it is a significant extension of the policy of protection afforded to them, as it now includes consumer contracts that do not fall into the traditional[82] categories of consumer contract in Articles

79 C. Reed, *Internet Law, Text and Materials*, 2nd ed (Cambridge, 2004) at p.5.

80 L.E. Gillies, 'Adapting International Private Law Rules for Electronic Consumer Contracts,' in C.E.F. Rickett, and T.G.W. Telfer (eds), *International Perspectives on Consumers' Access to Justice* (Cambridge, 2003) and J.S.T. Øren, 'International Jurisdiction Over Consumer Contracts in e-Europe' (2003) 52 *ICLQ* 665 *et seq.*

81 Gillies, 'Rules of Jurisdiction for Electronic Consumer Contracts – Scottish Perspectives,' at p.132; Øren, ibid at p.670–672; Gillies, 'Addressing the "Cyberspace Fallacy": Targeting the Jurisdiction of an Electronic Consumer Contract' (2008) 2 *Int Journal Law and Inf Tech*, 1 at p.10.

82 European Commission, 'Proposal for a Council Regulation (EC) on jurisdiction and the recognition and enforcement of judgments in civil and commercial matters,' COM (1999) 348 FINAL 99/0154(CNS), Brussels 14 July 1999, at p.15.

15(1)(a) or (b)[83] *and* the consumer no longer has to conclude the contract in their domicile in comparison to Article 13 of the Brussels Convention.[84] The European Commission confirmed that the latter requirement could be 'difficult or impossible to determine,' and was deemed superfluous in establishing jurisdiction under Article 15(1)(c).[85] For the 'first alternative'[86] of Article 15(1)(c) to operate, the business must have been pursuing, or seeking out, commercial activity in the Member State where the consumer is domiciled. As Øren points out, it would be necessary to consider if the business was pursuing commercial activities in a Member State in a 'continuous and systematic way.'[87] Alternatively, the business' commercial activity must have been *directed to* the Member State of the consumer's domicile in some way in order to instigate the protective provisions for consumers domiciled in that Member State. Therefore if a business uses a web site to direct its professional or commercial activities to, *inter alia*, a consumer domiciled in a Member State in such a way that a consumer contract[88] is concluded in accordance with that business' activities, then jurisdiction can be established against that business in the consumer's domicile in terms of Article 15(1)(c). A business situated or having a branch or agency in an EU Member State that uses the WWW[89] to promote and provide their goods or services via web sites to consumers domiciled in Europe must therefore be able to foresee or predict with certainty the implications of the Regulation's provisions.[90] Whilst the phrase 'any means' is very wide, it is the

83 Gillies, 'Rules of Jurisdiction for Electronic Consumer Contracts – Scottish Perspectives,' at p.132.

84 European Commission, 'Proposal for a Council Regulation (EC) on jurisdiction and the recognition and enforcement of judgments in civil and commercial matters,' COM (1999) 348 FINAL 99/0154(CNS), Brussels 14 July 1999, at p.16. Frederic Debussere, 'International Jurisdiction over E-Consumer Contracts in the European Union: Quid Novi Sub Sole?' (2002) 10 *IJLIT* 344 at p.351–355.

85 European Commission, ibid at p.16.

86 Øren, 'International Jurisdiction Over Consumer Contracts in e-Europe,' at p.677.

87 Øren, ibid at p.676.

88 Termed 'direct contracts with consumers,' in the Opinion of the Economic and Social Committee on the 1999 proposal for the Brussels 1 Regulation at para.2.2.4.

89 Or for that matter any other form of traditional or electronic media for marketing purposes.

90 European Commission, ibid at p.17. M. Docherty and R. Fletcher, 'Responding to the legal problems of electronic commerce' (2000) 5 *Communications Law* 5; Bristows, 'Consumer contracts and jurisdiction – changes to the Brussels Convention' (2001) IHL 66; Gillies, 'Rules of Jurisdiction for Electronic Consumer Contracts – Scottish Perspectives,' at p.133; J.-J. Forner, 'Special Jurisdiction in Commercial Contracts: From the 1968 Brussels Convention to Brussels-one Regulation' (2002) 13:3 ICCLR 131; Debussere, 'International Jurisdiction over E-Consumer Contracts in the European Union,' at p.361–362; Stone, 'The Treatment of Electronic Contracts and Torts in Private International Law under European Community Legislation,' at p.122 and Gillies, 'Adapting International Private Law Rules for Electronic Consumer Contracts,' at p.368; Øren, 'International Jurisdiction Over Consumer Contracts in e-Europe.'

extent to which a business directs its activities to a consumer via its web site that will determine jurisdiction[91] of the parties' dispute and ultimately what choice of law rules will be applied to the consumer contract."[92]

'The Philosophy of Article 15'

As the present author has recently remarked,

> (T)he European Commission regarded the 'directing activities' connecting factor as the 'philosophy of Article 15.'[93] However, despite the European Commission's obligation under Article 65 to have reported on Article 15 within two years of the Brussels 1 Regulation being introduced,[94] the meaning of 'directing activities' remains to be clarified.[95] In the context of contracting electronically via a web site,[96] the connecting factor 'directing activities' has been equated to different degrees or spectra[97] of web site activity. The courts in the United States have developed their established test for ascertaining personal jurisdiction, derived from *Zippo Manufacturing v Zippo Dot Com*,[98] by determining the level of activity generated by a business' web site and how that activity was directed to or 'targeted' [99] towards the particular State in question (i.e. where the plaintiff is domiciled).[100]

The Hague Conference has also considered case law from the United States' courts to determine the applicability of analogous consumer jurisdiction provisions in their

91 European Commission, 'Proposal for a Council Regulation (EC) on jurisdiction and the recognition and enforcement of judgments in civil and commercial matters,' at p.16.

92 Øren, 'International Jurisdiction Over Consumer Contracts in e-Europe,' at p.671; Gillies, 'Addressing the "Cyberspace Fallacy",' at p.10.

93 European Commission, 'Proposal for a Council Regulation (EC) on jurisdiction and the recognition and enforcement of judgments in civil and commercial matters,' at p.16.

94 Ibid at p.17.

95 Gillies, 'Rules of Jurisdiction for Electronic Consumer Contracts – Scottish Perspectives,' at pp.132–133; L. Gillies, 'New European Rules for Electronic Consumer Contracts' (2001) 17:6 *CLSR* 395 at p.397; Debussere, 'International Jurisdiction over E-Consumer Contracts in the European Union,' at p.360; Gillies, 'Adapting International Private Law Rules for Electronic Consumer Contracts,' at p.369.

96 Business marketing activities can of course be conducted via traditional (for example television, radio and newspapers) as well as new forms of media (for example e-mail and mobile telephones) analysis of which is outside the scope of this book; Øren, 'International Jurisdiction Over Consumer Contracts in e-Europe,' at p.678.

97 Chapter 8.

98 *Zippo Manufacturing v Zippo Dot Com, Inc.* 952 F.Supp, 1119.

99 Chapter Eight considers the targeting tests espoused in *ALS Scan v Digital Service Consultants Inc.*, 293 F.3d 707 (4th Circuit 2002) and M. Geist, 'Is There a There? Towards Greater Certainty for Internet Jurisdiction' (2001) 16 *Berkeley Tech Law Journal* 1345.

100 Gillies, 'Addressing the "Cyberspace Fallacy",' at p.10.

draft jurisdiction and judgments convention.[101] As the first chapter demonstrated, the level of activity of a web site has been frequently[102] distinguished as 'active', 'passive' or 'interactive.'[103] A web site that enables a consumer to conclude a contract by going through a series of steps or pages on that web site, such as <http://www.easyjet.co.uk>, is an 'active' web site.[104] Conversely where a web site is nothing more than an information source to those browsing its pages, it is regarded as a 'passive' web site. The European Commission's proposals had previously confirmed that '(T)he fact that a consumer simply has knowledge of a service or possibility of buying goods via a passive web site accessible in his country of domicile will not trigger the protective jurisdiction.'[105]

By comparison, when a web site contains information and facilitates communication with potential consumers such as information request options or sign up facilities to receive information on goods or services by email the web site constitutes an 'interactive'[106] web site. An interactive web site provides a method of communication between the parties, for example via a facility to receive email newsletters or request information, and may therefore lead to the conclusion of a contract between the parties. These definitions seek to distinguish [107] how businesses operate web sites as a means of transmitting information and contracting with potential consumers.[108] The 'Sliding Scale' test has been considered by the United States' courts in cases predominantly concerned with determining the jurisdiction of IP infringements, domain names disputes, defamation and personal injury cases as opposed to consumer contracts. The European Commission and Parliament did acknowledge the distinction between active and passive web sites in earlier drafts

---

101 For example, the remarks made by A. Haines in 'The Impact of the Internet on the Judgments Project: Thoughts for the Future, Hague Conference on Private International Law, Preliminary Document No. 17.

102 Chapter 8 examines what constitutes an active, passive or interactive web site in the context of determining specific personal jurisdiction in the United States.

103 Preliminary Draft Report for a Council Regulation (EC) (COM (1999) 348 final – C5-0619/1999–99/0154 (CNS)) by the Committee on Legal Affairs and the Internal Market at 'Explanatory Statement.'

104 <http://www.amazon.co.uk> and <http://www.easyjet.co.uk>.

105 European Commission, 'Proposal for a Council Regulation (EC) on jurisdiction and the recognition and enforcement of judgments in civil and commercial matters,' at p.16.

106 Debussere, 'International Jurisdiction over E-Consumer Contracts in the European Union'.

107 See the European Commission's comments on the interpretation of 'active' and 'passive' sales (derived from the application of Article 4(b) of the Block Exemption Regulation) in its 'Guidelines for Vertical Restraints' (on EC Competition Rules), 2000 C291/1.

108 Gillies, 'Rules of Jurisdiction for Electronic Consumer Contracts – Scottish Perspectives,' at p.132.

of the Regulation. However, despite Øren's view to the contrary,[109] reference to 'consumer contracts concluded via an interactive web site' in the comments on the European Parliament's amendments to the draft proposals should include reference to 'active' web sites. The reason for this view is that the Commission compares interactive web sites with the consumer's inability to contract via 'passive' web sites.[110] Since the consumer can communicate and enter into a contract with businesses via an interactive web site, the consumer should be able to establish jurisdiction on the basis that the interactive web site constitutes activity directed towards that consumer.

The Distinction between Active, Interactive and Passive Web sites

The European Commission's interpretation of 'active' and 'passive' sales[111] in its 'Guidelines for Vertical Restraints' provides an interesting illustration on to how such sales are treated under EU competition law rules.[112] Essentially, the Commission concludes that 'the use of the Internet is not considered a form of active sales into such territories or customer groups, since it is a reasonable way to reach every customer.'[113] However the definition of active sales in these Guidelines begins with a specific reference to 'actively approaching individual customers inside another distributor's exclusive territory or exclusive customer group.'[114] thereby limiting the definition of 'active' sales in this context.[115] The present author has previously noted that '(T)he European Commission regards passive selling as the situation where a customer views a website which leads to contact with the seller.'[116] The Commission went as far as to say that the language of a web site 'plays normally no role in that respect.'[117] Whilst the EU's Guidelines

109 Øren, 'International Jurisdiction Over Consumer Contracts in e-Europe,' at p.679.

110 Debussere, 'International Jurisdiction over E-Consumer Contracts in the European Union,' at p.357.

111 European Commission, 'Guidelines for Vertical Restraints,' at p.12, para. 50; Gillies, 'Rules of Jurisdiction for Electronic Consumer Contracts – Scottish Perspectives,' at p.132 and Gillies, 'Adapting International Private Law Rules for Electronic Consumer Contracts,' at p.369.

112 Gillies, ibid. The Guidelines refer to Article 4(b) of the Block Exemption Regulation.

113 Ibid.

114 European Commission, 'Guidelines for Vertical Restraints' 2000 C291/1, at p.12, para.50.

115 The Guidelines specify that the restriction of active sales is one exception to the Block Exemption Regulation, explained at C291/12 para.50.

116 Gillies, 'Adapting International Private Law Rules for Electronic Consumer Contracts,' at p.369.

117 Ibid. Note however that the European Commission regarded 'language barriers [as] still an obstacle to cross-border transactions' (word in brackets substituted) 'Jurisdiction and

are interesting, the present author has previously remarked that 'only define active and passive sales in relation to distributors targeting goods for sale to *customers or group of customers* in *another distributors' exclusive territories or customer group*,[118] hence the relevance to competition law.'[119]

There is no requirement to distinguish groups of customers and territories attributed to businesses for the purposes of international private law.[120] Therefore, similar guidance on what constitutes 'directing such activities' remains to be clarified in the context of jurisdiction rules in Article 15(1)(c) of the Brussels 1 Regulation. [121] In order to clarify the application of Article 15 applying to consumer contracts conducted by electronic means, the European Commission Justice and Home Affairs Directorate issued a Statement on Articles 15 and 73.[122] The Commission acknowledged that in accordance with Article 16 above, consumers would be able to sue businesses in their own jurisdiction but that this would be subject to the requirements set out in Article 15. The Commission confirmed that if a business had 'targeted' a consumer by means of the WWW, the contract would fall under the protection of Article 15. Given the Commission's rejection of 'ring-fencing' as an indicator of directing commercial activities, it is submitted that targeting must constitute a *positive act* by the seller to contract with the consumer. Therefore, from a practical perspective it is good practice for businesses to ensure that their web sites clearly state which jurisdictions they are targeting with a view to conducting commercial activities there. However, the Directorate stressed[123] the point that the before consumers would be entitled to sue businesses in their own jurisdiction, there had to be a contract concluded as a result of the previous directed activity.[124] Øren points out that this term is crucial to the operation of

applicable law in cross-border consumer complaints – Socio-legal remarks on an ongoing dilemma concerning effective legal protection for consumer-citizens in the European Union (ECLG/157/98–29/04/98),' at para.1.

118 European Commission, 'Guidelines for Vertical Restraints' 2000 C291/1, at p.12, para. 51.

119 Gillies, 'Adapting International Private Law Rules for Electronic Consumer Contracts,' at p.369.

120 Gillies, ibid at p.369.

121 Gillies, ibid at p.369; Øren, 'International Jurisdiction Over Consumer Contracts in e-Europe,' at p.683 and reiterated at p.686; Gillies, 'Addressing the "Cyberspace Fallacy",' at p.13.

122 European Commission, Justice and Home Affairs DG, 'Statement on Articles 15 and 73,' JUSTCIV 1413900 14/12/00, available at <http://register.consilium.eu.int/pdf/en/00/st14/14139en0.pdf>; P. Stone, 'The Treatment of Electronic Contracts and Torts in Private International Law under European Community Legislation' (2002) 11:2 *Information and Communications Technology Law* 121 at p.125. Appendix (i); Gillies, ibid.

123 The Statement reads '... the Council and Commission stress ...'; 'Statement on Articles 15 and 73.

124 Wendy Kennett (ed), 'Current Developments: Private International Law The Brussels 1 Regulation' (2000) 50 *ICLQ* 725 at p.728; Gillies, ibid.

Article 15 and that it should not be made "redundant" simply by the existence of a consumer contract. However, even if the consumer did not observe the business' web site (or contract via the web site), provided the business intentionally targeted its web site at the consumer's jurisdiction the contract is subject to Article 15. It is submitted that the alternative requirements of Article 15(1)(c) also reinforce the point made by the Commission that even if the consumer is technically prevented from contracting with the business via an interactive web site, the subsequent contract is still subject to the protective provision of Article 15 since the contract *'falls within the scope of such [previous] activity'*[125] *directed to the consumer*. The Directorate confirmed that the mere accessibility of a web site was insufficient to establish jurisdiction in the consumer's domicile.[126] It is suggested again that the reference to 'mere accessibility' was to 'passive' web sites. Nevertheless, the Directorate did concede that 'a factor will be that this Internet site solicits the conclusion of distance contracts and that a contract has actually been concluded at a distance, by whatever means.'[127]

Whilst an 'active' web site would have exemplified that point, the Commission did not confirm whether this view extended to 'interactive' web sites. Furthermore, the Statement did not confirm if the language choices or currency payment options on a web site were relevant factors in determining whether a business' web site constitutes activity directed towards foreign consumers. Bristows suggests that the language and currency of a web site would demonstrate that the business directed its activities to a particular country.[128] However, with respect, this underestimates the potential for multiple language and currency options on web sites. As the next Chapter will illustrate, Geist does not endorse the use of language or currency as factors determining targeting since such factors can now be adjusted in 'real time'[129] when the consumer is completing his order online. For example, a US business' web site could provide (automatically or on request) a currency conversion from US dollars to Euros when a Spanish or Italian consumer orders goods online. The Commission's statement 'by whatever means' appeared to place more weight on the intrinsic nature and effect of web site activity on a consumer contract (i.e. the extent to which the web site enables the consumer to contract with the business) as opposed to the (technological) features of a particular web site (i.e. language or currency options on the web site). Therefore, if a business' web site

125 Article 15(1)(c), word in bracket and italics added for emphasis; Gillies, ibid at p.13–14.

126 Affirming the (then) DTI's view in its Consultation Paper 'European Commission Proposals for Changes to Article 13 of the 1968 Brussels Convention.' Copyright Department of Trade and Industry, 12 April 2000; Gillies, ibid at p.14.

127 Statement on Article 15 and 73. Øren, International Jurisdiction Over Consumer Contracts in e-Europe,' at p.670; Gillies, ibid.

128 Bristows, 'Consumer contracts and jurisdiction – changes to the Brussels Convention'; Gillies, ibid.

129 Geist, 'Is There a There?'; Gillies, ibid.

enables a consumer in another jurisdiction to communicate with a business and a contract is concluded as a result of that activity *by any other means,* for example a telephone conversation or fax order form, the web site is interactive in nature and must enable the consumer to rely on the protective jurisdiction of Article 15(1)(c). Despite the Commission's statement, the connecting factor "directing activities" in Article 15(1)(c) remains ambiguous. Even if the ECJ interprets the connecting factor, such interpretation will inevitably remain behind web site technology. Furthermore, any interpretation will ultimately be reliant on cases being referred by national courts to the ECJ. In matters concerning judicial cooperation in civil and commercial matters Article 68 of the Treaty confirms that only national courts of last instance can make such references to the ECJ. Consequently, delays will result in determining an autonomous interpretation of 'directing such activities' in Article 15(1)(c). Such delays will contribute towards the gap between the continued development of web site technology and the legal basis of Article 15(1)(c). A delay in the precise interpretation of 'directing activities' will have an impact on consumer and business confidence in electronic commerce. If a business intentionally targets its activities towards consumers in foreign jurisdictions via an active or interactive web site, any dispute between the parties must be heard in the consumer's jurisdiction. Equally businesses must be able to determine with a degree of predictability whether the commercial activities they participate in via their web sites constitute activities directed towards consumers in foreign jurisdictions for the purposes of Article 15(1)(c). Øren repeats Geist's sentiment on the polarised views of the 'Country of Origin' and 'Country of Destination' principles. Øren confirms businesses investing in and using technology to contract with consumers in other jurisdictions ought to be aware of the risks inherent in such activities and should not expect to be relieved from being sued in the consumer's domicile if held to have directed commercial activities there.[130] It is submitted that the connecting factor 'directing activities' must enable the consumer who contracts via a foreign business' active or interactive web site to sue the business in his own jurisdiction. It is therefore imperative that, in the same way that a specific invitation or advertising that was intended for consumers had to be established in accordance with Article 13, businesses must intend that their active or interactive web sites targeted consumers in particular jurisdictions and that the consumer's contract was concluded as a result of the business targeting its web site towards them.[131]

---

130 Øren, 'International Jurisdiction Over Consumer Contracts in e-Europe'; Gillies, ibid.

131 Gillies, ibid.

Summary of Article 15(1)(c)

The EC Treaty has provided for the protection of consumers throughout Europe. The European Union has upheld the traditional view of the consumer as the contractually weaker party by providing consumers with juridical protection as well as substantive legal protection. Subject to Article 15, Article 16 of the Brussels 1 Regulation enables consumers to raise proceedings in their own jurisdiction against businesses situated in other EU Member States. In order to take advantage of advertising and selling via web sites to consumers across Europe, businesses will be required to comply with the rules of jurisdiction in Article 15(1)(c). Businesses with a branch or agency in an EU Member State will have to consider the benefits and risks of conducting business online with consumers domiciled in Europe. Small and medium sized enterprises, those very businesses that have been encouraged to take advantage of global electronic commerce, might be dissuaded from conducting their commercial activities via electronic commerce as a result of the Brussels 1 Regulation.[132] Nevertheless given the limited scope of Article 15, the meaning of the connecting factor 'directing such activities' and the distinction between active, passive and interactive web sites have all yet to be tested by either the UK courts or the ECJ. The distinction between the types of web sites used by businesses in promoting their business activities have been considered in several decisions from the federal and district courts in the United States. In due course the ECJ will have to provide guidance on the extent to which businesses are deemed to be directing their activities to consumers via web sites. Until that time, as Bristows attests,[133] uncertainty will remain as to whether businesses operating interactive web sites will be subject to the consumer's jurisdiction in accordance with Article 15(1)(c). If the EU does not amend Article 15(1)(c) or provide further detailed guidance on the scope of its application, the ECJ must provide an autonomous interpretation instead. Such interpretation will have to have due regard to the active-interactive-passive spectrum of web site activity. Furthermore – as the next Chapters will demonstrate – assuming the EU Commission or the ECJ endorses the active-passive spectrum of web site activity, the 'directing activities' connecting factor will require modification to incorporate a 'target'-based test to ensure that the scope of a business' online operations can be determined with far greater accuracy.[134] Finally, jurisdiction can also be established over a business not situated in an EU Member State when that business has a branch or agency in an EU Member State. However, this provision does not provide the legal certainty consumers need when contracting with a foreign seller in the globally equivalent electronic marketplace.[135]

---

132 N. Goldstein, 'Brussels 1: A Race to the Top' (2001) 2 *Chi. J. Int'l L* 521.

133 Bristows, 'Consumer contracts and jurisdiction – changes to the Brussels Convention.'

134 Geist, 'Is There a There?'

135 Gillies, ibid at p.16.

Alternative Connecting Factor – Jurisdiction from the Operations of the Business' Branch/Agency

Article 13 previously provided that jurisdiction could be established over a business on the basis of the actions of a business' branch, agency or other establishment. These provisions ensured that businesses could not argue that they did not target consumers and ensured that consumers were afforded protection in accordance with equivalent rules under Article 5(5) of the Convention. In the context of cross-border commerce, it is entirely feasible that consumers will enter into contracts with a business' branch or agency situated in an EU Member State via a web site.

In *Brenner and Peter Noller v Dean Witter Reynolds*,[136] the focus was whether the German court had jurisdiction over a contract when the other party to the contract was domiciled in a non-Contracting State and there was no branch, agency or other establishment involved. The Advocate General was initially concerned with what jurisdiction rules applied when one of the parties is domiciled in a non EU Member State.[137] The Advocate General confirmed that Article 13 was subject to Articles 4 and 5(5) as follows, '(T)he express reference to Article 4 in the first paragraph of Article 13 is thus a reminder that the scope of Articles 13 to 15 is limited to cases where the defendant is domiciled in a Contracting State.'[138]

Article 13–15 of the Brussels Convention could therefore be used against those defendants domiciled in a non-Contracting State that had a branch, agency or other establishment in a Contracting State. If such a branch or agency was involved in the contract with the consumer, then the seller could be subject to proceedings in the consumer's domicile. As there was no such branch or agency in the *Brenner* case, the Brussels Convention could not apply. This case provided a clear indication that the provisions relating to consumer contracts contained in Articles 13 to 15 only applied to consumers domiciled in a Contracting State if the defendant was also domiciled in a Contracting State or had a branch, agency or other establishment there. A consumer could only rely upon Article 13 to 15 of the Brussels Convention if he was able to demonstrate with certainty that the business or its branch sent an invitation or advertised to a consumer in his or her own domicile. A business' web site would, therefore, still have to constitute a specific invitation or advertising in the consumer's country[139] that enabled the consumer to

136 (C-318/93) *Brenner and Peter Noller v Dean Witter Reynolds* [1994] ECR I-4275. *Brenner* and *Noller* commenced court proceedings against *Dean Witter Reynolds* (an American company with an agency in Germany) for breach of contractual and tortuous obligations owed to them under their contract. After the case was dismissed at first instance and on appeal, *Brenner* and *Noller* appealed to the Bundesgerichtshof.

137 In his Opinion to the ECJ, Advocate General Darmon confirmed that the very same three questions, which arose in *Shearson*, also occurred in this case, ibid at p.I-4277 and 4278; *Shearson Lehmann Hutton v TVB*.

138 Ibid at p.I-4281.

139 For example a web site domain name ending with '.co.uk'.

contract with the agent or branch whilst in his or her own domicile.[140] The same concerns vis-à-vis web sites constituting specific invitations or advertising and the consumer concluding the contract in his own jurisdiction considered earlier would have been just as problematic had the business operated via an agent or branch in a Member State.

The provisions of Article 15(2) are just as significant for businesses situated in or outside an EU Member State. This section allows for jurisdiction to be established when the business' branch, agency or other establishment is situated in an EU Member State and the dispute is concerned with the operation of the 'branch, agency or other establishment.' Article 15(2) will operate even though the business' principle place of business is not in an EU Member State. The question is whether Article 15(2) extends to the activities of a business' agent or branch undertaken via a web site. As Chapter 1 indicated, web sites are a means of instantaneous communication between parties situated in different jurisdictions. If the agent or branch used a web site to direct and conduct commercial activities with foreign consumers and the dispute arose as a result of those activities, jurisdiction should be established where the branch, agency or other establishment is situated.

Is a Web Server a Branch or Agency?

An important question that follows from this is whether a web or host server located in an EU Member State constitutes a 'branch, agency or other establishment'. Schu did not view a web server as a branch, agency or other establishment. In his comparison of jurisdictions in Europe and the United States, he maintains that the physical location of a server is irrelevant to a contract.[141] Whilst the drafters of the Regulation did not take the opportunity to clarify this important matter, the point was affirmed in the Electronic Commerce Directive which states, *inter alia*, 'the place of establishment of a company providing services via an Internet website is not the place at which the technology supporting its website is located.'[142]

The 'location' or 'presence' of a web server in a Member State will not establish jurisdiction in that place. Firstly, as the present author has previously observed, 'the web server is a conduit of information, similar to a telephone or a fax machine.'[143] Secondly, the web server needs to receive information from the business if that web site is to be available and of commercial use to the business. That information may well come from the business via another web server or servers. Therefore, the server's location is of secondary importance to the nature

140 For example <www.amazon.com>.

141 R. Schu, 'The Applicable Law to Consumer Contracts Made Over the Internet: Consumer Protection Through Private International Law?' (1997) 5:2 *International Journal of Law and Information Technology* 192 at pp.204, 207 and particularly pp.221–222.

142 The Electronic Commerce Directive, 2000 OJ L178.

143 Gillies, 'Adapting International Private Law Rules for Electronic Consumer Contracts,' at p.367.

of the business' operations on their web site. Indeed, difficulties would arise in ascertaining jurisdiction of a branch, agency or establishment under Article 15(2) if more than one server was involved in transmitting the web site's content. Thirdly, what matters for the purposes of establishing jurisdiction under Article 15 is whether and to what extent a business' web site actively or passively directs that business' activities to consumers. Indeed, the web site owner's actions might fall in between these two recognised parameters of web site activity and content.[144] However, the web server's location does not appear to have concerned those who proposed the Regulation. The Regulation makes it clear that it is where the activities on a web site are *directed towards* as opposed to where they *come from* that will enable jurisdiction to be established in the case of electronic consumer contracts. Given the labyrinth of networks that make up the Internet and the time and money that would be required to establish where a server or servers are located, this is a realistic approach. Furthermore, in the time it could take for a server to be identified, another server or servers could be used and the rule establishing jurisdiction could be subjected to a form of online forum shopping. Therefore, the European Commission or the European Court of Justice should confirm that the location of a web server does not establish jurisdiction under Article 15(2).

The Effect of Jurisdiction Agreements in an Electronic Consumer Contract

Article 17 provides that where the parties have entered into a jurisdiction agreement,

Article 17

> "The provisions of this Section may be departed from only by an agreement:
> 1. which is entered into after the dispute has arisen; or
> 2. which allows the consumer to bring proceedings in courts other than those indicated in this Section; or
> 3. which is entered into by the consumer and the other party to the contract, both of whom are at the time of conclusion of the contract domiciled or habitually resident in the same Member State, and which confers jurisdiction on the courts of that Member State, provided that such an agreement is not contrary to the law of that Member State."[145]

When parties are at a distance to one another, the jurisdiction and choice of law clauses will be included in a standard form contract. Consumers are unlikely to be

144 As exemplified by B.K. Epps in '*Maritz, Inc, v Cybergold, Inc.*: The Expansion of Personal Jurisdiction in the Modern Age of Internet Advertising' (1997) 32 *Ga L Rev* 237 at p.255 *et seq* where he discusses US Supreme and Federal Court cases on this point.

145 Brussels 1 Regulation, 2001 OJ L12/1 at pp.6–7.

able to enforce any preference of a particular jurisdiction upon a foreign business. However, the principle of party autonomy is limited when jurisdiction rules provide consumers with juridical protection.[146] As Chapter One demonstrated, whilst a consumer and business can contract instantaneously via a web site, they do not do so on a face-to-face basis. Given that the legal and practical constrains which limit the consumer's ability to negotiate contractual terms with a foreign business are compounded by electronic commerce,[147] it is necessary to consider how consumers are protected from unfair terms such as a choice of forum clause in standard form, click-wrap agreements. Article 17 provides three alternative rules[148] to govern jurisdiction agreements and provides juridical protection for consumers only when the business is situated in an EU Member State or when each party is domiciled in a different part of the United Kingdom. The first alternative requires the agreement to have been made between the parties after the dispute arose.[149] The second enables the consumer to commence proceedings 'in courts other than those indicated in this Section.'[150] Thirdly, Article 17(3) allows jurisdiction to be conferred on a Member State provided that the consumer and business were domiciled or habitually resident in the same Member State.[151] The important point about Article 17(3) is that any jurisdiction agreement in a consumer contract cannot conflict with the consumer protection rules of the Member State concerned.[152] Whilst each of the requirements in Article 17 could easily operate when the consumer contracts with a business via a web site, the substantive criticism of Article 17 is that it only operates when the defendant business is situated in an EU Member State. Consumers are not therefore provided with adequate, certain and predictable juridical protection when they enter into a contract with a business situated in a non EU Member State. Withers has suggested that consumers can 'take it or leave it' in deciding whether to contract with a foreign business.[153] However, as Chapter One indicated, since the consumer is the legally inexperienced party and can only communicate with the foreign business by the WWW, such an attitude will impede consumer confidence and limit the commercial success of electronic commerce to businesses.

In determining whether a jurisdiction agreement is to be upheld, the courts of Member States have had to balance Article 15 of the Brussels Convention (now

146 C. Withers, 'Jurisdiction Clauses and the Unfair Terms in Consumer Contract Regulations' (2002) 1–160 *LMCLQ* 56 at p.61.

147 Withers, ibid at p.65.

148 Gillies, 'Rules of Jurisdiction for Electronic Consumer Contracts – Scottish Perspectives,' at p.132.

149 Article 17(1) Brussels 1 Regulation; Gillies, ibid at p.132.

150 Article 17(2) Brussels 1 Regulation; Gillies, ibid.

151 Gillies, ibid.

152 Gillies, ibid.

153 Withers, 'Jurisdiction Clauses and the Unfair Terms in Consumer Contract Regulations,' at p.61.

Article 17, Brussels 1 Regulation) with the requirements of the EC Directive on Unfair Terms in Consumer Contracts.[154] The Directive on Unfair Terms in Consumer Contracts seeks to regulate, *inter alia*, the operation of unfair terms in consumer contracts such as jurisdiction agreements and (by Regulation 6) choice of law clauses in favour of the law of a non-Member State. The ECJ case *Cape Snc v Idealservice Srl*[155] confirmed, in accordance with Article 2(b), that the Directive only applies to consumers as 'natural persons.' In *Oceano Grupo Editorial SA v Quintero and Others*,[156] the ECJ held that the jurisdiction clause in the contract used by *Oceano Grupo* was deemed to be unfair to consumers in accordance with the 1999 Regulations. The plaintiff company had previously entered into a number of contracts to sell encyclopaedias to consumers and tried to take action against them in the lower courts. However, the Spanish Tribuno Supremo had previously ruled that the jurisdiction clauses in these contracts were unfair in terms of the Directive. The local court then requested a Preliminary Ruling from the ECJ as to 'whether Courts of their own motion could decide whether or not the term in a contract was unfair.'[157] The ECJ held that if the term of the contract was unfair, then it was appropriate for the national court whether to refuse jurisdiction on that basis. Withers has criticised the *Oceano Grupo* decision. Since a jurisdiction agreement is subject to the tests of fairness and transparency under the 1999 Regulation, Withers was not convinced that considering fairness alone was the most appropriate method of determining the applicability of a jurisdiction agreement in that case.[158] Wither's rationale was premised on the "commercial value" of jurisdiction agreements to businesses.[159] Indeed, it is submitted that this value is enhanced further when businesses contract via web sites with consumers. Businesses need to be able to predict with certainty the legal effect of undertaking commercial activities with consumers in distant jurisdictions. To that extent, the ability of the business to specify a preferred forum in advance is crucial if the business wants a particular law to govern the parties' contract. When this observation is combined with Gatt's findings that consumers are not necessarily

154 1993 OJ L95/29.

155 (C-541/99) *Cape Snc v Idealservice Srl* [2001] ECR I-9049.

156 *Oceano Grupo Editorial SA v Quintero and Others* [2000] ECR I-4941; considered in 'Courts must decline unfairly conferred jurisdiction' (2000) 58 *EU Focus* 7. S. Whittaker, 'Judicial Interventionism and Consumer Contracts' (2001) 117 *LQR* 215. C. Chance, 'Case Comment Ocean Grupo Editorial SA v Quintero' (2000) 11:8 *Practice Law for Companies* 56; Editorial Comment, 'Unfair Terms and the Role of the Courts' (2000) 23 *Consumer Law Today* 1.

157 'Court obliged to join local authorities in fight against unfair contract terms,' case comment on *Oceano Grupo*, ibid, IHL (2000): 50.

158 Withers, 'Jurisdiction Clauses and the Unfair Terms in Consumer Contract Regulations,' at p.62.

159 Withers, ibid at p.61.

aware of the effect of click-wrap agreements,[160] the fairness and transparency of a choice of forum clause in a click-wrap agreement will become more difficult for businesses to establish. Withers maintained that since the 1999 Regulations can be upheld in terms of Article 57(3) of the Brussels Convention as a 'national law ... govern(ing) jurisdiction'[161] then

> ... Article 57(3) would have the dramatic effect of imposing, in addition to the formal requirements of Article 17, a new substantive requirement that the jurisdiction clause in question *(sic)* not cause a significant imbalance in the parties' rights and obligations arising under the contract, to the detriment of the consumer.[162]

A judicial determination of the relationship between the Directive and Articles 17 and of the Brussels 1 Regulation[163] has not yet been requested. Withers argued that the irrespective of Article 17, the effective operation of a jurisdiction agreement may, on the motion of a party or the court, be subject to the tests of fairness and transparency in accordance with the Directive. As the *Oceano* and *Standard Bank* cases demonstrate, the courts refused to uphold a choice of forum clause when in each case the clause, whilst valid under the Brussels regime, was held to be unfair under the Directive. It is submitted therefore that the 1999 Regulations provide a basis for refusal to uphold a jurisdiction agreement if the consumer can establish that the choice of forum is not fair and the clause was not intimated to the consumer with the effect that 'the clause will lead to a significant imbalance in the parties' rights and obligations.'[164] In the context of electronic commerce, a jurisdiction agreement should not prevent a consumer from being able to sue a foreign business in his own jurisdiction. As Withers suggests, a choice of forum will not be deemed fair if it restricts the consumer to suing the business in the business' jurisdiction alone.[165] If such a clause was inserted into a click-wrap agreement on a web site it would fail the first test of fairness, even if the click-wrap agreement was sufficiently transparent and all its terms could be viewed or retrieved before the consumer clicked 'I accept' in accordance with Article 8 of the Electronic Commerce Directive. Therefore it is right and fair that Article 17 should not prevent the consumer from being able to sue in his own jurisdiction.

---

160 A. Gatt, 'Electronic Commerce – Click-wrap agreements: The Enforceability of Click-Wrap Agreements' (2002) 18:6 *CLSR* 404 at p.408.

161 Withers, 'Jurisdiction Clauses and the Unfair Terms in Consumer Contract Regulations,' at p.64. Additional wording in brackets added.

162 Ibid.

163 Bearing in mind the changes to jurisdiction agreements in Article 17 and any change to Article 57/its equivalent.

164 Withers, 'Jurisdiction Clauses and the Unfair Terms in Consumer Contract Regulations,' at p.58.

165 Withers, ibid at p.58.

Chapter 6

Application of United Kingdom Jurisdiction Rules to Electronic Consumer Contracts

Intra-United Kingdom Rules of Jurisdiction: Schedule 4 to the 1982 Act

The 1982 Act provides rules of jurisdiction when the consumer and business are domiciled in different parts of the United Kingdom. These rules are the 'Intra-UK' rules[1] and are contained in Schedule 4 to the 1982 Act. Collins explained that these rules are 'closely modeled on the 1968 Convention.'[2] Following the Maxwell Committee Report, the United Kingdom adopted an Intra-UK model based and modified on the 1978 Accession Convention. The 1982 Act provided an 'opportunity'[3] to facilitate legal certainty and predictability of jurisdiction rules applicable between parties domiciled in different parts of the United Kingdom.[4] In the context of an electronic consumer contract, consumers in one part of the United Kingdom will rely on these rules when contracting over the web with a business situated in another part of the United Kingdom. The rules for consumer contract jurisdiction were set out in Schedule 4[5] to the Civil Jurisdiction and Judgments Act 1982 as follows:

Schedule 4

Title II of 1968 Convention as Modified for Allocation of Jurisdiction within UK

---

1 P.R. Beaumont, *Anton and Beaumont's Civil Jurisdiction in Scotland*, 2nd ed (Edinburgh, 1995) at p.49, and A. Mennie, 'Civil Jurisdiction and Consumer Contracts' (1987) *SLT (News)* 181.

2 Lawrence Collins, *The Civil Jurisdiction and Judgments Act 1982* (London, 1983), Chapter 6, at p.127.

3 Collins, ibid at pp.134-135 and Beaumont, *Anton and Beaumont's Civil Jurisdiction in Scotland*, at p.3.

4 P.M. North, 'Is European Harmonisation of Private International Law a Myth or Reality? A British Perspective,' in T.M. De Boer, *Forty Years On: The Evolution of Post War Private International Law in Europe, Symposium in Celebration of the 40th Anniversary of the Centre of Foreign Law and Private International Law, University of Amsterdam, on 27 October 1989* (Deventer, 1990) at p.33 *et seq*.

5 A.E. Anton, *Private International Law*, 2nd ed (Edinburgh, 1990) at pp.175–176 (where he discusses Schedule 8 rules, of which Schedule 8, Rule 3 is the same as it is in Schedule 4).

Section 4 – Jurisdiction over consumer contracts
Article 13

In proceedings concerning a contract concluded by a person for a purpose which can be regarded as being outside his trade or profession, hereinafter called "the consumer", jurisdiction shall be determined by this Section, without prejudice to the provisions of Articles … 5(5) and 8(b), if it is:

(1) a contract for the sale of goods on instalment credit terms, or

(2) a contract for the loan repayable by instalments, or for any other form of credit, made to finance the sale of goods, or

(3) any other contract for the supply of goods or a contract for the supply of services and … the consumer took in the part of the United Kingdom in which he is domiciled the steps necessary for the conclusion of the contract.

* * *

This Section shall not apply to contracts of transport or insurance.

Article 14

A consumer may bring proceedings against the other party to a contract either in the courts of the part of the United Kingdom in which that party is domiciled or in the courts of the part of the United Kingdom in which he himself is domiciled.
Proceedings may be brought against a consumer by the other party to the contract only in the courts of the part of the United Kingdom in which the consumer is domiciled.
These provisions shall not affect the right to bring a counterclaim in the court in which, in accordance with this Section, the original claim is pending.

Article 15

The provisions of this Section may be departed from only by an agreement:

(1) which is entered into after the dispute has arisen

(2) which allows the consumer to bring proceedings in courts other than those indicated in this Section, or

(3) which is entered into by the consumer and the other party to the contract, both of whom are at the time of conclusion of the contract domiciled or habitually resident in the same part of the United Kingdom, and which confers jurisdiction on the courts of that part, provided that such an agreement is not contrary to the law of that part.

These rules enabled consumers to bring their disputes before the courts of the part of the United Kingdom in which they were domiciled. However, very few reported cases considered the application of Articles 13 to 15 of Schedule 4 to the

1982 Act.[6] *Waverley Asset Management Ltd. v Saha*[7] is the only reported case that has considered whether the matter in dispute was a 'consumer contract' and if the Scottish court had jurisdiction. A dispute arose between a Scottish company and an individual domiciled in England. The pursuer sought to enforce the contract with the defender for the purchase of units in a unit trust and raised an action in the Sheriff Court. The court did not accept the defender's claim that the contract constituted a consumer contract since unit trusts were not 'goods.'[8] The case is interesting in a number of ways. First, it was the only case to consider Article 13 in Schedule 4 to the 1982 Act. Second, Article 13 of Schedule 4 was only considered as a result of the defender's (albeit unsuccessful) objection to the Scottish court having jurisdiction over the dispute. Third, the case is interesting as the Scottish court interpreted the meaning of 'goods' in Article 13 of Schedule 4 by reference to another UK statute without reference to EU authority on Article 13 to assist. If a consumer contract had been entered into by electronic commerce between parties domiciled in different parts of the United Kingdom, Article 13 of Schedule 4 could have been used provided the consumer concluded the contract where he was domiciled. The most significant aspects of Article 13 in Schedule 4 was that there was no requirement for a business in one part of the United Kingdom to have sent a specific invitation or advertised to a consumer in another part of the United Kingdom. In addition, the consumer had to conclude the contract where he was domiciled. Furthermore, the goods contracted for had to satisfy the definition of goods in the Sale of Goods Act 1979. Despite the Scottish Executive's suggestion that the changes to the consumer jurisdiction rules were 'minor'[9] in nature, reform of Articles 13–15 in Schedule 4 was necessary for the following reasons. First, Schedule 4 had to reflect the ability of consumers to contract with foreign businesses via web sites. Second, the intra-UK rules had to be aligned with analogous rules in Schedule 1 to the 1982 Act as amended by the Civil Jurisdiction and Judgments Order 2001. The amendments to Schedule 4 were also necessary since national law cannot circumvent Treaty objectives and furtherance of the Internal Market. Furthermore given the ECJ's refusal in *Kleinwort Benson v Glasgow City Council*[10] to interpret analogous jurisdiction rules applicable when the parties are situated in different parts of the same Member State, Schedule 4 had to be amended.

6 Attributed by the (perceived) low value of consumer contract disputes generally; M. Chissick and A. Kelman, *Electronic Commerce Law and Practice*, 3rd ed (London, 2001).

7 *Waverley Asset Management Ltd. v Saha* (1989) SLT (Sh Ct) 87.

8 Ibid at p.88A. The Sheriff pointed out that there was no definition of goods provided in the 1982 Act, and that reference required to be made to the Sale of Goods Act 1979. In the 1979 Act, 'goods' were defined in the following terms, '"Goods" includes all personal chattels other than things in action and money, and in Scotland, all corporeal moveables except money,' Sale of Goods Act 1979, section 61, cited in *Waverley Asset Management*, ibid at p.88B.

9 Scottish Executive Civil Justice Department, 'New Rules on Civil Jurisdiction' (2002) SLT (News) 39 at p.40.

10 [1997] 4 All ER 641 (HL).

In response to the Brussels 1 Regulation, the United Kingdom amended the jurisdiction rules for consumer contracts in Schedule 4 as follows:

Jurisdiction over consumer contracts

7(1) In matters relating to a contract concluded by a person, the consumer,for a purpose which can be regarded as being outside his trade or profession,jurisdiction shall be determined by this rule and rules 8 and 9, without prejudice to rule 3(e) and (h)(ii), if

(a) it is a contract for the sale of goods on instalment credit terms; or

(b) it is a contract for a loan repayable by instalments, or for any other form of credit, made to finance the sale of goods; or

(c) in all other cases, the contract has been concluded with a person who pursues commercial or professional activities in the part of the United Kingdom in which the consumer is domiciled or, by any means, directs such activities to that part or to other parts of the United Kingdom including that part, and the contract falls within the scope of such activities.

(2) This rule shall not apply to a contract of transport other than a contract which, for an inclusive price, provides for a combination of travel and accommodation, or to a contract of insurance.

8(1) A consumer may bring proceedings against the other party to a contract either in the courts of the part of the United Kingdom in which that party is domiciled or in the courts of the part of the United Kingdom in which the consumer is domiciled.

(2) Proceedings may be brought against a consumer by the other party to the contract only in the courts of the part of the United Kingdom in which the consumer is domiciled.

(3) The provisions of this rule shall not affect the right to bring a counter-claim in the court in which, in accordance with this rule and rules 7 and 9, the original claim is pending.

9. The provisions of rules 7 and 8 may be departed from only by an agreement

(a) which is entered into after the dispute has arisen; or

(b) which allows the consumer to bring proceedings in courts other than those indicated in those rules; or

(c) which is entered into by the consumer and the other party to the contract, both of whom are at the time of conclusion of the contract domiciled or habitually resident in the same part of the United Kingdom, and which confers jurisdiction on the courts of that part, provided that such an agreement is not contrary to the law of that part.[11]

11 Civil Jurisdiction and Judgments Order SI 2001/3929.

The amendments to Schedule 4 to the 1982 Act reflected Articles 15–17 of the Brussels 1 Regulation and apply when the consumer and business are domiciled in different parts of the United Kingdom. The main benefit to the consumer contracting online with a business in another part of the United Kingdom is that he is no longer required to conclude the contract where he is domiciled. However, it must be established that the business was either pursuing commercial activities or 'directing activities' to that part of the United Kingdom where the consumer was domiciled. As with Article 15(1)(c), the amendment by the 2001 Order in Council does not provide a definitive meaning of what constitutes 'directing activities' when the business seeks custom from consumers via a web site. The connecting factor in Schedule 4 will not provide a certain and predictable result in favour of the consumer's jurisdiction. Schedule 4 must be amended further to ensure that intentional targeting via active and interactive web sites establish jurisdiction when consumers and businesses are domiciled in different parts of the United Kingdom.

Jurisdiction over a Business Located in a Non EU Member State: Schedule 8 to the 1982 Act

The 1982 Act has provided rules of jurisdiction where one party is domiciled in the United Kingdom and the other party is domiciled in a non EU Member State.[12] The rules for such disputes are contained in Schedule 8 to the 1982 Act. It is important to note that the rules in this Schedule are particular to the law of Scotland. There are no corresponding rules for England and Wales in the 1982 Act.[13] Section 20 of the 1982 Act states that regard should be had, inter alia, to principles derived by and relevant decisions from the ECJ as well as the Official Reports to the Brussels Conventions. It is useful to consider how these sources have influenced the interpretation of the rules contained in Schedule 8 given that the rules only apply when the consumer is domiciled in Scotland and the business is situated in a non-EU Member State. As Chapter One confirmed, consumers are increasingly contracting via the WWW with businesses situated in non-EU Member States. Scottish consumers have to use the rules in Schedule 8 to the 1982 Act to establish that the Scottish court has jurisdiction over a foreign business. The rules were also recently amended by the 2001 Order in Council. The impact of these rules for consumers contracting electronically with foreign businesses has therefore increased and must be evaluated.

Prior to the amendments by the 2001 Order in Council, the special rules of jurisdiction for consumer contracts in Schedule 8 were contained in Rule 3 as follows.

12 The country in which the other party is either domiciled or situated (in the case of a business) is often referred to as a 'third country.'

13 W.W. McBryde, *The Law of Contract in Scotland*, 2nd ed (Edinburgh, 2001).

Jurisdiction over consumer contracts

3(1) In proceedings concerning a contract concluded by a person for a purpose which can be regarded as being outside his trade or profession, hereinafter called the "consumer", subject to Rule 4 (exclusive jurisdiction), jurisdiction shall be determined by this Rule if it is –

(a) a contract for the sale of goods on instalment credit terms; or

(b) a contract for a loan repayable by instalments, or for any other form of credit, made to finance the sale of goods; or

(c) any other contract for the supply of goods or a contract for the supply of services, if –

(i) the consumer took in Scotland the steps necessary for the conclusion of the contract: or

(ii) proceedings are brought in Scotland by virtue of section 10(3).

(2) This Rule shall not apply to contracts of transport or contracts of insurance.

(3) A consumer may bring proceedings against the other party to a contract only in –

(a) the courts for the place in which that party is domiciled

(b) the courts for the place in which he himself is domiciled: or

(c) any court having jurisdiction by virtue of Rule 2(6) or (9).

(4) Proceedings may be brought against a consumer by the other party to the contract only in the courts for the place where the consumer is domiciled or any court having jurisdiction under Rule 2(9).

(5) Nothing in this Rule shall affect the right to bring a counterclaim in the court in which, in accordance with this Rule, the original claim is pending.

(6) The provisions of this Rule may be departed from only by agreement –

(a) which is entered into after the dispute has arisen: or

(b) which allows the consumer to bring proceedings in a court other than a court indicated in this Rule.

Rules 3(1) and 3(2) defined the scope of the Rule 3's application. Rule 3 provided that a consumer could raise proceedings either in the courts where they are domiciled or where the other party is domiciled.[14] The requirement for the consumer contract to have been 'preceeded by a specific invitation addressed to him [i.e. the consumer] or by advertising' was omitted from Rule 3(1)(c).[15] The omission of that requirement from Rule 3 has significant implications for both the consumer and the business contracting via a web site. The consumer could assert jurisdiction over a foreign business without having to establish that the business sent

14 Rule 3(a) and (b) or indeed by virtue of Rule 2(6) or (9).

15 Anton, *Private International Law*, at p.176. Words in square brackets added. 'Report on the Scottish Committee on Jurisdiction and Enforcement, under the Chairmanship of The Honourable Lord Maxwell' (hereafter the Maxwell Committee Report) at para.13.88 *et seq*, pp.226–228 and Beaumont, *Anton and Beaumont's Civil Jurisdiction in Scotland*, at p.271.

a specific invitation or used advertising in accordance with analogous provisions in Schedule 1 to the 1982 Act. A Scottish consumer suing a Canadian business in Scotland would not therefore have had to demonstrate that the Canadian business' web site constituted a specific invitation, advertising or activity directed towards Scottish consumers. Whilst this omission may have facilitated legal certainty for the consumer, Rule 3 operated against foreign businesses seeking custom via web sites. Nevertheless, the scope of Rule 3 was restrictive as it required the consumer to conclude the contract in Scotland. As with Article 13 of the Brussels Convention, this requirement would have been unduly onerous for the consumer to establish when contracting with a foreign business via a web site. Alternatively, the Scottish consumer could have raised proceedings against the business in the business' jurisdiction. Given the time, expense and uncertainty in pursuing legal proceedings in another jurisdiction combined with the specific issues of identity and geographical location of the business operating via the WWW, the consumer who contracted via a web site was unlikely to take advantage of that alternative. Equally, a foreign business contracting with a Scottish consumer would not necessarily have been aware of the effect of Rule 3 in Schedule 8. Anton is therefore correct in his assertion that Rule 3 could have enabled a consumer to forum shop[16] in his own jurisdiction. The global, dematerialised nature of business activities via the WWW compounds the Scottish consumer's ability to raise proceedings against a foreign business in Scotland. Nevertheless, the Scottish court could have declined jurisdiction. Section 22(1) of the 1982 Act provides that '(N)othing in Schedule 8 shall prevent a court from declining jurisdiction on the ground of *forum non conveniens*.'

If the Scottish court held that it was not the most appropriate jurisdiction, then it would decline jurisdiction and remit the case to another more appropriate court. A foreign business was likely to argue in response to a case brought under Rule 3 that the consumer did not conclude the contract in Scotland. If changes to Rule 3 in Schedule 8 had not been made then foreign businesses contracting with Scottish consumers via the WWW would have relied more frequently on the plea of *forum non conveniens* to restrict the Scottish consumer's claim being heard in Scotland.

The case law on Schedule 8 to the 1982 Act appears to fall into two distinct categories. The first category is where the dispute is entirely within the jurisdiction of the Scottish courts rendering the dispute a purely domestic matter. In these cases it is not necessary to consider international private law rules unless the choice of law is in dispute or another law is to be applied. The second category applies when the defendant is not domiciled in Scotland or another part of the United Kingdom. However, there does not appear to be very many reported cases in the latter category that have had to consider or apply Rule 3 in Schedule 8. Nevertheless, the following cases provide some insight into the interpretation of the Schedule 8 rules by the Scottish courts prior to amendment by the Civil

16 Anton, *Private International Law*, at pp.176–177.

Jurisdiction and Judgments Order 2001. In *Chris Hart (Business Sales) v Niven*[17] the court held that the contract was a consumer contract. However, on appeal the Sheriff Principal noted that the appellant's argument relied upon the decision in the English case *R&B Custom Brokers Co Ltd v United Dominion Trust Ltd*[18] as well as the Schlosser Report, the Maxwell Report on jurisdiction in Scotland and the ECJ's decision in *Bertrand v Ott*.[19] In his determination of the appeal, the Sheriff Principal considered the particular nature of the consumer contract provisions that, according to the Jenard Report and *Bertrand v Ott* case, were designed to protect the consumer as the economically weaker party.[20] The Sheriff Principal held in this case that the defenders were buying privately and were accordingly in an economically weaker position than the pursuers. The appeal was refused on the grounds that the contract was a consumer contract. The interesting aspects of this case were the factors that the Sheriff Principal took into account when determining whether the contract was a consumer contract or not. The Sheriff Principal pointed out the nature of the contract and the defenders' conduct prior to the conclusion of the contract. The Sheriff Principal also made reference to the particular contract the defenders were required to sign, as well as the fee being charged by the pursuers in connection with the purchase and the limited grounds for revocation of the contract itself.[21] By taking all of those factors into account, combined with the guidance from the Official Reports and particular[22] case law of the ECJ on Article 13, the Sheriff Principal upheld the Sheriff's earlier decision and dismissed the action for lack of jurisdiction. This case demonstrates that the Scottish courts will uphold the independent meaning of Article 13 of the Brussels Convention in cases, such as this one, that are not strictly speaking of an 'international' nature.

Until recently, the decision in *BJ Mann (Advertising) Ltd v Ace Welding & Fabrications Ltd*,[23] demonstrated how the Scottish court extended the definition of consumer in Rule 3 of Schedule 8 to include a business that purchases goods outside its own trade. The definition of consumer was temporarily expanded and the remit of juridical protection for consumers extended by that case. The pursuers raised an action for recovery of sums owed by the defenders in Glasgow Sheriff Court in accordance with the parties' jurisdiction agreement. The defenders argued that the court should not have jurisdiction as the agreement between the parties

17 *Chris Hart (Business Sales) v Niven* (1992) SLT (Sh Ct) 53.

18 *R&B Custom Brokers Co Ltd v United Dominion Trust Ltd* [1988] 1 All ER 847.

19 (150/77) *Bertrand v Ott* [1978] ECR 1431, where the European Court gave a restrictive interpretation to the meaning of Articles 13 to 15 of the Convention.

20 Ibid at p.55D-F.

21 Ibid at p.55H-J.

22 *cf* the Sheriff Principal in *Prostar Management Ltd v Twaddle* (2003) SLT (Sh Ct) 11 at pp.14–15 commented that the Sheriff Principal in *Chris Hart* erred in not following the ECJ decision in (C-361/89) *France v Di Pinto* [1991] ECR I-1189 in determining whether the contract was a consumer contract.

23 *BJ Mann (Advertising) Ltd v Ace Welding & Fabrications Ltd* 1994 SCLR 763.

was a consumer contract. The court held at first instance and on appeal that the contract was a consumer contract. The most significant aspect of the decision for this analysis was that the defender was a limited company.[24] The Sheriff Principal upheld the Sheriff's earlier decision that the purchase of goods was outside the defender's trade.[25] Moreover, the Sheriff Principal also accepted that the pursuer had imposed a standard form contract on the defenders, rendering them the contractually weaker party.[26] The question remained whether legal persons could be deemed to be consumers if they purchase goods or services outside their trade or professional activities.[27] Indeed, depending on the terms of the contract, businesses of any size may be deemed to be in a contractually weaker position when contracting online with foreign businesses. This case conflicted with the earlier decision in *Benincasa* which confirmed that Articles 13–15 applied only to private, final consumers. The *BJ Mann* decision rendered it possible for businesses to be provided with the degree of protection intended for natural persons as traditional consumers. However, given more recent authority, this decision must be treated with caution. The definition of consumer in Rule 3 of Schedule 8 has now been clarified by two subsequent decisions. These decisions ensure that a consistent and predictable rule is provided for the juridical protection of Scottish consumers.

In *Semple Fraser v Quayle*,[28] the court applied *Benincasa* to determine whether the contract was a consumer contract. A firm of solicitors raised an action for payment of fees against a former client who had moved to England. The defender claimed that he should be sued, as a consumer, in the courts of his domicile. The court held that evidence was necessary to establish whether the defendant received services from the solicitor for his own private use or in connection with his role as a company director. The decision in *Semple Fraser* was specifically followed both at first instance and on appeal in *Prostar Management v Twaddle*.[29] In *Prostar*, the pursuer sued the defender for sums owed under an agency agreement. The defender argued that since the contract was for management services to assist him in his profession as a footballer, the contract was outside his trade or profession as a footballer and that since the contract was a consumer contract, the pursuers should have sued him in his domicile. However the appeal court in *Prostar* upheld the decision in *Semple Fraser* that a consumer must be purchasing goods or services

24 Indeed, the Sheriff Principal noted that this was the "first case in which it had been held that a limited company was a 'consumer' within the meaning of rules 3(1) of Sched.8 to the 1982 Act"; ibid at p.765. B.A. Stevenson, 'Businesses as "Consumers"; Jurisdiction Within Scotland' (2000) 33 *Civ P.B* 4.

25 Ibid at p.764–E.

26 Ibid, at p.764–F.

27 A matter pointed out by the Sheriff Principal in *Prostar Management Ltd v Twaddle*.

28 *Semple Fraser v Quayle* 2002 SLT (Sh Ct) 33 and *Prostar*.

29 *Prostar*.

for their own private use or consumption.[30] Furthermore, the Sheriff Principal in *Prostar* rejected the decisions in both the *Chris Hart* and *BJ Mann Advertising* cases on the basis that the meaning of 'consumer' in Rule 3 of Schedule 8 should not be extended to enable businesses to claim they are consumers in any contract deemed not within their immediate trade or profession. The decision in *Prostar* is correct as it reiterates the objective of Rule 3 to provide juridical protection for the private (Scottish) consumer acting outside his trade or profession when he contracts with a business for his own private consumption. The decision in *Chris Hart* extended juridical protection intended for traditional consumers to legal persons and would therefore have conflicted with EU law. The decision would have been to the detriment of juridical protection for traditional consumers and increased uncertainty for foreign businesses seeking business from Scottish consumers. Furthermore, the *Prostar* decision indirectly reiterated the importance of businesses being able to predict with certainty when their commercial activities will subject them to the jurisdiction of the Scottish courts.

The case of *Lynch & Co v Bradley*[31] demonstrated that despite the absence of a specific invitation or advertising, a consumer who concluded a contract in Scotland with a business could have relied on Rule 3 in Schedule 8. The pursuers were a firm of solicitors and raised proceedings for the payment of their fees. At a hearing before Sheriff Murphy, the defender contended that the matter was a consumer contract since he was the consumer of services provided by the pursuers. The pursuers contended that the matter was not a consumer contract as 'the services had been carried out in Glasgow Sheriff Court, that the defender had instructed the pursuers in Glasgow and that his instructions had not been solicited by advertisement or by any other method.' The pursuers brought Article 13 in Schedule 1 and Articles 13 and 14 in Schedule 4 to the attention of the Sheriff. Nevertheless, Sheriff Murphy held that the matter was a consumer contract as the defender was deemed to be a 'consumer' for the purposes of Rule 3 in Schedule 8. By instructing solicitors to act on his behalf in court (i.e. the provision of services), the Sheriff was satisfied that the consumer had done everything necessary to conclude the contract with the pursuers in Scotland. Accordingly, any action for non-payment of fees by the defender would have to be brought in the jurisdiction of his domicile in accordance with Rule 3 of Schedule 8. If a Scottish consumer concluded a contract via a foreign business' web site in Scotland, there was no requirement in Rule 3 that the business' web site had to constitute a specific invitation or advertising to Scottish consumers. Whilst Rule 3 provided greater protection for consumers than Articles 13–15 of the Brussels Convention, businesses situated outside Europe would have been exposed to the jurisdiction of the Scottish courts more frequently than businesses situated in an EU Member State. Rule 3 had to be amended to include

30 Referred to as the 'private consumption' test applied in *Semple Fraser* and also referred to in *Standard Bank (No.1)* (which was an unreported case at that time); *Prostar*, at p.11 and 14 respectively.

31 1993 SLT (Sh Ct) 2.

the requirement that a foreign business intended to target Scottish consumers via an active or interactive web site. As stated earlier, the requirement that the consumer must conclude the contract in his domicile is superfluous when the parties communicate via the global, dematerialised WWW and therefore had to be removed. Such a change would have increased legal certainty for the consumer and predictability of result for the business. Given that the WWW increases the opportunity for consumers to contract with businesses situated in non EU Member States, Rule 3 of Schedule 8 had to be amended. There are benefits to consumers and businesses with the revision of Rule 3. First, there will be an increase in legal certainty for the consumer if the principal requirement in Rule 3 is that the business' online activities have to target consumers. Second, the requirement for the consumer to have concluded the contract in Scotland is restrictive when the consumer does not need to be physically present in his own jurisdiction to contract with the business online. Third, such amendments will limit the possibility of the foreign business successfully pleading *forum non conveniens*. Nevertheless, the 2001 Order in Council replaced jurisdiction rules for consumer contracts in Schedule 8 with the following rules,

Jurisdiction over consumer contracts

> 3(1) In matters relating to a contract concluded by a person, the consumer, for a purpose which can be regarded as being outside his trade or profession, subject to rule 5, jurisdiction shall be determined by this rule if
>
> (a) it is a contract for the sale of goods on instalment credit terms; or
>
> (b) it is a contract for a loan repayable by instalments, or for any other form of credit, made to finance the sale of goods; or
>
> (c) in all other cases, the contract has been concluded with a person who pursues commercial or professional activities in Scotland or, by any means, directs such activities to Scotland or to several places including Scotland, and the contract falls within the scope of such activities.
>
> (2) This rule shall not apply to a contract of transport other than a contract which, for an inclusive price, provides for a combination of travel and accommodation.
>
> (3) A consumer may bring proceedings against the other party to a contract only in
>
> (a) the courts for the place in which that party is domiciled;
>
> (b) the courts for the place in which he is himself domiciled; or
>
> (c) any court having jurisdiction by virtue of rule 2(f) or (i).
>
> (4) Proceedings may be brought against a consumer by the other party to the contract only in the courts for the place where the consumer is domiciled or any court having jurisdiction under rule 2(i).
>
> (5) The provisions of this rule shall not affect the right to bring a counterclaim in the court in which, in accordance with this rule, the original claim is pending.
>
> (6) The provisions of this rule may be departed from only by an agreement
>
> (a) which is entered into after the dispute has arisen; or

> (b) which allows the consumer to bring proceedings in courts other than those indicated in this rule; or
> (c) which is entered into by the consumer and the other party to the contract, both of whom are at the time of conclusion of the contract domiciled or habitually resident in the same Regulation State, and which confers jurisdiction on the courts of that Regulation State, provided that such an agreement is not contrary to the law of that Regulation State.[32]

As the extract from the 2001 Order in Council above demonstrates, the same issues that arose with analogous rules in Schedules 1 and 4 to the 1982 Act as amended are also evident in the amendments to Schedule 8 to the 1982 Act. Akin to Schedule 4, the requirement that the Scottish consumer has to conclude the contract in Scotland has been removed from Schedule 8. This change ensures that the Scottish consumer does not have to be present in Scotland whilst contracting with a foreign business via a web site. However like Schedules 1 and 4, the consumer can only raise proceedings in his own jurisdiction provided the business had either pursued professional activities or 'directed activities' towards the jurisdiction. Again, the connecting factor "directing activities" must be amended to ensure that a business' active or interactive web site constitutes commercial activity targeted at Scottish consumers. Such an amendment is needed to ensure that a consumer can establish jurisdiction in Scotland with certainty and that a business can predict the potential for such claims with greater consistency. The rule governing jurisdiction agreements has also been clarified. Whilst the parties can agree a jurisdiction after their dispute has arisen, the other two alternatives are the most relevant for contracts conducted online. Schedule 8 will uphold a jurisdiction agreement in favour of another forum. For example, a Scottish consumer contracts with a Mexican business via that business' web site. If the Mexican business' click-wrap agreement includes a choice of forum clause in favour of the Mexican courts, Schedule 8 will uphold this choice. In the absence of any protection under the Unfair Terms in Consumer Contracts Regulations 1999, the Scottish consumer will have to bring proceedings in Mexico. From the Scottish consumer's perspective, the combined lack of physical contact with the business, the 'take it or leave it' nature of the click-wrap agreement and this rule in Schedule 8 are all disincentives to the consumer contracting with foreign businesses in the first place. The practical effect of this rule will hinder the Mexican business' endeavours to obtain business from Scottish consumers. Alternatively, the parties' agreement can only confer jurisdiction on another EU 'Regulation state' provided both parties are domiciled or habitually resident in that Regulation state and the agreement itself is not contrary to the law of that state. Given the inequality of bargaining power between the parties and the inherent uncertainties vis-à-vis location and identity of the parties, provided the business intended to target the Scottish consumer via its web site, a jurisdiction agreement in an online click-wrap agreement should not

32 Civil Jurisdiction and Judgments Order.

restrict the Scottish consumer from being able to raise proceedings in Scotland regardless of where the business is situated.

Summary of Rule 3 in Schedule 8 to the 1982 Act

Rule 3 in Schedule 8 to the 1982 Act will become increasingly important and relevant to consumers who want to sue a business situated in a non-EU Member State. Unless there is a jurisdiction agreement in favour of another jurisdiction, a Scottish court is unlikely to accept a plea of *forum non conveniens* when a consumer has entered into and concluded a contract with a business via the business' active or interactive web site intended for such consumers. If the business contracted to provide the goods or services to the Scottish consumer, such a plea is unlikely to succeed. The contract will be sufficiently connected with Scotland if the business targets and contracts with Scottish consumers via its web site and subsequently delivers the goods to the consumer in Scotland. Rule 3 of Schedule 8 must be amended further so that foreign businesses that operate active or passive web sites with the positive intention of targeting Scottish consumers are bound by it. Nevertheless, the greatest limitation in Rule 3 is the opportunity for businesses not situated in the EU to include a jurisdiction agreement in their click-wrap agreements which will limit the consumer's ability to raise proceedings in Scotland.

Application of the Common Law Rules by the English Courts

As has been demonstrated, Rule 3 in Schedule 8 to the 1982 Act only applies when the consumer is domiciled in Scotland and the business is situated in a non-Member State. Since these rules do not apply in England, English consumers must establish jurisdiction under the Civil Procedure Rules (CPR). It is appropriate to consider whether analogous rules in England require adaptation and whether Scots and English law should adopt a coordinated approach. The 'procedural character'[33] of the English common law rules assert jurisdiction on the basis of the defendant being served the proceedings whilst in England or, with leave of the court, outside England. Part 6 of the CPR sets out the different ways in which service of the proceedings may occur. These are listed in Part 6, paragraph 20(5) of the Rules. In addition to service by post, 'service by certain electronic means'[34] is possible. The CPR also contains particular provisions for service on companies in addition to requirements under the Companies Act 1985. Briggs points out that where the subject matter does not fall within the definition of a 'civil and commercial matter'

33 P.M. North, and J.J. Fawcett, *Cheshire and North's Private International Law*, 13th ed (London, 1999) at p.285. A. Briggs, *The Conflict of Laws* (Oxford, 2002) at p.91 *et seq*.

34 Briggs, ibid at p.92.

these rules are used by the English courts in order to determine jurisdiction of the dispute.[35] For service out of a jurisdiction to be invoked under the CPR, the court has to be satisfied not only that the claim has been brought in accordance with the rules, but also that England is the proper forum for the matter in dispute[36] and that the claim 'has a reasonable prospect of success on its merits.'[37] Further, paragraphs 5–7 of Part 6, CPR contains rules for service out of the jurisdiction where the matter is one involving a contract. There are a number of prerequisites to the application of paragraphs 5–7. The contract either has to have been entered into in the jurisdiction, or by agents in the jurisdiction, governed by English law or containing a choice of forum clause. Each of these connections could be established when a consumer contracts via the WWW. First, an English consumer could be deemed to have entered into the contract in England when they receive an acceptance from the foreign seller. Since the contract between the consumer and the foreign business is instantaneous, the consumer will conclude his contract with the seller wherever he is situated. However not every consumer will be able to establish that his contract was concluded in England. If a consumer takes the initiative to contract with a foreign seller on his laptop computer whilst travelling between jurisdictions or in a third jurisdiction, jurisdiction of the English courts will not be established. Second, a consumer could enter into a contract via the WWW with an agent of the seller if that agent was also situated in England. If the agent is instructed to obtain business from consumers in England, it should not matter whether the agent uses a telephone, fax or the WWW to do so. This alternative requirement may be of benefit to the consumer who cannot establish that his contract was concluded in England. However, this alternative will not be available to the consumer if the foreign business' agent or branch is not domiciled in England. Even if a web server was located in England, as with Article 17 of the Brussels 1 Regulation, a web server will not constitute a branch or agency. Third, if the click-wrap agreement contains a jurisdiction or choice of law clause in favour of England then the consumer could establish jurisdiction over the foreign seller. However a foreign business that wishes to avoid the possibility of service out under the CPR is unlikely to include such clauses in its click-wrap agreement. Nevertheless, this option should still be retained in Paragraph 6 of CPR. For these reasons, it is necessary for Paragraph 6 of the CPR to be amended, primarily to reflect the consumer's ability to contract with a foreign business via the WWW but also to ensure that the business can predict in advance whether the English court will grant service out. The English court should permit 'service out' under the CPR when the business or its agent uses an active or interactive web site with the intention of contracting with English consumers. For the reasons given earlier, the requirement that the consumer concludes the contract in his domicile should

35 Briggs, ibid at p.91.

36 Briggs, ibid at p.105 *et seq.*

37 Briggs, ibid at p.100 and p.106.

be abolished and replaced with the requirement that the business used its active or interactive web site with the intention of contracting with an English consumer.

The Application of the Lugano Convention in the United Kingdom

The Lugano Convention allocates jurisdiction when the dispute concerns a defendant domiciled in a European Free Trade Association (hereafter 'EFTA') state. A significant difference between the Brussels and Lugano Conventions is that cases under the Lugano Convention cannot be referred to the European Court of Justice for a Preliminary Ruling. Nevertheless, the decisions deriving from the European Court of Justice are often taken into account when similar matters arise under the Lugano Convention. Schedule 3 to the Civil Jurisdiction and Judgments Act 1991 contains the rules of jurisdiction for consumer contracts. The jurisdiction rules for consumer contracts are contained in Articles 13 to 15 of the Lugano Convention and are identical[38] to those Articles in the Brussels Convention. The Lugano Convention was amended on 30 October 2007 to reflect the changes made by the Brussels 1 Regulation.[39] Furthermore, the revised Lugano Convention will now apply vis-à-vis Denmark.[40] Furthermore, Articles 13–15 of the Lugano Convention must be adapted to ensure that the consumer's jurisdiction is established when a business uses an active or interactive web site to contract with consumers in other EFTA States or EU Member States.

Summary

The European Union has led the development of regional rules of jurisdiction for electronic consumer contracts.[41] This was in response to the European Union's Framework for Judicial Cooperation in both Civil and Commercial Matters and to provide updated jurisdiction rules for electronic consumer contracts. The Brussels 1 Regulation does not currently operate amongst all EU Member States. Until July 2007, Articles 13–15 of the Brussels Convention applied vis-à-vis Danish consumers. Despite the fact that the fragmentation of jurisdiction rules amongst

38 Civil Jurisdiction and Judgments Act 1991, c.12, Introduction and General Note, at 12–16.

39 'Council Decision on the signing, on behalf of the Community, of the Convention on jurisdiction and the recognition and enforcement of judgments in civil and commercial matters,' Brussels, 10 September 2007, 12247/07 JUSTCIV 218.

40 Ibid at Preamble, para.7.

41 J. Hörnle, 'The European Union Takes Initiative in the Field of E-Commerce,' Commentary (2000) *The Journal of Information, Law and Technology* JILT 3: <http://www2.warwick.ac.uk/fac/soc/law/elj/jilt/2000_3/hornle>; J.S.T. Øren, 'International Jurisdiction Over Consumer Contracts in e-Europe' (2003) 53 *ICLQ* 665 at p.695.

the EU Member States will be addressed by Denmark adopting the Regulation, the requirements of Articles 15–17 will continue to hinder the ability of the consumer to establish jurisdiction of an electronic consumer contract in his own jurisdiction. As far as the Brussels 1 Regulation is concerned, Articles 15–17 only apply where the business is either situated or has a branch or agency in an EU Member State. The rules of jurisdiction for consumer contracts in Schedules 4 and 8 to the 1982 Act and the CPR rules must also be amended to ensure that a Scottish or English consumer can establish jurisdiction over a foreign business in the part of the United Kingdom where the consumer is domiciled. Regardless of where the foreign business is situated, it should only be subject to the jurisdiction of the consumers' domicile when the business specifically intended to target consumers in their own jurisdiction via an active or interactive web site. The connecting factor 'directing activities' in Article 15(1)(c) of the Brussels 1 Regulation and Schedules 1,4 and 8 to the 1982 Act currently hinders the effective application of juridical protection for consumers. The second condition of Article 15(1)(c) of Regulation EC 44/2001 should be amended to reflect the need for a more foreseeable, precise connecting factor. Article 15(1)(c) should be amended to apply

> … in all other cases, the contract has been concluded with a person who pursues commercial or professional activities in the Member State of the consumer's domicile or, by any means, *intentionally targets business activities towards* that Member State or to several States including that Member State, [*via an active or interactive web site*] and the contract falls within the scope of such activities.

If the European Commission does not propose an amendment to this connecting factor, a lack of certainty and predictability will continue to prevail in establishing that the dispute should be heard in the consumer's jurisdiction.

Chapter 7

Choice of Law Rules for Electronic Consumer Contracts in the Rome 1 Regulation

Introduction[1]

The last three decades have demonstrated an increase in the legal protection directed towards consumers by the European Community.[2] The European Community has sought to ensure that the consumer, formally recognised as the contractually and economically weaker party[3] in a contract with a (foreign) business, is given legal protection when contracting with that business for goods or services. As stated earlier, the legal basis for the European Community's actions vis-à-vis consumer protection derives from Treaty obligations. In particular, Article 153 EC requires that in order to advance and safeguard consumers' interests, consumers are to be provided with, *inter alia*, a high level of consumer protection and a right to information and education on such protective measures.[4] Three pinnacles of consumer protection – 'information disclosure, *ius poenitendi* and juridical protection'[5] – aim to reflect and support consumer welfare at all stages of the consumer's contractual relationship with the seller. International private law rules

1 This chapter was previously published as an article entitled 'Choice of Law Rules for Electronic Consumer Contracts: Replacement of the Rome Convention by the Rome 1 Regulation' (2007) *Journal of Private International Law* 89. The Rome 1 Regulation was subsequently adopted as 'Regulation (EC) No.593/2008 of the European Parliament and of the Council of 17 June 2008 on the law applicable to contractual obligations (Rome I) OJ L177 6' to take effect from 17 December 2009. The ability of the parties to a consumer contract to select the applicable law was retained. At the time of writing, the UK Government is carrying out a consultation exercise on whether to adopt the Regulation.

2 European Commission, 'Communication From the Commission to the European Parliament, The Council, The Economic and Social Committee and The Committee of the Regions, Consumer Policy Strategy 2002–2006' (Tampere Council), Brussels COM (2002) 208.

3 A consumer is a natural person, acting outside their trade or profession in accordance with the Unfair Terms in Consumer Contract Regulations 1999 implementing Directive 93/13 EEC, 1993 OJ L95/29.

4 Article 153 (ex Article 129a), TEU.

5 G. Finocchiaro, 'European Law and Consumer Protection in the Information Age' (2003) 12:2 *Information and Communications Technology Law* 111. The Tampere Council's

must remain effective in regulating conflicts justice by providing an appropriate and effective choice of law rule for consumer contracts, even more so since the compatibility of conflicts laws between the Member States is an obligation under the Treaty. The use of electronic commerce via the World Wide Web (WWW) as a communication medium between businesses and consumers has posed challenges to the European Community's commitment of sustaining effective juridical protection when consumers contract across borders by electronic means. Three factors, in particular, illustrate the difficulties in determining the jurisdiction and applicable law of an electronic consumer contract. It is difficult to determine whether a business' web site is meant to be a globally accessible advertisement or specific invitation (the 'dematerialisation'[6] factor) to a consumer in a foreign jurisdiction. It is also difficult to determine where the parties to an electronic consumer contract are resident and whether special protection requires to be afforded to either party via choice of law rules (the 'location' and 'identity' factors). This chapter will demonstrate that proposals to replace the current Rome Convention on the Law Applicable to Contractual Obligations 1980 (hereafter the Rome Convention) with a Community Regulation was an opportunity to precisely define an effective connecting factor to apply the law of the consumer's domicile.

In January 2003, the EU Commission released a Green Paper which contained a proposal to replace the Rome Convention with a Community Instrument.[7] The proposal for modernisation of the Rome Convention was the first since the Convention's inception. At that time, the European Commission sought to introduce a Convention on the 'unification of private international law and codification of the rules of conflict of laws *within the Community*.'[8] Indeed, the emphasis of the proposal for the Rome Convention was specifically to address divergences[9] in *Member States' substantive laws* in order to achieve greater legal certainty in disputes between parties domiciled in different Member States. Legal certainty was deemed to be necessary particularly where the dispute involved a

---

Consumer Policy Strategy, confirmed '(T)he Commission will take into account the consumer's interest when Community rules on international private law are established.'

6 J. Rothchild, 'Protecting the Digital Consumer: The Limits of Cyberspace Utopianism' (1999) 44 *Indiana Law Journal* 893.

7 'Green Paper on the conversion of the Rome Convention of 1980 on the law applicable to contractual obligations into a Community instrument and its modernization,' COM(2002) 654 final, 14 January 2003 (hereafter 'Green Paper') and the Press Release 'Commission launches consultation on the law applicable to contractual obligations ('Rome I'),' Brussels, 14 January 2003.

8 'Council Report on the Convention on the law applicable to contractual obligations, by Professors Mario Giuliano and Paul Lagarde,' 1980 OJ C282 (hereafter the 'Giuliano and Lagarde Report'), 4. Words italicised for emphasis.

9 J. Meeusen, M. Pertegás and G. Straetmans (eds), *Enforcement of International Contracts in the European Union: Convergence and Divergence between Brussels I and Rome I* (Antwerp, 2004).

conflict as to which law was to apply[10] to a contract between parties resident in different Member States.[11] Despite a number of decisions on Article 3 and 4 by various national courts, and the adoption of the Protocol on Interpretation by the European Court of Justice,[12] there is a lack of case law on the interpretation, *inter alia*, of Article 5.[13] The World Wide Web has enabled consumers and businesses located in different jurisdictions to contract with each other for goods and services. An important issue that has emerged is determining an appropriate choice of law rule for consumer contracts conducted by electronic means. Indeed, the Green Paper acknowledged that the requirements of Article 5 of the Rome Convention do not compliment emerging 'distance selling techniques.'[14] The general adequacy of the Rome Convention in providing consistent and appropriate choice of law rules has been deemed worthy of 'careful examination.'[15] Given the need to provide effective juridical protection for consumers and the desire for legal certainty in determining the choice of law of a cross-border consumer contract, reform of choice of law rules for consumer contracts conducted electronically is now due.[16] In particular, attention must now be given to the conditions upon which a choice of law rule for electronic consumer contracts ought to operate. Given the incidence of electronic commerce activity between parties resident in different jurisdictions,[17]

---

10 P.M. North, 'The E.E.C Convention on the Law Applicable to Contractual Obligations (1980): Its History and Main Features,' in P.M. North (ed), *Contract Conflicts The EEC convention on the Law Applicable to Contractual Obligations: A Comparative Study* (Amsterdam, 1982), 5.

11 L. Collins, 'Contractual Obligations – The EEC Preliminary Draft Convention on Private International Law' (1976) 25 *ICLQ* 35 citing the 'Giuliano and Lagarde Report,' at p.1.

12 'Second protocol conferring on the Court of Justice powers to interpret the 1980 convention (Consolidated version),' OJ C334, 30 December 2005, at p.1.

13 Max Planck Institute for Comparative and International Private Law, 'Comments On The European Commission's Proposal For A Regulation Of The European Parliament And The Council On The Law Applicable To Contractual Obligations (Rome I).'

14 Green Paper, at p.29.

15 P. North, 'Private International Law: Change or Decay?' (2001) 50 ICLQ 477, 503.

16 The Green Paper goes as far as to suggest that reform has been overdue since re-assessment of Article 5 of the Rome Convention was a condition of the Greek Accession to the Rome Convention back in 1986; at p.29. The recent opinion of the EESC reiterates the necessity for revision of the Rome Convention to 'compliment […] the proposed Rome II regulation' and harmonise contractual choice of law rules generally amongst the Member States; 'Opinion of the European Economic and Social Committee on the Proposal for a Regulation of the European Parliament and of the Council on the law applicable to contractual obligations (Rome I),' COM(2005) 650 final – 2005/0261 (COD), 13 September 2006, available at <http://eescopinions.eesc.europa.eu/eescopiniondocument.aspx?language=en&docnr=1153&year=2006> (hereafter 'EESC Opinion'). Word in bracket removed for syntax.

17 According to a recent EEC-Net report 'The European Online Marketplace: Consumer Complaints 2005,' published June 2006, the number of complaints vis-à-vis

and the inherent risks of (*inter alia*) 'data protection and security concerns, fraud, breach of privacy, jurisdiction and [applicable] law'[18] consumers experience when contracting electronically,[19] a certain and predictable connecting factor which applies the law of the consumer's habitual residence to an electronic consumer contract is now of crucial importance.

The connecting factor for determining the applicable law of an electronic consumer contract must be adapted to provide appropriate juridical protection for consumers who contract with foreign businesses via web sites.[20] This Chapter argues that the juridical protection of consumers via a choice of law rule for electronic consumer contracts is a crucial legal mechanism to regulate consumers' cross-border activities and disputes, thereby enhancing judicial cooperation between Member States. Accordingly, a choice of law rule for consumer contracts must be capable of consistent application for it to apply to globally accessible and 'dematerialized'[21] forms of business activities directed towards consumers in foreign jurisdictions. In December 2005, the European Commission released a proposal for a Regulation on the Law Applicable to Contractual Obligations which was recently given approval by the European Economic and Social Committee (EESC).[22] Subject to certain conditions, the initial draft Rome 1 Regulation proposed that the law of the consumer's habitual residence would apply to all consumer contracts. Nevertheless, the argument successfully persisted that consumers and sellers should still be free to select the applicable law of a consumer contract.[23] The EESC argued that such freedom should operate for the protection

contracts between businesses and consumers online doubled from 831 in 2004 to 1834 in 2005 (at 3). The majority of those complaints related to defective or non-delivery of goods. Services were excluded from the analysis.

18 L.E. Gillies, 'Legal Regulation of Risk in B2C Electronic Commerce – From Top-Down Regulation to Promoting Consumer Trust' in I. Ramsay, J. Salloum, N. Horrox, G. Mowatt (eds), *Risk and Choice in Consumer Society*, Ant. Sakkoulas, Athens, 2007. Word in brackets added.

19 C. Coteanu, *Cyber Consumer Law and Unfair Trading Practices* (Aldershot, 2005).

20 L. Moerel, 'The Country-Of-Origin Principle in the E-Commerce Directive: The Expected "One Stop Shop?"' (2001) 7 *Computer and Telecommunications Law Review* 184, at p.190, note 53.

21 R. Fentiman, 'English Private International Law at the End of the 20th Century: Progress or Regress?' in S.C. Symeonides (ed), *Private International Law at the End of the 20th Century: Progress or Regress?* (London, 2000) at p.190.

22 EU Commission, 'Proposal for a Regulation of the European Parliament and the Council on the law applicable to contractual obligations (Rome 1),' COM (2005) 650 final, 2005/0261 (COD), 15 December 2005 (hereafter referred to as the draft Rome 1 Regulation). EESC Opinion.

23 Editorial, 'On the Way to a Rome 1 Regulation' (2006) 43:4 *CMLR* 913 (particularly at pp.918–922). See also Z. Tang, 'Parties' Choice of Law in E-Consumer Contracts' (2007) *Journal of Private International Law*.

of EU consumers, in recognition of Treaty obligations. A more far reaching view also recently argued that freedom to select the applicable law should operate *vis-à-vis* contracts with all consumers, not just those consumers resident in the EU.[24] The recently adopted Rome 1 Regulation has, as a result of an amendment by the European Parliament, been amended to reintroduce party autonomy to select the applicable law of a consumer contract.[25] However, in view of Treaty obligations and the need to ensure a fair and predicable choice of law rule, the initial proposal to restrict parties' freedom to select the applicable law in a consumer contract was preferable. For example, during the negotiations for the Brussels 1 Regulation, a representative of the Consumers Association in the United Kingdom reported that '[The Consumers Association's view is] that allowing consumers to make claims in their local courts is of limited value unless they can have the dispute decided according to their laws. Any other option requiring the input of foreign legal experts will not be viable.'[26]

Despite the 'thorough re-working' of Article 5 of the Rome Convention espoused by the EESC,[27] the conditions upon which the law of the consumer's habitual residence applies vis-à-vis electronic consumer contracts remain unclear. In particular, the Rome 1 Regulation should not replicate 'word for word'[28] the requirements for determining the jurisdiction of an electronic consumer contract in Article 15(1)(c) of the Brussels 1 Regulation. Rather than reproducing the condition that prior to the consumer contract the business 'directed its activities' towards the consumer's jurisdiction, there should instead be a more accurate pre-requisite premised on intentional targeting[29] to determine in what circumstances the law of the consumer's habitual residence applies to an electronic consumer contract. Choice of law rules must be adapted to provide both parties to an electronic consumer contract with a predictable basis for determining what law will apply to their online activities. Despite reference to the law of the consumer's habitual residence, the conditions upon which Article 6 of the draft Rome 1 Regulation applies will not provide sufficiently consistent results. In particular, inconsistency will result if the European Commission simply replicates the

24 Editorial, ibid at p.918.

25 Article 6, 'European Parliament legislative resolution of 29 November 2007 on the proposal for a regulation of the European Parliament and of the Council on the law applicable to contractual obligations' (Rome I) (COM(2005)0650 – C6-0441/2005 – 2005/0261(COD).

26 A. Patel, 'The Brussels Regulation...Good for business' (2000) 2:12 *E-commerce Law and Policy* 10, 13. Word in bracket amended. It is unfortunate that the United Kingdom has not (yet) indicated that it will, in due course, adopt the Rome 1 Regulation; EESC Opinion, at para.1.5

27 EESC Opinion, ibid at para.3.3.1.

28 P.M. North and J.J. Fawcett, *Cheshire and North's Private International Law*, 13th ed (London, 1999), 542.

29 A requirement acknowledged in the most recent amended draft Rome 1 Regulation – Recital 24.

requirements of Article 15(1)(c) of the Brussels 1 Regulation in Article 6 of the recently adopted Rome 1 Regulation. The regulation of choice of law rules for cross-border consumer contracts is an important corollary that, if left unattended, could limit the effectiveness of juridical protection for EU consumers who contract by electronic means with businesses situated in other EU Member States.

Juridical Protection for Consumers via EU International Private Law

The European Community has sought and, as Hörnle and Finnocchiaro have both argued, led[30] the implementation of consumer protection policies in the Information Society between the Member States. The European Community has introduced Directives on Unfair Terms in Consumer Contracts,[31] Distance Selling,[32] the Distance Marketing of Consumer Financial Services[33] and more recently a Regulation to control Unfair Commercial Practices.[34] Each of these Community instruments simultaneously regulate and promote consumer welfare in the online environment by imposing information disclosure duties upon the (predominantly foreign) seller[35] or providing the EU resident consumer with substantive legal protection including the right of withdrawal.[36] In addition to these instruments, and the fact that Article 3(3) of the Electronic Commerce Directive[37] expressly excludes international private law rules from the regulation of Information Society

30 J. Hörnle, 'The European Union Takes Initiative in the Field of E-Commerce' (2000) Commentary, 3 *The Journal of Information, Law and Technology* (JILT) <http://www2.warwick.ac.uk/fac/soc/law/elj/jilt/2000_3/hornle>. Finocchiaro, 'European Law and Consumer Protection in the Information Age.'

31 Unfair Terms in Consumer Contracts Regulations incorporating Directive 93/13/EC, 1993 OJ L95/29.

32 Distance Selling Directive, 1997 OJ L0007.

33 Directive EC 2002/65 on the Distance Marketing of Consumer Financial Services OJ L271/16, 23 September 2002.

34 The Unfair Commercial Practices Directive, 2005 OJ L149/22, which came into force in December 2007. The Directive will apply to misleading and aggressive practices which lead to pressure selling. The test in determining whether a commercial practice is unfair consists of assessing when it is contrary to professional diligence and materially distorts consumers' behaviour.

35 Ibid. J. Hamilton and L.E. Gillies, 'The Impact of E-commerce on Consumer Welfare – Information Disclosure Regimes' (2003) 11:4 *Journal of Financial Regulation and Compliance* 329.

36 For example, the Distance Selling Directive requires, *inter alia*, the business to provide certain information to the consumer. It also provides the consumer with a right of withdrawal and stipulates rules on performance of the contract.

37 The Electronic Commerce Directive, 2000 OJ L178.

Service Providers,[38] the European Community has also sought to provide an appropriate level of juridical protection for EU resident consumers contracting online with businesses.

In Europe, juridical protection for consumers contracting electronically or otherwise is three-fold. Firstly, as had been considered earlier, the European Community addressed the issue of jurisdiction and the recognition of judgments for, *inter alia*, electronic commerce by replacing the Brussels Convention with the Brussels 1 Regulation.[39] The United Kingdom DTI succinctly highlighted the need for re-regulation of jurisdiction rules for consumer contracts as follows '(T)he (Brussels) Convention pre-dates the Internet and in the absence of any case law it is not clear how Article 13 applies to electronic commerce and websites in particular.'[40] In 2001, Articles 15–17 of the Brussels 1 Regulation[41] replaced Articles 13–15 of the Brussels Convention to provide jurisdiction rules for consumer contracts, including those contracts conducted by electronic means.[42] Secondly, the European Community has sought to promote alternative means of resolving disputes concerning electronic consumer contracts.[43] However to date, no such measures have been implemented.[44] Finally, the third – and rapidly becoming

38 Electronic Commerce Directive, Article 3(3) and Recital 23, ibid; C.T. Poggi, 'Electronic Commerce Legislation: An Analysis of European and American Approaches to Contract Formation' (2000) 41 *Virginia Journal of International Law* 224, at p.247.

39 Brussels 1 Regulation, 2001 OJ L12/1.

40 United Kingdom Department of Trade and Industry Consultation Paper, 'European Commission Proposals for Changes to Article 13 of the 1968 Brussels Convention,' Copyright Department of Trade and Industry, 12 April 2000.

41 2001 OJ L12/1.

42 S. Dutson, 'E-Commerce – European Union Transnational E-Commerce' (2000) 16 *Computer Law and Security Report* 105; P. Stone, 'Internet Consumer Contracts and European Private International Law' (2000) 9:1 *Information and Communications Technology Law* 5; L.E. Gillies, 'A Review of the New Jurisdiction Rules for Electronic Consumer Contracts within the European Union' (2001) Commentary, *The Journal of Information, Law and Technology* (JILT) 1 <http://www2.warwick.ac.uk/fac/soc/law/elj/jilt/2001_1/gillies>; F. Debussere, 'International Jurisdiction over E-Consumer Contracts in the European Union: Quid Novi Sub Sole?' (2002) 10 *International Journal of Law and Information Technology* 344; P. Stone, 'The Treatment of Electronic Contracts and Torts in Private International Law under European Community Legislation' (2002) 11:2 *Information and Communications Technology Law* 121; J.S.T. Øren, 'International Jurisdiction Over Consumer Contracts in e-Europe' (2003) 52 *ICLQ* 665.

43 'Proposal for a Decision establishing a programme of Community action in the field of Health and Consumer Protection 2007–2013' (COM(2005) 115 final 2005/0042 (COD)), available at <http://europa.eu.int/comm/consumers/overview/programme_2007-2013_en.htm> at para.4.2.3.

44 A Regulation on a European Small Claims Procedure is currently in preparation: EU Commission, 'Regulation establishing a European Small Claims Procedure,' COM 2005 87 final, 2005/0220 (COD), 15 March 2005 <http://europa.eu.int/comm/justice_home/fsj/civil/recognition/fsj_civil_recognition_general_en.htm>. In 2004, the Commission proposed

the most significant – aspect of juridical protection for consumers are choice of law rules. Since 1980 the Rome Convention[45] has, *inter alia*, upheld the parties' freedom to agree the contractual choice of law and provided particular choice of law rules for certain consumer contracts. The impact of the Rome Convention was that it was, and still remains, a convention with international scope and application.[46] It need not matter whether the laws in question are Member States' laws or not. Article 1 of the Rome Convention applies to any contractual situation where there is a choice between the laws of different countries. The premise of the Convention is to uphold and apply the law(s) chosen by the parties. Articles 3 and 4 provide rules that determine the applicable law when the parties have selected a choice of law or not. The applicable law is therefore determined primarily by reference to the parties' intentions or, in the absence of choice, by localising the contract[47] with a particular law. The applicable law rules for 'certain consumer contracts'[48] are contained in Article 5 of the Rome Convention and apply to contracts for the supply of goods or services[49] to a consumer 'for a purpose which can be regarded as being outside his trade or profession.'[50] Article 5 does not define the other party to the consumer contract, i.e. the seller. Subject to particular connecting factors, the effect of Article 5 is either that the mandatory law(s) of the consumer's habitual residence and the contractual choice of law are both applied or the law of the consumer's habitual residence applies in the absence of choice. The three alternative connecting factors are either that the consumer's contract was preceded by a specific invitation or advertising and that the contract was concluded in the consumer's habitual residence, or the seller (or his agent) received the consumer's order in that country, or if the consumer travelled to another country in order to place his order for a contract for the sale of goods as a result of the seller inducing the consumer to travel.

---

a 'Directive on Certain Aspects of Mediation in Civil and Commercial Matters,' COM 2004/0718 final, 2004/0251 (COD) (which has yet to be approved); <http://ec.europa.eu/civiljustice/adr/adr_ec_en.htm>.

45 'Council Convention on the Law Applicable to Contractual Obligations,' opened for signature in Rome on 19 June 1980 (80/934/EEC), 1980 OJ L266.

46 North, 'The E.E.C Convention on the Law Applicable to Contractual Obligations (1980): Its History and Main Features,' at pp.11–12.

47 North and Fawcett, *Cheshire and North's Private International Law,* at p.552.

48 Article 5, Rome Convention.

49 Ibid. The modernisation of the Rome Convention should also provide the opportunity to enable Article 5 to apply to the sale of digital goods and services.

50 Article 5(1), Rome Convention. Article 5 does not apply to carriage contracts and contracts for the supply of services where the services are to be supplied to the consumer exclusively in a country other than that in which he has his habitual residence (Articles 5(4)(a) and (b) respectively). It does apply to contracts for package holidays (Article 5(5)).

North and Fawcett raise the important question whether 'special features of particular contracts necessitate special choice of law rules?'[51] Despite the low pecuniary value attributed to an individual electronic consumer contract,[52] it is the combination of an inherent difference in bargaining strength between the parties to a consumer contract and the 'dematerialised'[53] nature of electronic commerce which justifies[54] special consideration of the connecting factors to determine the choice of law of an electronic consumer contract. Since EU resident consumers who contract with foreign sellers online can, in principle, sue those sellers in their own jurisdiction, the future Rome 1 Regulation must provide a consistent and effective choice of law rule for EU resident consumers who contract electronically.

Restricting Party Autonomy to Select the Applicable Law

Despite the emphasis afforded to the parties' intentions, the ability of the parties to select a particular law has been restricted either by the operation of mandatory rules or by particular policy considerations. Article 3 of the Rome Convention defines mandatory rules as 'rules which cannot be derogated from by contract.' In practice, Article 3(3) is of limited application in cross-border disputes as the facts of such disputes will generally be connected to more than one country. In the context of consumer contracts, Articles 3(3) and 3(4) operate only in cases of purely internal conflicts where for example, the consumer and business were resident in the same jurisdiction (e.g. England) where performance of the contract was also to take place but the contract between the parties contained a choice of law clause in favour of another jurisdiction (e.g. India). In seeking to implement 'a new, simple and foreseeable conflict rule'[55] for consumer contracts, reference in the current Article 5 to Article 3(4) (Article 3(3)'s equivalent measure) should be deleted from a future Rome 1 Regulation in favour of the law of the consumer's habitual residence.

---

51 North and. Fawcett, *Cheshire and North's Private International Law*, at p.534.

52 The UK European Consumer Centre and EEJ-Net's Interim Report, January – July 2005, previously available at <http://www.euroconsumer.org.uk/index/publications/other_reports/activity_0805_eec_interim_report.htm> reported that 36 per cent of the pecuniary value of consumer disputes reported were less than £350. However, according to data recently obtained by IMRG, the long term growth in UK Internet sales is beginning to emerge; 'Internet Shopping Hits £3 Billion in November,' 14 December 2006, available at <http://www.imrg.org/ItemDetail.aspx?clg=News&cid=nws&pid=News_IMRG_Index&language=en-GB>.

53 Fentiman, 'English Private International Law at the End of the 20th Century: Progress or Regress?' and Rothchild, 'Protecting the Digital Consumer: The Limits of Cyberspace Utopianism.'

54 North and Fawcett, *Cheshire and North's Private International Law*, at pp.574–575; Editorial, 'On the Way to a Rome 1 Regulation.'

55 Draft Rome 1 Regulation, Explanatory Memorandum, *supra* n 22 at pp.6, 15.

Article 7 can override the parties' choice entirely and impose either the mandatory rules of another law (Article 7(1))[56] or the forum (Article 7(2)). If the consumer raised proceedings in his own jurisdiction, the effect of Article 7(2) could be that all of the laws of the consumer's habitual residence apply, overriding the contractual choice of law. However, in cases concerning consumer contracts, the ability of the parties to select a particular law is already limited[57] by Article 5. Article 5 is a narrow[58] mandatory rule that applies the mandatory laws of the consumer's habitual residence even if the parties have selected a choice of law. Article 5 was 'designed to guarantee a country's social and economic order'[59] by seeking compatibility with, but not identical to,[60] the analogous consumer contract jurisdiction rule in the Brussels Convention.[61] According to the Giuliano and Lagarde Report, the 'specific conflict rule for certain contracts made by consumers' was justifiably drafted to provide a consistent rule governing those contracts where one of the parties is contractually and economically weaker (i.e. the consumer) than the other (i.e. the seller).[62] The practical aim of this mandatory rule was to restrict the seller's ability to impose his law (and jurisdiction) in a contract of adhesion.

However in practice as a mandatory rule the current Article 5 is not particularly effective in achieving legal certainty or predictability of result. It is not easy for either an individual consumer or foreign seller to determine which laws of the consumer's habitual residence are mandatory in cross-border cases and what effect those mandatory rules have on the contractual choice of law: even more so when the identity and location of the parties to an electronic consumer contract are difficult to determine in the first place. The Green Paper on the Replacement of the Rome Convention considered the premise upon which Article 5 should operate in future. The Green Paper considered whether just the mandatory rules or all of the laws of the consumer's habitual residence should be applied in Article 5. Concerns were expressed regarding a clash between the tenet of party autonomy[63] to select the applicable law and juridical protection for consumers. As stated earlier, the purpose of Article 5 was to ensure that the mandatory rules of the consumer's habitual residence applied, whether or not the parties had selected a choice of

56 Article 7(1) was not implemented in the United Kingdom.

57 North and Fawcett, *Cheshire and North's Private International Law*, at p.577.

58 C. Knofel, 'Mandatory rules and choice of law: a comparative approach to Article 7(2) of the Rome Convention' (1999) May, *Journal of Business Law*, 239.

59 Green Paper, at p.33.

60 C.G.J. Morse, 'The EEC Convention on the Law Applicable to Contractual Obligations' (1982) 2 *Yearbook of European Law* 107, 134 *et seq*.

61 Giuliano and Lagarde report ; T.C Hartley, 'Consumer Protection Provisions in the E.E.C Convention,' in P.M. North (ed), 'The E.E.C Convention on the Law Applicable to Contractual Obligations (1980): Its History and Main Features,' at p.125; J. Blaikie, 'Choice of Law in Consumer Contracts' (1992) 60 *Scottish Law Gazette*; 6 at p.7.

62 Giuliano and Lagarde Report, ibid.

63 Deemed the 'keystone of the system'; Green Paper, at p.11.

law.[64] Since the implementation of Article 5, it has been questioned whether the consumer in fact gains greater protection via the contractual choice of law, rather than the (mandatory) law(s) of his habitual residence. Despite reference to the mandatory rules of the consumer's habitual residence, the contractual choice of law (usually the law where the seller is located) often still applies with the result that the contract is 'split' (*dépeçage*) between different laws, thereby further reducing the opportunity for legal certainty.[65] It has been argued that by referring to the mandatory rules of the consumer's habitual residence, the consumer is always provided with an appropriate (that is, from the consumer's perspective an effective and predictable) level of protection.[66] Such a view tends to support a minimal approach to the enforcement of substantive consumer protection laws operating between the Member States, particularly when the majority of such laws have been implemented via secondary EU legislation. Indeed, as Tang has remarked, it may be difficult to determine whether such consumer protection rules are intended to be mandatory laws in the context of cross-border electronic commerce.[67] It is right that any reference to 'mandatory rules' has been removed from the draft Article 5 particularly since the EU has, as stated earlier, sought to implement rules concerned with consumer protection in the information society. As Howells and Wilhemsson argue, there is a need to ensure that a maximum, in the sense of a mandatory, level of substantive consumer protection operates between the Member States.[68] Such protection must clearly apply in cross-border disputes where the consumer is resident in a Member State. Straetmans recently confirmed[69] that a maximum approach to consumer protection can be further enhanced by juridical rules that have the effect of applying all substantive (EU-led) consumer protection laws, irrespective of the existence of a contractual choice of law. To this extent, it is submitted the recent Opinion from the EESC that the parties (including the

64 Morse, 'The EEC Convention on the Law Applicable to Contractual Obligations,' at p.8 and 9 suggests that this operates to provide the consumer with 'minimum' protection.

65 A point reiterated by the EESC in its Opinion; at para.3.3.1.

66 According to Jaffey, the purpose of Article 5 was to ensure that the consumer had the 'convenience in consulting the [i.e. his] law', rather than being entitled to *whatever law* is more favourable to him (whether his domestic law or a foreign law); A.E. Jaffey, *Topics in Choice of Law* (London, 1996) at pp.49 and 51. Words in square brackets added. At p.49 Jaffey continues, 'the aim of the choice of law rule must be to select the appropriate governing law on criteria of justice and convenience for the parties' (a view expressed in his earlier article, 'The English Proper Law Doctrine and the EEC Convention' (1984) 33 *ICLQ* 531 at p.540). *cf* the potential implications of dépéçage in a consumer contract considered by Green Paper, at p.30, n 64.

67 Z. Tang, 'Parties' Choice of Law in E-Consumer Contracts.'

68 G. Howells and T. Wilhelmsson, 'EC Consumer law: has come of age?' (2003) 28 *European Law Review* 370.

69 G. Straetmans, 'The Consumer Concept in EC Law,' in J. Meeusen, M. Pertegas and G. Straetmans (eds), *Enforcement of International Contracts in the European Union: Convergence and Divergence between Brussels I and Rome I*, at p.315.

consumer) should still benefit from selecting a contractual choice of law in a consumer contract would have the opposite, and a potentially detrimental, effect in providing EU resident consumers with a consistent level of consumer protection.[70] As far as electronic consumer contracts are concerned, it appears to be generally accepted[71] that a restriction on the ability of the parties to select a law other than that of the consumer's habitual residence will, particularly in the context of 'new communication technologies and the globalisation of the economy,'[72] provide consumers with increased juridical protection and consequently offer the parties greater legal certainty than offered by the current Article 5. Therefore, the future Article 6 must limit the seller's ability to impose a law other than all of the laws of the consumer's habitual residence in a consumer contract.

The Need for an Appropriate Connecting Factor

As stated earlier, the connecting factors in Article 5 of the Rome Convention are currently established in a number of ways. The requirement for the consumer to be habitually resident in a given jurisdiction has always operated and, with respect to contrary suggestions, is not rendered obsolete[73] by the purpose of Article 5. The mandatory rules of the consumer's habitual residence will apply, subject to either the consumer having received a specific invitation or when the seller advertised in the consumer's jurisdiction. In either case the consumer must have concluded the contract in his habitual residence or travelled to the seller's jurisdiction in order to conclude the contract. As stated earlier, the effect of Article 5 is either to apply the law chosen by the parties subject to the mandatory rules of the consumer's habitual residence or the mandatory laws of the consumer's habitual residence only.

When the Rome Convention is converted to a Regulation its application will, in accordance with Articles 61(c) and 65 EC, be restricted (as far as the consumer contract choice of law rule is concerned) to situations where the consumer is habitually resident in a Member State. It is anticipated that analogous concerns that arose with the application of jurisdiction rules in the Brussels 1 Regulation to electronic consumer contracts vis-à-vis the application of the law of the 'Country

70 EESC Opinion, at para. 3.3.1.

71 Straetmans, 'The Consumer Concept in EC Law,' and Max Planck Institute, at pp.39–40. *cf* Editorial, 'On the Way to a Rome 1 Regulation,' EESC Opinion, and Tang, 'Parties' Choice of Law in E-Consumer Contracts.'

72 Straetmans, 'The Consumer Concept in EC Law,' at p.314.

73 C. Riefa, 'Article 5 of the Rome Convention on the Law Applicable to Contractual Obligations 1980 and Consumer E-contracts: The Need for Reform' (2004) 13:1 *Information and Communications Technology Law* 59 at p.68; C. Wild, S. Weinstein and C. Riefa, 'Council Regulation (EC) 44/2001 and Internet Consumer Contracts: Some Thoughts on Article 156 and the Futility of Applying 'In the Box; Conflict of Law Rules to the "Out of the Box" Borderless World' (2005) 19:1 *International Review of Law, Computers and Technology* 13 at p.17.

of Destination' (i.e. the law of the consumer's habitual residence) will be re-ignited by certain lobbyists with the conversion of the Rome Convention to a Regulation. Whilst electronic commerce activity is not restricted to situations where both parties are domiciled in a Member State, any concerns over the application of the law of the 'Country of Destination' in the draft Article 6 will not outweigh the juridical, and by implication substantive, protection to be given to the consumer and the difficulty and expense in applying more than one law to the consumer contract (*dépeçage*). Even though the consumer currently has the protection of the mandatory rules of his habitual residence, as Riefa explains,[74] he is unlikely to know the juridical and practical effect of (*inter alia*) the contractual choice of law(s). Given the dematerialised nature of electronic commerce and in the event of a dispute with a foreign seller, the consumer should be able to rely on all of the (substantive consumer protection) laws of his habitual residence. Contrary to explanations offered by both Riefa and Tellini,[75] the mandatory rules of the consumer's habitual residence operate *whether a choice of law has been specified in the contract or not*. When the parties have not made a choice, Article 4 is then used to determine the applicable law. Article 5 therefore requires businesses that contract with consumers in foreign jurisdictions to anticipate which aspects of the consumers' laws are (*internationally applicable*) mandatory rules.

As North and Fawcett explain, there are numerous connecting factors which may be used to determine what law governs a contract. The place where the parties are domiciled and the place where the contract is to be performed are two important connecting factors. These connecting factors are particularly relevant when the parties to a consumer contract are domiciled in different jurisdictions and have even greater significance when parties in different jurisdictions contract with each other by electronic means. Electronic commerce is a means of instantaneous communication that has rendered (traditional) connecting factors such as the location of the parties and the place where their commercial activities takes place more difficult to determine.[76] Consumers can contract with sellers who are resident in another EU Member State or a third (i.e. a non Member) state. Consequently, as Stone confirms, it has become increasingly important to ensure that a harmonised approach is taken when determining the jurisdiction of a consumer contract.[77] It is appropriate and necessary that the location of the parties and the place where

74 Riefa, ibid, at p.60.

75 Riefa, ibid and D.E. Tellini, 'Applicable Law and Electronic Consumer Contracts: A European Perspective' (2005) 16:1 *International Company and Commercial Law Review* 1, at p.7.

76 L.E. Gillies, 'An Analysis of Jurisdiction Rules for Electronic Consumer Contracts: United Kingdom, United States and Global Perspectives,' PhD Thesis, University of Strathclyde, 2005, 42.

77 P. Stone, 'The Treatment of Electronic Contracts and Torts in Private International Law under European Community Regulation' (2002) 11:2 *Information and Communications Technology Law* 121, 122; Gillies, ibid.

commercial activities take place are still used as connecting factors to determine the jurisdiction and choice of law of electronic consumer contracts for two reasons. First, given the 'dematerialised'[78] nature of electronic commerce, it remains necessary to connect the parties or their commercial activities to a particular jurisdiction. As regards rules governing jurisdiction, Article 15 of the Brussels 1 Regulation provides that the consumer can sue the professional seller in his own jurisdiction provided the foreign seller directed its (commercial) activities towards the consumer's domicile. Second, once such a connection has been established, 'the state can assert jurisdiction over a dispute and … apply its own laws.'[79]

The business will normally impose a choice of law clause in its online click-wrap agreement. Despite a choice of law clause in such agreements, businesses contracting online must still anticipate which consumers they *intend* to contract with. It is submitted that determining the consumer protection laws that will apply to the electronic consumer contract will *not* be difficult if the business is deemed to have *intentionally (i.e. positively) targeted* its online activities towards consumers in specific jurisdictions. To take this requirement to its logical conclusion, if a business has gone to the expense of identifying target markets or jurisdictions, assessed the operation and effect of substantive consumer protection laws applicable in those jurisdictions, advertised to and contracted with consumers resident in those jurisdictions, the business will not be disadvantaged if its contract is governed according to the law of the consumer's habitual residence[80] instead of (conceivably) *both* the contractual choice of law *and* the mandatory rules of the consumer's habitual residence. Indeed, support for this view is to be found in the Explanatory Memorandum of the initial draft Rome 1 Regulation where the Commission said

> (I)t also seems fair in economic terms: a consumer will make cross-border purchases only occasionally whereas most traders operating across borders will be able to spread the cost of learning about one or more legal systems over a large range of transactions. Finally, in practice this solution does not substantially modify the situation of the professional […] under the Convention, the mandatory provisions are already those of the country of the consumer's habitual residence.[81]

78 Fentiman, 'English Private International Law at the End of the 20th Century: Progress or Regress?' and Rothchild, 'Protecting the Digital Consumer: The Limits of Cyberspace Utopianism.'

79 Gillies, 'A Review of the New Jurisdiction Rules for Electronic Consumer Contracts within the European Union,' 47 referring to B.B. Sookman, 'Electronic Commerce, Internet and the Law – A Survey of the Legal Issues' (1999) *Computer and Telecommunications Law Review* 52, 54.

80 *cf* Riefa, 'Article 5 of the Rome Convention on the Law Applicable to Contractual Obligations 1980 and Consumer E-contracts: The Need for Reform,' at p.70.

81 Draft Rome 1 Regulation, Explanatory Memorandum. Brackets added.

However, there are two main difficulties with the current application of Article 5(2) of the Rome Convention. First, the mandatory rules of the consumer's habitual residence in Article 5(2) of the Rome Convention will only operate if the consumer has taken all the steps necessary to conclude the contract in his own jurisdiction. Second, the consumer must have previously received a specific invitation or advertising from the supplier. It is submitted that, given the dematerialised nature of an electronic consumer contract, both of these requirements will be difficult to establish especially when the business is located in another jurisdiction from the consumer. Consequently, as will now be considered, there are difficulties with the second condition proposed in Article 6 of the Rome 1 Regulation that the seller 'directed its activities' to consumers in foreign jurisdictions.

The Connecting Factor for Electronic Consumer Contracts in the Draft Rome 1 Regulation from 'Specific Invitation or Advertising' to 'Intentional Targeting'

The initial draft and subsequent amended draft Rome 1 Regulation[82] states, *inter alia*, that

> Article 6 – Consumer Contracts
>
> 1. Consumer contracts within the meaning and in the conditions provided for by paragraph 2 shall be governed by the law of the Member State in which the consumer has his habitual residence.
>
> 2. Paragraph 1 shall apply to contracts concluded by a natural person, the consumer, who has his habitual residence in a Member State for the purpose which can be regarded as being outside his trade or profession with another person, the professional, acting in the exercise of his trade or profession.

In order to rely upon Article 6 of the draft Rome 1 Regulation as a basis for determining the applicable law of a consumer contract, the consumer has to be a private, natural person[83] purchasing goods and services outside his or her trade or profession. Like the Brussels 1 Regulation and related Community instruments,[84] the draft Rome 1 Regulation should retain this definition of a consumer and it should *not* be extended to cover legal persons such as 'Small to Medium Sized Enterprises' (SMEs).[85] For the first time, the seller has been specifically defined in Article 6 as 'a professional, acting in the exercise of his trade or profession.' This clarifies that Article 6 will only apply to contracts between consumers and

82 *Ibid.*

83 (150/77) *Bertrand v Ott* [1978] ECR 1431.

84 See note 3.

85 Max Planck Institute, at p.41.

professional sellers and not private individuals. Whilst it is accepted that the provisions in Article 5 of the Rome Convention would only apply to certain consumer contracts,[86] it was also previously thought that the consumer provisions would not apply very often.[87] According to North

> … the conditions for the operation of the consumer protection rules in the Convention are narrowly drawn and the result is that Article 5 is likely to apply to a relatively small proportion of international contracts entered into by … consumers.[88]

However, given the increasing ways in which consumers can be targeted by foreign businesses today using technology such as web sites, an increasing proportion of consumers will expect protection from a choice of law rule as they enter into electronic contracts with businesses. Whilst Niemman's argument that the consumers' negotiating position is just as weak as if they were contracting by other means of communication is reasonable,[89] the nature of the dematerialised relationship between the consumer and the business contracting online renders this imbalance more acute. In addition to establishing the location and identity of the parties, the consumer who contracts with a business in another jurisdiction by electronic means is unlikely to have had prior dealings with the foreign business and often takes the economic risk by having to reveal – *in advance* – personal and financial information when ordering and paying for the goods or services.

The draft Rome 1 Regulation proposed by the Commission stated that the law of the consumer's habitual residence will apply

> provided that (a) the professional pursues his commercial or professional activities in the country where the consumer has his habitual residence, or (b) by any means, directs such activities to that country or to several countries including that country, and the contract falls within the scope of such activities.[90]

The two commercial situations in which the draft Article 6 would operate are either when the professional seller concludes a contract with a consumer in the same jurisdiction or has 'directed such activities to [the] Member State' in which the consumer is resident. There is no difficulty with the first option. When both

86 North, 'The E.E.C Convention on the Law Applicable to Contractual Obligations (1980): Its History and Main Features,' at p.43.

87 Morse, 'The EEC Convention on the Law Applicable to Contractual Obligations,' at p.11.

88 North, 1990 I *Hague Rec.* 13, 176. A point made by the same author previously; North, 'The E.E.C Convention on the Law Applicable to Contractual Obligations (1980): Its History and Main Features,' at pp.22–23.

89 J. Niemann, 'Webvertisements Covered by Art.5(2) Rome Convention?' (2000) 5:3 *Communications Law* 99.

90 Draft Rome 1 Regulation, Article 6(a) and (b).

parties are located in the same jurisdiction, the law of the consumer's habitual residence should apply. The key issue with the second scenario is whether the requirement for 'directing such activities' is akin to the seller having advertised or sent a specific invitation to the consumer *in his habitual residence*[91] as currently required by Article 5 of the Rome Convention.[92] The Giuliano and Lagarde Report affirmed that this provision would apply where the seller of goods or the provider of services aimed to sell those goods or services specifically towards consumers in foreign jurisdictions. The requirement for a specific invitation or advertising is particularly relevant to consumer contracts conducted by electronic commerce. Since web sites are widely accessible to consumers, the question arises whether web sites constitute a specific invitation or advertising as a means of directing such activities to consumers?[93] It is submitted that in the absence of precise[94] guidance on the meaning of 'directing such activities,' a web site constitutes neither a specific invitation nor a traditional advertisement to consumers. The Giuliano and Lagarde report commented on operation of the first condition of Article 5(2) of the Rome Convention as follows,

> (T)hus the trader must have done certain acts such as advertising in the press, or on radio or television, or in the cinema or by catalogues aimed specifically at that country, or he must have made business proposals individually through a middleman or by canvassing. If, for example a German makes a contract in response to an advertisement published by a French company in a German publication, the contract is covered by the special rule. If, on the other hand, the German replies to an advertisement in American publications, even if they are sold in Germany, the rule does not apply unless the advertisement appeared in special editions of the publication intended for European countries. In the latter case the seller will have made a special advertisement intended for the country of the purchaser.[95]

The seller must either use traditional advertising media aimed specifically at that country or send specific invitations to consumers. In both cases, the seller elects to use a specific commercial activity in order to attract sales. In comparison to traditional advertising, specific invitations are not difficult to establish if the consumer received a personal invitation from the seller. Morse has questioned whether the reference to advertising applies when the business actually '*intended*

91 R. Schu, 'The Applicable Law to Consumer Contracts Made Over the Internet: Consumer Protection Through Private International Law?' (1997) 5:2 *International Journal of Law and Information Technology* 192, 210 *et seq*.

92 O. Lando, 'Some issues relating to the law applicable to contractual obligations' (1996/97) 7 *King's College Law Journal* 55, 73.

93 C. Tillman, 'The relationship between party autonomy and the mandatory rules in the Rome Convention' (2002) (Jan) *Journal of Business Law*, 45 at p.57.

94 Draft Rome 1 Regulation, Explanatory Memorandum, *supra* n 22 at p.3.

95 Giuliano and Lagarde Report, at p.24.

to advertise?'[96] This question suggests that the business must have intended to advertise in the same way than if it sent specific invitations to consumers, i.e. were the advertisements aimed at consumers in specific countries? The first example offered by the Rapporteurs provides an affirmative answer and also reflects the commercial reality of how sellers seek to secure business in foreign jurisdictions. The second example in the quote correctly suggests that the seller should not be bound by Article 5 of the Rome Convention if the advertisement was *viewed but not actually meant for* the particular consumers in question. There must therefore be a *positive link* between the commercial activity undertaken by the seller (whether a traditional advertisement or invitation localised towards a particular jurisdiction or jurisdictions) and the subsequent contract with the foreign consumer (resident in that jurisdiction). When the business *either* sends specific information to consumers *or* authorises advertisements towards consumers in specific jurisdictions, the commercial strategy or *intention* of the seller is to seek out consumers habitually resident in those jurisdictions and Article 5(2) should apply. The commercial expectation of the seller is to obtain sales from consumers in those jurisdictions as a result of undertaking general or specific marketing activities intended for such consumers. To take this to its logical conclusion Article 5(2) of the Rome Convention, akin to the decision in *Shearson Lehman Hutton v TVB*,[97] should operate whether or not the consumer actually viewed the advertisement before contracting with the seller. However in the context of electronic commerce, consumers will probably have browsed a foreign business' web site prior to contracting with that business as the web site represents both the means of marketing to consumers in foreign jurisdictions and the *modus operandi* of the contract. Article 5 of the Rome Convention necessitates a positive act on behalf of the seller to advertise or send invitations on its goods or services to consumers. According to Blaikie,[98] the nature and extent of advertising determines whether the specific choice of law rules for consumer contracts are applied in the Rome Convention. It is relatively easy to imagine how many times consumers view advertising on a daily basis. Newspapers, television, radio and mail order are all forms of traditional (jurisdictionally confined) advertising media that encourage or entice consumers to respond to by requesting information or purchasing the goods or services concerned. Such forms of advertising media are selected in order to localise[99] the advertising within or towards a particular country or countries. Equally, there is no problem in determining that a consumer has been targeted by a specific invitation when that invitation has been addressed and sent to him or her personally.

---

96 Morse, 'The EEC Convention on the Law Applicable to Contractual Obligations,' at p.6.

97 *Shearson Lehman Hutton v TVB* C-89/91 [1993] ECR I-139.

98 Blaikie, 'Choice of Law in Consumer Contracts.'

99 Green Paper, at p.29; North and Fawcett, *Cheshire and North's Private International Law.*

However as a result of increasing technological developments, consumers can view foreign business' web sites to obtain information and offers on goods available or to enter into contracts via web sites no matter where they or the business are located. The drafting of Article 15(1)(c) of the Brussels 1 Regulation was a useful opportunity to identify the different types of web sites used by businesses to 'direct such activities' towards consumers. A web site that enables a consumer to conclude a contract by going through a series of steps or pages on that web site is an 'active' web site. Conversely where a web site is nothing more than an information source to those browsing its pages, it is deemed to be a 'passive' web site. In between this spectrum of commercial activity on web sites are 'interactive' web sites, providing information and a means of communication between the parties. Whilst interactive web sites do not enable consumers to make online purchases, they do provide an opportunity for the parties to communicate with each other which may lead to a contract.[100] In the United States, the ability to distinguish between these types of web sites has enabled the courts (to a greater or lesser degree) to determine whether a business purposefully availed itself of the jurisdiction of another state by doing business in that state.[101]

However, Geist[102] has suggested that it is no longer sufficient to consider the level of web site activity alone to determine whether a business 'directed its activities' to the jurisdiction of the consumer's domicile. As the Green Paper suggests, it will be necessary to formulate an assessment of business activities via web sites to determine if the business intentionally sought custom from consumers resident in those countries. It is submitted that the same issue that arose regarding the definition of 'directing such activities' in Article 15(1)(c) of the Brussels 1 Regulation must now be clarified in the context of a choice of law rule for electronic consumer contracts.[103] As the European Commission previously confirmed vis-à-vis Article 15 of the Brussels Regulation, '(T)he fact that a consumer simply has knowledge of a service or possibility of buying goods via a passive web site accessible in his country of domicile will not trigger the protective jurisdiction.'[104]

It will not therefore be sufficient to insert the same term 'directing such activities' into the first condition of Article 5(2)'s replacement unless specific direction or explanation (preferably in the text of the draft Rome 1 Regulation itself) is given as to what actually constitutes 'directed activity' via a web site or indeed a combination of a web site and other marketing activities. Indeed this

100 Derived from the US case *Zippo Manufacturing v Zippo Dot Com, Inc.* 952 F.Supp, 1119 (W.D. Pa. 1997).

101 *World Wide Volkswagen v Woodson*, 444 US 286, 100 S.Ct. 559 (1980).

102 M. Geist, 'Is There a There? Towards Greater Certainty for Internet Jurisdiction' (2001) 16 *Berkeley Technology Law Journal* 1345; Øren, *supra* n 42.

103 Niemann, 'Webvertisements Covered by Art.5(2) Rome Convention?' at p.100 (in particular).

104 European Commission, Justice and Home Affairs DG, 'Statement on Articles 15 and 73.'

very concern was highlighted by the Green Paper.[105] In addition to determining the appropriate level of web site activity adopted by the seller's web site, it is submitted that the new Article 6(b) (or its replacement) should stipulate that business activities were '*intentionally targeted towards consumers [in EU Member States] via traditional media or an active or interactive web site* and that a contract was concluded as a result of those activities.' Indeed, the Explanatory Memorandum in the draft Regulation specifically refers to a 'targeted activity criterion already present in Article 15 of the Brussels 1 Regulation.'[106] However, despite a contrary interpretation of Article 15(1)(c),[107] the Commission's earlier Statement on Article 15[108] of Brussels 1 does not positively confirm that targeting is *prima facie* required for Article 15(1)(c) to operate. Instead the Commission in its Statement explains that, in the absence of a contract having been concluded as a result of business activities in the consumer's jurisdiction, *targeting on its own is insufficient* to establish jurisdiction. A broad way in which a targeting approach could operate is if the consumer browses the business's web site or requests information via an email address or online form on its web site. In this way the active or interactive web site operates both as an effective communication method and a means of contracting between the seller and the consumer. There appears to be no difficulty that a business would (currently) be subject to the mandatory rules of the consumer's habitual residence being applied if the business provided information on goods or services that subsequently led to a contract between the parties. An interesting question is whether a request for information from the consumer who had previously browsed the business' passive web site would trigger the application of the consumer's law? Support for an affirmative answer to this question can be found in the Giuliano and Lagarde Report, which suggests that the consumer's conduct would require to be demonstrated *prior* to the contract between the parties. Rather than, in the present author's opinion, automatically applying the 'criteria'[109] of Article 15(1)(c) of the Brussels 1 Regulation, Article 6 should be adapted to apply when the business *intended to target* the consumer via an active or interactive web site, and the consumer responded by requesting information and subsequently ordered goods or services from the business. Alternatively, a narrower way in which the current Article 5(2) might operate is if the business' web site specified which countries they would accept orders from consumers via a drop-down list. Indeed, businesses may (and often do) 'select' their target market in advance by restricting (or ring-fencing) the countries from where they are prepared to receive orders via their web sites. However despite the apparent merits of a 'ring-fencing' approach,[110] the

105 Green Paper, at p.31, point vi.

106 Draft Rome 1 Regulation, Explanatory Memorandum, at p.6.

107 Editorial, 'On the Way to a Rome 1 Regulation,' at p.918.

108 EU Commission, 'Statement on Articles 15 and 73,' at p.6.

109 Tellini, 'Applicable Law and Electronic Consumer Contracts: A European Perspective,' at p.7.

110 Øren, 'International Jurisdiction Over Consumer Contracts in e-Europe.'

European Commission previously denounced 'ring-fencing' as being counter to the Community's approach to jurisdiction rules. Accordingly, Article 6 of the draft Rome 1 Regulation ought to be amended further to reflect the increased ability of sellers to target consumers, particularly as the consumer can receive a personal, automated response to information from a seller's web site, often instantaneously. If the draft Article 6 is not amended further, it will become increasingly difficult to establish the 'directing such activities' condition without further clarification. If the draft Article 6 cannot be established, the applicable law will be determined in accordance with the draft Article 4, namely the law of the characteristic performer of the contract. Such an approach is counter to the EU's desire to provide increased juridical protection for consumers.

All of this presupposes that the remainder of the first condition in Article 5(2) of the Rome Convention can also be satisfied, i.e. the business has advertised or sent an invitation to the consumer *and that the consumer has taken the steps to conclude the contract in his habitual residence*. Stone regards such a consumer as one who is 'static'.[111] With regard to electronic consumer contracts, the reality is that consumers can view web sites whether or not they are physically present in their habitual residence at the time.[112] The replacement of Article 5(2) will have to consider the extent to which it is necessary for the consumer to be specifically targeted by the seller whilst the consumer is in his habitual residence and whether analogous provisions in the Brussels 1 Regulation are preferable[113] in order to avoid, as Schu explains, 'fortuitous locations of connecting factors.'[114] The next part of the Giuliano and Lagarde Report is particularly interesting when considered from the perspective of electronic consumer contracts. The Report explains,

> (T)he Group expressly adopted the words 'steps necessary on his part' in order to avoid the classic problem of determining the place where the contract was concluded. This is a particularly delicate matter in the situations referred to, because it involves international contracts normally concluded by correspondence. The words 'steps' includes inter alia writing or any action taken in consequence of an offer or advertisement.[115]

111 Response by Professor Peter Stone, Department of Law, University of Essex, to the Green Paper COM(2002) 654 final of 14 January 2003 available at <http://europa.eu.int/comm/justice_home/news/consulting_public/rome_i/doc/university_essex_en.pdf>.

112 Schu, 'The Applicable Law to Consumer Contracts Made Over the Internet: Consumer Protection Through Private International Law?' at p.211 *et seq*.

113 As party expectations are and should be no different when a consumer contract is conducted online or offline; *cf* Schu, 'The Applicable Law to Consumer Contracts Made Over the Internet: Consumer Protection Through Private International Law?' at p.225 *et seq*.

114 Schu, ibid.

115 Ibid.

It is not clear to what extent the consumer in an electronic consumer contract would have to firstly take '*all*' the necessary steps to conclude the contract and secondly how the consumer could demonstrate that those steps had actually been taken in his habitual residence. In the context of electronic consumer contracts, the suggestion by Van Der Hof that this requirement of Article 5(2) should simply be deleted is preferred.[116] Since this requirement has been deleted, there is therefore no need to consider the current distinction between the 'static' (or passive) and 'mobile' (or active) consumer. Indeed, the Green Paper suggested that the distinction between the 'mobile' and 'static' consumer should be removed. There is no reason to justify the non-application of the laws of the consumer's habitual residence if a consumer happens to browse and place an order for books via a web site whilst present in another jurisdiction when he could do so in his own jurisdiction or when travelling between jurisdictions. In the context of electronic commerce, and Article 11(1) of the Electronic Commerce Directive,[117] such a limitation is now superfluous and may operate as a disincentive to consumers and businesses contracting via web sites.

However, the draft Rome 1 Regulation does not alter the first condition of Article 5(2) of the Rome Convention. The consumer will therefore have to complete the electronic contract by means of a secure server or exchange of emails in his own jurisdiction and be able to prove this in the event of a dispute. Businesses are not likely to favour such a means of contracting with consumers as it may also be difficult for them to ascertain with certainty that the consumer concluded the contract in his own jurisdiction. Therefore a requirement for the business to demonstrate that it intentionally targeted consumers in particular jurisdictions via an active or interactive web site should replace the current Article 5(2) effectively for the benefit of both parties, without the need for the condition that the consumer entered into a contract whilst present in his own jurisdiction. It should be sufficient that the consumer can establish that he is habitually resident in the Member State targeted by the business.

Are the Alternative Connecting Factors in Article 5(2) of the Rome Convention Still Necessary?

(i) Contracts Between the Consumer and the Seller's Agent

The alternative condition to a specific invitation or advertising in Article 5(2) of the Rome Convention states ' … if the other party or his agent received the consumer's order in that country.' Again, this condition requires the consumer to send his or her order to the business from the consumer's jurisdiction. According to

116 S. Van Der Hof, 'European Conflict Rules Concerning International Online Consumer Contracts' (2003) 12:2 *Information and Communications Technology Law* 165 at p.172.

117 'Directive 2000/31/EC on certain legal aspects of information society services, in particular electronic commerce, in the Internal Market.'

the Giuliano and Lagarde Report, the agent in Article 5(2) is someone who simply represents the seller.[118] The Giuliano and Lagarde Report asserts two points; the seller must either 'visit' the consumer's jurisdiction or have a 'permanent branch or agency' there. If a branch or agent used an active or interactive web site to communicate with consumers then this would satisfy Article 5(2). However it is unlikely that a web site *per se* would satisfy Article 5(2). The point was affirmed in the Electronic Commerce Directive which states, *inter alia*, that ' … the place of establishment of a company providing services via an Internet website is not the place at which the technology supporting its website is located.'[119] Furthermore, the European Commission's Statement on Article 15 of the Brussels 1 Regulation confirms that a web site does not constitute a branch, agency or other establishment for the purposes of asserting the jurisdiction of the consumer's domicile.[120] It is submitted that the status of a web site or web server ought to be regarded in the same way for consumer choice of law rules. A web site does not have the sufficient degree of 'permanency' that is required to demonstrate that a branch or agency has been established in the jurisdiction. Furthermore, the concern over the location of mail servers[121] is, with respect, not therefore as such as significant an issue in determining the applicable law of an electronic consumer contract as it might have first appeared. For these reasons, it is appropriate that the Commission deleted the reference to contracts between consumers and agents as an alternative condition in the draft Article 5.

(ii) 'The Mobile Consumer'

Article 5 of the Rome Convention currently applies to contracts with mobile consumers 'if the contract is for the sale of goods and the consumer travelled from that country to another country and there gave his order, provided that the consumer's journey was arranged by the seller for the purpose of inducing the consumer to buy.'

This condition can therefore only be satisfied if the (mobile) consumer travelled to another country, at the seller's arrangement, for the purposes of placing an order for goods and services there. It is submitted that with the onset of electronic commerce, this alternative condition is also now superfluous[122] as electronic commerce enables contracts to be entered into without the parties requiring

118 Giuliano and Lagarde Report, at p.24 and affirmed by Morse, 'The EEC Convention on the Law Applicable to Contractual Obligations,' at p.7.

119 2000 OJ L178.

120 Statement on Articles 15 and 73.

121 Riefa, 'Article 5 of the Rome Convention on the Law Applicable to Contractual Obligations 1980 and Consumer E-contracts: The Need for Reform,' at p.67.

122 Niemann, 'Webvertisements Covered by Art.5(2) Rome Convention?' at p.100; Riefa, ibid at p.65.

face-to-face contact with each other.[123] Rather than *extending* the application of Article 5 to mobile consumers,[124] if the connecting factor in Article 5 is clearly defined, the distinction between a mobile and a static consumer is not necessary. In the context of electronic commerce, it should not matter (and may indeed prove problematic to prove) the location where the consumer entered into the contract. The business may be able to anticipate where the consumer placed his order by requiring the consumer to provide details of his residence as a condition of the contract, such as for the purpose of delivering goods to the consumer. Alternatively, the provision could be retained to enable the consumer to continue travelling to another jurisdiction with the assurance that if they contracted online the law of his habitual residence would still apply.[125] This certainly appears to be proposed in the draft Regulation vis-à-vis timeshare contracts. Finally, since the Distance Selling Directive specifically excludes contracts for travel and food entered into online from its scope, there is in fact neither ambiguity nor concern[126] in excluding contracts of carriage from the scope of Article 6. This has subsequently been reflected in the inclusion of a separate Article 5 of the amended draft Rome 1 Regulation for contracts of carriage. Whilst this may be unfair to those of us who purchase low-cost flights online on a regular basis, the European Court of Justice recently confirmed[127] that the effect of cancellation rights under the Directive were of greater detriment to suppliers than consumers.

Summary

As the previous section sought to demonstrate, the application of connecting factors in Article 5 of the Rome Convention to electronic consumer contracts remains contentious. The conditions upon which the choice of law rule in the Rome Convention for consumer contracts operates are no longer sufficient to apply to those consumer contracts conducted by means of electronic commerce. Furthermore, the conditions upon which Article 6 of the draft Rome 1 Regulation will operate are not as precise as they ought to be. Choice of law rules need to be adapted to be capable of consistent and effective application to such consumer

123 Debussere, 'International Jurisdiction over E-Consumer Contracts in the European Union: Quid Novi Sub Sole?'

124 Riefa, 'Article 5 of the Rome Convention on the Law Applicable to Contractual Obligations 1980 and Consumer E-contracts: The Need for Reform,' at p.64.

125 A.E. Jaffey, 'The Foundations of Rules for the Choice of Law' (1982) 2 *Oxford Journal of Legal Studies* 368, N. Reich, 'Germany: Time Sharing Contract Consumer Protection and the Rome Convention' (1997) 5 *Consumer Law Journal* 6 at p.40.

126 Riefa, 'Article 5 of the Rome Convention on the Law Applicable to Contractual Obligations 1980 and Consumer E-contracts: The Need for Reform,' at p.64.

127 *Easycar (UK) Ltd v Office of Fair Trading* (C336/03) [2005] All E.R. (EC) 834, [2005] ECR I-1947 [2005] 2 CMLR 2.

contracts to ensure that the law of the consumer's habitual residence[128] applies to online as well as offline contracts.

The current choice of law rules for consumer contracts must be adapted to provide efficient juridical protection for consumers who contract with businesses electronically. A significant step has been taken to address this by proposing that the law of the consumer's habitual residence applies to all consumer contracts. Nevertheless, further consideration must be given to the fact that web site activity is neither analogous to advertising nor a specific invitation to a consumer. As Article 15(1)(c) of the Brussels 1 Regulation has demonstrated, the term 'directing such activities' is of little use as a connecting factor in an electronic consumer contract unless it is clearly defined. The term 'directing such activities' in the draft Rome 1 Regulation should be replaced with a more precise criteria that 'businesses must have "intentionally targeted", via an active or interactive web site, consumers habitually resident in a Member State at the time the contract was entered into between the parties.'

128 Regarded by Tillman as the law in 'which the weaker party normally has confidence. This appears to be the law of his or her environment,'; 'The relationship between party autonomy and the mandatory rules in the Rome Convention,' at p.53.

Chapter 8

Rules of Personal Jurisdiction for Electronic Consumer Contracts in the United States

Introduction[1]

For over a decade the courts in the United States have had to tackle the 'fundamental'[2] issue of Internet jurisdiction premised on traditional principles of personal[3] jurisdiction. At the same time, the amount of electronic commerce activity in the United States has continued to increase.[4] The emergence of rules of jurisdiction for contracts conducted online in the United States demonstrate the way in which traditional (internal) state jurisdiction rules have been singularly adapted by the courts to include commercial activity being conducted over the WWW across state and national borders in accordance with the US Constitution.[5] The modification of existing jurisdiction rules to encompass commercial activity directed via web sites to a party (such as a consumer) domiciled in another state have been crucial in determining whether businesses intended to pursue commercial activities there. As the present author has recently remarked, compared to the approach of the United Kingdom courts where there has been very little case law on electronic commerce disputes (including those involving consumers),[6] it has

1 Sections of this chapter were recently published in L.E. Gillies, 'Addressing the "Cyberspace Fallacy": Targeting the Jurisdiction of an Electronic Consumer Contract' (2008) 2 *Int Journal Law and Inf Tech* 1.

2 R. Yagura, 'Does Cyberspace Expand the Boundaries of Personal Jurisdiction?' (1998) 38 *IDEA* 301, at p.301. D.T. Rice, 'A Cyberspace Odyssey Through US and EU Internet Jurisdiction,' Practising Law Institute, Patents, Trademarks and Literary Property Course Handbook Series, Fifth Annual Internet Law Institute, New York 9–10 July 2001, San Francisco, 23–24 July 2001: 421 at p.429.

3 Rules of jurisdiction for tortious disputes are outside the scope of this book.

4 OECD, 'Measuring the Information Economy' report, Chapter 1. A. Siddiqi, 'Welcome to the City of Bytes? An Assessment of the Traditional Methods Employed in the International Application of Jurisdiction Over Internet Activities – Including A Critique of Suggested Approaches' (2001) 14 *N.Y. Int'l L. Rev.* 43 at p.64.

5 J.T. Westermeier, 'Personal jurisdiction: Today's Hot Issue in E-Commerce,' JILT, <http://www2.warwick.ac.uk/fac/soc/law/elj/jilt/1998_3/westermeier>.

6 Yagura, 'Does Cyberspace Expand the Boundaries of Personal Jurisdiction?' at p.309.

been the courts in the United States[7] that have had to consider the application and 'adaptation'[8] of existing principles of jurisdiction in the context of electronic commerce. In comparison to case law under the Brussels Convention, the US cases concerned with jurisdiction issues on the Internet have covered a far wider subject area than consumer protection, with the majority of disputes seeking determination of specific jurisdiction on intellectual property rights, particularly trademark infringements[9] and domain name disputes[10] through to claims in tort for defamation[11] and personal injury.[12] Such cases highlight the lower court's application and modification of existing jurisdiction rules to disputes concerning electronic consumer contracts. The common focus of these cases is that they seek to establish personal jurisdiction where the plaintiff is situated, thereby of benefit to the majority of consumers who would want to raise proceedings in their own jurisdiction. In particular, the cases demonstrate the courts' tendency to focus on whether constitutional 'Due Process' is satisfied when the dispute involves, *inter alia*, the defendant's online commercial activities. The cases illustrate that the courts have assessed whether the two main requirements of specific personal jurisdiction, namely purposeful availment and 'fair play and substantial justice' in accordance with constitutional 'Due Process,' have been satisfied.[13] In order to ensure that consumers and businesses are provided with a certain and predictable jurisdiction rule for consumer contracts, the following question posed by Lockerby (and repeated by Rochlin)[14] needs to be addressed: ' … just how much of a nexus is required between the electronic transaction and the forum seeking to exercise jurisdiction?'[15] Lockerby reinforces the importance of a choice of forum clause to associate the parties' online activities with a particular location. However, the US

7 S. Wilske and T. Schiller, 'International Jurisdiction in Cyberspace: Which States May Regulate the Internet?' (1997) 50 *Fed Comm LJ* 117.

8 R. Rochlin, 'Cyberspace, International Shoe and the Changing Context for Personal Jurisdiction' (2000) 32 *Conn LR* 653 at p.654.

9 For example, *Maritz v Cybergold*, 947 F. Supp.1328 (E.D.Mo.1996).

10 For example, *No Mayo-San Francisco v Memminger*, 1998 U.S. Dist. LEXIS 13154 (N.D. Cal. 1998) where the US District Court for the Northern District of California held that there was no jurisdiction in Hawaii over a registered trademark and domain name dispute.

11 For example, *Heroes Inc. v Instruction Set*, 958 F. Supp.1 (D.D.C. 1996) and *Revell v Lidov* 317 F.3d 467 C.A.5 (Tex.), 2002 Dec 31, 2002, a Fifth Circuit defamation case.

12 For example *In re Ski Train Fire in Kaprun Austria* on 11 November 2000, 2003 WL 22909153 S.D.N.Y 09/12/03.

13 Perry *et al*, 'Personal Jurisdiction in Cyberspace Where Can you be Sued, And Whose Laws Apply?' New York Law School Communications Media Centre, Volume VII, No.1, Fall 1998.

14 Rochlin, 'Cyberspace, International Shoe and the Changing Context for Personal Jurisdiction,' at pp.665–667.

15 M.J. Lockerby, 'Non-Contractual Legal Problems' (1999) IBL 244; Gillies, 'Addressing the "Cyberspace Fallacy",' at pp.16–17.

courts will only uphold a choice of forum clause as reasonable if there is a sufficient *link* between the forum selected and the parties' dispute. Determining the extent of activities directed to individuals in a particular state via web sites requires a coordinated and harmonised approach[16] to ensure consistency[17] in asserting jurisdiction and maintaining consumer confidence and business investment in electronic commerce. A coordinated, consistent and predictable approach is required regardless of whether the defendant business is situated in another US state or outside the US. As Fitzmaurice and Mody explain, to date, the Supreme Court has 'disallowed clear cut rules' of personal jurisdiction.[18] A consistent and predictable approach can be achieved in two ways. Firstly, the Supreme Court must endorse the 'Sliding Scale' test as amended by the Fourth Circuit Court of Appeal in the *ALS Scan v Digital Service Consultants Inc.*[19] This amendment would incorporate the specific requirement from *ALS Scan* that a business who uses a web site with the manifest intent of pursuing commercial activity in the forum should be subject to the jurisdiction of that forum. Secondly, if the rules of jurisdiction for electronic consumer contracts are to provide legal certainty and predictability, such rules must apply to businesses not situated in a US state. As Silberman and Lowenfeld confirm ' ... principles of conflicts do not operate only within the boundaries of the United States [...] private international law has a role to play in thinking about choice of law, jurisdiction and the enforcement of judgments.'[20]

Effective Specific Personal Jurisdiction

Over the years, a number of factors have impinged upon the quest for cohesive specific personal jurisdiction rules for electronic commerce contracts in the United States. One factor is the different emphasis attributed to intra-state disputes[21] in comparison to disputes between parties domiciled in different countries, essentially

16 J.R. Aguilar, 'Over the Rainbow. European and American Consumer Protection Policy and Remedy Conflicts on the Internet and a Possible Solution' (1999/2000) (Winter) *International Journal of Communications Law and Policy*.

17 J.S. Millstein, J.D. Nueburger and J.P. Weingart, *Doing Business on the Internet Forms and Analysis* (New York, 1997) at p.11–1.

18 K.M. Fitzmaurice and R.M. Mody, 'International Shoe Meets the World Wide Web. Whither Personal Jurisdiction in Florida in the Age of the Internet?' (1997) 71 Fla BJ 22.

19 *ALS Scan v Digital Service Consultants Inc.*, 293 F.3d 707 (4th Circuit 2002).

20 L.J. Silberman and A.F. Lowenfeld, 'A Different Challenge for the ALI: Herein of Foreign Country Judgments, an International Treaty, and on American Statute' (1998) 74:1 *Indiana LJ* 635 at p.647. Word in brackets modified.

21 E.F. Scoles and P. Hay, *Conflict of Laws*, 2nd ed (St Pauls, Minnesota, 1992); Gillies, ibid at p.17.

'true conflicts.'[22] In the former case, Cavers describes the situation where the judge is 'confronted by the laws of two states.'[23] However as Anton explains, 'true conflicts' arise when the parties to a cross-border dispute are situated in different countries.[24] As stated earlier, the parties who contract by electronic means may be domiciled in different parts of the same country, for example the United Kingdom or the United States, or in completely different countries. Another explanation is that both the tests and decisions in these cases predominantly turn on their facts and are (arguably) 'lacking in predictability and precision.'[25] Despite the fact-based nature of the specific personal jurisdiction tests, Abramson believes that the tests provide flexibility which is advantageous as electronic commerce continues to develop.[26] Another factor is that these rules, like the Brussels Convention 1968, pre-dated the Internet and WWW. Furthermore, a justifiable criticism of the courts in the early years of applying rules of personal jurisdiction to cases involving web sites was that decisions such as *Inset System, Inc. v Instruction Set*[27] demonstrated 'inconsisten[cy]'[28] and a lack of understanding regarding the effect and accessibility of a web site.[29]

In response, states have either upheld or refused jurisdiction based (albeit not entirely) on the level, extent and purpose of web site accessibility and activity directed to persons in those states in accordance with existing specific personal jurisdiction tests, partly derived from the US Constitution. The 'active – passive' web site distinction, more commonly referred to as the 'Sliding Scale,' used to differentiate web site activities whilst useful, is now not the only factor used to establish jurisdiction over a business situated in another state or outside the United States. Furthermore, despite the increasing number of cases premised on web site activities in the forum at both Federal and Circuit Court level, both the 'Sliding

22 A.E. Anton, *Private International Law*, 2nd ed (Edinburgh, 1990) at pp.3–4; R.J. Weintraub, *Commentary on the Conflict of Laws*, 4th ed (New York, 2001) at p.1 (where he refers to the Restatement (Second) Conflict of Laws §2 (1971)); Silberman and Lowenfeld, 'A Different Challenge for the ALI,' at p.647; Gillies, ibid.

23 D.F. Cavers, *The Choice of Law Process* (Michigan, 1965) at p.9; Gillies, ibid.

24 Anton, *Private International Law*; Gillies, ibid.

25 L. Abramson, 'Clarifying 'Fair Play and Substantial Justice: How the Courts Apply the Supreme Court Standard for Personal Jurisdiction' (1991) 18 *Hastings Const LQ* 441 at p.446.

26 Abramson, ibid; Gillies, ibid at p.18.

27 *Inset System, Inc. v Instruction Set* 937 F.Supp.161 164 (D.Conn. 1996); Gillies, ibid.

28 J.S. Burns and R.A. Bales, 'Personal Jurisdiction and the Web' (2001) 53 *Me. L. Rev.* 29 at pp.30–31 and p.46. Word modified for syntax. C.E. Mayewski, 'The Presence of a Web Site as a Constitutionally Permissible Basis for Personal Jurisdiction' (1997) 73:1 *Indiana LJ* 297 and A. Mitrani, 'Regulating E-commerce, E-contracts and the controversy of Multiple Jurisdiction' (2001) 7:2 *Int TLR* 50 at p.59; Gillies, ibid.

29 Rice, 'A Cyberspace Odyssey Through US and EU Internet Jurisdiction,' at p.429; Gillies, ibid.

Scale' (as modified) and the 'effects' tests have yet to be affirmed by the US Supreme Court as suitable tests for determining the constitutionally significant[30] matter of jurisdiction over electronic commerce disputes. As Rochlin confirms, another reason for the 'difficult and arbitrary nature'[31] of the 'Sliding Scale' test is because the Supreme Court has 'not yet had occasion to shape the contours of jurisdictional analysis for cyber-claimants, most if not all of these issues are being decided at the district court level with very little guidance.'[32]

Rather than looking to the Supreme Court for endorsement of the 'Sliding Scale' test or 'new or applicable precedent,'[33] Rochlin argues that an 'earnings analysis' test should determine whether a separate 'cyber-court' has jurisdiction. With respect, an analysis of business earnings would be a subjective method of establishing whether the business purposefully availed itself by doing business in the jurisdiction. There must be a clear and predictable jurisdiction rule for electronic consumer contracts regardless of the value of the transaction concerned. Businesses could use Rochlin's 'earnings analysis' test to forum shop and avoid jurisdictions with the lowest business earnings threshold. Green also criticises the 'Sliding Scale' test as 'insufficient' and advocates a 'real space' argument based on targeting. Whilst evidence of the business' intention to target consumers is desirable, Green's criticism is premised on the existence[34] of interactive web sites. However, such a criticism does not appreciate the express reference to interactive web sites in the 'Sliding Scale' test and the fact that many web sites are 'interactive' in nature. The lack of endorsement by the highest courts in the United States is also Geist's key criticism of the 'Sliding Scale' test.[35] Geist argues that the question the courts should pose is whether a business intended to target its web site towards a particular jurisdiction by applying a three-stage test.[36] Since *Zippo*, numerous cases in the United States have examined whether the content and activities of a web site are sufficient to establish jurisdiction in the forum where web site activity has occurred.[37] By analogy, there are important implications for the consumer. If

30 R.A. Brand, 'Due Process, Jurisdiction and a Hague Judgments Convention' (1999) 60 *U Pitt LR* 661; Gillies, ibid.

31 Rochlin, 'Cyberspace, International Shoe and the Changing Context for Personal Jurisdiction,' at p.665.

32 Rochlin, ibid at p.654; Gillies, ibid.

33 Rochlin, ibid at p.654.

34 J. Green, 'Is Zippo's Sliding Scale a Slippery Slope of Uncertainty? A Case For Abolishing Web Site Interactivity As A Conclusive Factor in Assessing Minimum Contacts in Cyberspace' (2001) 34 *J Marshall L Rev* 1051, at p.1075.

35 M. Geist, 'Is There a There? Towards Greater Certainty for Internet Jurisdiction' (2001) 16 *Berkeley Tech Law Journal* 1345.

36 Geist, ibid at p.1363.

37 Referred to as the 'highway approach' by Burns and Bales, 'Personal Jurisdiction and the Web,' at p.32; L.E. Gillies, 'Adapting International Private Law Rules for Electronic Consumer Contracts,' in C.E.F. Rickett, and T.G.W. Telfer (eds), *International Perspectives on Consumers' Access to Justice* (Cambridge, 2003) at p.374.

the business intentionally targets its activities at the consumer's jurisdiction via a web site, the consumer should be provided with juridical protection.[38] The present author has previously remarked that '(E)stablishing jurisdiction at the consumer's domicile would clearly be advantageous to the consumer, given that they are more likely to know the rules and procedures of their own jurisdiction or at least can identify them more quickly than if the jurisdiction was elsewhere, such as where the business is located.'[39] The present author has also previously argued that 'most consumers will be unable to fund the cost of pursuing a case either in another US state or country.'[40] Whilst an approach that includes intentional targeting is now required, the modified 'Sliding Scale' test provided by the Fourth Circuit in *ALS Scan v Digital Service Consultants Inc.*[41] is preferred to Geist's three stage targeting test. If a business intended to target consumers in particular jurisdictions via an active or interactive web site and the communication between the parties leads to a contract, a consumer must be able to sue the business in his own jurisdiction.

Despite the extent to which the 'Sliding Scale' test in *Zippo Manufacturing v Zippo Dot Com*[42] has been used to determine the level of web site activity in a particular case, its continued application has been recently reassessed in *ALS Scan v Inc.*[43] At the same time, the lower courts have also endorsed the 'effects'[44] test as a basis of personal jurisdiction predominantly for tort disputes. The most important responses by the US Supreme Court were in *Young v New Haven Advocate*[45] and *Healthgrades.com v Northwest Healthcare Alliance.*[46] In *Young*, the Supreme Court refused to consider the Fourth Circuit's earlier decision in *ALS Scan Inc*[47] as to whether the *Zippo* 'Sliding Scale' of Internet jurisdiction breached constitutional 'Due Process.' Despite this, the *ALS Scan* decision has been subsequently acknowledged by several other Circuit Court of Appeals. In *Healthgrades*, the Supreme Court refused to review the Ninth Circuit Court of Appeal's decision to permit the Washington District Court to assert jurisdiction using the 'effects test.'[48] Rice has remarked that whilst the 'effects' test has been equated to 'targeting' activities towards a jurisdiction, he regards the two as different. Aciman and Vo-Verde also agree that the tests are different and suggest that targeting requires

38 Gillies, ibid at p.377.

39 Gillies, ibid.

40 Gillies, ibid. Chapter One above.

41 *ALS Scan Inc.*

42 *Zippo Manufacturing v Zippo Dot Com, Inc.* 952 F.Supp, 1119; Gillies, ibid at p.19.

43 *ALS Scan Inc*; Gillies, ibid at p.20.

44 Rice, 'A Cyberspace Odyssey Through US and EU Internet Jurisdiction,' at p.437 and 517 *et seq*; Gillies, ibid.

45 *Young v New Haven Advocate* US No 02-1394; Gillies, ibid.

46 *Healthgrades.com v Northwest Healthcare Alliance* US 02–1250.

47 *ALS Scan Inc.*

48 *Northwest Healthcare Alliance v Healthgrades.com* 2002 WL 31246123 (9th Circuit Washington); see 'post *Zippo*' discussion later; Gillies, ibid.

'specifically reach(ing) persons in a forum,'[49] for example via a web site. By comparison, the 'effects' test did not traditionally, until *Blumenthal v Drudge*, refer to technology[50] but was focussed on whether the effects of the parties conduct could be felt in the forum. However, the emergence of a requirement to directly target activities at a particular state in *Graduate Management Admission Council v Raju*[51] demonstrates how the 'effects' test and the modified 'Sliding Scale' test (as adapted by *ALS Scan*) both seek to satisfy the same end. In any event, there have been two tests[52] – the 'Sliding Scale' and 'effects' tests – which the courts have used to satisfy 'Due Process' and thereby determine jurisdiction over an electronic commerce dispute.

For these reasons, harmonisation of jurisdiction rules for electronic consumer contracts must be achieved by retaining the 'Sliding Scale' test and incorporating a 'directly targeting activities' test. Such a test would be satisfied when a business intended to contract with foreign consumers via an active or interactive web site accessible in the consumers' jurisdiction. Jurisdiction ought to be established when the parties or their activities are 'intuitively'[53] connected to a particular jurisdiction. Alternatively if such an option is neither politically[54] nor legally endorsed, the test of personal jurisdiction for electronic consumer contracts must be sufficiently consistent across the spectrum of web site activity[55] that is neither circumvented by a lack of guidance from the Supreme Court[56] nor the level of activity required

---

49 Aciman and D. Vo-Verde, 'Refining The Zippo Test: New Trends on Personal Jurisdiction for Internet Activities' (2002) 19 *Computer and Internet Law* 19.

50 *Blumenthal v Drudge* 992 F. Supp.44 (D.D.C. 1998). Aciman and D. Vo-Verde, ibid *et seq*. The extent to which this difference remains will be considered in the discussion of decisions post-*Zippo* later in this chapter.

51 *Graduate Management Admission Council v Raju*, E.D.Va No.02-581-A 23 January 2003.

52 M. C. Dearing, 'Personal Jurisdiction and the Internet: Can the Traditional Principles and Landmark Cases Guide the Legal System into the 21st Century?' (1999) 4:4 *J Tech L & Pol'y.*

53 Green, 'Is Zippo's Sliding Scale a Slippery Slope of Uncertainty?' at p.1055.

54 Aguilar, 'Over the Rainbow,' who points out the US government's preference for self-regulation. Department of State, Office of the Legal Adviser Memorandum Regarding International Electronic Commerce Projects 'Review of possible future Ecom Projects,' '(M)any issues have arisen as well as a growing body of jurisprudence in the US and some other countries over the last two years, but few internationally recognised answers exist.'

55 Siddiqi, 'Welcome to the City of Bytes?' at p.75 advocates modification of the 'Sliding Scale' test. Green, 'Is Zippo's Sliding Scale a Slippery Slope of Uncertainty?'

56 A matter that has been highlighted already in terms of general inconsistencies in the Supreme Court's purported 'preoccupation with domestic constitutional puzzles,' forfeiting their potential use in a ' … model for international cooperation' in comparison to the EU; F. K. Juenger, 'A Shoe Unfit for Globetrotting' (1995) 25 *UC Davis LR* 1027 at p.1037 and 1044. See also F.K. Juenger, 'Jurisdiction, Choice of Law and the Elusive Goal of Decisional Harmony,' in M. Sumampouw, L.A.N.M. Barnhoorn, J.A. Freedberg-Swartzburg, J.J.M. Tromm, and J.A. Wade (eds), *Law and Reality, Essays on National and*

to satisfy constitutional 'Due Process.'[57] Whilst the lack of endorsement could be attributed to a historical lack of agreement on whether the government or industry should regulate electronic commerce,[58] that debate has now been superceded by the need to provide a consistent and predictable jurisdiction rule for electronic consumer contracts. As the cases *Hanson v Denckla*[59] and *Weber v Jolly Hotels* confirmed, '(T)he Supreme Court has long recognised that personal jurisdiction must adapt or progress in technology.'[60] This view is reinforced by Gasparini's comment that rules of personal jurisdiction are not static and need to adapt to changes in the speed and frequency of cross-border communications and commercial activities.[61] Nevertheless as Siddiqi stresses, '(T)he Supreme Court has not discussed the impact that Internet technology might have on the analysis of personal jurisdiction.'[62] A 'reassessment'[63] of personal jurisdiction is necessary and that directing or targeting commercial activities at a particular state via an active or interactive web site must be the basis of a harmonised approach in determining jurisdiction of an electronic consumer contract.

Synopsis of Consumer Protection and Law in the United States

The US Federal Trade Commission's ('FTC') Bureau for Consumer Protection enforces federal consumer protection laws 'to protect consumers against unfair, deceptive or fraudulent practises'[64] throughout the United States. Matters relating

---

International Procedural Law in Honour of Cornelis Carel Albert Voskuil (London, 1992); Yagura, 'Does Cyberspace Expand the Boundaries of Personal Jurisdiction?' at p.309.

57 Rice deems constitutional principles (i.e. Due Process) a 'limit[ation]' compared to the EU; Rice, 'A Cyberspace Odyssey Through US and EU Internet Jurisdiction,' at p.453. Word modified for syntax. However this has been regarded as an advantage of due process; M.L. Russell, 'Back to Basics: Resisting Novel and Extreme Approaches to the Law of Personal Jurisdiction and the Internet' (1999) 30 *U.Mem.L.Rev* 157 at p.177.

58 Aguilar, 'Over the Rainbow.'

59 *Hanson v Denckla*, 357 US 235 (1958).

60 *Young* and *Healthgrades.com, Inc. Weber v Jolly Hotels* 977 F.Supp 327 334 (D.N.J, 1997).

61 L.U. Gasparini, 'The Internet and Personal Jurisdiction: Traditional Jurisprudence for the Twenty-first Century Under The New York CPLR' (2001) 12 *Alb L J Sci & Tech* 191 at p.195.

62 Siddiqi, 'Welcome to the City of Bytes?' at p.68.

63 K.S. Dubanevich and A.J. Shebiel, 'Personal Jurisdiction in the Silicon Forest' (2001) 62 *Or. St. B. Bull* 21 at p.22.

64 Federal Trade Commission, 'Guide to the Federal Trade Commission,' <http://www.ftc.gov/bcp/edu/pubs/consumer/general/gen03.shtm>. Word in brackets modified and added respectively.

to consumer protection and electronic commerce fall within this remit.[65] In September 2000, the FTC issued a report[66] that recommended effective core consumer protections premised on the OECD's recommendation that consumers should be provided with the same level of protection whether they contract via the WWW or by other traditional means of communication. The FTC's report also recommended greater use of ADR as methods of 'partial convergence' of laws 'in appropriate areas' including jurisdiction rules for contracts conducted by electronic means. The Office of the Legal Adviser in the Department of State is also responsible for gathering and disseminating information on matters concerning international private law.[67] An example of this was the consultation on the Hague Conference's Judgments Convention project. In addition, each state has its own consumer protection laws analogous to the Federal Trade Commission Act. The Uniform Commercial Code protects the consumer in respect of sale of goods matters. In brief, sections 2–601 and 2–719 provide that the consumer can return non-conforming goods and that the seller is bound to inform the consumer what remedies (including level of damages) are available respectively. Jurisdiction agreements in consumer contracts are generally upheld by the Unites States courts provided (as will be considered later) that such agreements are not obtained by unfair or deceptive means. It is with this in mind that the consumer who contracts with a foreign business by electronic means will have to carefully consider how he can establish jurisdiction where he is domiciled. Aguilar[68] demonstrated that whilst the US e-commerce policy has addressed 'cybercrime … and unfair e-business practices,'[69] there was a need to address 'e-consumer protection' or remain behind other regional areas such as the EU. Furthermore, since 'Due Process' requires an element of fairness to the foreign defendant, it is necessary that the 'Sliding Scale' test is modified to incorporate the business' intention to target foreign consumers.

---

65 Federal Trade Commission Act 15 USC ss.41–58. The FTC also has a Bureau of Consumer Protection, examples of its range of work can be viewed at <http://www.ftc.gov/bcp/index.shtml>.

66 The FTC considered different views with respect to e-commerce regulation and agreed as a minimum that consumers should receive the same level of protection online as they receive offline, analogous with the OECD's Guidelines for Consumer Protection in Electronic Commerce, Chapter 1 above.

67 The Private International Law Database of the Department of State's Office of Legal Adviser.

68 Aguilar, 'Over the Rainbow,' at p.8 and 12.

69 Aguilar, ibid at p.12.

The Regulation of Electronic Commerce in the United States

The United States is widely regarded[70] as one of the most active countries participating in electronic commerce.[71] As the first Chapter demonstrated, the onset of electronic commerce facilitates the 'disintermediation'[72] of the consumer contract and consumer protection laws. The disintermediation of the consumer contract continues to question the effectiveness of current juridical protection for consumers.[73] Whilst the consensus in the United States is that the Internet as a whole requires to be regulated,[74] how regulation should be imposed and enforced and by whom (whether industry or government) has historically been part of a wider debate on the regulation of jurisdiction for cyberspace.[75] The position of online sales and fraud,[76] tax matters[77] and security and privacy are some of the key issues that the United States has addressed. However, Aguilar has argued that a lack of agreement on how the Internet should be regulated contributes to a lack of 'e-consumer protection' in the United States.[78] Compared to the intrinsic institutional basis for EU consumer protection, there are fewer legislative measures providing juridical protection for consumers in the US.

In the 1997 'Framework for Global Electronic Commerce' (the then) President Clinton and Vice-President Gore maintained that 'governments should encourage

70 OECD, 'Consumers in the Online Marketplace: The OECD Guidelines Three Years Later,' Report by the Committee on Consumer Policy on the Guidelines for Consumer Protection in the Context of Electronic Commerce, DSTI/CP(2002)4/FINAL, 3 February 2003 (hereafter referred to as the 'OECD 2003 Report'); OECD, 'Measuring the Information Economy 2002', Chapter IV Electronic Commerce, August 2002, available at <http://www.oecd.org./dataoecd/34/35/2771139.pdf> (hereafter 'OECD 2002 Report) where it was reported that '(I)n January 2000, the United States had 65% of the total OECD-area of secure servers' (at p.60) second only to Iceland. All copyright OECD.

71 OECD 2002 Report, ibid at p.66 where it states that (alongside Denmark, Sweden and the United Kingdom) 'about 38% of individuals using the Internet ordered products in 2001' in the United States. Furthermore the report confirms that '(E)-commerce retail sales in the second quarter of 2002 accounted for 1.2% of total sales.'

72 J. Rothchild, 'Protecting the Digital Consumer: The Limits of Cyberspace Utopianism' (1999) 74 *Ind LJ* 893 at p.895–897.

73 Rothchild, ibid at p.912.

74 Chicago-Kent Project on Internet Jurisdiction at <http://www.kentlaw.edu/cyberlaw/resources/guide.html>. Internet and the Resources pages.

75 Chapter 1 above.

76 Rothchild, 'Protecting the Digital Consumer: The Limits of Cyberspace Utopianism,' at p.904 *et seq* where he cites Cella and Reed, '(T)he swindles over the Internet are no different from the confidence games of the past: the only difference is the medium.'

77 A. Horn, 'Internet Transaction Taxes: The Need for Jurisdictional Integration' (2001) 9 *CommLaw Conspectus* 29.

78 Aguilar, 'Over the Rainbow,' at p.14.

industry self-regulation wherever appropriate.'[79] Later in the same paper, Clinton and Gore 'urge[d] UNCITRAL, other appropriate international bodies, bar associations, and other private sector groups to continue their work in this area.'[80]

Whilst rules of specific personal jurisdiction have been used to establish jurisdiction when the parties contract via the WWW, the US Government and external organisations have undertaken separate initiatives that have all advocated a global solution to jurisdiction issues raised by the WWW. In 1999, the Federal Trade Commission held a workshop entitled 'US Perspectives on Consumer Protection in the Global Electronic Marketplace,'[81] which acknowledged the need for an international solution to the issue of Internet jurisdiction generally.[82] Interestingly, their subsequent report[83] 'Consumer Protection in the Global Electronic Marketplace: Looking Ahead,' argued against imposing the country of origin rule as the basis of jurisdiction, with preference in the report for 'partial convergence.'[84]

In 1992, the Hague Conference on Private International Law commenced work on the United States' proposal for a worldwide judgments convention.[85] The then proposed Hague jurisdiction and judgments convention was regarded as being similar to the Brussels Convention in form[86] and general purpose,[87] and included proposed jurisdiction rules in Article 7 for electronic consumer contracts.[88] The United States has considered the related internal, constitutional[89] and external

79 President W.J. Clinton and Vice-President A. Gore, Jr., *A Framework for Electronic Commerce*, The White House, 1997.

80 Ibid. Word in brackets modified for syntax.

81 Federal Trade Commission, Public Workshop and Report on 'Consumer Protection in the Global Electronic Marketplace: Looking Ahead,' 6 September 2000.

82 Ibid.

83 See Federal Trade Commission's Bureau of Consumer Protection at <http://ftc.gov/bcp/bcp.html> and in particular their Public Workshop and Report, ibid.

84 Ibid.

85 Preliminary Document No.11, 'The Future Hague Convention on International Jurisdiction and the Effects of Judgments in Civil and Commercial Matters,' Report of the Special Commission by P. Nygh and F. Pocar (hereafter the Nygh and Pocar Report). A.T. Von Mehren, 'Drafting A Convention on International Jurisdiction and the Effects of Foreign Judgments Acceptable Worldwide: Can the Hague Conference Project Succeed?' (2001) 49 *Am J Comp L* 191.

86 Von Mehren ibid. L.E. Gillies, 'The Impact of the Hague Conference's Proposed Judgments Convention for Electronic Commerce and Intellectual Property Disputes' (2002) 16:3 *Int Rev L Comps and Tech* 233.

87 Nygh and Pocar Report.

88 June 2001 draft Convention; Gillies, 'The Impact of the Hague Conference's Proposed Judgments Convention for Electronic Commerce and Intellectual Property Disputes.'

89 Brand, 'Due Process as a Limitation on Jurisdiction in U.S Courts and a Limitation on the United States at the Hague Conference on Private International Law.' On the implications of the proposed Hague Judgments Convention for the First Amendment see

implications of acceding to and ratifying such a convention. Svantesson has argued that since the *Zippo* case requires prior commercial activity via a web site for jurisdiction to be established, criteria such as 'quantity [and] nature of contacts with the forum' were 'irrelevant'[90] to Article 7 of the 2001 draft convention and 'should not bear any weight in the international context.'[91] However, Brand remarked that '(D)ue process [is] a concept important beyond the borders of the United States.'[92] Brand's remark highlights the significance of the 'Due Process' requirement in establishing jurisdiction when the foreign business in situated outside the United States. Furthermore, despite Svantesson's opinion, the intention in addition to the quantity and nature of the foreign business' contacts with US consumers are crucial when the parties contract via a globally equivalent, dematerialised medium such as a web site. Such contacts must demonstrate the business' positive intention to contract with a consumer in another jurisdiction. Furthermore, as Silberman and Lowenfeld confirmed, '(M)ost of the jurisdictional provisions in the proposed Hague Convention would seem to meet US Constitutional standards.'[93]

Despite symposia[94] and general consultation exercises,[95] much work remained outstanding before a compromise could have been agreed for the Convention to be acceded by a sufficient number of countries, including the United States. The

---

for example S. Hudleston, 'Preserving Free Speech in a Global Courtroom: The Proposed Hague Convention and the First Amendment' (2001) 10 *Minn. J. Global Trade* 403. On the implications for the Fourteenth Amendment see Von Mehren, 'Drafting A Convention on International Jurisdiction and the Effects of Foreign Judgments Acceptable Worldwide.'

90 D. Svantesson, 'Jurisdiction Issue in Cyberspace What Should Article 7 – Consumer Contracts, of the Proposed Hague Convention, Aim to Accomplish in Relation to E-Commerce?' (2001) 5 *CLSR* 318, at p.323. Word in brackets added.

91 Svantesson, ibid.

92 Brand, 'Due Process as a Limitation on Jurisdiction in U.S Courts and a Limitation on the United States at the Hague Conference on Private International Law.' Word in bracket added.

93 Silberman and Lowenfeld, 'A Different Challenge for the ALI' (and also referring to Brand's article on tort jurisdiction entitled 'Tort Jurisdiction in a Multilateral Convention: The Lessons Of The Due Process Clause and the Brussels Convention' (1998) XXIV/1 *Brook J Int'l L* 125.

94 Symposium held by Brooklyn Law School and the Brooklyn Law School Center for the Study of International Business Law, 'Enforcing Judgments Abroad: The Global Challenge' (1998) XXIV/1 *Brook J Int'l L*; Annual Meeting of the Association of American Law Schools, Section on Conflict of Laws' articles on their Symposium 'Conflict of Laws in the Global Village: International Conflicts Issues for the General Course in Conflicts of Laws' in (1995) 28 *Vand J Transnat'l L* 3.

95 Symposium held by Brooklyn Law School and the Brooklyn Law School Center for the Study of International Business Law, 'Enforcing Judgments Abroad: The Global Challenge' (1998) XXIV/1 *Brook J Int'l L*; Annual Meeting of the Association of American Law Schools, Section on Conflict of Laws' articles on their Symposium 'Conflict of Laws in the Global Village: International Conflicts Issues for the General Course in Conflicts of Laws' in (1995) 28 *Vand J Transnat'l L* 3.

significance of the Unites States' agreement to the Hague's proposed convention was crucial to the success of the entire project.[96] The initial contention appeared to be on reaching agreement on which bases of jurisdiction[97] should be obligatory ('white'[98]), exorbitant ('black'[99]) or discretionary ('grey'[100]) under the proposed convention, later to be superceded by questions on the exact nature (and purpose) of the Convention. Burbank argued that the proposed convention should be agreed at the expense of 'understanding current approaches to jurisdiction ... and the need for international legal order in the future.'[101] If adaptation of existing UK and US jurisdiction rules do not occur, the work carried out by the Hague Conference should form the basis for a specific international convention on jurisdiction rules for electronic consumer contracts, premised on intentional targeting.

In any event, the overarching necessity of international private law rules to provide just solutions to disputes with a foreign element, was succinctly summed up by Weintraub as follows.

> Conflicts problems are too widespread, of too great practical importance to be ignored by anyone who would call himself a lawyer. The problems must be thought out and solved in clear and understandable terms. The rules in this area must be shaped and often reshaped to yield not only solutions, but solutions that are responsive to modern social realities.[102]

Weintraub's remark highlights the need for a predictable or foreseeable jurisdiction rule when the parties contract via a global, dematerialised medium such as a web site. Despite all of these efforts to integrate e-commerce issues into policy,[103] the US has made limited legislative changes with regard to electronic commerce issues.

---

96 Brand, 'Due Process as a Limitation on Jurisdiction in U.S Courts and a Limitation on the United States at the Hague Conference on Private International Law,' has said that the 'United States could not be a party under [the 2001 draft] option.' Word in brackets added. S.B. Burbank, 'Jurisdictional Equilibration, the Proposed Hague Convention and Progress in National Law' (2001) 40 *Am J Comp L* 203.

97 S. Murphy, 'Negotiation of Convention on Jurisdiction and Enforcement of Judgments' (2001) 95 *Am J., Int'l L.* 418.

98 A.T. Von Mehren, 'Recognition and Enforcement of Foreign Judgments: A New Approach for the Hague Conference?' (1994) 57 *L and Contemp Probs* 271.

99 Von Mehren, ibid. Murphy, 'Negotiation of Convention on Jurisdiction and Enforcement of Judgments,' at p.420.

100 Von Mehren, ibid. Murphy, ibid at p.420.

101 Burbank, 'Jurisdictional Equilibration, the Proposed Hague Convention and Progress in National Law.'

102 R.J. Weintraub, *Commentary on the Conflict of Laws*, 3rd ed (New York, 1986) at p.4 (and reiterated in the 4th ed of Weintraub's text, *Commentary on the Conflict of Laws*, at p.5).

103 Electronic commerce has not been at the top of the agenda of the current US President.

For example, the Uniform Electronic Transactions Act (UETA) provides rules on electronic signatures[104] whilst the Uniform Computer Information Transactions Act (UCITA) provides a general contract law framework for transactions conducted by electronic commerce falling within its scope[105] including rules to complement, *inter alia*, choice of law rules in the Uniform Commercial Code.[106] In recent years, instead of legislation, many cases at federal and appeal courts have considered and applied personal jurisdiction rules in disputes concerning electronic commerce to resolve such issues. Siddiqi has argued that the 'vast experience of courts can be used to find a global approach to obtaining jurisdiction over internet activities.'[107] Ensuring customer trust and satisfaction must be a key to business profit and success, and ultimately the success of electronic commerce.[108] In the absence of any global agreement to date, the 'Sliding Scale' test should be adapted to incorporate the requirement that a business intended to target consumers via its active or interactive web site.

Synopsis of Rules of Personal Jurisdiction in the United States

Asserting General Personal Jurisdiction

The court derives its ability to assert personal jurisdiction over a defendant situated in a different state from the plaintiff from *Pennoyer v Neff*.[109] However, in *Calder v Jones*, the Supreme Court has acknowledged that it has 'disallowed any clear cut [personal] jurisdiction rules.'[110] In a dispute over a consumer contract (whether the contract was entered into on or offline), a consumer is likely to want to raise

104 Drafted by the National Conference of Commissions on Uniform State Laws (NCCUSL), <http://www.nccusl.org>.

105 Uniform Computer Information Transactions Act, section 103(a); M.J.H. Dively, 'The New Laws That Will Enable Electronic Contracting: A Survey of the Electronic Contracting Rules in the Uniform Electronic Transactions Act and the Uniform Computer Information Transactions Act' (2000) 38 *Duq L. Rev* 209.

106 For example, the UCITA provides rules prohibiting the application of choice of law clauses in respect of consumer contracts (§ 109). C.T. Poggi, 'Electronic Commerce Legislation: An Analysis of European and American Approaches to Contract Formation' (2000) 41 *Va J Int'l L* 224 at p.243 *et seq*.

107 Siddiqi, 'Welcome to the City of Bytes' at pp.64–65.

108 T.P. Vartanian in 'Whose Internet is it Anyway? The Law of Jurisdiction in Cyberspace: Achieving Legal Order Among the World's Nations,' American Bar Association, Section on Business Law, Committee on Cyberspace Law, Subcommittee on Transnational Issues, 2000 Global Internet Summit, 13–14 March 2000 <http://www.kentlaw.edu/cyberlaw/resources/globalsummit.rtf>.

109 *Pennoyer v Neff*, 95 US 714, 24 L.Ed. 565, 95 Otto 714 (1878).

110 *Calder v Jones*, 465 US 783, 788, 104, S.Ct. 1482, 1486, 79 L.Ed.2d. 804 (1984) referred to in. Fitzmaurice and Mody, 'International Shoe Meets the World Wide Web.'

proceedings in his own jurisdiction. The decisions in these cases are therefore useful as they demonstrate the extent to which a plaintiff can assert jurisdiction in his own domicile based on the accessibility of a foreign business' web site. The case *Helicopteros Nationales de Colombia, S.A v Hall*[111] provided that there are two types of personal jurisdiction, general and specific. The *Helicopteros* case confirmed that general personal jurisdiction is established if the defendant has systematic and continuous contact with the forum.[112]

The Ninth Circuit of the Court of Appeal in *Bancroft and Masters*[113] considered how general personal jurisdiction was established over a trademark infringement case. The defendants were alleged to have misused their trademark ('Masters'), which also happened to be the plaintiff's domain name ('masters.com'). The Californian court held that the defendants were not subject to the jurisdiction of the courts as the contacts were insufficient to establish personal jurisdiction. However, the court also ruled that there was general jurisdiction. The Ninth Circuit provided a coherent summary of how general jurisdiction is established.

> A defendant whose contacts with a state are 'substantial' or 'continuous and systematic' can be [*sic*] hauled into court in that state in any action, even if the action is unrelated to those contacts. This is known as general jurisdiction. The standard for establishing jurisdiction is 'fairly high', and requires that the defendant's contacts be the sort that approximate physical presence. Factors to be taken into account are whether the defendant makes sales, solicits or engages in business in the state, serves the state's markets, designates an agent for the service or process, holds a license or is incorporated there.[114]

There must be 'extensive and persuasive'[115] evidence or connections[116] demonstrating 'continuous and systematic' business activities within the forum for general personal jurisdiction. According to the court in both *Helicopteros Nationales*[117] and *Bancroft and Masters*, the standard of proof required to establish general jurisdiction is fairly high, equating to physical presence. For the purposes of this analysis, the most important aspect of general jurisdiction is that evidence

---

111 *Helicopteros Nationales de Colombia, S.A v Hall* 466 US 408, 414–416, 104 S.Ct 1868, 1872–73, 80 L.Ed.2d 404 (1984).

112 *Helicopteros*, ibid; G.B. Born, *International Civil Litigation in Unites Stated Courts*, 3rd ed (The Hague, 1996) at p.104; Westermeier, 'Personal jurisdiction: Today's Hot Issue in E-Commerce.'

113 *Bancroft & Masters Inc. v Augusta National Inc.*, No.99-15099 223 F.3d 1082.

114 *Bancroft and Masters*, ibid.

115 *Desktop Technologies Inc. v Colorworks Reproduction & Design* 1999 WL 98572 E.D.Pa., 25 February 1999 citing *Reliance Steel Prod. Co., v Watson, Ess, Marshall and Engass*, 657 F.2d 587, 589 (3rd Cir.1982).

116 Born, *International Civil Litigation in Unites Stated Courts*, at p.95.

117 The *Helicopteros* case stated that in the case of a business there had to be 'sufficient permanent connection with the forum.'

can be taken into account of the extent to which the defendant has engaged in business in the jurisdiction. However, these are only factors that can be taken into account in the particular case. Given the onerous requirement to establish general jurisdiction over any dispute, it is to be expected that the majority of cases dealing with jurisdiction for electronic commerce disputes have focussed on whether the plaintiff can establish either general or specific personal jurisdiction over the defendant.

Asserting Specific Personal Jurisdiction

Specific personal jurisdiction arises from or in relation to the particular cause of action in dispute between the parties. 'Substantially less' is required to establish specific jurisdiction than general jurisdiction.[118] The courts in both *Helicopteros*[119] and *Bancroft*[120] considered the tests required to establish specific personal jurisdiction. Specific personal jurisdiction firstly requires that the defendant 'purposefully availed' himself by conducting business in the jurisdiction. The 'purposeful availment' requirement was derived in *Hanson v Denckla*,[121] and *World Wide Volkswagen Corp. v Woodson.*[122] Secondly, the dispute must be related to the actual basis of claim and thirdly, the exercise of jurisdiction must be reasonable.

In general, each state has discretion[123] to assert jurisdiction over an out-of-state defendant via its long arm statute in two ways.[124] Born distinguishes long arm statutes in two general categories, namely those 'incorporat[ing] the due process limits of the fourteenth amendment … [and those which] detail the circumstances in which state courts may assert personal jurisdiction over foreign defendants.'[125] The state can either specify the categories in which jurisdiction can be asserted or permit jurisdiction over an out-of-state defendant as far as 'Due Process' permits.[126] As a plaintiff who is usually deemed to be the weaker party to the contract, the consumer is likely to want to raise proceedings in his own jurisdiction, whether or not the contract was conducted via the WWW.[127] In order to determine whether the

118 Born, *International Civil Litigation in Unites Stated Courts*, at p.78.

119 *Helicopteros*.

120 *Bancroft and Masters*.

121 *Hanson v Denckla*.

122 *World Wide Volkswagen v Woodson*, 444 US 286, 100 S.Ct. 559 (1980).

123 Gasparini, 'The Internet and Personal Jurisdiction: Traditional Jurisprudence for the Twenty-first Century Under The New York CPLR,' at p.208.

124 Gasparini, ibid at p.209.

125 Born, *International Civil Litigation in Unites Stated Courts*, at p.68. Word(s) in brackets modified and added for syntax respectively.

126 T.S. Trout-McIntyre, 'Personal Jurisdiction and the Internet: Does the Shoe Fit?' (1997) 21 *Hamline L Rev* 223 at pp.227–228.

127 Trout-McIntyre, ibid. G.M. Kalow, 'From the Internet to Court: Exercising Jurisdiction Over World Wide Web Communications' (1997) 65 *Fordham L.Rev.* 2241 at p.2251.

defendant is subject to the jurisdiction of another state, the court has to determine whether the defendant made contact with a party situated in the forum state. To do this, the court considers whether the defendant has sought to create continuing relationships and obligations with residents of the forum state, for example by entering into contracts to provide goods or services to residents in the forum. If the defendant has done this, then the state may invoke its long arm statute to assert jurisdiction on the forum state, subject to constitutional 'Due Process.' According to *International Shoe v State of Washington*, the exercise of personal jurisdiction should be 'directly proportionate to the nature and quality of commercial activity that an entity conducts over the Internet.'[128] The fact that a party can assert jurisdiction based on the forum's long-arm statute may encourage businesses to restrict which parties (such as consumers) they choose to contract with. As the *International Shoe* case demonstrates below, there is a strong connection between the application of a state's long arm statute and the constitutional requirement of 'Due Process.' As subsequent cases will also demonstrate, many disputes involving web site activities satisfy the state's long arm statute (often close to the requirement of 'Due Process'[129]) with the majority of the court's analysis on whether 'Due Process' permits application of the state's long arm statute.

The next question that the court considers in determining personal jurisdiction is whether the exercise of jurisdiction meets the 'Due Process' requirement of (but not defined by) either the Fifth[130] or Fourteenth[131] Amendments of the United States Constitution.[132] As Brand explains, the 'Due Process' clauses 'exist to protect individuals from excessive exercises of governmental authority.'[133] The case law has developed the 'Due Process' requirement for disputes concerning electronic commerce.

Due Process

Depending on the type of jurisdiction to be established, two tests may satisfy the requirement of 'Due Process.' For general personal jurisdiction, there must be 'substantial, continuous and systematic presence in the forum state' that would give

128 *International Shoe v State of Washington*, 326 US 310, 316, 66, S.Ct. 154, 158, 90, L.Ed. 95 (1945). Aciman and Vo-Verde, 'Refining The Zippo Test: New Trends on Personal Jurisdiction for Internet Activities.'

129 Born, *International Civil Litigation in Unites Stated Courts*, re the different basis of implementing long arm statutes, at p.68.

130 Applicable where the defendant is domiciled in another US state.

131 Applicable where the defendant is domiciled in another country.

132 Both Amendments specify reference to due process in the event that a person's life, liberty or property is in dispute.

133 Brand, 'Due Process as a Limitation on Jurisdiction in US Courts and a Limitation on the United States at the Hague Conference on Private International Law.'

the court jurisdiction.[134] In order to render specific personal jurisdiction reasonable, the court must determine firstly whether the defendant had 'minimum contacts' or 'purposeful contacts'[135] with the forum state. The well-known case *International Shoe* illustrates the second test of 'Due Process.' In that case, jurisdiction over a defendant not resident in the forum was established since contact made with the forum did not go against 'notions of fair play and substantial justice' in accordance with the Fourteenth Amendment.[136] Abramson has suggested that the 'fair play' test 'continues to develop independently from the minimum contacts enquiry.'[137] However, in the context of jurisdiction over electronic commerce disputes, the courts have given greater consideration to the minimum contacts test. Since *International Shoe*, the Supreme Court has sought to develop the 'Due Process' test by ensuring that it could apply 'in response to technological and commercial changes.'[138] The 'minimum contacts' with the forum test (so required to establish 'Due Process') has been affirmed by the Supreme Court in *International Shoe*, *McGhee v International Life Ins. Co.*,[139] *Hanson v Denckla*,[140] *World Wide Volkswagen Corp.v Woodson,*[141] and *Burger King Corp.v Rudewicz*,[142] where the Supreme Court confirmed that states retain 'sovereign power' to hear disputes within their borders. In *World Wide Volkswagen*, Justice Marshall said that in accordance with the *International Shoe* test 'the quality and nature of commercial activity is more likely to cause effects in a larger sphere ... ma[king] it fair to require [the defendant/business] to answer for [its] conduct where its effects are felt.'[143]

134 For example, *Desktop Technologies Inc.*, note 126 supra, *Robert and Lauren Efford t/a Goldhope Farm v The Jockey Club*, 2002 Pa.Super. LEXIS 462, 796 A.2d 370, 375 (2002). and *Mar-Eco, Inc. v T&R and Sons Towing and Recovery Inc,* considered below.

135 Born, *International Civil Litigation in Unites Stated Courts,* at p.76.

136 *International Shoe*, note 139 supra. Interestingly there were no long arm statutes when *International Shoe* was decided.

137 Abramson, 'Clarifying 'Fair Play and Substantial Justice,' at p.469.

138 Rochlin, 'Cyberspace, International Shoe and the Changing Context for Personal Jurisdiction,' at p.653 and 660. Rochlin's article explains in previous years that there were economic, commercial and 'societal' (at p.661) justifications for expanding *International Shoe's* personal jurisdiction tests. In terms of 'technical developments,' see for example the decision of the Sixth Circuit in *Neogen Corp.v Neo Gen Screening* No.00–217 (reversing the earlier decision of the Western District of Michigan) where the web site that provided web users with passwords to access a web site constituted minimum contacts in the forum.

139 *McGhee v International Life Ins. Co.*, 355 US 220 (1957).

140 *Hanson v Denckla.*

141 *World Wide Volkswagen Corp.*

142 *Burger King Corp.v Rudewicz* 471 US 462, 105 S.Ct. 2174, L.Ed.2d.528 (1985).

143 Rochlin, 'Cyberspace, International Shoe and the Changing Context for Personal Jurisdiction' (words in brackets added and amended).

International Shoe and the Internet

The test of personal jurisdiction in *International Shoe* entered the electronic realm in the case *Compuserve v Paterson.*[144] In that case, the Sixth Circuit Court of Appeal was asked to consider whether the dispute brought against the defendant complied with the three requirements of the 'Due Process' test in order for the Ohio district court to assert jurisdiction over the dispute. Paterson (a Texan resident) alleged that he had ownership of software that he made available to third parties via an agreement with Compuserve. Compuserve subsequently offered products that Paterson regarded as being too akin to his own and sought a settlement from Compuserve. Compuserve raised proceedings in Ohio and Paterson disputed the court's jurisdiction. The Sixth Circuit held that the court could assert jurisdiction over Paterson as all three requirements for 'Due Process' had been satisfied. Paterson had purposefully availed himself by sending his software via a shareware facility to Ohio and since this was done only via Compuserve in Ohio, the second requirement was satisfied. Accordingly, the court held that the 'substantial connection' with Ohio had been met and it was reasonable for Paterson to defend a dispute raised in Ohio.

The decision in *Compuserve* developed from the Supreme Court decision *World Wide Volkswagen Corp.v Woodson*, which confirmed that the degree of contact a defendant had with the forum meant 'he should reasonably anticipate being hauled [*sic*] into court there.'[145] For the test of minimum contacts to apply, three 'fact-specific'[146] conditions must be satisfied. In *Digital Equipment Corp.,* the court referred to these conditions as 'relatedness, purposeful availment and reasonableness.'[147]. Firstly, in accordance with authority from *Hanson v Denckla,*[148] *Calder v Jones,*[149] *Burger King,*[150] and *Compuserve,*[151] it must be demonstrated that the defendant has 'purposefully availed'[152] himself by 'deliberately'[153] doing business in the forum state. According to *Digital Equipment Corporation* '(I)t is

144 *Compuserve v Paterson* 89 F.3d 1257 (6th Circuit 1996).

145 *World-Wide Volkswagen Corp.*

146 *Cybersell v Cybersell*, F.3d (1997 WL 739021 9th Cir.) and 130f.3d 414 (9th Cir. 1997), at p.416. See also Millstein, Nueberger, and Weingart, *Doing Business on the Internet Forms and Analysis*, at p.11–6 and Rice, 'A Cyberspace Odyssey Through US and EU Internet Jurisdiction,' at p.616.

147 *Digital Equipment Corporation v. Alta Vista Technology Inc.*, Civil Action No.96-12192NG 13 March 1997, at E.

148 *Hanson v Denkla.*

149 *Calder v Jones.* Its 'effects test' was subsequently altered by *ALS Scan Inc. v Digital Service Consultants Inc.*, note 19 supra which also adapted the *Zippo* 'Sliding Scale' test.

150 *Burger King.*

151 *Compuserve v Paterson.*

152 *Hanson v Denckla.* Words italicised for emphasis.

153 *Digital Equipment.*

essential … that there be some act by which the *defendant* purposefully avails itself of the privilege of conducting activities thus invoking the benefits and protections of its laws.'[154]

In accordance with the Supreme Court's rulings in *World Wide Volkswagen* and *Burger King*, the defendant's contacts with a particular forum must not be 'random, fortuitous or attenuated.'[155] A business should be subject to the jurisdiction if, as Green rightly point out, it chose to do business there.[156] Essentially, if the parties entered into a contract with each other, the terms[157] of this contract could be highly demonstrative of 'doing business' in the forum state.[158] As the next sections of this Chapter will illustrate the existence of a contract, whether agreed online or offline, is clear evidence of purposeful availment. The second requirement is that the dispute must be sufficiently connected or related to the defendant's activities in the forum.[159] The *Carnival Cruise Lines Inc. v Shute* [160] case described the relatedness requirement as a 'but for' test. The *Digital Equipment* case confirmed that the purpose of this test is to separate general and specific personal jurisdiction.[161] It is important that legal certainty and predictability is provided by jurisdiction rules when parties in different jurisdictions contract electronically with each other. However as the case authority demonstrates, unlike analogous provisions of the Brussels 1 Regulation, the relatedness requirement is only satisfied when a *link* has been established between the business' web site activity and the subsequent contract between the parties. It is submitted that the link should be satisfied if the business intended to target and has contracted with the consumer. The third requirement, derived by 'inference'[162] from the first two requirements, is whether the connection between the defendant's actions and the forum, to justify establishing jurisdiction, is reasonable. The test of minimum contacts is subject to a presumptive[163] reasonableness test that examines whether the exercise of jurisdiction in the particular circumstances of the case[164] 'comport with notions

154 *Digital Equipment*, ibid, emphasis added.

155 *Burger King*, at p.475.

156 Green, 'Is Zippo's Sliding Scale a Slippery Slope of Uncertainty?' at p.1056.

157 Millstein, Nueberger and Weingart, *Doing Business on the Internet Forms and Analysis*, at p.11–8.

158 *Burger King*, supra.

159 *Digital Equipment*. 'Tag jurisdiction' (premised on presence in the forum) is sufficient for purposeful availment in *Sulton v Ashley* SDNY No.01 Civ 8179 (JSM) 22 January 2002.

160 *Carnival Cruise Lines Inc. v Shute* 499 US 585 (1991) 9th Circuit.

161 *Digital Equipment*, note 158 supra; derived from *Helicopteros Nationales*, note 122 supra and *Nowak v Tak How Investments Ltd.*, 94F.3d708712 (1st Circuit) where the court said 'relatedness is the "driving rod" separating specific and general jurisdiction.'

162 *Compuserve v Paterson*, per Judge Bailey Brown.

163 Abramson, 'Clarifying 'Fair Play and Substantial Justice,' at pp.445–446.

164 Abramson, ibid.

of fair play and substantial justice.'[165] According to both Abramson and Rice, the reasonableness test is most significant when the defendant is resident in another country. As Rice confirmed '(T)he net effect of the reasonableness standard is to require more close contact between a foreign defendant and the forum country than is required under constitutional due process.'[166] Therefore, the reasonableness test is as significant as the relatedness test when the parties have contracted across borders by electronic means. The test of reasonableness for minimum contacts involving a business' web site was affirmed in *Zippo Manufacturing Co. v Zippo Dot Com, Inc.*[167] The *Zippo* case involved a trademark dispute over the defendant's use of the name 'Zippo' on their web site. The defendant's web site offered different service levels, two of which required viewers to pay for via an online subscription service. The Western District Court of Pennsylvania held that the state's long arm statute applied as the defendants were found to have contracted with several thousand Pennsylvanian residents. Since the long arm statute applied, the court also held that the constitutional test of 'Due Process' had also been met. In finding that the defendants had sufficient 'minimum contacts' with residents in the forum, the court introduced a 'Sliding Scale' differentiating levels of web site activity. The court confirmed that to ensure compatibility with constitutional 'Due Process' the nature and quality of the commercial activity had to be considered in each case. With regard to web sites in particular, the court distinguished activities on a web site that enabled a business to communicate and contract with a buyer through to those web sites that were akin to advertisements.[168] These web sites were categorised by the court in *Zippo* as 'active,' 'interactive' or 'integral,'[169] and 'passive' web sites.

> At one end of the spectrum are situations where a defendant clearly does business over the Internet. If the defendant enters into contracts with residents of a foreign jurisdiction that involve the knowing and repeated transmission of computer files over the Internet, personal jurisdiction is proper. At the opposite end are situations where a defendant has simply posted information on an Internet Web site which is accessible to users in foreign jurisdictions. A passive Web site that does little more than make information available to those who are interested in it is not grounds for the exercise of personal jurisdiction. The middle ground is occupied by interactive Web sites where a user can exchange information with the host computer. In these cases, the exercise of jurisdiction

---

165 *International Shoe.*

166 Rice, 'A Cyberspace Odyssey Through US and EU Internet Jurisdiction,' at pp.433–434

167 *Zippo*; Millstein, Nueberger, and Weingart, *Doing Business on the Internet Forms and Analysis*, at p.11–7.

168 Thereby insufficient in themselves to satisfy constitutional 'Due Process.'

169 *Agar v Multi-Fluid Inc.*, DC Texas Civil Action No.95–5105, an early case which on the facts held that the Norwegian defendant's web site was passive (since there were no purchases/contracts with the site).

> is determined by examining the level of interactivity and commercial nature of the exchange of information that occurs on the Web site. [170]

The 'Sliding Scale' effectively differentiates between advertising and commercial activities in the forum. A passive web site is a form of one way advertising from the business to the consumer. On the other hand, the other web sites enable the parties to contract with each other via an active web site or not, for example via email or other traditional means of communication. Abramson has raised a significant point about the relationship between relatedness and reasonableness. Abramson maintained that jurisdiction would only be 'defeated'[171] when 'fair play and substantial justice factors would render jurisdiction unreasonable.'[172] Abramson suggested that jurisdiction would be unreasonable if a foreign defendant's contact with the forum is 'minimal.'[173] Nevertheless, even if jurisdiction is unreasonable, jurisdiction will still be established when the business has purposefully availed itself by directing commercial activities towards that jurisdiction.[174] For that reason the connection between the activity and the dispute should remain second to the requirement for purposeful availment. Millstein, Nueberger and Weingart suggest that the state's long arm statute may operate to assert jurisdiction in the event that the contract is in dispute, whether or not the defendant is resident in the state[175] or not.[176] As the *World Wide Volkswagen* and *Burger King* cases confirm, the requirement of reasonableness is the second aspect or 'step'[177] in establishing 'Due Process.' In *Burger King*, a dispute arose over breach of a franchise agreement. On appeal the Eleventh Circuit held that the defendant's continuous conduct had to be directed, 'deliberate and repeated contacts'[178] towards the forum even if the defendant was not resident in the forum.

170 Zippo.

171 Abramson, 'Clarifying 'Fair Play and Substantial Justice,' at p.446.

172 Abramson, ibid.

173 Abramson, 'Clarifying 'Fair Play and Substantial Justice,' at p.450.

174 Abramson, ibid.

175 *Bensusan Restaurant Corp.v King*, 937 F. Supp 295 (S.D.N.Y 1996). Linked to the *Bensusan* case was the NY case *Telebyte Inc. v Kendaco Inc. d/b/a Telebyte Northwest and Telebyte NW*, EDNY 99-CV-3866 (ADS) 24 July 2000 which held that mere accessibility of a web site does not equate jurisdiction.

176 *Inset System v Instruction Set.*

177 B.K. Epps, 'Maritz, Inc v Cybergold, Inc: The Expansion of Personal Jurisdiction in the Modern Age of Internet Advertising' (1997) 32 *Ga L Rev* 237at p.251.

178 Millstein, Nueberger and Weingart, *Doing Business on the Internet Forms and Analysis*, at p.11–9.

In determining whether it is *reasonable* to assert jurisdiction over the foreign defendant,[179] the court is obliged to consider[180] a range of 'gestalt'[181] factors. In order to determine whether jurisdiction is reasonable, the 'gestalt' factors that are considered include:

> The forum state's interests in adjudicating the dispute; the plaintiff's interest in obtaining convenient and effective relief, at least when that interest is not adequately protected by the plaintiff's right to choose the forum; the interstate judicial system's interest in obtaining the most efficient resolution of controversies; and the shared interests of the several states in furthering substantive social policies.[182]

The gestalt factors are examples of how conflicts justice ensures that the forum with the closest or most appropriate connection adjudicates a cross-border dispute. As Epps explained, the test of reasonableness ensures that the foreign defendant is 'protected against inconvenient litigation'[183] in a foreign forum. All of these gestalt factors are relevant to electronic consumer contracts. With respect to the first factor, Abramson regards this requirement as 'one of the most important factors in the balancing process for determining the reasonableness of jurisdiction over a non-resident defendant.'[184] It is submitted that Abramson's remark is significant when the consumer and business contracted via a web site. The 'legitimate concern'[185] of the forum is to provide conflicts justice in situations where defendants, whilst not physically present, conduct their commercial activities. The forum's interest in resolving cross-border disputes has been compounded as a result of foreign businesses using electronic commerce more often to target, communicate and contract with consumers. The second and third gestalt factors can be considered together. It is inconvenient, costly and time consuming for individual consumers to raise proceedings in a foreign jurisdiction. Furthermore, if the consumer could only sue the business where it is situated, it will also be difficult and inconvenient for a consumer as a weaker party to know with certainty where that foreign

179 Deemed 'the most important factor,' by G.A. Zaphiriou in 'Basis of the Conflict of Laws: Fairness and Effectiveness' (1988) 10 *Geo Mason UL Rev* 301, at p.310; Trout-McIntyre, 'Personal Jurisdiction and the Internet: Does the Shoe Fit?' at p.230.

180 Trout-McIntyre, ibid.

181 *Asahi Metal Industry Co. v Superior Court*, 480 US 102, 109, 107 S.Ct. 1026, 1033 94 L.Ed.2d 92 (1987). Indeed reinforcement of the reasonableness test was regarded as a helpful factor provided by the court in *Asahi*, at p.167.

182 Affirmed by the Supreme Court in *World Wide Volkswagen*, note 133 supra at p.292 and *Burger King*, note 153 supra and termed 'gestalt' factors in *Digital Equipment*, note 158 supra. Abramson, 'Clarifying 'Fair Play and Substantial Justice,' at p.443 *et seq* and Trout-McIntyre, 'Personal Jurisdiction and the Internet: Does the Shoe Fit?'.

183 Epps, 'Maritz, Inc v Cybergold, Inc: The Expansion of Personal Jurisdiction in the Modern Age of Internet Advertising,' at p.48.

184 Abramson, 'Clarifying 'Fair Play and Substantial Justice,' at p.451.

185 Abramson, ibid at p.452.

business is located. Given the globally accessible and dematerialised nature of electronic commerce, the consumer's position is more acute if he or she has to raise proceedings in another jurisdiction. This is an example of how Abramson locates the plaintiff's interest in a 'comparison [of] convenience ... with another forum.'[186] Fourthly, it is important generally that the forum provides consumers with a consistent and predictable basis for asserting jurisdiction when foreign businesses have undertaken commercial activity in the forum. For example, in *State by Humprey v Granite Gate* Resorts,[187] the Minnesota court held that since the business' web site offered global gambling opportunities twenty-four hours a day, the business had forfeited its 'privilege of conducting activities within every state.' The court upheld the application of its long arm statute. The minimum contacts enquiry was satisfied having regard to the quantity of the contacts and the link between the contract and the dispute. By comparison, *American Network Inc. v Access America/Connect Atlanta Inc.*[188] the minimum contacts test was established when six web site users signed up to business services. Finally, both the forum and other states share an interest in providing a consistent and predictable rule for establishing jurisdiction when a consumer, as the weaker party, contracts with a foreign business via the WWW. A consumer will want to take advantage of being able to sue a foreign business in his own jurisdiction, especially if that business is located in another US state or outside the US. As stated earlier, the United States must ensure that existing consumer protection policies adapt to provide effective, consistent and predictable juridical protection for consumers who contract electronically with foreign businesses. Since the minimum contacts test must be established for personal jurisdiction, the remainder of this book will consider firstly how the accessibility of web sites, including passive web sites, should be distinguished from commercial activities conducted via active and interactive web sites and secondly that active and interactive web sites can effectively demonstrate purposeful availment if the business intended to target consumers in foreign jurisdictions. It will be concluded that the 'Sliding Scale' test should be amended, in line with the Fourth Circuit decision in *ALS Scan*, to incorporate the requirement that the business intended to target consumers via such web sites.

---

186 Abramson, ibid at p.458.

187 *State by Humprey v Granite Gate* Resorts N.W.2d, 1997 WL 557670 (Ct. App., Minn.) and 568 N.W. 2d 715 (Ct App., Minn., 1997).

188 *American Network Inc. v Access America / Connect Atlanta Inc.*, DC SNY 96 Civ 6823 13 August 1997.

Developments in International Private Law Rules for Electronic Commerce in the United States

Accessibility of Web Sites and the 'Stream of Commerce'

The essential aspect of commercial activity over the WWW is whether web site accessibility or interactivity constitutes purposeful availment in the forum and is thereby sufficient to establish jurisdiction in that state. The point was developed from Scoles and Hay who asked 'whether a foreign business entity has purposefully produced effects in the forum state of such significance that it is not manifestly unfair to require him to resolve a resulting legal dispute in this state.'[189] The jurisdictional effect of economic activity in the forum was expressed in *McGhee v International Life Ins. Co*. In that case, the Supreme Court asserted that 'it is sufficient for purposes of due process that the suit was based upon a contract which had a substantial connection with that state.'[190] The issue to be resolved is whether there is a 'substantial connection' to the forum in order to assert jurisdiction and how such a substantial connection is defined. That issue highlights the necessity for minimum contacts with the jurisdiction requiring 'additional activities'[191] to be directed within the 'stream of commerce.' On one level, such a requirement has helped to distinguish between the accessibility and the activity of a business' web site. In addition such a requirement has, according to Stott, helped to distinguish further between the active and passive nature of web site activities. Stott maintained that if additional activity demonstrates that a business' web site has entered the 'stream of commerce' in line with the decision *in Asahi*,[192] then personal jurisdiction ought to be upheld.[193] Whilst the *Asahi* decision is authority for this correct proposition, it will be demonstrated that 'something more' as provided by the decision in *ALS Scan* is now necessary.

In *Asahi Metal Industries v Superior Court*, the Supreme Court ruled that personal jurisdiction is not established over a defendant who simply operates a web site that is accessible in the forum.[194] If businesses were to be held liable in every jurisdiction in which their web sites were capable of being viewed, many businesses would withdraw their web sites since businesses would be subjected to unforeseen risks and potential liabilities. Burns and Bales expressed concerns that

---

189 Scoles and Hay, *Conflict of Laws*, at p.308.

190 *McGhee*.

191 *Maritz, Inc v Cybergold, Inc*., note 8 supra and *Asahi Metal Industries v Superior Court*. D.L. Stott, 'Personal Jurisdiction in Cyberspace: The Constitutional Boundary of Minimum Contacts Limited to a Web Site' (1997) 15 *Marshall J Computer and Info L* 819 at p.840.

192 *Asahi v Superior Court*.

193 Stott, 'Personal Jurisdiction in Cyberspace,' at p.853.

194 *Asahi*. The 'spider's web' approach according to Burns and Bales, 'Personal Jurisdiction and the Web,' at p.31.

jurisdiction over a web site could be established wherever that site was situated or accessible, i.e. worldwide jurisdictional reach.[195] Mitrani supports the view that the mere accessibility of a web site is an 'expansive' approach to jurisdiction.[196] The fact that the parties have entered into a contract with each other does not appear to affect this rule.[197] It must be demonstrated that the parties have a relationship that is connected to the forum in a foreseeable and material way.[198]

In *Asahi Metal Industry Co. v Superior Court*,[199] the court reaffirmed[200] the 'purposeful availment' requirement and confirmed that a business merely being in the 'stream of commerce'[201] was not enough to establish minimum contacts in the jurisdiction. By that, it was meant that placing an advertisement in a newspaper or magazine[202] to alert possible consumers to goods for sale does not render the business subject to the jurisdiction wherever that advertisement may arise. The court's decision in *Asahi* was crucial. In *Asahi*, the court referred to two distinct 'approaches' to jurisdiction. Justice O'Connor supported the 'Highway approach' which considered whether conduct in addition to placing a product in the stream of commerce supported jurisdiction. Justice O'Connor's view formed the majority decision that purposeful availment was not established. In comparison, Justice Brennan supported the 'Spider's Web approach' whereby jurisdiction is established wherever a business' commercial activities can be accessed. The 'Highway' approach has received support both from the case law and academics.[203] As stated earlier, the European Commission confirmed the mere accessibility of a web site was not sufficient to establish jurisdiction under the Brussels 1 Regulation. Burns and Bales have criticised the *Asahi* decision for two main reasons. First, those authors maintained that the court in *Asahi* did not unequivocally resolve whether putting items for sale in the stream of commerce was sufficient alone to establish

195 Epps, 'Maritz, Inc v Cybergold, Inc: The Expansion of Personal Jurisdiction in the Modern Age of Internet Advertising,'; Stott, 'Personal Jurisdiction in Cyberspace,' and S. Puathasnanon, 'Cyberspace and Personal Jurisdiction: The Problem of Using Internet Contacts to Establish Minimum Contacts' (1998) 31 *Loy.L.L.L.Rev* 691.

196 Mitrani, 'Regulating E-commerce, E-contracts and the controversy of Multiple Jurisdiction,' at p.56.

197 A 'simplistic notion' according to Rice, 'A Cyberspace Odyssey Through US and EU Internet Jurisdiction,' at p.429.

198 *McGhee*.

199 As with *World Wide Volkswagen*.

200 Born, *International Civil Litigation in Unites Stated Courts*, at p.76.

201 A term previously used in product liability cases.

202 *Weber v Jolly Hotels*, also said that advertisement in magazine not sufficient for purposeful availment, akin to decision by the US District Court of the Northern District of Illinois in *Transcraft Corp. v Doonan Trailer Corp.*, DC Nill No 97C 4943 12 November 1997 and *Blackburn v Walker Oriental Rug Galleries* ED. Pa. No.97 – CV – 5704 7 April 1998.

203 Burns and Bales, 'Personal Jurisdiction and the Web,' at p.44–45.

personal jurisdiction.[204] Second, those authors argue that the *Asahi* decision has been interpreted in different ways and those different interpretations render inconsistent results. For example, the cases to be discussed later demonstrate that the 'something more' than just web site accessibility is definitely required, whereas in *Ruston Gas Turbines*,[205] the court said that something more was not required. The authors also point out that that in *Carnival Cruise Lines*, the court did not consider the issue at all.[206] Despite the different judicial opinions expressed in *Asahi* and given the subsequent authority considered below, the *Asahi* decision confirms that mere accessibility of a foreign business' web site will not establish jurisdiction. Burns and Bales regard the 'Spider's Web' approach used by the courts in *Inset* as 'flawed.'[207] This is correct since jurisdiction must be established, *inter alia*, on the level of interactivity and not simply the accessibility of a web site. Burns and Bales argue for a three-stage test that distinguishes between passive, active and financial web sites, the latter of which would always establish jurisdiction. However, despite the incidence of interactive web sites and explicit reference to them in the 'Sliding Scale' test, the key weakness of the Burns and Bales' model is the omission of any reference to interactive web sites.

The decision in *Asahi* confirmed that 'minimum contracts' would not be satisfied when the defendant simply placed its services in the 'stream of commerce.' Without something more,[208] a web site is merely accessible in the particular state and there is no evidence to substantiate business activity.[209] As Kalow has suggested, the courts adopted two 'patterns of analysis' in determining jurisdiction.[210] The first pattern required purposeful availment and reasonableness for minimum contacts to be established. This first pattern, of which *Asahi* is an example, used *Zippo's* 'Sliding Scale' to determine whether the business' use of a web site constituted purposeful availment. In addition the court could consider other factors, such as quantity of contacts and the gestalt factors mentioned earlier in this analysis. The second pattern, or 'stream of commerce' analysis, of which *Inset System, Inc. v Instruction Set*[211] is an example, required the business to consider whether it could anticipate being sued in a particular US court or courts. The Connecticut District Court's decision in *Inset* has been the subject of particular criticism. In *Inset*, the court asserted jurisdiction over a non-resident defendant who had not conducted business in Connecticut and did not have assets there. The business was deemed to

204 Burns and Bales, ibid at p.38.

205 *Ruston Gas Turbines v Donaldson Company Inc.*, 9 F.3d 415, 418 (5th Cir.1993).

206 *Carnival Cruise Lines v Shute.*

207 Burns and Bales, 'Personal Jurisdiction and the Web,' at p.44.

208 Stott, 'Personal Jurisdiction in Cyberspace,' at p.839–840.

209 *Asahi.*

210 Kalow, 'From the Internet to Court: Exercising Jurisdiction Over World Wide Web Communications,' at p.2265.

211 *Inset System, Inc. v Instruction Set.* Y.A. Tamayo, 'Who? What? When? Where? Personal Jurisdiction and the World Wide Web' (1998) 4 *Rich J L & Tech* 7.

have purposefully availed itself since its 'solicitation[s] [were] of a sufficient[ly] repetitive nature,'[212] to justify minimum contacts. According to Green, '(T)he [*sic*] precedential effect rendered by the *Inset Systems* holding is chilling … assail(ing) the very essence of due process.'[213] The long-term effect of the *Inset* decision would have meant that any foreign business operating a web site, regardless of the nature (i.e. *accessibility*) of that web site, would have been subject to the jurisdiction of any court in the United States. As Probasco confirmed, the decision demonstrated how the US courts initially had difficulty in asserting jurisdiction over foreign businesses that conducted commercial activity via web sites.[214] Such a decision was clearly contrary to the observation made earlier that 'Due Process' is designed to protect defendants from 'excessive governmental authority.'[215] This point was reiterated in *Zippo* when the court said that *Inset* 'represented the outer limit of the exercise of personal jurisdiction on the Internet.'[216] It is imprudent that all web sites are regarded as advertising[217] to consumers wherever they are capable of being viewed or accessed.[218] Businesses would have difficulty knowing or reasonably anticipating where their web sites were being accessed to the extent that '(W)ithout such indications of active (or perhaps 'interactive') efforts to secure customers in the forum state through [a] website, the use of the internet alone is no more indicative of local jurisdictional contacts than an isolated advertisement in a nationally distributed magazine.'[219] Reliance on such precedent would undermine both the economic[220] and marketing value of using web sites and the role of 'Due Process' in protecting foreign defendants. As Stott remarked, 'due process could hardly be served if each state can exercise personal jurisdiction over an Internet user who maintains a web site.'[221]

Furthermore, subsequent cases have not supported the decision in *Inset* and have relied upon the 'Highway approach' advocated by Justice O'Connor in *Asahi*.

212 *Asahi*; Rice, 'A Cyberspace Odyssey Through US and EU Internet Jurisdiction,' at p.463.

213 Green, 'Is Zippo's Sliding Scale a Slippery Slope of Uncertainty?' at p.1064. Word modified for syntax.

214 A.R. Probasco, 'Due Process Analysis in *Millennium Enterprises, Inc. v Millennium Music*, LP' (2000) 40 *Jurimetrics* 457, at pp.462–463.

215 Brand, 'Due Process as a Limitation on Jurisdiction in US Courts and a Limitation on the United States at the Hague Conference on Private International Law.'

216 *Zippo* and Perry *et al*, 'Personal Jurisdiction in Cyberspace Where Can you be Sued, And Whose Laws Apply?'

217 In reference to the case *Winfield Collection v McCauley*, 105 F. Supp 2d 746, 750 (E.D.Mich., 2000).

218 Ibid.

219 Rice, 'A Cyberspace Odyssey Through US and EU Internet Jurisdiction,' at p.508. Word in brackets added.

220 Yagura, 'Does Cyberspace Expand the Boundaries of Personal Jurisdiction?' at p.327.

221 Stott, 'Personal Jurisdiction in Cyberspace,' at pp.852–853.

The case *McDonagh v Fallon McElligott Inc*[222] reiterates that the mere availability of a web site to residents in a forum state is not sufficient in itself to establish personal jurisdiction over the creator of the site where the dispute is not concerned with how the web site itself is operated. Additionally, the case *Hearst Corporation v Goldberger*[223] confirmed that simply the availability of a web site to forum residents is not sufficient in a case alleging infringement of a trademark dispute. The court in Hearst refused to follow earlier authority from the Minnesota Court of Appeal held in *Minnesota v Granite Gate Resorts Inc State of Minn Dist Crt.*[224] In that unusual case, the court held that advertisements on an active web site that were accessible to and directed at Minnesota residents were deemed 'sufficient contacts' with consumers in the state to subject the defendant to the jurisdiction of that state. In determining whether jurisdiction was reasonable, the court considered the five 'gestalt' factors including subsequent contact with the forum via the web site and the quality of the conduct. Importantly the court also said the state's consumer protection rules advocated the argument for jurisdiction.

The decisions in *Maritz v Cybergold* and *Bensusan v King* demonstrate the antagonism when web sites are equated to advertisements. In the *Maritz v Cybergold* case, it was held that the web site was neither active nor passive given that viewers were able to add their names to a mailing list on the site.[225] Clearly, this might therefore apply to many web sites that provide a similar service. The court in *Maritz*[226] upheld the important test of 'fairness' and jurisdiction was established. By contrast, the case of *Bensusan Restaurant Corp.v King*[227] demonstrated that the passive web site is simply an information provider. In *Bensusan*,[228] the court considered web site activity in the context of the New York long arm statute. No consideration was given to the 'Due Process' requirement as the tort claim failed since the defendant was not 'physically present' in New York when the alleged act was committed as required by the state's long arm statute. The court confirmed

222 *McDonagh v Fallon McElligott Inc* 1996 US Dist Lexis 15139 (S.D. Cal 5 August 1996).

223 *Hearst Corporation v Goldberger*, 96 Civ. 3620(PKL) (AJP), 1997 WL 97097 S.D.N.Y 26/02/97.

224 *Minnesota v Granite Gate Resorts Inc. State of Minn Dist Crt.*, Ramsey County Court File No.C6-95-7227, 568 N.W.2d 715 (11 December 1996) aff'd No.C6-97-89, 576 N.W 2d 747 (Minn Ct App.5 September 1997).

225 Epps, 'Maritz, Inc v Cybergold, Inc: The Expansion of Personal Jurisdiction in the Modern Age of Internet Advertising.' F. Debussere, 'International Jurisdiction over E-Consumer Contracts in the European Union: Quid Novi Sub Sole?' (2002) 10 IJLIT 10 344.

226 Gasparini, 'The Internet and Personal Jurisdiction: Traditional Jurisprudence for the Twenty-first Century Under The New York CPLR,' at p.207 as regards the decision in *Maritz* as being 'on shaky ground.'

227 *Bensusan v King*. Tamayo, 'Who? What? When? Where?' regards *Bensusan* as providing a 'satisfactory examination' of the use of to Internet web sites.

228 *Bensusan v King*.

that '(M)ere foreseeability of an in-State consequence is not sufficient to establish personal jurisdiction. Creating a site is like placing a product in the stream of commerce, maybe felt nationwide – or even worldwide – but, without more, it is not an act purposefully directed towards the forum state.'[229]

Many web sites do not enable businesses to interact or communicate directly with viewers browsing those web sites. Such sites may provide facilities for those browsing to register minimum details such as their name or email address with the site for future information or special offers.[230] This is one of the reasons the decision in *Maritz* has been criticised.[231] Stott maintains that, unlike the decision in *Hearst*, the court applied the 'Spiders Web' approach to jurisdiction in finding that purposeful availment was satisfied. As stated earlier, the 'Spider's Web' approach enables jurisdiction to be established wherever a web site is accessed. Epps succinctly explained the effect of the 'Spider's Web' approach in the *Maritz* decision as follows. 'If the Maritz court's reasoning is adopted by other US courts, it could affect companies advertising on the Internet around the world. Non resident defendants could be hauled [*sic*] into any court in the United States.'[232] The decision in *Maritz* was not the most certain and predictable way of establishing that a business intended to undertake commercial activities in a particular jurisdiction. Essentially, this case illustrates the important distinction between the nature and content of web sites and advertising.[233] As the previous Chapters demonstrated, given their globally accessible nature, web sites are not the same as individual invitations or advertising via traditional media to consumers in specific jurisdictions. Epps maintains that the court in *Maritz* went too far in extending personal jurisdiction[234] because it failed to consider the relationship between web site content, advertising and constitutional 'Due Process.' Nevertheless, Epps concluded that *Maritz* would 'continue to influence many courts and commentators in their reasoning and their findings.'[235]

---

229 *Bensusan*, ibid.

230 An example of 'a user [being able to] exchange information with the host computer.' Epps, 'Maritz, Inc v Cybergold, Inc: The Expansion of Personal Jurisdiction in the Modern Age of Internet Advertising,' at p.255. Words in brackets added.

231 Epps, ibid and Stott, 'Personal Jurisdiction in Cyberspace,' at p.822 and 846 *et seq*.

232 Epps, 'Maritz, Inc v Cybergold, Inc: The Expansion of Personal Jurisdiction in the Modern Age of Internet Advertising,' at p.241.

233 In his paper, Epps refers to 'globally and nationally distributed magazines' as such an analogy; ibid at p.266 and 268.

234 Epps, ibid at pp.269-279.

235 Ibid at p.279. For example, see *Mieczkowski v Masco Corp.*, DC ETexas No.5: 96cv286 18 March 1998. In Mieczkowski, the defendant made numerous business contacts with the forum and the court cited *Maritz* in support of asserting jurisdiction.

In *Stephen C. Edberg et al v Neogen Corporation*[236] the Connecticut District Court confirmed that it was not possible to assert jurisdiction over a non-resident defendant who maintained a web site that was accessible to residents in the forum. The web site facilitated the advertisement of products, enabled users to request information about products and offered a free telephone number for the placing of orders, although the order could not be completed or submitted online. There was one sale to a resident in the forum and this was held to be insufficient to find jurisdiction, as it did not satisfy the test of 'minimum contacts.'[237] Meanwhile, the US Court of Appeal of the District of Columbia in *GTE New Media Servs., Inc. v Bell South Corp.,*[238] also confirmed that the 'mere accessibility' of a web site was not sufficient to assert specific personal jurisdiction. More recently in *Digital Control v Boretronics Inc.*,[239] the District Court for the Western District of Washington held that no personal jurisdiction could be asserted over the defendant. In criticising the *Inset* case, the court said that 'something more' was necessary to establish sufficient contacts with the forum. Therefore the *Inset* case serves as a useful reminder that both the approach and decisions in *Asahi* and *Bensusan* were correct in so far as placing a web site in the 'stream of commerce' will not satisfy purposeful availment.

'Mere Accessibility' of a Web Site Does Not Establish Personal Jurisdiction

Subsequent cases have, in accordance with *International Shoe*[240] and *Zippo*, focussed on the extent to which a business has conducted business in the forum, beyond merely advertising their services or making their web site accessible in the 'stream of commerce.' The mere accessibility of a web site can be attributed in the same way as a passive web site.[241] A passive web site is essentially an information provider that does not allow the web site owner and viewer to communicate or contract with each other via that site. In *Cybersell, Inc. v Cybersell, Inc.*[242] the District of Arizona and the Ninth Circuit held that since the web site was passive there were no 'continuous and systematic contacts' with the forum to establish

236 *Stephen C. Edberg et al v Neogen Corporation* 17 F.Supp.2d 104 (D.Conn. 1998).

237 For minimum contacts, see P.J. Borchers, 'Judgments Conventions and Minimum Contracts' (1998) 61:4 *Alb L Rev* 1161.

238 *GTE New Media Servs., Inc. v Bell South Corp.,* 199 F.3d 1343 (D.D.C. 2000).

239 *Digital Control v Boretronics Inc.*, WD Wash No.C01-0074L 6 September 2001.

240 *Worldwide Volkswagen v Woodson*, per Justice Marshall.

241 Rice, 'A Cyberspace Odyssey Through US and EU Internet Jurisdiction,' at p.521.

242 *Cybersell, Inc. v Cybersell, Inc.* subsequently referred to in *Barrett v Catacombs Press* E.D Pa. Civ. No.99-736 12 April 1999 where the passive web site was deemed a fortuitous contact with the forum. See also D.W. Falcon, 'A Nice Place to Visit But I Wouldn't Want to Litigate There: The Effect of *Cybersell v Cybersell* on the Laws of Personal Jurisdiction' (Spring 1999) 5 *Rich J L & Tech* 11.

jurisdiction. The court also stipulated that targeting activities in the state was necessary to establish jurisdiction.[243] The requirement for 'something more' was expressly made by the court in *Telco Communications Group, Inc. v An-Apple-a-Day, Inc.*[244] Whilst the court confirmed and accepted the web site activity distinction in *Inset* it said that 'repeated solicitation(s)' were necessary as 'foreseeability [was] not sufficient'[245] in that case.

The trend of decisions in relation to passive web sites has generally taken a three-fold approach. Firstly, the courts have likened such web sites with advertisements, readily available[246] or accessible to viewers in multiple locations and therefore not demonstrating purposeful availment towards the forum. For example, *Weber v Jolly Hotels* confirmed that a passive web site was akin to an advertisement in a national magazine.[247] In *Hearst Corporation v Goldberger*,[248] despite New York residents viewing the web site, the court held that the defendant was not doing business in the forum. This case also confirmed that the availability of a web site to forum residents is not sufficient in a case alleging infringement of a trademark dispute. Secondly, the trend of court decisions has also distinguished web sites providing no more than information[249] from those directly targeting business activities in the forum. In *Soma Medical International v Standard Chartered Bank*[250] the Tenth Circuit Court of Appeal held that the web site was passive since it merely provided information. In *CFOs 2 Go, Inc. v CFO 2 GO, Inc.*[251] the court examined the method of communication with the plaintiff and held that purposeful availment

243 Aciman and Vo-Verde, 'Refining The Zippo Test: New Trends on Personal Jurisdiction for Internet Activities.'

244 *Telco Communications Group, Inc. v An-Apple-a-Day, Inc.* 977 F. Supp.404 (E.D.Va. 1997).

245 *Telco*, ibid. Word added for syntax.

246 *Edberg*.

247 *Weber v Jolly Hotels*.

248 *Hearst Corporation v Goldberger*.

249 For example, *John G. Green et al v William Manson & Co et al* (1998 US Dist Lexis 331, 996 F. Supp.394 (D.N.J 5 March 1998) where the court determined that it was insufficient to establish personal jurisdiction by simply maintaining a passive web site that was available to residents in the forum without something more – at all stages of the Zippo enquiry. In *Envirotech Pumpsystems Inc. v Sterling Fund Systems AG* (No.2:99CV814K 2000 US Dist. LEXIS 16942 (D.Utah 16 November 2000)), the plaintiff sued for patent infringement on the defendant's web site but the court held that the web site only provided information and therefore did not satisfy either general or specific personal jurisdiction. *Med-Tec Iowa Inc. v Computerized Imaging Reference Systems Inc.* (S.D.Iowa No.4-02-CV-90338 3 October 2002), was an example of a passive web site which only provided information and did not facilitate interaction with web users.

250 *Soma Medical International v Standard Chartered Bank*, 196 F.3d 1292, 1295 (10th Cir.1999).

251 *CFOs 2 Go, Inc. v CFO 2 GO, Inc.*, 1998 U.S. Dist. LEXIS 8886 (N.D. Cal. 1998).

could not be premised simply on web site and email communication. Thirdly, and linked to the first two points, the decisions to refuse jurisdiction over a passive web site have been premised upon constitutional considerations. For example, in *Ecotecture Inc. v Wenz*[252] a passive web site which provided free subscriptions to a journal and information did not meet purposeful availment requirements according to the US District Court of Maine. In reaching their decision, the court observed that the state's Long Arm Statute provided the 'widest possible basis'[253] for establishing jurisdiction over a foreign defendant in accordance with the Fourteenth Amendment. The court was satisfied that the defendant had no way of knowing, *i.e. foreseeing*, the geographical location of those subscribing to its subscription service.[254] In *SF Hotel Co. L.P. v Energy Investments, Inc.*,[255] the US District Court of Kansas said that, in line with *Zippo* and *Weber*, it would offend 'Due Process' for personal jurisdiction in a trade mark dispute to be upheld when the web site was passive. Interestingly, the District Court for the Northern District of Mississippi held in *Lofton v Turbine Design*[256] that by its passive web site the Florida defendant was subject to the Long Arm Statute. However, since there was no purposeful availment (i.e. purposeful contact in the State), 'Due Process' was not satisfied and accordingly specific jurisdiction could not be established.

As consideration of the other levels of web site activity will demonstrate, the courts have looked for 'something more' to satisfy purposeful availment and 'Due Process.' The Fifth Circuit dismissed the *Mink v AAAA Development et al*[257] case for lack of jurisdiction since the plaintiff could not order online but only by email. In *Mink* the court commented that the exercise of jurisdiction over web sites that came in between the 'active' and 'passive' distinctions depended upon 'the level of interactivity and commercial nature of the exchange of information.'[258] The Vermont-based defendant's web site was held to be passive. Whilst there was an e-mail facility and a toll-free number there was no evidence of contacts with residents in the forum, such as contracts, in accordance with the *Zippo* scale.[259] The case *American Homecare Federation Inc v Paragon Scientific Corporation et al*[260] concerned allegations of a trademark infringement. The web site was available to all US residents but the court classified the nature of its activity as passive.

252 *Ecotecture Inc. v Wenz*, F Supp 2d. 2000 W760961 D.Me 16 May 2000.

253 *Ecotecture*, ibid at p.4.

254 Ecotecture, ibid at p.6.

255 *SF Hotel Co. L.P. v Energy Investments, Inc.*, 985 F. Supp.1032 (D.Kan. 1997).

256 *Lofton v Turbine Design, F. Supp.2d* (2000 WL 6364711 N.D., Miss., 2000).

257 *Mink v AAAA Development et al* 190 F.3d 333 (5th Cir.1999).

258 *Mink*, ibid at p.336 and in the process quoted *Zippo*, at 1124 – this was also referred to in the case of *People Solutions Inc. v People Solutions Inc.*, No.Civ.A. 399-CV-2339-L. 2000 WL 1030619 (N.D.Tex).

259 This was the first time that the Fifth Circuit considered and adopted Zippo's 'Sliding Scale.'

260 *American Homecare Federation Inc v Paragon Scientific Corporation et al* Case No CV-893 (WWE) 1998 US Dist Lexis 17962 (D.Conn 26 October 1998).

As a result, the court also held that the activity of the web site and the use of a free telephone number were insufficient to establish personal jurisdiction over a defendant who was not resident in the state.

In *Fix My P.C. LLC d/b/a/ Fixx My PC v N.F.N. Associates, Inc. d/b/a Pure Logic Computers*,[261] the Texas court held that it did not have jurisdiction over a non-resident defendant. The defendant's web site advertised services on the Internet that were available to Texas residents. The defendants also operated a free telephone number, but this was not accessible from its web site. The court rejected the decision in *Inset* which, as stated earlier, found jurisdiction on the basis of a passive web site and the availability of a free phone number. In addition to the *Fix My PC* case, the United States District Court for the District of East Virginia in *Rannoch, Inc. v Rannoch Corp.*,[262] confirmed that the defendant's conduct was in accordance with the state's long arm statute. The court's main consideration was whether the defendant's conduct in the forum constituted minimum contacts. The court held that by posting the web site, the defendants had merely entered the 'stream of commerce' and therefore did not purposefully avail themselves of doing business which would have subjected them to the jurisdiction of East Virginia. Furthermore, the court confirmed that a 'passive' web site still meant that the web site was accessible in the forum but that this was not enough for personal jurisdiction. The court also criticised the *Inset* case on the basis that *Inset* didn't distinguish between purposeful availment in that state and purposeful availment in other states.[263] In *Schweers v Hovaton*[264] the court held that the defendants had not purposefully availed themselves of doing business in the forum. The plaintiff alleged trademark infringement over the name 'Eagle Farm Ranch' but the District Court of New Mexico held that the defendant's web site was not directed towards New Mexico. The court followed the *Zippo* 'Sliding Scale' and confirmed that web site activity itself is not enough to establish personal jurisdiction.

The US District Court for the Eastern District of Virginia held that a web site in the case *Newspaper Association of America Inc. v Mancusi*[265] was too passive for jurisdiction to be asserted. The web site neither sold goods nor sought information from those browsing its pages. The Newspaper Association sued the defendants for unfair competition as the defendant used a very similar domain name in one of his web sites to that used (but not owned by) the plaintiffs. The court considered

---

261 *Fix My P.C. LLC d/b/a/ Fixx My PC v N.F.N. Associates, Inc. d/b/a Pure Logic Computers*, 48 F.Supp.2d 640 (N.D.Tex. 1999).

262 *Rannoch, Inc. v Rannoch Corp.*, 52 F. Supp.2d 681 (E.D.Va. 1999).

263 A similar case on the latter point was *Roche v Worldwide Media*, E.D.Va. No.99-1534-A 27 March 2000, which involved a 'passive' pornography site which linked automatically to the defendant's web site. The court classified the activity specifically as less than that in *Rannoch*.

264 *Schweers v Hovaton*, D NM No.Civ 99-162 MV/DJS 31 August 1997.

265 *Newspaper Association of America Inc. v Mancusi*, E.D.Va No. 01-1635-A 8 May 2002.

the Virginia long arm statute and held that its requirements had been met. The court's next consideration was whether jurisdiction was permitted in accordance with the constitutional 'Due Process' test and referred to *America Online Inc. v Huang*[266] on the level of activity of the web site. The court held that since the web site did not facilitate sales or information transfer, jurisdiction was not established. Interestingly, the court also held that jurisdiction would not be established over the defendant's web sites that was not the subject of the actual dispute. It is submitted therefore that a link has to be established between the defendant's intention to target consumers in the forum and the level of web site activity used by the business to meet that commercial objective.

'Something More' Required to Establish Personal Jurisdiction

The courts have therefore looked at different factors to demonstrate 'something more' for purposeful availment. Another example of 'something more' was the defendant's actual knowledge of the plaintiff's well-known trademark in *Amazon.com v Webovation*.[267] The District Court of the Western District of Washington upheld jurisdiction after considering the Ninth Circuit decision in *Panavision* (albeit a tort case) regarding purposeful availment. The *Zippo* 'Sliding Scale' was used in the case *Desktop Technologies Inc. v Colorworks Reproduction and Design Inc*.[268] to determine whether general or specific personal jurisdiction could be established. The court held that the defendant's web site was passive. The dispute arose when the non-resident defendant allegedly used the plaintiff's trademark in its domain name. In this case, the court held that it could not assert general or specific jurisdiction over the defendant. The court took into account the existence of a passive web site and the advertisements issued by the defendants in respect of its services and for employment. In this case, the degree of interactivity did not affect the fact that the site was still deemed to be passive. The facts demonstrated that those visiting the web site could communicate with the defendants by email or telephone. There was even an online order form available, but this could not be completed or sent online.

In *Butler v Beer Across America* the US District Court of the Northern District of Alabama was not satisfied that general or specific jurisdiction had been established. In comparison to *Wise* (considered below in the context of general personal jurisdiction), the defendants had a web site but did not seek to conduct business via that web site to Alabama residents. The passive nature of the web site in the *Butler* case was subsequently referred to by the Supreme Court of Alabama in *Ex P. Troncalli Chrysler Plymouth Dodge, Inc In re David J. Case v Alexander Dodge*

266 *America Online Inc. v Huang*, E.D.Va 00-290-A, 13 July 2000.

267 *Amazon.com v Webovation*, W.D.Wash., C00-1173C 2 November 2000.

268 *Desktop* – subsequently followed by *Mar-Eco, Inc. v T&R and Sons Towing and Recovery Inc.*, A.2d 2003 WL 22718179, 2003 PA Super 444, Pa. Super, 19 November 2003.

Chrysler Plymouth, Inc.[269] In referring to *Burger King*, the Court said 'something more than an isolated contact initiated by an in-state plaintiff is required to satisfy the "purposeful-availment" prong of the due-process analysis. "Something more" might involve "prior negotiations and *contemplated future consequences*," along with ... the parties' actual course of dealing.'[270] This case reiterates the view that *prior negotiations or future contemplated consequences* demonstrate 'something more' for purposeful availment. The business' intention to contract with a foreign consumer is the common denominator to both of these examples. Since the 'Sliding Scale' of Internet activities pronounced in the *Zippo* case, courts throughout the United States have pursued a qualitative analysis of the defendant's conduct in the forum, concerned with more than just web site accessibility (and indeed interactivity), to justify asserting jurisdiction in accordance with 'Due Process.'[271] Both the court's application and subsequent development of the 'Sliding Scale' test will be examined, demonstrating the court's continued overarching desire to satisfy constitutional 'Due Process.'

The 'Effects Test'

At the same time as the courts were considering whether the use of web sites contributed to activities in the forum for non-tortious claims, the courts also considered how the 'effects test' establishes jurisdiction over tort claims.[272] In *Calder v Jones*, the court confirmed that personal jurisdiction would be established if its three tests were satisfied as follows, namely the 'relationship among the defendant, the forum and the litigation.' The 'effects test' was applied in *Panavision Intl L P v Dennis Toeppen*.[273] The court in *Panavision* used the

---

269 *Ex P. Troncalli Chrysler Plymouth Dodge, Inc In re David J. Case v Alexander Dodge Chrysler Plymouth, Inc.*, 876 So.2d 459, Ala., 12 September 2003.

270 *Ex P. Troncalli Chrysler Plymouth Dodge, Inc.*, ibid at p.465.

271 Other cases which illustrate the point that mere accessibility would not establish jurisdiction ; *Drucker Cornell v Assicurazioni General SpA Consolidates* SDNY No.98-CIV 9186 16 March 2000, *Telebyte Inc.*, and *Enterprise Rent-A-Car v Stowell* Ed.Mo. No.4:00CV0555 TCM 5 April 2001 (where there was no communication or contract via email with the plaintiff). See also *V'soske Inc. v Vsoske.com* SDNY No.00 CIV 6099 (DC) 23 May 2001 where the District Court for the Southern District of New York held that the court could not assert jurisdiction on the basis that a New York resident could access the Irish defendant's web site. A further reason for refusing jurisdiction was that there were no contracts with residents in New York on the basis of non-compliance with the long arm statute (as opposed to purposeful availment as in other cases).

272 Yagura, 'Does Cyberspace Expand the Boundaries of Personal Jurisdiction?' at p.310 *et seq*.

273 *Panavision Intl L P v Dennis Toeppen*, 938 F. Supp.616 (C.D. Cal., 1996), aff'd 141 F.3d 1316 (9th Cir. 1998). Dearing, 'Personal Jurisdiction and the Internet: Can the Traditional Principles and Landmark Cases Guide the Legal System into the 21st Century?'

three part test to establish specific jurisdiction not only on the basis of the web site but also that 'something more' was evident, i.e. that the defendant knew that harm would occur in California.[274] The requirements for purposeful availment in *Panavision* were re-confirmed in *American Hondo Motor Co Inc. v Rinkied Inc.*[275] The defendant's web site generated business in the forum state (California) when more than eighty residents contracted with the defendant. The dispute however concerned a trademark infringement and the court held that it had jurisdiction since the defendants had purposefully availed themselves in the forum. The court referred to the *Panavision* case requirements for purposeful availment, the defendant's activities in the forum and the jurisdiction of the court and held since the defendant made no other attempts to advertise in California their web site was regarded as having generated the business. The 'effects test,' has re-emerged[276] in recent decisions to clarify further the extent to which a business has purposefully availed itself by its conduct in the forum state. For example, the requirement for 'something more' was expressly confirmed by the Fourth Circuit Court of Appeal in *Carefirst of Maryland Inc. d/b/a Carefirst Blue Cross/Blue Shield v Carefirst Pregnancy Centers Inc. d/b/a Carefirst and Netimpact Inc* which will be considered later.[277] Furthermore, Rule 4(k)(2) of the Federal Rule of Civil Procedure has also recently been used as a basis of federal jurisdiction over an out of state defendant. As will be considered later in this Chapter, the case *Graduate Management Admission Council v Raju*, demonstrates how 'Rule 4(k)(2)'s most obvious application [...] permit[s] specific jurisdiction over foreign defendants who have 'minimum contacts' with the entire United States [...] [T]his was the purpose for which Rule 4(k)(2) was specifically intended.'[278] The federal courts can apply Rule 4(k)(2) on two conditions. Firstly, it can be used when a state court cannot assert personal jurisdiction. Secondly, it can only be used when the dispute relates to federal law. The extent to which the potential future application of Rule 4(k)(2) to electronic commerce disputes could be utilised will be considered later.

274 Subsequently considered in *Healthgrades.com* case, and expressly confirmed by the Fourth Circuit Court of Appeal, *Carefirst of Maryland Inc. d/b/a Carefirst Blue Cross/ Blue Shield v Carefirst Pregnancy Centers Inc. d/b/a Carefirst and Netimpact Inc.* (CA-01-1578-CCB) 2 July 2003, considered later.

275 *American Hondo Motor Co Inc. v Rinkied* C.D. Cal. CV 98-7315 DDP 3 March 1999.

276 Siddiqi asserts that most jurisdictional issues were controlled by *Calder v Jones* which now is used mostly for intellectual property disputes; 'Welcome to the City of Bytes? at p.68. Green confirmed that (previously) the effects test was used in a 'fairly narrow' way by the courts to 'intellectual property and intentional tort claims'; 'Is Zippo's Sliding Scale a Slippery Slope of Uncertainty?' at p.1062.

277 *Carefirst.*

278 Born, *International Civil Litigation in United States Courts*, at p.196. Word in bracket modified.

Summary

In the absence of specific national (or international) guidance on jurisdiction for electronic commerce disputes, the courts in the United States have applied[279] the 'Sliding Scale' or the 'effects' tests to determine if jurisdiction has been established against a foreign business that operates a web site. However the test of personal jurisdiction is challenged in the context of electronic commerce. The reasons for this include firstly that the Supreme Court had not affirmed the 'Sliding Scale' test and secondly that the scale itself is by no means all encompassing.[280] A consideration of subsequent cases will demonstrate that even at the most active end of the spectrum, such activities are not in themselves always sufficient to assert specific personal jurisdiction over a foreign defendant.[281] Probasco maintains 'interactivity serves little or no purpose.' With respect, this view is at odds with the nature and purpose of electronic commerce to facilitate cross-border marketing activities and instantaneous communication. In the same paper, Probasco then stresses that if a business operating a web site now necessitates that the business targeted residents in a particular state, the level of activity (together with other factors and an intention) will contribute towards determining personal jurisdiction. From the analysis of the cases, the test of minimum contacts is most concerned with the intention and impact of the web site activity towards the forum state no matter whether the defendant is located in another state or country. Thereafter the remainder of this book will briefly consider the analogous issues of whether jurisdiction can be established where a web site is physically located and the role and effect of choice of forum clauses[282] before assessing the impact of the trends from recent cases that have questioned the need for adaptation of the 'Sliding Scale' test.

279 *Panavision*, where the court said, '(W)e are asked to apply existing rules of personal jurisdiction to conduct that occurred, in part, in "cyberspace."'

280 The 'Sliding Scale' has not gone without its critics, e.g. particular contributions to the Consumer Project on Technology's newsgroups on the Hague Conference's proposed judgments convention (which can be found at <http://www.cptech.org/ecom/jurisdiction/hague.html>) expressed the opinion that these tests do not make adequate reference to the actual technology used. See Green, 'Is Zippo's Sliding Scale a Slippery Slope of Uncertainty?'; *Hurley v Cancun Playa*, E.D.Pa. 99–574 31 August 1999 and Geist, 'Is There a There? Towards Greater Certainty for Internet Jurisdiction.'

281 Probasco, 'Due Process Analysis in *Millennium Enterprises, Inc v Millennium Music*, LP,' at p.467.

282 Millstein, Neuburger and Weingart, *Doing Business on the Internet Forms and Analysis*, at p.11–11.

Chapter 9

Adaptation of Personal Jurisdiction Rules for Electronic Consumer Contracts in the United States

Introduction – Activities of an Out-of-State Defendant's Web Site: Adapting Zippo's 'Sliding Scale'[1]

Minimum Contacts and 'Interactive' Web Sites

Despite many cases establishing the degree of web site interactivity combined with other factors required for 'Due Process,' an 'ambiguous concern'[2] remains with the 'Sliding Scale' test. According to Westermeier, the 'most troublesome' aspect of the 'Sliding Scale' is that it has only been concerned with extremes of web site activity. Geist similarly refers to the 'Sliding Scale' as a 'passive-active' test. Accordingly, the court's decisions to assert jurisdiction or not have, in the majority of instances,[3] been premised on *both* the nature of web site activity *and* other factors demonstrating *quality* of contact with residents in the forum. It is submitted that the most important factor now (in addition to the level of web site activity) is demonstrating the business' *intention to target* commercial activity in a particular jurisdiction, in line with the decisions in *Asahi* and *ALS Scan*. For example, the combination of the interactive web site and the defendant's conduct via its web site and newspapers in the forum were sufficient to demonstrate persistent conduct in *Heroes, Inc. v Heroes Foundation.*[4] Similarly, the US District Court of Massachusetts in *Hasbro, Inc. v Clue Computing, Inc.*,[5] held that specific personal jurisdiction could be upheld over a trademark dispute since the defendant

---

1 Sections of this Chapter were recently published in L.E. Gillies, 'Addressing the "Cyberspace Fallacy": Targeting the Jurisdiction of an Electronic Consumer Contract' (2008) 2 *Int Journal Law and Inf Tech*, 1.

2 Stott, 'Personal Jurisdiction in Cyberspace,' at p.843.

3 *Starmedia Network Inc. v Star Media Inc.*, SDNY case No.00 CIV 4647 23 April 2001, distinguished from the *Cybersell* case. In *Starmedia*, it was held that the web site was interactive, with minimum contacts and purposeful availment established in New York even though no contracts were entered into in the forum.

4 *Heroes, Inc. v Heroes Foundation,* 958 F.Supp. 1, 14 (D.D C.1996).

5 *Hasbro, Inc. v Clue Computing, Inc.*, 994 F. Supp. 34 (D. Mass. 1997).

advertised for customers from all states. In *Clipp Designs v Tag Bags*,[6] jurisdiction was established since in addition to advertising, the defendant business could obtain orders via their web site. Other examples of an interactive web site establishing jurisdiction were demonstrated by *Blumenthal v Drudge*[7] where the District Court for Columbia District held that since the defendant 'had an interactive web site ... accessible [in the forum] ... and, in addition ... sufficient non-Internet related contacts,'[8] the exercise of jurisdiction was reasonable. In *People Solutions Inc. v People Solutions Inc.*[9] (a trademark infringement case), the Northern District of Texas held that there was no purposeful availment even though the defendant had, in accordance with *Zippo*, an interactive or 'middle ground' web site.[10] The court followed the Fifth Circuit in *Mink* and held that there were no repeated contacts to justify specific personal jurisdiction. Furthermore, the court confirmed that jurisdiction cannot be premised on a 'mere possibility, with nothing more that the defendant may be able to do business with [forum residents] over its web site. '[11] This case reinforces the importance of a contract to *ALS Scan*'s intentional targeting test which will be considered later. In the more recent case *Washington State Department of Revenue v <www.dirtcheapcig.com> Inc.*,[12] the Washington District court confirmed that the sale of goods via an interactive web site by a Missouri defendant, in accordance with *Stomp Inc. v NeatO LLC*,[13] satisfied purposeful availment. The test of 'Due Process' was also satisfied on the premise that there was a sufficient connection between the contacts in the forum and the dispute to support specific personal jurisdiction as reasonable.

As the following cases on interactive web sites show, the quality and nature of the *defendant's* contacts are imperative to the courts' analysis and reasoning when determining either general or specific jurisdiction. In *Resuscitation Technologies Inc v Continental Health Care Corp.* ,[14] the court held that the defendants ought to be subject to the personal jurisdiction of the courts even though they did not have offices in the jurisdiction, nor conducted business there. The court

---

6 *Clipp Designs v Tag Bags* 996 F. Supp. 766 (N.D. Ill. 1998).

7 *Blumenthal.* Rice, 'A Cyberspace Odyssey Through US and EU Internet Jurisdiction,' Practising Law Institute, Patents, Trademarks and Literary Property Course Handbook Series, Fifth Annual Internet Law Institute, New York 9-10th July 2001, San Francisco, 23-24 July 2001: 421.

8 Blumenthal, ibid at p.56.

9 *People Solutions.*

10 *People Solutions*, ibid at p.3.

11 *People Solutions*, ibid at p.4 and *Mink.*

12 Recently referred to by the US District Court for the Southern District of New York in *City of New York v Cyco.Net, Inc.*, Slip Copy, 2005 WL 174482, RICO Bus.Disp. Guide 10, 824, S.D.N.Y., 27 January 2005.

13 *Stomp Inc. v NeatO LLC*, 61 F.Supp. 2d 1074, 1078, n.7 (C.D.Cal.1999).

14 *Resuscitation Technologies Inc v Continental Health Care Corp* IP 96-1457 – C-M/S, 1997 US Dist Lexis 3523 (So. Dist. Indiana 24 March 1997) 1997 WL 148567 (S.D Ind 24 March 1997).

based their decision on the emails (eighty in total) and telephone conversations that the defendants had with an Indiana resident to form a company there. The defendant's web site was held to be interactive. The question thereafter was whether the defendant's actions were in accordance with 'Due Process.' The court used the 'Sliding Scale' and again was concerned with the quality of the activities in relation to the activity in question. In *International Star Registry v Bowman-Haight Ventures, Inc.*,[15] the US District Court for the Northern District of Illinois held that the defendants were subject to the jurisdiction of the court since they sold defective goods to residents in that state. Again, the court upheld the *Zippo* 'Sliding Scale' and to determine purposeful availment, the court reiterated the importance of the defendant's quality of contacts with the forum. In *American Eyewear Inc. v Peepers Sunglasses*[16] the Federal District Court in the Northern District of Texas considered the jurisdictional analysis in the *Mink* case to determine whether the state's long arm statute and 'Due Process' tests were satisfied in a dispute involving the defendant's[17] web site. The court held that the defendant's web site fell into the middle of the 'Sliding Scale', and referred to the Fifth Circuit's decision in *Ruston Gas Turbines v Donaldson Company Inc.*,[18] on the extent to which the gestalt factors satisfied the test of reasonableness. The District Court for the Northern District of Texas upheld the *American Eyewear* case in *Carrot Bunch Co., Inc. v Computer Friends, Inc.*[19] In *Carrot Bunch*, the court held purposeful availment was satisfied since the defendant's 'website sen[t] an e-mail confirmation of purchase to those customers who provide[d] their e-mail addresses. This direct contact result[ed] in an exchange of information between the website and the consumers who order[ed] the inkjet printer cartridges.'[20] The court was satisfied that the sales constituted something more, in comparison to the mere possibility of sales in *People Solutions*.[21] These decisions demonstrate how significant the existence of communication or a contract between the parties is to the 'Due Process' enquiry. Indeed, sufficient communication and the existence of a contract are strong indicators of the foreign business' intention to contract with a consumer in the forum.

The search for facts demonstrating qualitative contacts has also been evident in cases seeking to establish *general* personal jurisdiction. The following two

15 *International Star Registry v Bowman-Haight Ventures, Inc.*, 1999 U.S. Dist. LEXIS 7009 (N.D. Ill. 1999).

16 *American Eyewear Inc. v Peepers Sunglasses*, 106 F.Supp. 2d 895, 901 (N.D.Tex.2000).

17 The defendant was a subsidiary of Eyecity.com but jurisdiction was not established over that company since it did not make continuous and substantial contacts in Texas.

18 *Ruston Gas Turbines Inc.*

19 *Carrot Bunch Co., Inc. v Computer Friends, Inc.*, 218 F.Supp. 2d 820, N.D.Tex., 14 August 2002.

20 *Carrot Bunch*, at p.826. Words modified for syntax.

21 *People Solutions*.

examples confirmed the Third Circuit's endorsement of the 'Sliding Scale' test. The first case, *Desktop Technologies, Inc. v ColorWorks Reproduction & Design*,[22] considered what other factors demonstrate contacts with the forum. The Third Circuit court mentioned the Superior Court case *Efford v The Jockey Club*[23] that considered the 'Sliding Scale' and concluded that even though the web site was passive (since the order form was accessible online but could not be submitted online), there were still insufficient additional factors to establish purposeful availment. The defendants did not have an office or property in the forum, nor did they have agents or employees or pay taxes in the jurisdiction either.[24] Despite web users' ability to interact with the business, it was not sufficient for minimum contacts in *Efford v the Jockey Club*.[25] The Superior Court held that the web site was interactive in accordance with the 'Sliding Scale' and satisfied the long arm statute but did not satisfy the 'Due Process' minimum contacts requirement. The reasons for this were premised on the facts that the plaintiffs were not sent information by email and the defendant was not regarded as targeting Pennsylvanian residents. Both the *Desktop* and *Efford* cases were subsequently followed by the Superior Court of Pennsylvania in *Mar-Eco, Inc. v T & R and Sons Towing and Recovery, Inc.*[26] In that case, whilst the web site was 'undisputedly'[27] interactive, the court had to be satisfied that 'something more' existed for jurisdiction. The court was satisfied that the quality of contact operable via the defendant's web site was more than adequate for general personal jurisdiction. In the second example, *Molnlycke Healthcare AB v Dumex Medical Surgical Procedures*,[28] the existence of an interactive web site available in Pennsylvania did not mean however that the defendant had demonstrated continuous and systematic contacts with the forum[29] to satisfy the requirement for general personal jurisdiction. The court was not prepared to hold that such sites (where goods could be ordered) could expose businesses to general personal jurisdiction. The court said that *Zippo*'s 'Sliding Scale' test could be used to establish general as well as specific jurisdiction, but affirmed that a high standard was still required to establish general jurisdiction.

22 *Desktop Technologies, Inc.*

23 *Robert and Lauren Efford t/a Goldhope Farm v The Jockey Club*, 2002 Pa.Super. LEXIS 462, 796 A.2d 370, 375 (2002).

24 Both this case and the decision in *S. Morantz Inc. v Hang & Shire Ultrasonics, Inc.* ((1999) U.S. Dist. LEXIS 19412 (E.D. Pa. 1999) where the web site of the defendant enabled customers to download an enquiry form but this was not enough for personal jurisdiction) below were subsequently referred to in *Accuweather Inc. v Total Weather Inc*, M.D Pa. No.4:DV-02-0006 2 October 2002.

25 *Efford v The Jockey Club*.

26 *Mar-Eco, Inc. v T & R and Sons Towing and Recovery, Inc.*, 837 A.2d 512, 2003 PA Super 444, Pa.Super., 19 November 2003.

27 *Mar-Eco Inc.*, ibid at p.517.

28 *Molnlycke Healthcare AB v Dumex Medical Surgical Procedures* No. CIV. A. 99-1725 64 F.Supp. 2d 448 7 September 1999.

29 *Molnlycke Healthcare AB*, ibid at p.453.

Despite advances in technology, the court was not satisfied that 'general personal jurisdiction could be established *solely by the existence of web sites such as these*.'[30]

The decision in *Molnlycke* was affirmed in *Snyder v Dolphin Encounters Ltd.*,[31] where the court reconfirmed the high standard that had to be met to establish general personal jurisdiction. The District of Columbia Circuit held that the web site in *Gorman d/b/a Cashbackrealty.com v Ameritrade Holding Corporation and freetrade.com Inc.*[32] was in between the passive and interactive distinction. The court considered whether the defendant was doing business in the forum and confirmed 'doing business [in accordance with the District of Columbia long arm statute] is co-extensive with the reach of constitutional due process.' Since the web site enabled parties to contract online it held that conduct was 'continuous and systematic' premised on the 'examination of frequency and volume of the firm's transactions with District residents.' Meanwhile in both *Hurley v Cancun Playa Oasis International Hotel*[33] and *Coastal Video Communications v Staywell Corp.* ,[34] the court held that the *potential to contact* residents in a forum was not sufficient even though the web site was interactive,[35] contacts had to be 'continuous and systematic' to demonstrate the defendant's actual contact with residents in the forum to establish general personal jurisdiction. 'The mere existence of an interactive web site, without proof that there was continuous and systematic contact between the forum state and web site, is not sufficient for a court to exercise general jurisdiction.'[36] A similar case was *Dagesse v Plant Hotel NV*.[37] In *Dagesse*, the District Court for New Hampshire was asked to consider whether the business specifically directed its activities to the forum for the purposes of establishing jurisdiction.[38] The court held that the plaintiffs did not use the defendant's web site before the parties' dispute arose. Whilst the court did not approve *Zippo* – it deemed it applied to extreme cases – it nevertheless regarded the defendant's web site as falling in the middle of that spectrum. However, since the plaintiffs had not accessed the defendant's web site before the dispute, the court held that there were

30 *Molnlycke Healthcare AB*, ibid at p.455. Italics added for emphasis.

31 *Snyder v Dolphin Encounters Ltd.*, E.D. Pa. No.02-CV-1264 10 December 2002. In *Snyder*, the plaintiff sought to assert jurisdiction over the defendant as the defendants received payment for their services from the plaintiff via an agent in the forum.

32 *Gorman d/b/a Cashbackrealty.com v Ameritrade Holding Corporation and Freetrade.com Inc.*, 293 F.3d 506, 513 (D.C.Cir.2002).

33 *Hurley*.

34 *Coastal Video Communications v Staywell Corp.*, 1999 U.S. Dist. LEXIS 11827 (E.D. Va. 1999).

35 In addition to the interactive nature of the web site, the court referred to the number of hits on the web site and the volume of business.

36 *Coastal Video Communications,* at p.571.

37 *Dagesse v Plant Hotel NV* DNH No. CV-98-713-B 05/01/00 at p.1224.

38 Perhaps in response to the difficulties or a lack of preference for the 'Sliding Scale' test.

insufficient facts to uphold the requirement of 'relatedness' for specific personal jurisdiction. The ruling in *Dagesse* confirms that in addition to the level of activity of the web site, the plaintiff must have accessed the web site in order to associate the business' web site activities with a particular jurisdiction. This point is important as it demonstrates the different approaches in the EU and US on the need for relatedness between the business' commercial activities and the dispute. As the chapter on the Brussels 1 Regulation observed, it should only be necessary that the business' web site was intended for consumers in that jurisdiction before the parties' contracted with each other. Purposeful availment is more important than relatedness for 'Due Process.' In accordance with the court's approach in *Digital Equipment*, if the business intended to 'target'[39] particular states via an interactive web site, the lack of *prior* contact should not prevent purposeful availment from being established provided the business intended to target consumers in the forum and the parties have subsequently contracted with each other. The level of web site activity is entirely under the selection, direction and control of a business. As Rice explains, an interactive web site is 'used by the operator to conduct transactions with persons in the forum state, receiving on-line orders and posting confirmation or other messages directly to specific customers.'[40]

If the business intended to contract with consumers in particular jurisdictions, its contacts with consumers in different fora must not, as *Burger King* affirmed, be 'random, fortuitous or attenuated.'[41] Therefore if the business has chosen to operate its business activities via an interactive web site, and a contract is subsequently concluded with a consumer in a foreign jurisdiction via another means of communication (for example, email, telephone or fax message), purposeful availment should be established.

The 'primary analysis' of 'Due Process' in *Dagesse* was reaffirmed by the Supreme Court of New Hampshire in *Metcalf v Lawson*[42] and again in *The Lyme Timber Co. v DSF Investors LLC.*[43] In *Metcalf*, the Supreme Court of New Hampshire held that the case was an 'isolated' situation as it involved conduct on a public auction site (Ebay) as opposed to considering the level of activity of a private business' own web site. The *Metcalf* case raised a significant point. It confirmed the application of *Compuserve v Paterson* test that the defendant has to have 'knowingly contracted' in the forum by 'directed activities' at the forum or by 'engaging in ongoing commercial relationship through the use of the

39 *Digital Equipment*, at p.472.

40 Rice, 'A Cyberspace Odyssey Through US and EU Internet Jurisdiction,' Practising Law Institute, Patents, Trademarks and Literary Property Course Handbook Series, Fifth Annual Internet Law Institute, New York 9–10 July 2001, San Francisco, 23–24 July 2001: 421 at p.464.

41 *Burger King*.

42 *Metcalf v Lawson*, 148 N.H. 35, 802 A.2d 1221, N.H., 25 June 2002.

43 *The Lyme Timber Co. v DSF Investors LLC,* 150 N.H. 557, 842 A.2d 115, N.H., 17 February 2004.

Internet.'[44] Since the defendant in *Metcalf* did not know who would bid for the goods she was selling, and where those bidders were situated, she was not deemed to have purposefully availed herself of doing business in New Hampshire via a public auction web site. The *Metcalf* case implicitly illustrates the significance of foreseeable and intended targeting in accordance with *ALS Scan Inc.* and *Graduate Management Admission Council v Raju.*[45] In the latter case, the court confirmed that in order '(T)o determine whether an "interactive" website is grounds for personal jurisdiction, a court must consider the "level of interactivity and the commercial nature of the exchange of information that occurs on the Web site."'[46] In *The Lyme Timber Co.*, the Supreme Court of New Hampshire confirmed that since the defendant's web site was interactive *and* the defendant had 'directed its communications to [the plaintiff] … the alleged impact cannot be said to be fortuitous … [and that the defendant] availed itself of the privileges and protections of New Hampshire law.'[47] In *Wise, et al. v Lindamood, et al.*,[48] the Canadian defendant's web site that enabled viewers to request materials and information as well as registering for services was deemed mid way and moderately interactive on the 'Sliding Scale' by the District Court of Colorado. The court also took into account the requirement that the plaintiff had to provide a contact email address to be able to communicate with the business. By considering both the web site's activity in the forum and other contacts that demonstrated the business' intention, the court held that general jurisdiction had been established.

In *Millennium Enterprises, Inc. v Millennium Music, L.P,*[49] a South Carolinian business sold compact discs and jurisdiction was sought as result of one compact disc being sold in the forum. The court held that it could not accept jurisdiction in this case since the defendant's contacts were clearly not deemed systematic and continuous for general jurisdiction with the result that there was no purposeful availment to attach specific jurisdiction to the defendant's conduct. In line with the Ninth Circuit, the *Millennium* case endorsed the *Zippo* 'Sliding Scale' of web site activity but stressed that in accordance with *Cybersell* 'something more' was necessary if the constitutional requirement of 'Due Process'[50] was also to be satisfied. For example, actual sales to residents in the forum or a site more *specifically targeted* at that forum state[51] would constitute something more. Indeed, the fact that the plaintiff has simply bought one compact disc in an attempt

44 *Compuserve.*

45 *Graduate Management.*

46 *Graduate Management,* ibid at 594.

47 *The Lyme Timber Co.*, at p.120.

48 *Wise et al. v Lindamood, et al.*, 89 F. Supp. 2d. 1187 (D. Col. 1999)

49 *Millennium Enterprises, Inc. v Millennium Music, L.P.* 33 F.Supp. 2d 907 (D. Or. 1999). A.R. Probasco, 'Due Process Analysis in Millennium Enterprises, Inc v Millennium Music, LP' (2000) 40 *Jurimetrics* 457.

50 Probasco, ibid at p.464 *et seq*.

51 Probasco, ibid.

to establish jurisdiction[52] did not demonstrate that the defendants has purposefully availed themselves of the protection of the forum. In particular, the court said that:

> … the middle interactive category of Internet contacts as described in Zippo needs further refinement to include the fundamental requirement of personal jurisdiction: 'deliberate action' within the forum state in the form of transactions between the defendant and residents of the forum or conduct of the defendant purposefully directed at residents of the forum state.[53]

Probasco has commented that the *Millennium* case 'failed to acknowledge the *unimportance* of web site level of interactivity.'[54] However, with respect, the *Millennium* case demonstrates that had there been additional activity such as sales in the forum, jurisdiction would have been established. For that reason, the *Millennium* case demonstrates how significant a business' intention is in establishing purposeful availment.

In addition to the quality of the defendant's contacts, the *plaintiff's actual use* of the defendant's interactive web site has also been indicative of the quality of contacts with persons in the forum state. The following cases demonstrate that as part of the 'something more' analysis, the courts are not inclined to assert jurisdiction if there is an ambiguity regarding the business' intention to target particular jurisdictions *and* the plaintiff has not accessed the defendant's web site. In *Deckler v Circus Circus Hotels* personal jurisdiction could not be exercised in New Jersey for two reasons. Firstly, the court was not satisfied that the defendant's national advertising demonstrated an intention to purposefully avail itself in New Jersey. Secondly, the plaintiffs had not demonstrated that they had accessed the business' web site. For example, the plaintiff had not made her reservation online. Thirdly, there was a choice of forum clause in favour of Nevada on the defendant's web site. In *Uncle Sams Safari Outfitters Inc v Uncle Sams Army Navy Outfitters Manhattan Inc*[55] the web site was potentially interactive but jurisdiction was not upheld since there was no evidence that it was accessed in Missouri. The Eastern District Missouri Court confirmed that something more was needed than the mere existence of a web site. Since the defendant intended that its interactive web site could be accessed in the forum, personal jurisdiction could be established. However, the court distinguished *Maritz* since the defendant had no other contact with residents in the state. Therefore, if the consumer wishes to assert jurisdiction over a business premised on its interactive web site, evidence of the plaintiff's

52 In that case a friend of the plaintiff's lawyer made the purchase.

53 *Millennium*, at p.921.

54 Probasco, 'Due Process Analysis in Millennium Enterprises, Inc v Millennium Music, LP,' at p.468. Word italicised for emphasis.

55 *Uncle Sam's Safari Outfitters Inc v Uncle Sam's Army Navy Outfitters Manhattan Inc.*, E.D.Mo CV 1633 DDN 13 April 2000.

use of the web site will, and should, contribute towards satisfying purposeful availment.

Further assertion of the significance of the plaintiff's use of the web site to demonstrate 'something more' was confirmed in *Advanced Software Inc. v Datapharm Inc.*[56] Even though the defendant operated an interactive web site which could be accessed in California, the US District Court for the Central District of California said that it did not have jurisdiction in the trade mark infringement case unless there was evidence that the site was used in the forum i.e. 'something more' (as in *Panavision* and *Cybersell*) required in terms of 'Due Process.' Despite an interactive web site that contained a hyper-link and a free telephone number, the court followed *Mink* and held that unless the plaintiffs had actually used the web site, the defendant had not purposefully availed itself of doing business in the forum. The court concluded, '(I)t should be of no consequence that a site is interactive unless it is shown that people within the forum state have utilized the interactive features of the site.' The court's opinion was grounded in the prevention of every web site accessible (thereby refuting mere accessibility) in the forum rendering a business subject to the jurisdiction of that forum and protection of the business' prerogative to do business with others domiciled in different states.

Finally, application of the effects test has also begun to emerge with respect to an interactive web site. In the *iAccess Inc v Webcard Technologies Inc,*[57] case, the US District Court for Utah granted a motion to dismiss the plaintiff's claim on the validity of a patent. The court held that as the web site was moderately interactive, it was 'insufficient to subject it to court's personal jurisdiction.'[58] The decision in the *iAccess* case confirmed that the plaintiff had to demonstrate a sufficient 'nexus'[59] between the defendant's specifically directed activities and the forum in accordance with *Asahi* and *Calder*.[60] The court was not satisfied that, in accordance with *Millennium Enterprises*, the defendant had targeted Utah residents or that Utah residents had interacted with the defendant's web site.[61] Therefore, as far as interactive web sites are concerned, the nexus required between the foreign business' web site and jurisdiction of the parties' dispute must be premised on the business' intention to target consumers in particular jurisdictions, the nature of the web site, any exchange of communication and the existence of a contract between the parties.

56 *Advanced Software Inc. v Datapharm Inc.* C.D Cal. No. CV 98-5943 DDP 3 November 1998.

57 *iAccess Inc v Webcard Technologies Inc*, 182 F. Supp. 2d 1183, 24 January 2002.

58 Ibid.

59 *iAccess*, note 57 supra at p.1189. M. J. Lockerby, 'Non-Contractual Legal Problems' (1999) IBL 244.

60 *iAccess*, note 57 supra at p.1186.

61 *iAccess*, note 57 supra at pp. 1187–1188.

Minimum Contacts and 'Active' Web Sites

If the 'passive-active' or 'Sliding Scale' test focuses only on extremes of web site activity, the courts would only be concerned with determining the level of such activity for purposeful availment. The following cases demonstrate that despite evidence of a high level of web site activity, the courts consider traditional advertising or other contacts as much when determining that the business has demonstrated purposeful availment. In *International Star Registry v Bowman-Haight Ventures, Inc.*,[62] the court considered whether long arm jurisdiction was permitted. Since the defendant's web sites were available to view in the United States, the plaintiff alleged that there was a 'false association' between the parties. Despite 'little appellate authority' and inconsistent district court decisions, the court upheld jurisdiction in accordance with *Zippo* and *Maritz*. In *Quokka Sports v Cup Int'l. Ltd.*,[63] the plaintiffs sought to restrict the New Zealand defendants' use of the domain name <www.americascup. com>. The defendants were regarded as actively directing business activities to US consumers in a number of ways. Firstly, the defendants used a domain name that infringed the plaintiff's licence with America's Cup Properties Inc. Secondly, the defendants had used a variety of different marketing techniques targeting US customers and had contracted with advertisers in a number of states, including the forum. The District Court for the Northern District of California held that the defendants were actively seeking business in the forum and that purposeful availment had been met. The case was recently referred to by the *Mashantucket Pequot Tribe v Redican*,[64] where the Connecticut District Court was also satisfied that the defendants had purposefully availed themselves by the combination of their interactive web site and traditional forms of contacts (i.e. advertising) in the forum.

The intention of a business to obtain sales in the forum can be demonstrated when it provides services online via its web site. If a consumer subscribes to an online service and pays a subscription or membership fee, purposeful availment will be established. For example, in *Online Partners.com Inc. v Atlanticnet Media Corp,*[65] the court held that the business' web site had been actively directed towards San Francisco. The defendants advertised and offered subscription services to residents in the forum, thereby demonstrating a high level of activity to satisfy purposeful availment in accordance with *Zippo*'s 'Sliding Scale.' In *Digital Equipment Corp. v Altavista Technology Inc.*,[66] the court had to determine

---

62 *International Star Registry v Bowman-Haight Ventures, Inc.*, 1998 U.S. Dist. LEXIS 10459 (E.D.Va. 1998).

63 *Quokka Sports v Cup Int'l. Ltd.*, 1999 U.S. Dist. LEXIS 21000 (N.D. Cal. 1999).

64 *Mashantucket Pequot Tribe v Redican*, 309 F.Supp. 2d 309, 70 U.S.P.Q.2d 1549, D.Conn., 18 March 2004.

65 *Online Partners.com Inc. v Atlanticnet Media Corp.* , 2000 U.S. Dist. LEXIS 783 (N.D. Cal. 2000).

66 *Digital Equipment.*

whether a dispute concerning a breach of trademark by Alta Vista could satisfy both Massachusett's long arm statute and constitutional 'Due Process.' The court held that there were sufficient facts to support both tests as Alta Vista's web site contained the Alta Vista trademark which was also used in Digital's web site (as permitted by the prior agreement between the parties) and which over time would have required Alta Vista to defend any claim in that state.

The District Court for the Eastern District of Michigan in *Audi AG v Izumi*[67] held that the web site constituted minimum contacts in the forum to establish jurisdiction. The plaintiffs disputed the defendants' use of the domain name in the defendant's web site and claimed that it breached their trademark. In order to determine personal jurisdiction, the parties had to be able to contract with the defendants via their web site. The court confirmed that since the state's long arm statute permitted a 'broad' application of the 'Due Process' requirement, the three tests for 'Due Process' had to be satisfied. The court held that these tests were satisfied; the defendants had purposefully availed themselves by doing business in the forum via an interactive web site,[68] thereby linking the dispute with the forum and rendering jurisdiction reasonable. This case was subsequently relied on by the Eastern District of Michigan Court in *Audi AG and Volkswagen of America, Inc. v D'Amato.*[69] In that case, the court held that ability of consumers in the forum to 'purchase services and products on the web site'[70] was sufficient for purposeful availment.

In addition to actual sales via active web sites constituting purposeful availment, other interactive features on a business' web site have demonstrated 'something more' for purposeful availment. It is submitted that these features are akin to actual sales since they demonstrate the business' intention to communicate and contract with residents in particular jurisdictions. The plaintiffs in the case *Computeruser.com Inc. v Technology Publications LLC*[71] sued Texan defendants for using their trademark in breach of the licensing agreement between the parties. They also sought an injunction against the defendants from using that trademark.[72] The U.S District Court for the District of Minnesota held that the defendant's web site was sufficiently active to permit jurisdiction in the forum. The web site ('Sexist Geek Alive') contained several interactive features available to users including email accounts and message boards. The court considered the 'Due Process' requirement and compared the case to *Burger King*: the existence of the agreement between the parties permitted jurisdiction. Furthermore, in comparison with the

67 *Audi AG v Izumi,* E.D Mich No.01-CV-74520-DT, 23 May 2002.

68 Akin to *Cybersell Inc. v Cybersell Inc.*

69 *Audi AG and Volkswagen of America, Inc. v D'Amato* 341 F.Supp. 2d 734, E.D.Mich., 19 October 2004 at p.744.

70 *Audi*, ibid.

71 *Computeruser.com Inc. v Technology Publications LLC,* D.Minn., Civil File No. 02-832 (MJD/JGL) 20 July 2002.

72 The trademark was 'Computer Geek.'

Mink case, the quality of the defendant's contact with the forum via their web site also satisfied the minimum contacts requirement. However, in *Accuweather Inc. v Total Weather Inc.*[73] a web site that included an email facility was not sufficient alone for minimum contacts. Before transferring the case to a District Court in the defendant's state (Oklahoma), the US District Court for the Middle District of Pennsylvania considered the earlier cases *Desktop Technologies* and *S. Morantz.*[74] The court affirmed the decision in *Desktop* that there needed to be 'something more' than use of another business' trademark as a name for a web site. The case *Multi Tech Systems Inc. v Net 2 Phone Inc.*[75] serves as a reminder of the need to demonstrate a link between the business activities and the dispute in question. The US District Court for the Federal District of Minnesota held that contacts with Minnesota residents and visits to Minnesota constituted minimum contacts. In reaching its decision that the web site was active, the court considered the 'Sliding Scale' and *Maritz*. The court also pointed to a range of activities in the state which supported a link between the contact made and the dispute in question that passed the reasonableness test. If a business provides facilities such as an order form, email account or message board that can be used and accessed by parties in different jurisdictions to communicate with the business, such activity demonstrates the business' prior intention to target and contract with residents, such as consumers, in the forum.

More recent cases involving active web sites have demonstrated an increasing trend of the courts to examine whether the defendant undertook some kind of targeted activity towards the forum, including the extent to which their web site contributed towards such activities. In the *Toys 'R' Us Inc et al v Step Two SA et al*,[76] the Court of Appeal for the Third Circuit confirmed that even if the defendant's web site was active, the crucial requirement is the defendant's purposeful availment of doing business in the jurisdiction for specific personal jurisdiction to be established. The court concurred with the decisions in *Cybersell* and the *ALS Scan* case where the court said that if a defendant

> direct[ed] electronic activity into the State, with the *manifest intent[ion]* of engaging in business or other interactions within the State *and that activity creat[ed] ... a potential cause of action ...*

---

73 *Accuweather Inc. v Total Weather Inc.*

74 Albeit in *Morantz*, the web site was not as active as the one in the instant case.

75 *Multi Tech Systems Inc. v Net 2 Phone Inc.*, Case 00-346 ADM/RLE.

76 *Toys 'R' Us Inc et al v Step Two SA et al* SA 3rd Cir. No. 01-3390 27 January 2003, followed by District Court of Rhode Island in *Swarovski Optik North America Ltd v Euro Optics Inc.*, 2003 WL 22014581, D.R.W., 25 August 2003 (Westlaw). Words in italics emphasised and words in brackets modified for syntax.

and jurisdiction could be established against him, or to put it another way, 'targeting.'[77] The court therefore reiterated that 'something more' than an active web site was necessary, suggesting that the defendant would have to have intentionally targeted residents in the forum. Interestingly, the court explained that whilst targeting could include either online or offline activities, the most important point was that the business' activities had to be targeted towards the forum state. In the recent case *Hartoy Inc. v Thompson d/b/a Truckin' Little Co.,*[78] the US District Court for the Southern District of Florida applied the 'Sliding Scale' test to determine if the defendant business from Wisconsin had sought out business from residents in Florida. The court held that the web site was active and in combination with (albeit only five) contracts with forum residents, the minimum contacts test jurisdiction was established over the defendant.

Summary of Minimum Contacts and Web Site Activities

The previous sections of this Chapter have considered how a court in a particular State can assert jurisdiction over a defendant when the parties have contracted via the WWW. It is now accepted by the lower US courts at least, that neither the mere accessibility of a web site nor a passive web site is enough to substantiate general or specific personal jurisdiction. By applying the 'Sliding Scale' the courts have sought to distinguish between different levels of web site activity. However as the cases have demonstrated, this is not the end of the analysis either, for *businesses* (and not web sites alone) must target the forum. Essentially, to ensure that the defendant's activities are localised in the forum as far as technology facilitates, the courts have considered a range of facts which may either tip the balance in favour of personal jurisdiction or otherwise. Whilst this may provide some consistency as a general approach, the truism remains that such analysis is entirely fact-reliant and lacking express endorsement from the Supreme Court. A business pursuing deceptive practices[79] over unsuspecting customers or consumers may be able to take advantage of such an approach by forum shopping and ensuring that as few connections with his online customers' state are made. In recent years the courts have considered approaches to personal jurisdiction beyond both *Zippo* and 'something more' espoused in *Compuserve*; possibly in a bid to promote e-commerce activity whilst reinforcing the constitutional requirement for 'Due

77 See an early reference to a business being subject to the jurisdiction of the forum where their business activities were intentionally directed. G.M. Kalow, 'From the Internet to Court: Exercising Jurisdiction Over World Wide Web Communications' (1997) 65 Fordham L.Rev. 2241 at p.2253.

78 *Hartoy Inc. v Thompson d/b/a Truckin' Little Co.,* S.D. Fla No.02-80454-CIV-Middlebrooks 29 January 2003; Gillies, ibid at p.21.

79 J. Rothchild, 'Protecting the Digital Consumer: The Limits of Cyberspace Utopianism' (1999) 74 *Ind LJ* 893 at p.897 *et seq*; Gillies, ibid.

Process.' Both the 'effects test' and 'targeting' whilst different,[80] share the same ends by seeking to demonstrate that the defendant's deliberate conduct towards the state renders him liable to the jurisdiction of the courts in that state. Indeed, as Salavado confirms, the 'combination' of those tests '*together form a formidable personal jurisdiction doctrine for use over cases involving Internet contacts*.'[81] Whilst Salvado argues that the modified 'Sliding Scale' test is akin to the effects test, the distinction Rice provides is even more effective. Rice confirms that the purpose of a web site is to '"target" residents of a given jurisdiction.' Rice argues that whilst a targeting test suggests 'an effort to specifically to reach persons in the forum,' the effects test 'might be produced within a given forum by acts that, at least on the surface, are not aimed there.'[82] Before the incorporation for intentional targeting in the 'Sliding Scale' test is considered, two smaller aspects to determining Internet jurisdiction ought to be considered from the perspective of contracts conducted online and consumer contracts.

Jurisdiction Where a Web Site Server is Located

As demonstrated earlier, the question of whether a web site's location could confer jurisdiction has yet to be determined by the European Court of Justice.[83] It should not be possible for jurisdiction to be conferred where the web server (or servers) is located.[84] To do so would certainly lead to forum shopping, for it would enable a business to select a web server or servers located in a jurisdiction with less favourable laws to the consumer. In *CFOS 2 GO Inc v CFO 2 GO Inc.*[85] it was not held sufficient to establish personal jurisdiction of a web site wherever it could be located simply because a draft client web site was posted by a web designer at the designer's own domain name. The case of *Amberson Holdings LLC v Westside Story Newspaper*[86] considered the jurisdictional position of a business' web server.

80 Rice, 'A Cyberspace Odyssey Through US and EU Internet Jurisdiction,' at p.437, 512 and 517.

81 C.J.R. Salvado, 'An Effective Personal Jurisdiction Doctrine For The Internet' (2003) 12 *U. Balt. Intell. Prop. L.J* 75: at p.80. Italics added for emphasis.

82 Rice, 'A Cyberspace Odyssey Through US and EU Internet Jurisdiction.'

83 Chapter Two above. See also Rothchild, 'Protecting the Digital Consumer: The Limits of Cyberspace Utopianism,' at p.981 *et seq*, where he says '(T)he location of the *parties* to a communication is far more relevant under traditional jurisdiction doctrine than is the location of the *computers* through which they communicate,' at p.982.

84 Chapter Two above.

85 *CFOS 2 GO Inc.*

86 *Amberson Holdings LLC v Westside Story Newspaper*, D.N.J, Civil Action No.00-1108 (NHP), 22 August 2000. R.J. Peach 'Dot-com's Host Server in N.J. Isn't a Foothold for Jurisdiction,' *New Jersey Law Journal*, http://www.law.com, 29 August 2000. L.E. Gillies, 'Adapting International Private Law Rules for Electronic Consumer Contracts,' in C.E.F. Rickett, and T.G.W. Telfer (eds), *International Perspectives on Consumers' Access to Justice* (Cambridge, 2003) at p.379.

Following this case, it is doubtful whether jurisdiction could be established over a business that uses a web server located in the forum. In *Amberson Holdings*, since the contract between the parties was a *de minimis* contract the court held that personal jurisdiction could not be found under the *International Shoe* minimum contacts test. This case demonstrates the likelihood of difficulties in satisfying the minimum contacts and fair play and substantial justice tests for jurisdiction premised on the location of a web server. Whilst the *Christian Science Board* case[87] regarded 'constitutional reasonableness' as a 'somewhat nebulous concept,' the court held that, in accordance with *International Shoe,* minimum contacts were not established at the place where the web server of a passive web site was located. The court held that when the host server transferred information to the web site this was akin to information being sent down a telephone line. By contrast in *Intercon v Bell Atlantic Internet Solutions Inc.*,[88] the US Court of Appeal for the Tenth Circuit upheld jurisdiction over an ISP based in Oklahoma. The defendant used an email server located in the forum which was deemed to be continuous use in accordance with *Compuserve* and *Zippo*. However, in *Jewish Defense Org., v Superior Court of Los Angeles*,[89] the contract with a Californian-based ISP was not sufficient to establish jurisdiction. In holding the web site as passive and referring to the 'effects test' in *Calder v Jones* to establish purposeful availment, the appeal decision overturned the earlier decision. In *Cable News Network v Go SMS.com Inc.*,[90] the question was whether the location of servers (in San Diego and Israel) used by Israeli defendant and Californian plaintiff established jurisdiction in New York. The US District Court of the Southern District of New York held that there was purposeful availment since the defendant sent information on services to New York residents. Meanwhile, the Californian Court of Appeal for the Second District in *Nam Tai Electronic Inc. v Titzer*[91] held that the physical location of a server was not relevant for the purposeful availment requirement. The court was predominantly concerned with whether the defendant targeted defamatory statements in the forum and in determining purposeful availment applied the effects test. In essence, the 'effects test' could therefore emerge as a means of determining jurisdiction where a web server is located.

There have been few cases in point that have considered the application of a jurisdiction agreement between the parties when Internet jurisdiction is disputed. Nevertheless, the court in *Bensusan* ruled that since consent had been given to

87 *Christian Science Board* 259 F3d 209.

88 *Intercon v Bell Atlantic Internet Solutions Inc.*, 205 F.2d 1415, 1417 (10th Cir.1998).

89 *Jewish Defense Org., v Superior Court of Los Angeles* Cal Ct App B129319 8 June 1999, California Court of Appeal, Second District.

90 *Cable News Network v Go SMS.com Inc.*, SDNY No. 00 CIV 4812 (LMM) 6 November 2000.

91 *Nam Tai Electronic Inc. v Titzer* California Court of Appeal 2d Dist. No. B149382 26 November 2001.

a jurisdiction agreement, this equated to consent to personal jurisdiction. This decision reiterates the general rule to uphold jurisdiction agreements provided they were not initiated by 'fraud, undue influence or overweening bargaining power,'[92] and satisfy both state law and 'Due Process.'[93] There is therefore an element of reasonableness in determining whether 'overweening bargaining power' prevails when the consumer – the party in a weaker bargaining position – contracts with a business. In *America Online Inc. v Superior Court [Mendoza]*[94] the forum selection clause was held unenforceable. The court held that the jurisdiction agreement violated public policy and rendered it the 'functional equivalent of a contractual waiver of the consumer protections under the [state's own Consumer Legal Remedies Act].' In *Decker v Circus Circus Hotel*,[95] the hotel's web site had a jurisdiction clause stating that the Nevada courts would resolve any disputes. Nevertheless, the New Jersey court upheld that in accordance with *Carnival Cruise Lines*[96] case, a link between the jurisdiction agreement and the use of the defendant's web site had to be shown. In that case, the Supreme Court ruled that the jurisdiction agreement on the defendant's tickets issued to the plaintiffs were valid since they were already printed on them.[97] However, the plaintiff had failed to demonstrate that the business' web site had actually been used. Equally, in *Westcode Inc. v RBE Electronics Inc*,[98] US District Court for the Eastern District of Pennsylvania did not uphold the choice of forum clause in the click-wrap agreement. According to the court, there was 'no relationship to the sale of goods' contract and the agreement seeking to confer jurisdiction.[99] Therefore if a business wishes to impose a choice of forum clause in a click-wrap agreement it is imperative that two criteria are satisfied. First, the choice of forum clause must be brought to the consumer's attention before the consumer clicks 'I accept' and makes payment. Otherwise, as Geist reiterates, the manner in

92 *Bremen v Zapata Off-Shore Co.*, 407 US 1, 12, 92 S.Ct., 1907, 1914, 32 L.Ed.2d. 513 (1972) and *Carnival Cruise Lines, Inc. v Shute*. J.S. Millstein, J.D. Nueburger and J.P. Weingart, *Doing Business on the Internet Forms and Analysis* (New York, 1997) at p.11–11; *Jacobson v Mailboxes, Etc USA., Inc.*, 419 Mass. 572 (1995) where a jurisdiction agreement in contract was deemed to be unreasonable.

93 Born, *International Civil Litigation in Unites Stated Courts,* at p.104.

94 *America Online Inc. v Superior Court [Mendoza]* No A 092813 Cal 1st Appeal District Division 2 21 June 2001. Words in brackets added.

95 *Decker v Circus Circus Hotel* D NJ Civ 97-1848 (WHW) 12 May 1999.

96 *Carnival Cruise Lines Inc, v Shute*.

97 R.n Yagura, 'Does Cyberspace Expand the Boundaries of Personal Jurisdiction?' (1998) 38 IDEA 301 at pp. 319–324. Yagura indicated how a jurisdiction agreement has an important role in determining the choice of law applied to contractual disputes in terms of the Restatement Second ss.187–188, particularly, as Yagura suggests, where there is no jurisdiction agreement, at p.321.

98 *Westcode Inc v RBE Electronics Inc.*, 2000 WL 124566 (E.D.Pa. 1 February 2000).

99 *Westcode*, ibid.

which the choice of forum clause is brought to the consumer's attention might be deemed unreasonable.[100] Second, when selecting or relying on a particular forum, the business must be able to demonstrate a link between the forum in the choice of law clause and the place where it does business via its web site. Such a link must be preserved to provide the consumer with the juridical protection of having a dispute heard in his own jurisdiction and, as Geist confirms, prevent choice of forum clauses providing the means for forum shopping.[101] If the business chooses to operate via an active or interactive web site, it is crucial that the business knows which jurisdiction it intends to target.

Post Zippo's 'Sliding Scale': Requirement for Intention to Target Activities Towards Residents in the Forum

In recent years, a number of recent cases have looked to either modification or replacement of the 'Sliding Scale' as a factor in determining purposeful availment and minimum contacts for personal jurisdiction. Undoubtedly, the 'Sliding Scale' is a significant aspect of the minimum contacts enquiry. However to ensure that jurisdiction is established with certainty and predictability, the courts should adopt a target based approach which examines the defendant's intention to direct its business activities towards residents, such as consumers, in a particular state. As the previous sections of this Chapter have indicated, the 'effects test' has emerged at the same time as the adaptation of the 'Sliding Scale' test.[102] The 'effects test' was applied in the e-commerce context[103] in *Blumenthal* and the *Yahoo!* case[104] (when the French anti-racism organisation sought to register the French judgment in California and the US District Court) for the Northern District of California held that on the basis of the effects test, the act of registering the judgment was 'wrongful' since it deprived Yahoo! of its constitutional rights. The effects test was also used in *American Information Corporation v American Infometrics*, citing *Bancroft and Masters*, which in turn said that there was a requirement of 'express aiming' or 'individualised targeting in addition to a foreseeable effect in the forum

100 M. Geist, 'Is There a There? Towards Greater Certainty for Internet Jurisdiction' (2001) 16 *Berkeley Tech Law Journal* 1345.

101 Geist, ibid.

102 The *Yahoo!* case was an example of the 'effects test' used in the internet context albeit it questioned the extent to which the US court could enforce a French judgment in accordance with the First Amendment. *Yahoo! Inc v La Ligue contre le racisme et l'antisemitisme* Case No.C-00-21275 US N.D Cal 7 November 2001 (Order granting motion for summary judgment). Gillies, ibid at p.20.

103 K.M. Fitzmaurice and R.M. Mody, 'International Shoe Meets the World Wide Web. Whither Personal Jurisdiction in Florida in the Age of the Internet?' (1997) 71 *Fla BJ* 22 at p.24. Gillies, ibid.

104 *Yahoo! Inc v La Ligue contre le racisme et l'antisemitisme*. Gillies, ibid.

state under the Calder effects test.'[105] The following cases show how the 'Sliding Scale' has been adapted by *ALS Scan Inc. v Digital Service Consultants Inc.*[106] to include a version of the 'effects test' in the form of 'targeting' or 'directing business activities towards a state.' Kohl has recently observed that the *ALS Scan* decision is significant since it prevents web site activity establishing 'jurisdiction everywhere.'[107] Authority for Kohl's endorsement of *ALS Scan* can be found in the Seventh Circuit Court of Appeal's recent case *Jennings v AC Hydraulic.*[108] In *Jennings*, the Seventh Circuit gave further credence to the Supreme Court's decision in *Mink* and Fourth Circuit Court of Appeal's decision in *ALS Scan*. The Seventh Circuit held that the defendant's maintenance of a passive web site did not support the exercise of personal jurisdiction over that defendant in a particular forum just because the web site can be accessed there. It is submitted that intentional targeting should emerge as the threshold requirement to satisfy purposeful availment and establish personal jurisdiction.

In *GTE New Media Servs Inc. v Bellsouth Corporation*[109] the US District Court for Columbia held that a telephone call and web site is not a 'persistent course of conduct in the District.'[110] The court referred to a number of cases, namely *Bensusan*, *Mink*, *Compuserve* and *Cybersell*[111] in refusing to dismiss the claim on the grounds of lack of personal jurisdiction. The defendants were alleged to have breached the Sherman Antitrust Act by committing tortious acts in the District of Columbia. The court held that it was not sufficient for the residents of the forum state simply to be able to access the web site.[112] Whilst suggesting a return to traditional jurisdiction rules,[113] the court in *GTE* made an important observation. 'The Due Process clause exists, in part, to give a degree of predictability to the legal system that allows potential defendants to structure their primary conduct

105 *American Information Corporation v American Infometrics*, No.CIV JFM-00-3288 139 F.Supp 2d 696. Gillies, ibid.

106 *ALS Scan Inc.* Gillies, ibid.

107 U. Kohl, 'The rule of law, jurisdiction and the Internet' (2004) 12:3 *I.J.L & I.T.* 365 at p.367. Gillies, ibid.

108 *Jennings v AC Hydraulic* No. 03-2157 383 F.3d 546, Prod.Liab.Rep. (CCH) P 17,084 2 September 2004. Gillies, ibid.

109 *GTE New Media Servs Inc. v Bellsouth Corporation.*

110 *GTE New Media*, ibid at pp. 338–399.

111 *Cybersell*, at pp. 338–399.

112 The court held that an alternative, and effectively national, basis for jurisdiction under the Clayton Act was warranted as service was effected against the defendants.

113 J. Green, 'Is Zippo's Sliding Scale a Slippery Slope of Uncertainty? A Case For Abolishing Web Site Interactivity As A Conclusive Factor in Assessing Minimum Contacts in Cyberspace' (2001) 34 *J Marshall L Rev* 1051 at p.1071 *et seq*, where the 'intent of the defendant' in the *Millennium* case at p.1073, rather than what the web site can do, is what matters.

with some minimum assurance as to where that conduct will and will not render them liable to suit.'[114]

As this author has previously submitted, adapting the 'Sliding Scale' test to incorporate the requirement that the business intended to target consumers will provide greater certainty for consumers and predictability for businesses. If a business chooses to use a passive web site then it should be inferred that the business did not intend to target its activities at a particular forum but merely to provide information about itself or its services. Indeed, in *Hartoy Inc. v David Thompson d/b/a Truckin' Little Company*,[115] the United States District Court for the Southern District of Florida confirmed in accordance with the Third Circuit in *Gorman* and the Fourth Circuit in *ALS Scan* that the manifest intent of a business to contract with residents in the forum is not demonstrated by a passive web site. However if a business uses an active or interactive web site to target and conduct business with consumers in different fora, the requirement for 'something more' should focus on whether the business intended to target consumers in those fora. For example, in *Gator com Corp. , v L.L. Bean Inc.*,[116] the Ninth Circuit Court of Appeal was happy to apply the adapted 'Sliding Scale' test from *ALS Scan* to assert general personal jurisdiction over the defendants. The court said:

> 'something more' than systematic transmission of electronic signals would be required in order to assert general jurisdiction [...] (B)usinesses who structure their activities to take full advantage of the opportunities that virtual commerce offers can reasonably anticipate that these same activities will potentially subject them to suit in the locales that they have targeted.[117]

The *Robbins v Yutopian Enterprises Inc.*[118] case demonstrates how the District Court in Maryland denied jurisdiction in a breach of copyright case against a Californian company despite the fact that the defendants contracted with forty-six residents in the forum and the defendants operated a web site, also accessible in the forum. In reaching its decision, the court considered whether the state's long arm statute and the constitutional 'Due Process' test had been met. Since the plaintiff did not claim specific personal jurisdiction, the court had to consider whether general personal jurisdiction could be established. On the point of general personal jurisdiction, the court cited the earlier case *Atlantech Distributors v*

114 *World Wide Volkswagen v Woodson* referred to in *GTE New Media Services Inc.*

115 *Hartoy Inc.* Gillies, ibid at p.21.

116 *Gator com Corp. , v L.L. Bean Inc.*, No. 02-15035 2001 WL 1528393 2 September 2003. Gillies, ibid.

117 *Gator*, ibid at p.1082. Gillies, ibid.

118 *Robbins v Yutopian Enterprises Inc.*, D.Md., Civil No. CCB-01-3096 15 May 2002.

Credit General Insurance Co.[119] where minimum contacts were not established by the existence of a passive web site and an agent in the forum. In *Robbins*, the court held that by applying the *Zippo* 'Sliding Scale,' the defendant's web site was active. However, the court did not follow this through to rule that this level of accessibility justified jurisdiction in the forum state. Where the case appeared to turn was on the fact that none of the forty-six transactions in the forum were alleged to have infringed the plaintiff's copyright. The court took the view that if jurisdiction was to be upheld, the defendants would be liable in any state. This case demonstrates the extent to which a District Court considers the three requirements of 'Due Process' and that the cause of action is linked to the plaintiff in a specific way. The fact that minimum contacts were not satisfied and the dispute did not relate to the cause of action justifies the court's decision to refuse jurisdiction. Any adaptation of the 'Sliding Scale' must therefore ensure the link between the business' on-line activities and the parties' dispute.

The *ALS Scan* case challenged the constitutional basis of the *Zippo* 'Sliding Scale' test.[120] The US Supreme Court was asked to consider the decision of the Fourth Circuit Court which held that the defendant (an ISP) was not subject to the specific jurisdiction of the court.[121] The court at first instance accepted and adapted the 'Sliding Scale' test. However, the Supreme Court refused to consider the decision of the Fourth Circuit, despite the petitioner's claim that the 'Sliding Scale' 'violated' the 'Due Process' test. The court in *ALS* also said that the *ESAB Group Inc. v Centricut Inc.*[122] case developed the effects test in *Calder v Jones* in respect of directing activities. The requirement of 'something more' in the *ALS Scan* case was also confirmed in the US Court of Appeal for the Fourth Circuit in *Young v New Haven Advocate*.[123] In the *Young* case, the plaintiff alleged defamation contained in newspaper articles published on the defendant's web site that was 'aimed at a Connecticut audience.'[124] The Appeal court reversed the decision of the Virginia court and confirmed that in accordance with *Calder*, the defendants would have had to have purposefully availed themselves by operating in the jurisdiction. The Fourth Circuit held that it could not exercise personal jurisdiction over the Connecticut defendants because 'they did not manifest an intent[ion] to aim their websites or the posted articles at a Virginia audience.'[125] On the requirement of doing business in the forum, the court said that the defendants

119 *Atlantech Distributors v Credit General Insurance Co.,* 30 F.Supp. 2d 534 (D.Md.1998).

120 *ALS Scan Inc*. Gillies, ibid at p.22.

121 The defendants operated a passive web site. Gillies, ibid.

122 *ESAB Group Inc. v Centricut Inc.* (4th Circuit) 126 F.3d 6 17, C.A 4 (SC), 1997, 17 October 1997. Gillies, ibid.

123 *Young*. Gillies, ibid.

124 *Young*, ibid. Gillies, ibid.

125 *Young*, ibid at p.475. Word in square brackets modified for syntax. Gillies, ibid.

had neither solicited business nor had assets there.[126] The court said 'considering both the effects test of *Calder* and the web site bulletin board ... there is a low level of interactivity.'[127] Furthermore, the court reasoned that the 'application of *Calder* in the Internet context requires proof that the out-of-state defendant's Internet activity is expressly directed at or directed to the forum state.' It also observed that more than simply making the news article accessible to Virginians by defendants' posting of the article on their Internet sites was needed for assertion of jurisdiction: 'The newspapers must, through the Internet postings, manifest an intent[ion] to *target* and *focus* on Virginia readers.'[128] The court in *Young* articulated the analogy for an adapted 'Sliding Scale' test – incorporating 'targeting' from *ALS Scan* – as follows,

> a state may, consistent with due process, exercise judicial power over a person outside of the state when that person (1) directs electronic activity in the State (2) with the manifest intent of engag[ing] in business or other interactions within the State and (3) that activity creates, in a person within the state, a potential cause of action cognisable in the state's courts.[129]

As this author has recently remarked, the *ALS Scan* intentional targeting test therefore constitutes three key components, namely *(on-line) activity, intention and a foreseeable or causal link to the dispute*. The first two requirements satisfy the requirement that the foreign business' activities in the forum were foreseeable. The first requirement should be satisfied when a business uses an active or interactive web site which is available and directed towards consumers in the forum. Rather than focussing on where the business chose *not* to target its activities (exemplified in Geist's 'de-targeting' and Svantesson's 'dis-targeting' approaches),[130] it is submitted that the test must be based on the *positive act* of the seller to engage in commercial activities in the forum. The second requirement will be satisfied if the active or interactive web site offers the potential for the consumer to contract with the business either on-line (via the business' active web site) or offline (via

---

126 *Young*, ibid. Gillies, ibid.

127 *ALS Scan*. Gillies, ibid.

128 *Young*. ibid,Words italicised for emphasis and word in brackets modified for syntax. Gillies, ibid.

129 *ALS Scan*. This three-part test to establish specific personal jurisdiction was subsequently applied by, *inter alia*, the District of Virginia in *Allen v James* 381 F.Supp. 2d 495 (E.D.Va., 29 July 2005)(NO. 2:05CV297) and *Williams v Reynolds*, Slip Copy, 2006 WL 3007347 (W.D.Va., Oct 20, 2006)(NO. 4:06CV00020), the District of Southern Carolina in *Gateway Gaming, L.L.C. v Custom Game Design, Inc.* Slip Copy, 2006 WL 2781043 D.S.C. 2006., 25 September 2006. Gillies, ibid at pp. 22-23.

130 Geist, 'Is There a There? Towards Greater Certainty for Internet Jurisdiction,' and D. Svantesson, 'Jurisdiction Issue in Cyberspace What Should Article 7 – Consumer Contracts, of the Proposed Hague Convention, Aim to Accomplish in Relation to E-Commerce?' (2001) 5 CLSR 318. Gillies, ibid at p.23.

other traditional communication methods such as a telephone or fax machine). 'Due Process' may still demand evidence that the consumer accessed the web site to establish a link between the defendant's activities in the forum and the dispute. The third requirement will be satisfied when the parties have contracted with each other by electronic or traditional means. If the first and third requirements are satisfied there could be a sufficient causal link between the location of the business' intended commercial activities and the parties' dispute for 'Due Process' to be satisfied. Indeed, Geist implicitly prioritises the significance of the parties' contract and the existence of a choice of forum clause as the first aspect of his three-stage targeting test. In *ALS*, the court said that it could not assert jurisdiction since the defendant 'did not manifest an intent to aim their web site or the articles posted at a Virginia audience.'[131] In referring to the *Christian Science* case,[132] the court in *Young* held that '(T)he newspaper did not post materials on the internet with the manifest intent of targeting Virginia residents.' The decision in *ALS* therefore combined both the 'Sliding Scale' and the 'effects test' to produce a new basis of satisfying the purposeful availment requirement in the form of intentional targeting. Furthermore, the second aspect of Geist's targeting test is based on neutral technology. Geist argues that technology enables businesses to limit or 'de-target' certain jurisdictions. However, the *ALS Scan* case by comparison endorses the need for a positive act on behalf of the foreign business to communicate and contract with the consumer in another forum. For example, a business could use a 'drop-down' list on its web site which specifies which consumers it intends to target. In addition, this requirement would encourage the consumer to 'self-declare' where he is located. Geist highlights consumer 'self-declaration'[133] as an 'additional advantage' of the technology aspect of his test. However, in the interests of fairness, certainty and predictability the primary focus of targeting must be on the business' commercial intentions in the jurisdiction and not the consumer's self-declaration. Finally, the third aspect of Geist's targeting test considers the parties' 'actual or implied knowledge' of the targeting of a particular jurisdiction. However, Geist admits that this is a 'catch-all' requirement which 'does not prescribe a particular type of technology *but rather the outcome*.'[134] On that basis, it is submitted that whilst the third requirement of Geist's targeting test is perhaps superfluous, it does contribute to demonstrating what commercial outcome the business intended (whether 'mere advertising' in the state or intention to target and contract) when using a web site to target foreign consumers.

131 *ALS Scan*, at p.3. Gillies, ibid.

132 Which in turn referred to *Calder v Jones* 465 US 783, 788, 104, S.Ct. 1482, 1486, 79 L.Ed.2d. 804 (1984). Gillies, ibid.

133 Geist, 'Is There a There? Towards Greater Certainty for Internet Jurisdiction.' Gillies, ibid at p.24.

134 Geist, ibid. Gillies, ibid.

After the *Zippo* case, the options appear to be to endorsement or more likely replacement of the 'Sliding Scale'[135] test which articulates the defendant's business conduct and activities towards residents in another state.[136] As an addition requirement for minimum contacts and purposeful availment, evidence must be shown that business targeted residents in the forum in accordance with *Millennium* and *ALS Scan*. Alternatively, the courts could continue to implement the 'effects test,' in accordance with *Calder* (as affirmed by *Blumenthal*). However, this is not preferred for two reasons. Firstly, as a note in the Harvard Law Review argued, the *Young* 'effects test' is still appropriate for internet defamation. The note confirms that the 'Sliding Scale' can still be used to distinguish between web sites on whether they demonstrate commercial and non-commercial activity.[137] Indeed, an interactive and active web site can be used to conduct commercial activities across borders. A passive web site is akin to an advertisement for jurisdictional purposes, or it might not be used for commercial purposes at all. Secondly, the requirement for targeting espoused by *ALS Scan* has been subsequently endorsed by several other Circuit and District court decisions, perhaps most noticeably in *Carefirst of Maryland Inc. d/b/a Carefirst Blue Cross/Blue Shield v Carefirst Pregnancy Centers Inc. d/b/a Carefirst and Netimpact Inc.*[138] In *Carefirst*, the plaintiffs brought a trademark infringement case in Maryland against an Illinois business. The question that the Fourth Circuit Court had to consider was whether the defendant 'expressly aimed' its web site at Maryland and referred again to *ALS*. However, the court considered the 'Sliding Scale,' the post-Zippo *ALS* 'targeting test' *and* the *Young* 'effects test' to uphold that there were no minimum contracts. The court said:

> (A)pplying these precedents to this case, it is clear that in order for CPC's web site to bring CPC within the jurisdiction of the Maryland courts, the company must have done something more than merely place information on the Internet. Rather, CPC must

135 Geist has suggested that the active / passive distinction is no longer a true indicator of web site activity. He maintains that the courts should examine to what extent the defendant targeted residents in the forum, thereby making personal jurisdiction more stringent, ibid. Gillies, ibid.

136 Rice, 'A Cyberspace Odyssey Through US and EU Internet Jurisdiction,' at pp. 517–518. Gillies, ibid.

137 J.H. Beck, 'A "Category-Specific" Legislative Approach to the Internet Personal Jurisdiction Problem in U.S. Law' (2004) 117 *Harvard Law Review Notes* 1617 at pp. 1621–1622. Gillies, ibid.

138 *Carefirst of Maryland Inc. d/b/a Carefirst Blue Cross/Blue Shield v Carefirst Pregnancy Centers Inc. d/b/a Carefirst and Netimpact Inc.* (CA-01-1578-CCB) 02/07/03, subsequently endorsed by *Electronic Broking Services Ltd v E-Business Solutions & Services*, 285 F. Supp. 2d 686 U.S.P.Q.2d 1531. D.Md, 30/09/03, *United Cutlery Corp. v NFZ Inc.*, 2003 WL 22851946, 2003 Corp. L. Decp.28,709, D.,Md., 1 December 2003, *Beyond Systems, Inc. v Realtime Gaming Holding Co.,* LLC, 388 Md. 1, 878, A.2d 567 (Md., 22 June 2005)(NO. 119 SEPT.TERM 2004) (all cases in the District of Maryland). Gillies, ibid at p.25.

> have acted with the 'manifest intent' of targeting Marylanders. Whether CPC intended to target Marylanders can be determined only from the character of the website at issue.[139]

This reiterates the significance of both the foreign business' intention and conduct in establishing minimum contacts in another jurisdiction. For example, in *Lakin v Prudential Securities* the Eighth Circuit Court of Appeals endorsed the *Zippo* 'Sliding Scale' and its application to specific jurisdiction as in *ALS Scan*.[140] In *Jennings v AC Hydraulic*[141] the Seventh Circuit Court of Appeal referred to *Carefirst* and two other Circuit court cases, the Sixth Circuit in *Bridgeport Music, Inc. v Still N The Water Publ'g,*[142] and the District of Columbia Circuit in *Gorman*,[143] as authority that the defendant is subject to the court's jurisdiction when goods or services can be ordered by consumers via the operation of an interactive web site. The court rejected an appeal dismissing the case for lack of jurisdiction since it was not satisfied that there was sufficient 'interactivity' between the parties, in accordance with *ALS Scan*, for jurisdiction to be established.

Targeting

It is necessary to consider what would constitute targeting. Rice suggests that if targeting is more readily used to determine jurisdiction, language (especially when it is not English), currency and tax are 'relevant' factors that should be taken into account.[144] Geist has highlighted how language and currency can now change in real time and should not be used to determine jurisdiction.[145] Evidence that the business intended to target particular jurisdictions should optimally seek to

139 Carefirst, ibid at p.400. The case *Allison v Lomas* 387 F.Supp. 2d 516 M.D.N.C., 2005, 25 August 2005 referred to *Carefirst* as authority for federal courts to apply state law in determining personal jurisdiction under Federal Rule of Procedure 4(k)(1)(A). Gillies, ibid.

140 *Lakin v Prudential Securities* No. 02-2477 348 F.3d 704 4 November 2003. Gillies, ibid.

141 *Jennings v AC Hydraulic*, .03-2157 383 F.3d 546, Prod.Liab.Rep. (CCH) P 17,084 2 September 2004. Gillies, ibid.

142 *Bridgeport Music, Inc. v Still N The Water Publ'g* 327 F.3d 472, 483 (6th Cir.2003) (per curiam). Gillies, ibid.

143 *Gorman d/b/a Cashbackrealty.com, d/b/a Cashbackrealty.com v Ameritrade Holding Corp.* , D.C. Cir. No. 01-7085 14 June 2002. Gillies, ibid.

144 Rice, 'A Cyberspace Odyssey Through US and EU Internet Jurisdiction,' at p.513.

145 Geist, 'Is There a There? Towards Greater Certainty for Internet Jurisdiction.' Chapter Two, supra.

localise web site activity with territories since territoriality 'intuitive(ly)'[146] alerts the defendant to where he may be hauled into court. In any event, consistency in the approach to targeting should be pursued. If not, then other decisions similar to *American Information Corporation v American Informetrics Inc.*,[147] could occur. In that case, a dispute occurred between two ISPs regarding an alleged infringement of the plaintiff's trademark on the defendant's web site. The Maryland District Court dismissed the case on the grounds of lack of personal jurisdiction. The court held that the defendant's web site did not satisfy the requirement of minimum contacts with the forum. Further, the forum was not deemed to be the 'focal point' for the harm which the plaintiff was alleged to have suffered.[148] This case demonstrates that if the web site used advertising to target large numbers of potential customers, in the absence of other factors that contribute to targeting commercial activity, the level of advertising could contribute to doing business in the jurisdiction.[149] Rather than following a decision which is reminiscent of the expansiveness of *Inset Systems,*[150] the requirements from *ALS Scan* should be used by the courts to adapt the 'Sliding Scale' test. In *Bates v Starnes*,[151] in accordance with *ALS Scan* and *Carefirst*, the United States District Court for the District of Maryland said that it was necessary to consider any 'specific efforts made by the defendant to obtain business from persons within the state in which personal jurisdiction is sought to be asserted.' The court demanded more information from the plaintiffs before determining whether the burden of purposeful availment had been sufficiently established. According to Vartanian, '(A) set of uniform principles could be established to govern how sellers should electronically target, screen and filter users so that they could predictably know where they will be subject to laws and regulations.'[152]

If parties to an electronic consumer contract are to be able to foresee where their disputes could be heard, the question that this author recently asked was what should constitute targeting commercial activities in foreign jurisdictions? The Oxford Dictionary defines a 'target' as

146 According to *Pennoyer v Neff*; Green, 'Is Zippo's Sliding Scale a Slippery Slope of Uncertainty?' at p.1055.

147 *American Information Corporation.*

148 *American Information Corporation,* ibid.

149 *GTE New Media Services.*

150 *Inset*, regarded in *Zippo*, as 'the outer limits of the exercise of personal jurisdiction based on the Internet.' If *Inset* and *Cybersell* had been followed, the point made by Eckert, Seamons, Cherin and Mellott, that *Inset* 'may also retard commercial exploitation of the Internet by raising the spectre of unlimited jurisdictional exposure.' Eckert, Seamons, Cherin and Mellott Supreme Court decision in Worldwide Volkswagen that 'foreseeability' alone has never been a sufficient constitutional benchmark for jurisdiction.'

151 *Bates v Starnes* No. Civ.JFM-04-1956. 2005 WL 705345 (D.Md.) 24 March 2005.

152 American Bar Association, Section on Business Law, Committee on Cyberspace Law, Subcommittee on Transnational Issues; Vartanian, 'Whose Internet is it Anyway?'

1. [to] select as an object of attention or attack,
2. [to] aim or direct.[153]

The key purpose of targeting therefore is to aim or direct towards a particular object. In the case of electronic commerce, businesses that aim their marketing and commercial activities towards particular jurisdictions would be deemed to be targeting consumers in those jurisdictions. Geist has argued that the test of targeting should encompass the knowledge and contract of the parties and technology (to assert state jurisdiction). As Boone has argued, there should be a universally applicable standard of assessment for targeting' that also facilitates foreseeability.[154] However, it is suggested that targeting commercial activities via web sites must encompass the following key requirements to enable the consumer to bring proceedings against the business in his own jurisdiction. First, there should be a positive act (i.e. an aim) by one party – that is, the use of an active or interactive web site by a business for marketing and commercial activities in another jurisdiction. The consumer need not therefore be an active or passive participant, i.e. it should not be necessary to provide that the consumer sought out the business' web site if, as suggested below, a contract is entered into via that web site. Second, the positive act must demonstrate an intention by the business to enter into contractual relations with consumers in the jurisdictions where the foreign markets / consumers are located. This does not mean however that the consumer has to be present in the jurisdiction when the contract was entered into. Instead, the consumer must be able to demonstrate that he was domiciled or resident in the jurisdiction that was targeted by the business via its web site at the time the parties entered into a contract with each other. This would deal with the situation where a consumer uses wireless technology to contract with a business via its web site whilst travelling between jurisdictions (eg during a flight between London and New York) or when present in another jurisdiction for a short time (eg on a business trip or vacation). Therefore, since the business must take positive steps to seek out foreign markets via its web site, and the definition of target highlights the need for the selection of an object of interest, it is submitted that 'ring-fencing' in order to avoid contracting with consumers resident in particular jurisdictions should not constitute targeting.

Third, the type of web site used by the business must be considered in the test of intentional targeting. Geist says that the test of targeting must be technologically neutral since, he argues, the 'Sliding Scale' of web site activity does not provide consistent results and more importantly cannot be foreseeable. Whilst reliance on the 'Sliding Scale' test *alone* may not provide the consistency argued for by Geist, combined with the other requirements of targeting suggested here, the 'Sliding

153 Oxford Dictionary and Thesaurus.

154 B. Boone, 'Bullseye!: Why A "Targeting" Approach To Personal Jurisdiction In The E-Commerce Context Makes Sense Internationally' (2006) 20 *Emory Int'l L. Rev*. 241 Gillies, ibid at p.26 *et seq*.

Scale' test must still form part of the test of intentionally targeting commercial activities as it provides and demonstrates the communicative 'means' by which the business' commercial activities are conducted with consumers. Fourth, a contract must be entered into between the parties as a tangible result of the business seller via the operation of an active or interactive web site. Fifth, the parties' dispute must relate to the contract which was entered into as a result of the targeted activity. This would demonstrate the causal connection between the activities of the business in the foreign jurisdiction and the parties' dispute. Waelde has questioned[155] whether the test of targeting must be objective or subjective. It is submitted that the sixth and final requirement for the targeting test must be objective, taking into account all of the circumstances *vis-à-vis* the electronic consumer contact upon which the parties' dispute is based and the requirements for intentional targeting put forward here.

In the United States, the requirement for specific personal jurisdiction should be amended further beyond the requirements of the *ALS Scan* case to subject a business to the jurisdiction of the state where the consumer is domiciled when it

> (1) *targets electronic activity towards* a State *or several States* [*via an active or interactive web site*] (2) with the manifest intent of engaging in business or other interactions within the State and (3) that activity creates, in a person within the state, a potential cause of action cognisable in the state's courts.

Summary

The United States has sought to address electronic commerce issues by creating a framework for electronic commerce and by modifying existing personal jurisdiction principles. However, jurisdiction rules for electronic consumer contracts must be developed further. In accordance with the OECD and the Trans Atlantic Consumer Dialogue's proposals, as a minimum, consumers ought to receive the same level of protection offline as they currently receive online. The United States case law demonstrates a need to endorse 'targeting' to provide greater consistency and predictability in determining jurisdiction over an electronic consumer contract. It appears that the European Union was influenced by the US 'Sliding Scale' approach to web site activity as a basis of jurisdiction for electronic consumer contracts by imposing the requirement that businesses must 'direct their activities' to Member States. As Chapter Five demonstrated, Article 15(1)(c) of the Brussels 1 Regulation needs to incorporate a target-based approach to ensure it can be applied regardless of where the defendant is domiciled. The same approach needs to be consistently incorporated into the 'Sliding Scale' test and approved by the Supreme Court. In

155 C. Waelde, 'International Private Law, Consumer and the Net: A Confusing Maze or a Smooth Path Towards a Single European Market?' in L. Edwards (ed), *The New Legal Framework For E-Commerce In Europe* (Oxford, 2005). Gillies, ibid at p.26 *et seq.*

the absence of specific guidance and endorsement by the Supreme Court, the lower courts in the United States have sought to implement and re-assess the application of existing rules of personal jurisdiction over a defendant conducting business in a particular state via a web site. In order to ensure a consistent approach to jurisdiction over electronic consumer contracts, the 'Sliding Scale' must include an intentional targeting component derived from *ALS Scan* and subject a business to the consumer's jurisdiction if the business intended to direct its commercial activities there via an active or interactive web site.

Chapter 10
Towards Harmonised International Private Law Rules for Electronic Consumer Contracts

Introduction

> The trans-national character of E-commerce makes its governance a matter of international trade policy and law. At least, questions regarding the nature and substance of the applicable commercial law and matters of jurisdiction and enforcement relating to on-line transactions need to be resolved satisfactorily if the medium is to gain credence and broader acceptability among parties from different states.[1]

Given the onset of electronic commerce,[2] governmental and non-governmental organisations, consumers, businesses and their representatives have a vested interest in how international private law rules apply to electronic consumer contracts. Efforts by the European Community and the United States' courts have contributed to developing rules of jurisdiction and choice of law for electronic consumer contracts to an extent. However, disparities in the interpretation and application of these rules for electronic consumer contracts still remain to the detriment of the parties and electronic commerce activity generally. Current jurisdiction and choice of law rules must incorporate a requirement of intentional targeting in order that a consistent, foreseeable connecting factor can be applied effectively in the on-line environment. Given the global, dematerialised nature of electronic commerce, a universalist, harmonised approach[3] would facilitate the modification of such rules.

1 A. Endeshaw, 'The Proper Law for Electronic Commerce' (1998) 1 ICTL 5 at p.10.

2 Chapter 1, above.

3 As with other areas of international private law; H. Van Loon, 'Globalisation and The Hague Conference on Private International Law' (2000) 2 *International Law Forum du droit international* 230; C.T. Poggi, 'Electronic Commerce Legislation: An Analysis of European and American Approaches to Contract Formation' (2000) 41 *Va J Int'l L* 224 at p.277.

Justifications for a Global Approach to Jurisdiction and Choice of Law Rules for Electronic Consumer Contracts

The rules in the Brussels 1 Regulation remain restrictive in three ways. First, the rules only apply to consumers domiciled in an EU Member State and businesses that are domiciled or have a branch in and direct their activities to, an EU Member State. Second, the rules only apply to certain consumer contracts. Third, the rules of jurisdiction are subject to particular conditions which are not conducive to electronic consumer contracts. Schedules 4 and 8 to the 1982 Act and Paragraph 6.20(5) CPR must also be adapted to ensure that the consumer can establish jurisdiction in his domicile regardless of whether the defendant is domiciled in another part of the United Kingdom, an EU Member State or a non-Member State. Chapter Four demonstrated that further adaptation and harmonisation of these rules is required to ensure that the consumer's jurisdiction can be established with certainty and predictability. Firstly, the consumer jurisdiction rules should continue to apply only to private (i.e. natural), final consumers purchasing for their own private use or consumption. Secondly, the term 'directing such activities' in Article 15(1)(c) must be clarified to ensure it is consistently applied when businesses undertake commercial activities via their active or interactive web sites. Consumers must therefore be specifically targeted by businesses via such web sites in order to benefit from the juridical protection of the courts where they are domiciled. If businesses intentionally direct their online activities towards consumers in this manner, any dispute must be heard in the consumer's jurisdiction. Thirdly, a jurisdiction clause in a click-wrap agreement on a business' web site must not restrict or prevent the consumer's dispute from being heard in his jurisdiction.

Whilst the European Union has led the development of regional rules of jurisdiction for electronic consumer contracts,[4] the requirements of Articles 15–17 will continue to hinder the ability of the consumer to establish jurisdiction of an electronic consumer contract in his own jurisdiction. As far as the Brussels 1 Regulation is concerned, Articles 15–17 only apply where the business is either situated or has a branch or agency in an EU Member State. The rules of jurisdiction for consumer contracts in Schedules 4 and 8 to the 1982 Act and the CPR rules must also be amended to ensure that a Scottish or English consumer can establish jurisdiction over a foreign business situated in another part of the UK or a non-Member State respectively. Regardless of where the foreign business is situated, it should only be subject to the jurisdiction of the consumers' domicile when the business specifically intended to target consumers in their own jurisdiction via an active or interactive web site. The connecting factor 'directing activities' in Article 15(1)(c) of the Brussels 1 Regulation and analogous provisions in Schedules 1, 4 and

4 J. Hörnle, 'The European Union Takes Initiative in the Field of E-Commerce,' Commentary 2000 (3) *The Journal of Information, Law and Technology* (JILT), <http://www2.warwick.ac.uk/fac/soc/law/elj/jilt/2000_3/hornle>; J.S.T. Øren, 'International Jurisdiction Over Consumer Contracts in e-Europe' (2003) 52 ICLQ 665 at p.695.

8 to the 1982 Act currently hinders the effective application of juridical protection for consumers. If this connecting factor is not amended further by the European Commission or ECJ and the UK government, a lack of certainty and predictability will prevail in establishing that the dispute should be heard in the consumer's jurisdiction. In accordance with the OECD and the Trans Atlantic Consumer Dialogue's (TACD)[5] proposals, as a minimum, consumers ought to receive the same level of protection offline as they currently receive online. The United States case law demonstrated a need to endorse a requirement for 'intentional targeting' to provide greater consistency and predictability in determining jurisdiction over an electronic consumer contract. It appears that the European Union was influenced by the US 'Sliding Scale' approach to web site activity as a basis of jurisdiction for electronic consumer contracts by imposing the requirement that businesses must 'direct their activities' to Member States. Article 15(1)(c) of the Brussels 1 Regulation needs to incorporate a target-based approach to ensure it can be applied regardless of where the defendant is domiciled. It is submitted that the same approach now needs to be consistently incorporated into the United States 'Sliding Scale' test and approved by the United States Supreme Court. In the absence of specific guidance and endorsement by the Supreme Court, the lower courts[6] in the United States have sought to implement and re-assess the application of existing rules of personal jurisdiction over a defendant conducting business in a particular state via a web site. In order to ensure a consistent approach to jurisdiction over electronic consumer contracts, the 'Sliding Scale' must be modified to incorporate an intentional targeting component derived from *ALS Scan* and applied by other United States' Circuit Courts which subjects the business to the jurisdiction of the consumer's domicile if the business intended to direct its commercial activities there via an active or interactive web site.

Global Developments: The Hague Conference on Private International Law's Judgments Convention

The impact of the World Wide Web and global trade has reinforced the need for globally consistent juridical protection for consumer contracts. Chapter One argued that juridical protection for consumers who contract with foreign businesses via the WWW can no longer be influenced by national, particularist

5 The Trans-Atlantic Consumer Dialogue (TACD, <http://www.tacd.org>). The TACD was launched in September 1998 as 'a forum of US and EU consumer organisations which develops and agrees joint consumer policy recommendations to the US government and European Union to promote the consumer interest in EU and US policy making,' at <http://www.tacd.org/about/about.htm>. The TACD web site confirms that around '45 EU and 20 US consumer organisations have joined TACD.'

6 A trend that appeared to be mirrored in Canada: M. Geist, 'Court cases taming 'wild west' Web and: Decisions benefit business, consumers,' *The Toronto Star*, 7 July 2003.

objectives in isolation to jurisdiction rules in other countries. A universalist, consistent, predictable approach must operate across different jurisdictions to provide effective juridical protection for consumers. As Chapter One observed, the approaches to the legal regulation of electronic commerce activity have been individual state regulation (illustrating a particularist approach), model laws and harmonisation (demonstrating a universalist approach). Indeed, the development of international private law rules has not simply been confined to particularist objectives. As North confirms,

> (A) most striking feature of the development of private international law over the last century has been that statute law has been the primary instrument of change – far more so … than judicial activism … [and] … that their genesis lies almost exclusively in the work of agencies outside central government.[7]

The OECD has released a number of position papers on consumer protection in the context of electronic commerce, one of which recently assessed the extent to which different countries have refined consumer protection law and policics for electronic commerce contracts including rules of jurisdiction for such contracts.[8] However, over the last ten years the Hague Conference on Private International Law has completed an international convention on choice of court agreements[9] which, until 2002, included jurisdiction rules for (electronic) consumer contracts. The next section of this Chapter will argue that given appropriately modified rules, one of the proposed Articles in the 2001 draft Convention could have contributed to ensuring clear and consistent jurisdiction rules for electronic consumer contracts.[10] It is submitted that the role of international organisations such as the Hague Conference should become even more prevalent in adapting existing international private law rules. As the previous Chapters have considered, it is crucial that jurisdiction rules provide clear and consistent juridical protection for consumers whilst providing businesses with an ability to foresee when the dispute will be heard in the consumer's jurisdiction.

By 1993, the United States' proposal[11] for a judgments convention had been included on the Special Commission's agenda. The initial purpose of the

7 P. North, 'Private International Law: Change or Decay?' (2001) 50 ICLQ 477 at p.496.

8 OECD, 'Consumers in the Online Marketplace: The OECD Guidelines Three Years Later, Report by the Committee on Consumer Policy on the Guidelines for Consumer Protection in the Context of Electronic Commerce,' DSTI/CP(2002)4/FINAL, 3 February 2003.

9 The Choice of Court Convention can be found at <http://www.hcch.net>.

10 L.E. Gillies, 'The Impact of the Hague Conference's Proposed Judgments Convention for Electronic Commerce and Intellectual Property Disputes' (2002) 16:3 *Int Rev L Comps and Tech* 233 at p.243.

11 US recommendation to the Hague Conference to put such a Convention on its agenda; Preliminary Document No.11, 'The Future Hague Convention on International

Hague Conference's proposed Convention was to ensure that judgments in 'civil and commercial matters' derived from Contracting States are capable of being recognised and enforced in other Contracting States. Civil and commercial matters were not defined in the draft Convention. However, according to the Report of the Special Commission by Nygh and Pocar (hereafter the 'Nygh and Pocar Report') such matters were likely to be determined in an 'autonomous manner'[12] and subject to a 'liberal interpretation'.[13] Despite concerns regarding the lack of an international court to interpret the proposed convention, the Hague Conference suggested that interpretative references could be made to an expert panel or the Hague Conference itself. The scope of the 1999 draft Convention was contained in Article 1.[14] Article 4 set out the proposed exclusive[15] rules on choice of court.[16] The 1999 draft Article 4 stated that if the parties agreed on which court would have jurisdiction over the dispute, then that court would have jurisdiction. Article 4 upheld the validity of a jurisdiction agreement where the contract was conducted by electronic means, provided the information could be retained for future or 'subsequent' reference.[17] For example, the provision would have applied to the situation where information about an online contract could be retained in an email, or by saving a copy of the web page. There was also a reference made to the selection of courts in non-Contracting States. In that instance, Article 4 required courts in Contracting States to either decline or suspend proceedings if the court in the non-Contracting States had not declined jurisdiction. Article 4(2) sought to be applicable in the context of electronic commerce, providing that the formal validity of a contact (and any agreement on jurisdiction contained in it) would be upheld if 'it was entered into or confirmed [...] (b) by any other means of communication

---

Jurisdiction and the Effects of Judgments in Civil and Commercial Matters,' Report of the Special Commission by P. Nygh and F. Pocar, at p.27. (Hereafter the Nygh and Pocar Report).

12 Preliminary Document No.11, Nygh and Pocar Report, ibid at p.33.

13 Ibid. Preliminary Document No.7, 'International Jurisdiction and Foreign Judgments in Civil and Commercial Matters,' report drawn up by C. Kessedjian, revised translation October 1997, at pp53-54 and the response to the suggestion for an expert panel in Preliminary Document No.9, 'Synthesis of the Work of the Special Commission of March 1998 on international jurisdiction and the effects of foreign judgments in civil and commercial matters,' drawn up by C. Kessedjian, at pp. 45-46. W.E. O'Brien Jr., 'The Hague Convention on Jurisdiction and Judgments: The Way Forward' (2003) 66 MLR 491at p.503.

14 Article 1, 1999 Hague Conference draft convention.

15 Nygh and Pocar Report, at p.45.

16 Article 4 of the 1999 draft Convention, see Appendix.

17 Contributions to the Consumer Project on Technology's discussion forum on the Hague Conference's proposed judgments convention with respect to internet jurisdiction and the Hague Conference on Private International Law's worldwide judgment's convention project available at <http://lists.essential.org/pipermail/hague-jur-commercial-law/>.

which renders information accessible so as to be usable for subsequent reference.'[18] The 1999 draft contained jurisdiction rules for consumer contracts in Article 7 to enable the consumer to sue in his own jurisdiction.[19] Article 7(1) of the 1999 draft convention defined a consumer in largely the same manner as the Brussels Convention.[20] A consumer must be contracting outside its[21] trade or profession in order for him to be able to sue in the court of its habitual residence.[22] Whilst the report briefly questioned the meaning of a 'consumer' in the context of electronic commerce, it conceded that consumers should be afforded juridical protection in the courts of their domicile regardless of whether their contract was online or offline.[23] However, like the Brussels Convention at the time, Article 7(1) of the 1999 draft required certain conditions to be satisfied before the consumer could sue in his habitual residence. Firstly, Article 7(1)(a) proposed the consumer to sue in his habitual residence if the other party was acting within its trade or profession, i.e. it was a business, and that the 'contract on which the claim is based'[24] was connected to the business' activities in that State.[25] Whilst particular emphasis was given to business activities conducted by means of 'publicity,' the term was not defined in the draft Article 7. Nevertheless, the Nygh and Pocar report provides a helpful, but nevertheless basic, explanation of 'publicity' in this context,

> ... any means of publicity whereby the consumer can be reached[[26]] at his place of residence is covered by the clause; alongside the traditional means of communication (such as the post, the press, the telephone or television), electronic means of communication may also be used, where for instance publicity or an offer to contract are posted on the Internet.[27]

---

18 Article 4(2)(b), 1999 draft convention.

19 Article 7, 1999 draft convention, see Appendix.

20 The Preliminary Document No.7, 'Electronic Data Interchange, Internet and Electronic Commerce,' at p.20.

21 Preliminary Document No.7, at point 100,p.31 stated '(M)oreover, jurisdiction introduced to protect the consumer must be individual to him, and not be used for anyone acting on behalf of the consumer or in his stead.'; and Preliminary Document No.8, 'Synthesis of the Work of the Special Commission of June 1997 on International Jurisdiction and the Effects of Foreign Judgments in Civil and Commercial Matters,' drawn up by C. Kessedjian, November 1997, at point 49, '(T)he rule ought to be limited to natural persons entering into an obligation ... for their personal, domestic or financial use.'

22 Preliminary Report No.7 at point 101,p.31 confirmed that habitual residence is that where the consumer is resident at the time *proceedings arose*, ' ... *not* the one which exists on the date when the contract is *concluded* ... ' ibid. Italics added for emphasis.

23 Coinciding with the OECD's general position in its 'Guidelines for Consumer Protection in the Context of Electronic Commerce,' Chapter One above.

24 Compare Article 7(1)(a) of the 2001 draft convention, considered infra.

25 Nygh and Pocar Report, at p.53.

26 Suggesting that the consumer is initially passive in the process, i.e. that the consumer does not 'seek out' the business but vice versa.

27 Nygh and Pocar Report, at p.53.

The report attributed a wide interpretation of publicity to encompass the Internet (i.e. the use of web sites) as well as traditional methods of advertising such as television and radio. It is interesting to note that the first requirement of Article 7(1)(a) could have been satisfied if the business had *either* 'engaged in' *or* 'directed activities to' the consumer's habitual residence. The former, perhaps broader, option could have subjected the business to the jurisdiction of the consumer's habitual residence without the business having necessarily directed its activities towards consumers in that country. The identical term 'directing activities' contained in the Brussels 1 Regulation was also used in the draft Hague convention. Whilst there was no definition of 'directing activities,' guidance can be derived again from the Nygh and Pocar Report on the draft convention. Nygh and Pocar confirmed that for the consumer jurisdiction rule to apply

> [The] defendant [i.e. the business] should have *acted positively* towards the plaintiff [i.e. the consumer] and that the consequence of this activity should be that an offer to contract should have reached the plaintiff on his territory by one of the possible means of communication (... offer to contract and advertisement via the Internet ..., making it possible to reach the consumer at his or place of habitual residence.)[28]

Given the arguments earlier that the businesses must positively intend to target consumers in foreign jurisdictions, the first requirement in Article 7(1)(a) would have had to be re-drafted to reflect this. Secondly, Article 7(1)(b) required the consumer to take the steps necessary to conclude the contract in his habitual residence in a virtually identical fashion to Article 13 of the Brussels Convention. As Chapter Four demonstrated vis-à-vis Article 13 of the Brussels Convention, such a requirement could have proved problematic for consumers to satisfy when contracting with a foreign business via its web site. The Hague Conference in a subsequent report on electronic commerce mirrored a similar concern.[29] The business would have had to ensure that the consumer was contracting from his habitual residence. It would be difficult and time consuming to ascertain with certainty in the context of a contract conducted online. All that a business would have been able to rely on was the address provided by the consumer in conjunction with a contractual term requiring the consumer to affirm that he was resident in a particular country at the time the contract was entered into.

In terms of jurisdiction agreements, Article 7(3) proposed that the parties could have entered into such agreements provided certain requirements were satisfied. Firstly, such agreements had to conform with the general rules for jurisdiction agreements contained in Article 4. Secondly, the agreement could be entered into after the dispute arose between the parties. The third requirement of Article 7(3) was to ensure that the consumer (and not the business) had an alternative forum

28 Preliminary Document No.8, at point 49. Words in square brackets added and words italicised for emphasis.

29 Preliminary Document No.7, at p.20.

in which to bring a claim. It is submitted that the value of the latter requirement to consumers contracting online would have been questionable given the consumer's weaker contractual position. Furthermore, it would have been unlikely that a business and consumer would subsequently agree to refer their dispute to a third country, particularly if it had no substantial connection to the parties, their contract or the dispute itself. Therefore, in a number of key respects, Article 7 in the 1999 draft convention was not appropriate for electronic consumer contracts.

The entire 1999 draft Convention was not adopted at the Special Commission meeting held in October 1999. Many aspects of the Convention remained unresolved, including which rules should be included in a white, grey or black list and which jurisdiction rules were deemed to be 'exorbitant.' In the absence of consensus, further work on the Convention was clearly required. In particular, it was recognised by the Hague Conference that electronic commerce had to be included[30] in the draft convention, as confirmed in their preliminary conclusions prior to the Ottawa Diplomatic meeting in February 2001. 'In view of the anticipated upsurge of electronic commerce in the immediate future, it would be unwise to exclude it from the substantive scope of the Convention.'[31] From that stage, a number of international governmental and non-governmental organisations began to acknowledge the potential impact of the proposed convention. Whilst the United States somewhat ironically led the wholesale opposition to the draft convention, denouncing it in its entirety,[32] the EU was particularly concerned with the particularly 'controversial'[33] provisions for consumer contracts.[34] Indeed, the Trans-Atlantic Consumer Dialogue responded to the proposals by acknowledging that even their own preference for ADR schemes ' ... [would] not diminish the need of consumers for access to judicial redress.'[35] Furthermore, an Australian government paper on the issues posed by the draft convention observed that

> (E)lectronic commerce brings the jurisdictional issues in relation to consumer protection sharply into focus because:

30 It is suggested that e-commerce required to be included expressly. Øren, 'International Jurisdiction Over Consumer Contracts in e-Europe.'

31 Preliminary Document No.7, at p.35 and 'Issues Paper 3, International Electronic Commerce,' November 2000, ibid.

32 'Issues Paper 3, International Electronic Commerce,' November 2000.

33 Issues Paper 3, ibid.

34 Council of the European Union, 'Conclusions concerning work in The Hague, with a view to preparing a draft Convention on international Jurisdiction and the Effects of Foreign judgments in civil and commercial matters,' 25–30 October 1999, JUSTCIV 139 11751/99, 11 October 1999, and 'Draft Hague Convention on Jurisdiction and the recognition and enforcement of foreign judgments,' JUSTCIV 172, 13225/99, 22 November 1999.

35 Trans Atlantic Consumer Dialogue, 'Resolution on the Proposed Hague Convention on Jurisdiction and Foreign Judgments in Civil and Commercial Matters,' Ecom-22–01, May 2001, available at <http://www.tacd.org>.

- the internet significantly expands the scope for consumers to purchase goods and services direct from overseas suppliers;
- it significantly expands the ability of small to medium business to sell direct to consumer overseas;
- the nature of web advertising is that business may be unable to ascertain the location of consumers and therefore have no choice over the consumers they contract with and therefore their resulting liabilities. [36]

The first informal meeting in Ottawa considered electronic commerce and the draft convention,[37] by focussing on 'three fundamental issues'[38] pertaining to contracts conducted online between businesses. The issues seemed to be more focussed on place of contracting and performance than investigating the most appropriate connecting factor for jurisdiction over an electronic consumer contract. With regard to the specific implications of Article 7 for consumer contracts conducted online the Ottawa meeting report[39] was, with respect, vague and uncertain in its assertions. For example, given the points raised in the earlier analysis of Article 7(1) of the 1999 draft, it is difficult to see how the draft Article 7(1)(a) 'would not seem to have any further relevance for the purposes of electronic commerce.'[40] Indeed, it appeared that the whole ethos behind Article 7 was that if the foreign consumer was sought out by a business and as a result contracted with that business for goods or services, then the business' activities are crucial to establishing jurisdiction. Whilst the Ottawa report demonstrated that no consensus had 'as yet'[41] been reached on the extent to which businesses used their web sites to target consumers, the lack of unanimity appeared to be premised on the existence of passive web sites.[42] It is unfortunate that the Ottawa Informal meeting did not examine the significance of web site activities at the time the draft convention was being revised.

Article 7 of the June 2001 draft Convention contained a proposal for consumer contract jurisdiction and three alternative proposals for jurisdiction agreements.[43] Article 7(1)(a) of the 2001 draft retained the definition of a consumer ('a natural person acting primarily for personal, family or household purposes' (Article 7(1)) and a 'business' (i.e. 'another party acting for the purposes of its trade or profession' (Article 7(1)) previously in the 1999 draft. However, this was further qualified

36 'Issues Paper 3, International Electronic Commerce,' November 2000, note 31 supra, where reference was also made to the DTI's comments on the archaic nature of Article 13 of the Brussels Convention.

37 'Electronic Commerce and International Jurisdiction,' summary of discussions prepared by C. Kessedjian, Ottawa, 28 February to 1 March 2000, Preliminary Document 12 August 2000.

38 Preliminary Document No.12, ibid at p.4.

39 Ibid.

40 Preliminary Document No.12, at p.6.

41 Ibid at p.9.

42 Preliminary Document No.12, ibid at p.7.

43 Article 7 of the 2001 draft Convention is in the Appendix.

to the extent that Article 7 would not apply if the 'other party' would not have entered into the contract if they had known that the consumer was contracting for the purposes of personal, family or household reasons. Such a get-out appeared to protect businesses that did not seek to contract with consumers by permitting them to 'dis-target' particular jurisdictions.[44] However, jurisdiction must be premised on a positive act by the business to undertake commercial activities as a legitimate alternative to the business' physical presence in the jurisdiction. The potential difficulty with this opt out would have been ensuring its effective operation in the context of an electronic consumer contract. For example, it would be difficult to determine whether consumers had sufficient knowledge of such an opt-out (and its effect) and whether they could circumvent it by, using a foreign ISP to access the web site or providing an address situated in another jurisdiction (acceptable to the business). A connecting factor which subjects the business to the consumer's jurisdiction must require a positive act on behalf of the seller to target consumers in their own jurisdiction.

The draft Article 7(2) proposed that the consumer could bring either 'proceedings' or 'an action in contract' where he was habitually resident 'if the claim relates to a contract which arises out of activities, including promotion or negotiation of contracts, which the other party conducted in that State, or directed to that State.'[45] It remained outstanding whether the consumer was entitled to raise 'proceedings,' or the more restricted alternative 'action in contract' against the business in his own jurisdiction. It is submitted that the proposals ought to have preserved the 1999 draft convention to enable a consumer to raise proceedings in his or her own jurisdiction provided those proceedings relate to the dispute in question. The most important aspect of Article 7(2) was that 'the claim related to a contract which arose out of activities, including promotion or negotiation of contracts, which the other party conducted in that State, or directed to that State.'[46]

The requirement for prior promotion or negotiation of contracts either *conducted in* or *directed to* that State was of particular significance to electronic consumer contracts. Again, as with Article 7(1) of the 1999 draft (as well as 15(1)(c) of the Brussels 1 Regulation), no definitions of 'promotion' or 'directing' activities were offered. Interestingly, whilst the term publicity was removed from Article 7(2) of the 2001 draft convention, it appears to have been replaced by the analogous term 'promotion.' Nevertheless, the possibility that businesses could direct their activities to states in which consumers were habitually resident still required to be precisely determined by the Hague Conference.

44 D. Svantesson, 'Jurisdiction Issue in Cyberspace What Should Article 7 – Consumer Contracts, of the Proposed Hague Convention, Aim to Accomplish in Relation to E-Commerce?' (2001) 5 *CLSR* 318 at p.323.

45 Article 7(2), 2001 draft convention, Appendix.

46 Ibid.

Despite all of the documents published during 1999–2001 on the draft convention, the Hague Conference did not consider the impact of electronic commerce in sufficient depth.[47] Furthermore, there was only one brief discussion reported on the meaning of 'directing activities.'[48] Whist passing reference was made in Preliminary Document No.17 to the different grounds of jurisdiction applied by courts in Canada, Germany, France, China and Australia in relation to the Internet, the majority of the discussion was premised on the United States' court analysis of the accessibility of a web site and emerging significance of the active and passive distinction between web sites. The Hague Conference made no effort to consider the ways in which the Hague Conference could have contributed to alleviating the fact that 'the Internet disturbs conventional notions of private international law.'[49] Despite the challenges of negotiating and drafting the Convention, Haines suggested that 'it is clear that these challenges are worth overcoming ... [since] ... (T)he e-commerce industry is becoming an increasingly vital part of economic and intellectual development in the Member States of the Hague Conference.'[50]

Given the lack of definition of directing activities, had the Convention been approved, Article 7 had to include the requirement that the business intentionally targeted the consumer's jurisdiction. In any event, the ability of the consumer to raise such proceedings could have been subject to the other party being able to establish that the consumer took the steps necessary for the conclusion of the contract in another State and that the goods or services were supplied to the consumer while the consumer was present in the other State.[51] These provisions were similar to Article 15 of the Brussels 1 Regulation. The draft Convention proposed that businesses could be exempt from the provisions of the Article if they could demonstrate that they did not intend to direct their activities, such as advertising, to consumers in certain jurisdictions. It is not surprising that in a footnote to Article 7(3) the Hague Conference acknowledged that '(T)here is no consensus on this provision.' Indeed, as stated previously and in the quote from the Nygh and Pocar Report in this Chapter, the requirement for intentional targeting must be premised on businesses positively seeking out and targeting consumers in foreign jurisdictions.

47 S.P. Baumgartner, 'The Proposed Hague Convention on Jurisdiction and Foreign Judgments: Where We Are and the Road Ahead' (2002) 4:1 E.J.L.R. 219 at p.225.

48 A. Haines, Hague Conference on Private International Law, 'The Impact of the Internet on the Judgments Project: Thoughts for the Future' Preliminary Document No.17, February 2002, at pp. 19–22 inclusive.

49 Ibid at p.22.

50 Ibid. Word in brackets added.

51 The requirement for the consumer to have received the goods in the other state was a bracketed, optional requirement in the draft convention.

As a result of two Diplomatic Meetings,[52] three alternative proposals for jurisdiction agreements were proposed for inclusion in Article 7.[53] The alternative proposals relate to determining the applicability of jurisdiction agreements in consumer contracts. The importance of these proposals could not be underestimated as they would have invariably affected the application of Article 7(2) considered earlier. It is submitted that Variant One of Alternative B (failing which Alternative C) would have been the most appropriate option to establish a rule on jurisdiction agreements for consumer contracts.[54] Variant One of Alternative B (and Alternative C) restricted the parties' jurisdiction agreement to the jurisdiction of the consumers' habitual residence. Variant One also enabled a Contracting State to uphold a jurisdiction agreement between the parties only if a dispute had arisen first, and to refuse recognition of a judgment if Article 7 had not been adhered to. By comparison, Variant Two of Alternative B was extremely similar to Article 17 of the Brussels 1 Regulation. It is submitted that rules for consumer contracts should have been obligatory (or white) in the Convention for, as the present author has previously argued, 'to leave such rules to the discretion of Contracting States would certainly inhibit any efforts at global harmonisation of jurisdiction and the recognition of judgments for such contracts in the first place.'[55]

It is questionable and unfortunate that the Hague Conference removed juridical protection for consumers from its draft convention for the following reasons. First, as this section demonstrated, the Hague Conference included jurisdiction rules for consumer contracts in the 1999 draft. Second, the Hague Conference recognised the importance of integrating juridical protection for consumers in the convention and acknowledged the importance of regulating cross-border commercial activities via the WWW.[56] The World Intellectual Property Organisation's Primer report supported the universalist approach in the Hague Conference's proposed convention as a means of ensuring legal predictability for businesses.

> (W)ith an adequate understanding, [businesses] can begin to organize the conduct of their affairs in order to achieve some assurance that they will not be subject to potential lawsuits in multiple and remote locations … should they fail to do so, the resulting confusion may discourage enterprises from using this efficient and internationally accessible avenue of commerce.[57]

---

52 These alternative drafts were the result of the Diplomatic meetings held in Ottawa in March 2000 and Edinburgh in April 2001.

53 Article 7, Alternatives A, B and C are reproduced as they were presented in the draft 2001 Convention in Appendix.

54 Gillies, 'The Impact of the Hague Conference's Proposed Judgments Convention for Electronic Commerce and Intellectual Property Disputes,' at p.243.

55 Gillies, ibid.

56 Haines, Preliminary Document No.17, at pp. 4, 5, 6 and *cf* p.7.

57 WIPO, 'Primer on Electronic Commerce and Intellectual Property Issues,' at p.8. Word in brackets amended.

Third, the Hague Conference undertook additional meetings and produced reports and various options for consumer contracts in Article 7 of the 2001 draft convention. Fourthly, the Hague Conference acknowledged the necessity for a consistent approach to jurisdiction rules for electronic (consumer) contracts.[58] As the Ottawa report confirmed,

> (T)he debate which followed made clear the interests at stake: States want to encourage electronic commerce, especially in the area of consumer contracts. ... From another point of view, it is clear that the Internet will only take off, in the context of trade with consumers, if consumers themselves have confidence in it. And one of the essential points for the consumer is to be sure that is a problem arises in his relationship with the business, he can obtain redress both rapidly and cost-effectively.[59]

The position papers issued by the Hague Conference indicated that to ensure completion of the project on time, contentious matters[60] (such as rules for consumer contracts)[61] would be sacrificed and removed from the scope of the convention. The contentious nature of the consumer contract jurisdiction rules appeared, in the Hague Conference's opinion, to be premised on whether Contracting States preferred a 'Country of Origin' or 'Country of Destination' approach to their jurisdiction rules for consumer contracts and the extent to which the EU's 'Country of Destination' approach may or may not affect the long-term impact of electronic commerce activity as a disincentive to businesses. However, the 'Country of Origin' and 'Country of Destination' approaches do not, and should not, conflict in the context of juridical protection for consumers. Regardless of the increased choice available to the consumer via the WWW, consumers must still be provided with effective juridical protection that enables them to sue in their own jurisdiction. Haines suggested that a targeting test would be an effective 'compromise' between the 'Country of Origin' and 'Country of Destination' approaches.[62] In support of that proposition, Haines cited the Ottawa report which said '(I)f the enterprise had specifically targeted consumers in a particular country, it would be consistent to decide that the courts of that country have jurisdiction for consumers residing on its territory.'[63] Haines was concerned with how targeting would be constituted. With the greatest of respect, Haines appeared to confuse the issue when she questioned how a *web site* targets a consumer. As Chapter Three argued, the modification to current jurisdiction rules should focus on whether the *business* intentionally

58 Haines, Preliminary Document No.17, at p.5 and 7.

59 Kessedjian, Preliminary Document 12, at p.7.

60 Baumgartner, at p.225.

61 Preliminary Document No.7, at p.7, 15 *et seq*.

62 A.D. Haines, 'Why is it so difficult to construct an international legal framework for e-commerce? The draft Hague Convention on Jurisdiction and the Recognition and Enforcement of Foreign Judgments: a case study' (2002) 3:1 *E.B.O.R.* 157–194 at p.179.

63 Haines, ibid at p.179.

targeted the consumer via its web site and *not* whether the web site (as a method of communication) targeted consumers. The Hague Conference appeared to justify their eventual position by advocating that Contracting States must address the issues and implications of electronic commerce in their own jurisdictions.[64] Nevertheless, the Hague Conference remarked,

> (B)earing in mind the international nature of electronic commerce, and its essentially multidisciplinary character, it may be as well to point out that much of this work could be undertaken jointly be several different organisations, thus enhancing the efficiency of the work and the management of the funds allotted for the purpose. Moreover, for work pertaining to international private law, collaboration with the Hague Conference would be desirable.[65]

Whilst international commercial activities including those conducted via electronic commerce[66] need global regulation of jurisdiction, recognition and enforcement rules, after more than a decade a cohesive desire for such rules eludes the Hague Conference's efforts in reaching agreement on a global 'justice product.'[67] To that extent, the importance of the Hague Conference's project goes beyond its 'scholarly orientation.'[68] Even though the project abandoned jurisdiction rules for consumers, the project itself highlighted how governments must modify juridical protection for consumers who contract with foreign businesses via the WWW.

Conclusion

Despite recent adaptation, existing jurisdiction and choice of law rules for consumer contracts in the United Kingdom and the United States are not conducive to electronic consumer contracts. Whilst these countries already have highly developed consumer protection rules, international private laws must ensure conflicts justice is maintained by reflecting the consumer's ability to contract by electronic means. Given the global, dematerialised nature of electronic commerce, harmonisation of juridical protection for consumers contracting via the WWW is necessary and desirable. As Poggi has remarked, '(A)ny international E-Commerce Convention will probably therefore have to exclude either consumer issues altogether, or simply continue to relinquish jurisdictional enforcement to

64 Haines, ibid at p.7 and 10.

65 Ibid at p.7.

66 Haines.

67 V. Black, 'Commodifying Justice For Global Free Trade: The Proposed Hague Judgments Convention' (2000) 38:2 *Osgoode Hall Law Journal* 237 at p.266.

68 Black, ibid.

the consumer's home country.'[69] Accordingly, jurisdiction and choice of law rules for such contracts should be further amended to ensure that the consumer can sue in his own jurisdiction and rely on the law of his domicile when a foreign business has targeted the consumer via an active or interactive web site. Furthermore given the global, dematerialised nature of electronic commerce and the lack of coherent international regulation to date, the amendment of such rules should be harmonised via an international instrument in accordance with universalist objectives to ensure that conflicts justice and international[70] 'decisional harmony'[71] are achieved.

69 Poggi, 'Electronic Commerce Legislation: An Analysis of European and American Approaches to Contract Formation,' at p.249.

70 A.P.M.J. Vonken, 'Balancing Processes in International Family Law, On the determination and weighing of interests in the conflicts of laws and the "openness" of the choice of law system,' in T.M. De Boer (ed), *Forty Years On: The Evolution of Post War Private International Law in Europe, Symposium in Celebration of the 40th Anniversary of the Centre of Foreign Law and Private International Law*, University of Amsterdam, on 27 October 1989 (Deventer, 1990) at p.178.

71 T.M. De Boer, 'The Evolution of Postwar Private International Law,' ibid at p.2, citing Meijers.

Appendix (i)

European Commission Statement on Articles 15 and 73

"1. The Council and the Commission are aware that the development of electronic commerce in the information society facilitates the economic growth of undertakings. Community law is an essential if citizens, economic operators and consumers are to benefit from the possibilities afforded by electronic commerce.

They consider that the development of distance marketing techniques based on the use of the Internet depends in part on the mutual confidence which may grow up between undertakings and consumers. One of the major elements in this confidence is the opportunity offered to consumers by Article 16 of the Regulation to bring possible disputes before the courts of the Member States in which they reside, where the contract concluded by the consumer is covered by Article 15 of the Regulation.

The Council and the Commission point out in this connection that for Article 15(1)(c) to be applicable it is not sufficient for an undertaking to target its activities at the Member State of the consumer's residence, or at a number of Member States including that Member State; a contract must also be concluded within the framework of its activities. This provision relates to a number of marketing methods, including contracts concluded at a distance through the Internet.

In this context, the Council and the Commission stress that the mere fact that an Internet site is accessible is not sufficient for Article 15 to be applicable, although a factor will be that this Internet site solicits the conclusion of distance contracts and that a contract has actually been concluded at a distance, by whatever means. In this respect, the language or currency which a web site uses does not constitute a relevant factor.

2. The Council and the Commission take the view that in general it is in the interest of consumers and undertakings to try to settle their disputes amicably before resorting to the courts.

The Council and the Commission stress in this connection that the purpose of the Regulation, and in particular Articles 15 and 17 thereof, is not to prohibit the parties from making use of alternative methods of dispute settlement.

The Council and the Commission accordingly wish to reiterate how important it is that work on alternative methods of dispute settlement in civil and commercial matters should continue at European Community level, in keeping with the Council's conclusions of 29 May 2000.

They are aware of the great significance of this work and stress the useful complementary role represented by alternative methods of dispute settlement in civil and commercial matters, in particular with regard to electronic commerce.

3. Pursuant to Article 73 of the Regulation, the Commission is to submit a report on the application of the Regulation, accompanied, if need by, by proposals for adaptations, to the European Parliament, the Council and the Economic and Social Committee.

The Council and the Commission consider that in preparing the report especial attention should be paid to the application of the provisions of the Regulation relating to consumers and small and medium-sized undertakings, in particular with respect to electronic commerce. For this purpose, the Commission will, where appropriate, propose amendments to the Regulation before expiry of the period referred to in Article 73 of the Regulation."

Source: European Commission (Copyright European Commission).

Appendix (ii)

Draft Article 4 (Agreements on Choice of Court) in the 1999 Draft Hague Convention on Jurisdiction and the Recognition of Judgments in Civil and Commercial Matters

"Article 4

1. If the parties have agreed that a court or courts of a Contracting State shall have jurisdiction to settle any dispute which has arisen or may arise in connection with a particular legal relationship, that court or those courts shall have jurisdiction, and that jurisdiction shall be exclusive unless the parties have agreed otherwise. Where an agreement having exclusive effect designates a court or courts of a non-Contracting State, courts in Contracting States shall decline jurisdiction or suspend proceedings unless the court or courts chosen have themselves declined jurisdiction.

2. An agreement within the meaning of paragraph 1 shall be valid as to form, if it was entered into or confirmed –

(a) in writing;
(b) by any other means of communication which renders information accessible so as to be usable for subsequent reference;
(c) in accordance with a usage which is regularly observed by the parties;
(d) in accordance with a usage of which the parties were or ought to have been aware and which is regularly observed by the parties to contracts of the same nature in the particular trade or commerce concerned.

3. Agreements conferring jurisdiction and similar clauses in trust instruments shall be without effect if they conflict with the provisions of Article 7, 8 or 12."

Source: Hague Conference on Private International Law.

Appendix (iii)

Draft Article 7 (jurisdiction for consumer contracts) in 1999 Draft Hague Convention on Jurisdiction and the Recognition of Judgments in Civil and Commercial Matters

"Article 7 Contracts concluded by consumers

1. A plaintiff who concluded a contract for a purpose which is outside its trade or profession, hereafter designated as the consumer, may bring a claim in the courts of the State in which it is habitually resident, if:

   (a) the conclusion of the contract on which the claim is based is related to trade or professional activities that the defendant has engaged in or directed to that State, in particular in soliciting business through means of publicity, and

   (b) the consumer has taken the steps necessary for the conclusion of the contract in that State.

2. A claim against the consumer may only be brought by a person who entered the contract in the course of its trade or profession before the courts of the State of the habitual residence of the consumer.

3. The parties to a contract within the meaning of paragraph 1 may, by an agreement which conforms with the requirements of Article 4, make a choice of court –

   (a) if such agreement is entered into after the dispute has arisen, or

   (b) to the extent only that it allows the consumer to bring proceedings in another court."

Source: Hague Conference on Private International Law.

Appendix (iv)

Draft Article 7 (including the alternative proposals for jurisdiction agreements)[1] in the 2001 Draft Hague Convention on Jurisdiction and the Recognition of Judgments in Civil and Commercial Matters

"Article 7 Contracts concluded by consumers

> 1. This Article applies to contracts between a natural person acting primarily for personal, family or household purposes, the consumer, and another party acting for the purposes of its trade or profession, [unless the other party demonstrates that it neither knew nor had any reason to know that the consumer was concluding the contract primarily for personal, family or household purposes, and would not have entered into the contract if it had known otherwise].
>
> 2. Subject to paragraphs [5–7], a consumer may bring [proceedings] [an action in contract] in the courts of the State in which the consumer is habitually resident if the claim relates to a contract which arises out of activities, including promotion or negotiation of contracts, which the other party conducted in that State, or directed to that State, [unless [that party establishes that] –
>
> > (a) the consumer took the steps necessary for the conclusion of the contract in another State: [and
> > (b) the goods or services were supplied to the consumer while the consumer was present in the other State]].
>
> [3. For the purposes of paragraph 2, activity shall not be regarded as being directed to a State if the other party demonstrates that it took reasonable steps to avoid concluding contracts with consumers habitually resident in the State.]
>
> 4. Subject to paragraphs [5–7], the other party to the contract may bring proceedings against a consumer under this Convention only in the courts of the State in which the consumer is habitually resident."

1 Square brackets were used in the original draft Article to highlight alternatives.

"[Alternative A

5. [Article 4 applies to a jurisdiction agreement between a consumer and the other party if the agreement is entered into after the dispute has arisen.

6. Where a consumer and the other party have entered into an agreement which conforms with the requirements of Article 4(1) and (2) before the dispute has arisen, the consumer may bring proceedings against the other party in the courts of the State designated in that agreement.

7. Where a consumer and the other party have entered into an agreement which conforms with the requirements of Article 4(1) and (2) before the dispute has arisen, Article 4 applies to the agreement to the extent that it is binding on both parties under the law of the State in which the consumer is habitually resident at the time the agreement is entered into.
Add at the beginning of Article 25,
'Subject to Article 25, *bis*'
Insert [*Article 25 bis*
1. A Contracting State may make a declaration that it will not recognise or enforce a judgment under this Chapter, or a declaration specifying the conditions under which it will recognise or enforce a judgment under this Chapter, where –

(a) the judgment was rendered by the court of origin under Article 7(2) [or Article 8(2)];

(b) the parties had entered into an agreement which conforms with the requirements of Article 4 designating a court other than the court of origin.]]"

[Alternative B

[Variant 1
5. This provision may be departed from by a jurisdiction agreement provided that it conforms with the requirements of Article 4.

6. A Contracting State may declare that –

(a) it will only respect a jurisdiction agreement if it is entered into after the dispute has arisen or to the extent that it allows the consumer to bring proceedings in a court other than a court indicated in this Article or in Article 3; and

(b) it will not recognise and enforce a judgment where jurisdiction has been taken in accordance with a jurisdiction agreement that does not fulfil the requirements in sub-paragraph (a).]

[Variant 2
5. Article 4 applies to an agreement between a consumer and the other party if the agreement is entered into after the dispute has arisen; or to the extent that the agreement permits the consumer to bring proceedings in a court other than the consumer's habitual residence.

6. A Contracting State may declare in the circumstances specified in that declaration –

(a) it will respect a jurisdiction agreement entered into before the dispute has arisen;
(b) it will recognise and enforce a judgment in proceedings brought by the other party given by a court under a jurisdiction agreement entered into before the dispute has arisen;
(c) it will not recognise and enforce a judgment given by a court in which proceedings could not be brought consistently with a jurisdiction agreement entered into before the dispute has arisen]]."

[Alternative C

5. Article 4 applies to a jurisdiction agreement between a consumer and the other party if the agreement is entered into after the dispute has arisen.

6. Where a consumer and the other party have entered into an agreement which conforms with the requirements of Article 4(1) and (2) before the dispute has arisen –

(a) the consumer may bring proceedings against the other party under the Convention in the courts of the State designated in that agreement
(b) the consumer may not bring proceedings against the other party under this Convention in any other court unless the agreement permits the proceedings to be brought in that court;
(c) the other party may bring proceedings against the consumer under this Convention only if the agreement permits the proceedings to be brought in the courts of the State in which the consumer is habitually resident]]."

Source: Hague Conference on Private International Law.

Bibliography

Articles

Abramson, Leslie W., 'Clarifying "Fair Play and Substantial Justice": How the Courts Apply the Supreme Court Standard for Personal Jurisdiction' (1991) 18 *Hastings Const LQ* 441.

Aciman, Carole and Vo-Verde, Diane, 'Refining The Zippo Test: New Trends on Personal Jurisdiction for Internet Activities' (2002) 19 *Computer and Internet Law* 16.

Aguilar, John R., 'Over the Rainbow. European and American Consumer Protection Policy and Remedy Conflicts on the Internet and a Possible Solution' (Winter 1999/2000) *International Journal of Communications Law and Policy* Issue 4.

Akehurst, Michael 'Jurisdiction in International Law' (1972–73) 46 *BYBIL* 145.

Auf der Mar, Rolf, 'Internet-Enabled Distribution Models,' 1999 *IBL* 264.

Basedow, Jürgen 'The Communitarisation of The Conflict of Laws Under The Treaty of Amsterdam' (2000) 37 *CMLR* 687.

Baumgartner, Samuel P., 'The proposed Hague Convention on Jurisdiction and Foreign Judgments: Where we are and the road ahead' (2002) 4:1 *E.J.L.R.* 219.

Beaumont, Paul R., 'A United Kingdom Perspectives on the Proposed Hague Judgments Convention' (1998) XXIV *Brook Int'l L* 1–75.

Beaumont, Paul R., 'European Court of Justice and Jurisdiction and Enforcement of Judgments in Civil and Commercial Matters' (1999) 48 *ICLQ* 223.

Black, Vaughan, 'Commodifying Justice For Global Free Trade: The Proposed Hague Judgments Convention' (2000) 38 *Osgoode Hall Law Journal* 237.

Blaikie, J., 'Choice of Law in Consumer Contracts' (1992) 60 *SLG* 6.

Boone, Brian, 'Bullseye!: Why A "Targeting" Approach To Personal Jurisdiction In The E-Commerce Context Makes Sense Internationally' (2006) 20 *Emory Int'l L. Rev.* 241.

Borchers, Patrick J., 'The Internationalization of Contractual Conflicts Law,' in 'Symposium: Conflict of Laws in the Global Village: International Conflicts Issues for the General Course in Conflict of Laws' (1995) 28 *Vand J Transnat'l L* 421.

Borchers, Patrick J., 'Judgments Conventions and Minimum Contracts' (1998) 61 *Alb L Rev* 1161.

Borchers, Patrick J., 'A Few Little Issues for the Hague Judgments Negotiations' (1998) XXIV *Brook J Int'l L* 157.

Bowett, D.W., 'Jurisdiction: Changing Patterns of Authority over Activities and Resources' (1982) *BYBIL* 1.

Brand, Ronald A., 'Tort Jurisdiction in a Multilateral Convention: The Lessons Of The Due Process Clause and the Brussels Convention' (1998) XXIV *Brook J Int'l L* 125.

Brand, Ronald A. ,'Due Process, Jurisdiction and a Hague Judgments Convention' (1999) 60 *U Pitt LR* 661.

Briggs, A., 'The Brussels Convention' (1993) 13 *YEL* 511.

Bristows, 'Consumer contracts and jurisdiction – changes to the Brussels Convention' (2001) *IHL* 66.

Brown, Tim and Hamer, Alex, 'Jurisdiction and the Internet: the EC Perspective' (2000) 28 *IBL* 439.

Burbank, Stephen B., 'Jurisdictional Equilibration, the Proposed Hague Convention and Progress in National Law' (2001) 40 *Am J Comp L* 203.

Burman, Harold S., 'International Conflict of Laws, The 1994 Inter-American Convention on the Law Applicable to International Contracts, and Trends for the 1990s,' in 'Symposium: Conflict of Laws in the Global Village: International Conflicts Issues for the General Course in Conflict of Laws' (1995) 28 *Vand J Transnat'l L* 367.

Burman, Harold S., 'Building on the CISG: International Commercial Law Development and Trends For The 2000's' (1998) 17 *J L and Commerce* 355.

Burns, Joseph S., and Bales, Richard A., 'Personal Jurisdiction and the Web' (2001) 53 *Me. L. Rev.* 29.

Burnstein, Matthew R., 'Conflicts on the Net: Choice of Law in Transnational Cyberspace' (1996) *Vand J Transnat'l L* 75.

Byassee, William S., 'Jurisdiction of Cyberspace: Applying Real World Precedent to the Virtual Community' (1995) 30 *Wake Forrest L Rev* 197.

Catchpole, James, 'The Regulation of Electronic Commerce: A Comparative Analysis of the Issues Surrounding the principles of Establishment' (2001) 9 *Int J Law and Info Tech* 1.

Chance, Clifford, 'Unfair Terms in Consumer Contracts Case *Oceano Grupo Editorial SA v Quintero and Others* C-240/98 TO 244/98, 27 June 2000' (2000) 11 *Practice Law for Companies* 56.

Collins, Lawrence, 'Contractual Obligations – The EEC Preliminary Draft Convention on Private International Law' (1976) 25 *ICLQ* 35.

Debussere, Frederic, 'International Jurisdiction over E-Consumer Contracts in the European Union: Quid Novi Sub Sole?' (2002) 10 *IJLIT* 344.

Dively, Mary Jo Howard, 'The New Laws That Will Enable Electronic Contracting: A Survey of the Electronic Contracting Rules in the Uniform Electronic Transactions Act and the Uniform Computer Information Transactions Act' (2000) 38 *Duq L. Rev* 209.

Docherty, Michael and Fletcher, Roland, 'Responding to the legal problems of electronic commerce' (2000) 5 *Communications Law* 2.

Dubanevich, Keith S., and Shebiel, Alec J., 'Personal Jurisdiction in the Silicon Forest' (2001) 62 (Dec) Or. St. B. Bull 21.

Dutson, Stuart, 'The Internet, the conflict of Laws, international litigation and intellectual property: the implications of the international scope of the Internet on intellectual property infringements' (1997) *JBL* 495.

Dutson, Stuart, 'International E-Commerce' (2000) 6:3 *CTLR* 76.

Duston, Stuart, 'Transnational E-Commerce' (2000) 16 *CLSR* 105.

Editorial Comment, 'Unfair Terms and the Role of the Courts' (2000) 23 *Consumer Law Today* 1.

Editorial, 'On the Way to a Rome 1 Regulation' (2006) 43:4 *CMLR* 913

Endeshaw, Assafa, 'The Proper Law for Electronic Commerce' (1998) 1 *Information and Communications Technology Law* 5.

Epps, Brian K., '*Maritz, Inc v Cybergold, Inc*: The Expansion of Personal Jurisdiction in the Modern Age of Internet Advertising' (1997) 32 *Ga L Rev* 237.

Falcon, W. David, 'A Nice Place to Visit But I Wouldn't Want to Litigate There: The Effect of *Cybersell v Cybersell* on the Laws of Personal Jurisdiction' (Spring 1999) 5 *Rich J L & Tech* 11.

Fawcett, James, 'The Interrelationships of Jurisdiction and Choice of Law in Private International Law' (1991) 44 *Current Legal Problems* 39.

Fennelly, Nial, 'The Area of "Freedom, Security and Justice," and the European Court of Justice – A Personal View' (2000) 49 *ICLQ* 1.

Fentiman, Richard, 'Commercial Expectations and the Rome Convention' (2002) 61:1 *CLJ* 50.

Finocchiaro, Giusella, 'European Law and Consumer Protection in the Information Age' (2003) 12:2 *Information and Communication Technology Law* 111.

Fitzmaurice, Kevin M., and Mody, Renu M., 'International Shoe Meets the World Wide Web. Whither Personal Jurisdiction in Florida in the Age of the Internet?' (1997) 71 *Fla BJ* 22.

Flaming, Todd, H., 'The Rules of Cyberspace: Informal Law in a New Jurisdiction' (1997) 85 *Ill BJ* 174.

Forner, Joaquim-J., 'Special Jurisdiction in Commercial Contracts: From the 1968 Brussels Convention to Brussels-One Regulation' (2002) 13:3 *ICCLR* 131.

Foss, Morten and Bygrave, Lee A., 'International Consumer Purchases through the Internet: Jurisdictional Issues pursuant to European Law' (2000) 8:2 *Int J Law & Info Tech* 99.

Furrer, Andreas, 'European Law Without Peak and Centre? Observations on the Europeanization Process in Private Law Towards a Supranational Multi-level System,' in Joerges, Christian and Gerstenberg, Oliver (eds), 'Private governance, democratic constitutionalism and supranationalism,' Proceedings of the COST A7 Seminar, Florence, 22 to 24 May 1997.

Gaja, Giorgio, 'How Flexible is Flexibility Under the Amsterdam Treaty?' (1998) 35 *CMLR* 855.

Gallagher, Steven, 'Contracting in Cyberspace – A Minefield for the Unwary' (2000) 16 *CLSR* 101.

Gasparini, Louis, U., 'The Internet and Personal Jurisdiction: Traditional Jurisprudence for the Twenty-first Century Under The New York CPLR' (2001) 12 *Alb L J Sci & Tech* 191.

Gatt, Adam, 'Electronic Commerce- Click Wrap Agreements, The Enforceability of Click-Wrap Agreements' (2002) 18:6 *CLSR* 404.

Geist, Michael, 'Is There a There? Towards Greater Certainty for Internet Jurisdiction' (2001) 16 *Berkeley Tech Law Journal* 1345.

Gillies, Lorna E., 'A Review of the New Jurisdiction Rules for Electronic Consumer Contracts within the European Union,' Commentary, 2001 (1) *The Journal of Information, Law and Technology (JILT)* <http://www2.warwick.ac.uk/fac/soc/law/elj/jilt/2001_1/gillies>, 28 February 2001.

Gillies, Lorna E., 'Rules of Jurisdiction for Electronic Consumer Contracts – Scottish Perspectives' (2001) 2 *SLPQ* 124.

Gillies, Lorna E., 'New European Rules for Electronic Consumer Contracts' (2001) 17:6 *CLSR* 395.

Gillies, Lorna E., 'The Hague Conference's Proposed Judgments Convention: Issues and Implications for Electronic Commerce and Intellectual Property Disputes,' 17th BILETA Conference, Amsterdam, April 2002 <http://www2.warwick.ac.uk/fac/soc/law/elj/jilt/2001_1/gillies>.

Gillies, Lorna E., 'The Impact of the Hague Conference's Proposed Judgments Convention for Electronic Commerce and Intellectual Property Disputes' (2002) 16:3 *Int Rev L Comps and Tech* 233.

Gillies, Lorna E. 'Choice of Law Rules for Electronic Consumer Contracts: Replacement of the Rome Convention by the Rome 1 Regulation' (2007) 4 *Journal of Private International Law* 89.

Gillies, Lorna E., 'Legal Regulation of Risk in B2C Electronic Commerce – From Top-Down Regulation to Promoting Consumer Trust' in Ramsay, Iain, Salloum, John, Horrox, Naomi, Mowatt, Geoff (eds), *Risk and Choice in Consumer Society*, Ant. Sakkoulas, Athens, 2007.

Gillies, Lorna E., 'Addressing the "Cyberspace Fallacy": Targeting the Jurisdiction of an Electronic Consumer Contract' (2008) 2 *Int Journal Law and Inf Tech*, 1.

Goldstein, Nicole, 'Brussels 1: A Race to the Top' (2001) 2 *Chi. J. Int'l L.* 521.

Green, Jason, 'Is Zippo's Sliding Scale a Slippery Slope of Uncertainty? A Case For Abolishing Web Site Interactivity As A Conclusive Factor in Assessing Minimum Contacts in Cyberspace' (2001) 34 *J Marshall L Rev* 1051.

Hamilton, Jenny and Gillies, Lorna E., 'The Impact of E-commerce on Consumer Welfare – Information Disclosure Regimes' (2003) 11:4 *Journal of Financial Regulation and Compliance* 329.

Haines, Avril D., 'Why is it so difficult to construct an international legal framework for e-commerce? The draft Hague Convention on Jurisdiction and the Recognition and Enforcement of Foreign Judgments: a case study' (2002) 3:1 *E.B.O.R.* 157–194.

Horn, Anita, 'Internet Transaction Taxes: The Need for Jurisdictional Integration' (2001) 9 *CommLaw Conspectus* 29.

Hörnle, Julia, 'The European Union Takes Initiative in the Field of E-Commerce,' Commentary 2000 (3) *The Journal of Information, Law and Technology (JILT)* <http://elj.warwick.ac.uk/jilt/00-3/hornle.html>.

Howells, G., and Wilhelmsson, T.,'EC Consumer law: has come of age?' (2003) 28 *European Law Review* 370.

In Focus, 'Defining E-Commerce' (2000) *First Quarter I-Ways* 32.

Israël, Jona, 'Conflicts of Law and the EC after Amsterdam: A Change for the Worse?' (2000) 7 *MJ* 81.

Janssens, Thomas, 'The Shearson judgment of the European Court of Justice: Problems raised by the "Europeanisation" and "Communitisation" of the Term "Consumer" in the Brussels Jurisdiction and Judgments Convention' (1995) 4 *ERPL* 605.

Juenger, Friedrich, K., 'A Shoe Unfit for Globetrotting' (1995) 25 *UC Davis LR* 1027.

Kalow, Gwenn M., 'From the Internet to Court: Exercising Jurisdiction Over World Wide Web Communications' (1997) 65 *Fordham L.Rev.* 2241.

Kennett, Wendy (ed), 'Current Developments: Private International Law' (1999) 48:2 *ICLQ* 465.

Kennett, Wendy (ed), 'Current Developments: Private International Law' (1999) 48:4 *ICLQ* 966.

Kennett, Wendy (ed), 'Current Developments: Private International Law The Brussels 1 Regulation' (2000) 50:3 *ICLQ* 725.

Knöfel, Suzanne, 'Mandatory Rules and Choice of Law: A Comparative Approach to Article 7(2) of the Rome Convention' (1999) *JBL* 239.

Kohl, Uta, 'Eggs, Jurisdiction and the Internet' (2002) 51 *ICLQ* 555.

Kohl, Uta 'The rule of law, jurisdiction and the Internet' (2004) 12:3 *I.J.L & I.T. 2004* 365.

Kortenberg, Helmut, 'Closer Cooperation in the Treaty of Amsterdam' (1998) 35 *CMLR* 833.

Kotuby, Jr., Charles T., 'External Competence of the European Community in the Hague Conference on Private International Law: Community Harmonization and Worldwide Unification' (2001) *NILR* 1.

Lando, Ole, '*Lex Fori* in *Foro Proprio*' (1995) 2 *MJ* 359.

Lando, Ole, 'Some Issues Relating to the Law Applicable to Contractual Obligations' (1996-97) *King's College Law Journal* 55.

Lehmann, Prof. Dr. jur. M., 'Electronic Commerce and Consumer Protection in Europe' (2000) 17 *Comp High Tech Law Journal* 101.

Lockerby, Michael J., 'Non-Contractual Legal Problems' (1999) *IBL* 244.

Mayer, Franz C., 'Europe and the Internet: The Old World and the New Medium' (2000) 11 *EJIL* 149.

Mayewski, Christine E., 'The Presence of a Web Site as a Constitutionally Permissible Basis for Personal Jurisdiction' (1997) 73 *Indiana LJ* 297

Mendes, Errol P., 'The Troublesome Workings of the Judgments Convention of the European Economic Community' (1980) 13 *Vand J Transnat'l L* 75.

Mennie, Alistair, 'Civil Jurisdiction and Consumer Contracts' (1987) SLT (News) 181.

Mitrani, Ahi, 'Regulating E-commerce, E-contracts and the controversy of Multiple Jurisdiction' (2001) 7 *Int TLR* 2, 50.

Mody, Sanjay S., 'National Cyberspace Regulation: Unbundling the Concept of Jurisdiction' (2001) 37 *STJIL* 365.

Moerel, Lokke, 'The Country-Of-Origin Principle in the E-Commerce Directive: The Expected "One Stop Shop?"' (2001) 7 *CTLR* 184.

Monar, Jörg, 'Justice and Home Affairs in the Treaty of Amsterdam: Reform at the Price of Fragmentation' (1998) 23 *EL Rev* 320.

Morse, C.G.J., 'The EEC Convention on the Law Applicable to Contractual Obligations' (1982) 2 *YEL* 107.

Morse, C.G.J., 'Consumer Contracts, Employment Contracts and The Rome Convention' (1992) 41 *ICLQ* 1.

Murphy, Sean, 'Negotiation of Convention on Jurisdiction and Enforcement of Judgments' (2001) 95 *Am J., Int'l L.* 418.

Murray, Andrew and Scott, Colin, 'Controlling the New Media: Hybrid Reponses to New Forms of Power' (2002) 65 *MLR* 491.

MacQueen, Hector L., and Azim-Khan, Rafi, 'The Argos free TV debacle: two legal opinions' (1999) 1 *Electronic Business Law* 9, 9.

Niemann, Jan-Malte, 'Cybercontracts – A Comparative View On The Actual Time of Formation' (2000) 5 *Communications Law* 48.

Niemann, Jan-Malte, 'Webvertisements Covered By Art.5(2) Rome Convention?' (2000) 5 *Communications Law* 99.

North, Peter, 'Private International Law: Change or Decay?' (2001) 50 *ICLQ* 477.

O'Brien Jr., William E., 'The Hague Convention on Jurisdiction and Judgments: The Way Forward' (2003) 66 *MLR* 491.

Øren, Joakim S.T., 'International Jurisdiction Over Consumer Contracts in e-Europe' (2003) 52 *ICLQ* 665.

Patel, Ajay, 'The Brussels Regulation ... Good for business' (2000) 2:12 *E-commerce law and policy* 10.

Pearce, Graham and Platten, Nicholas, 'Promoting the Information Society: The EU Directive on Electronic Commerce' (2000) 4 *ELJ* 363.

Peers, Steve, 'Justice and Home Affairs' (2000) 49 *ICLQ* 222.

Poggi, Christopher T., 'Electronic Commerce Legislation: An Analysis of European and American Approaches to Contract Formation' (2000) 41 *Va J Int'l L* 224.

Probasco, Angela R., 'Due Process Analysis in *Millenium Enterprises, Inc v Millenium Music*, LP' (2000) 40 *Jurimetrics* 457.

Puathasnanon, Sam, 'Cyberspace and Personal Jurisdiction: The Problem of Using Internet Contacts to Establish Minimum Contracts' (1998) 31 *Loy L A L Rev* 691.

Puurunen, Tapio, 'The Legislative Jurisdiction of States Over Transactions in International Electronic Commerce' (2000) XVIII *John Marshall Journal of Computer and Information Law* 688.

Reich, Norbert, 'Germany: Time Sharing Contract Consumer Protection and the Rome Convention' (1997) 5 *Consumer L J* 6, 40.

Reimann Mathias, 'American Private Law and European Legal Unification – Can the United States be a Model?' (1996) 3 *MJ* 217.

Remien, Oliver, 'European Private International Law, The European Community and its Emerging Area of Freedom, Security and Justice' (2001) 38 *CMLR* 53.

Rice, Denis T., 'A Cyberspace Odyssey Through US and EU Internet Jurisdiction,' Practising Law Institute, Patents, Trademarks and Literary Property Course Handbook Series, Fifth Annual Internet Law Institute, New York 9–10 July 2001, San Francisco, 23–24 July 2001.

Rice, Denis T., 'Jurisdiction in Cyberspace: Which Law and Forum Apply to Securities Transactions on the Internet?' (Fall, 2001) 21:3 *University of Pennsylvania Journal of International Economic Law* 585.

Riefa, C., 'Article 5 of the Rome Convention on the Law Applicable to Contractual Obligations 1980 and Consumer E-contracts: The Need for Reform' (2004) 13:1 *Information and Communications Technology Law* 59.

Rochlin, Richard, 'Cyberspace, International Shoe, and the Changing Context for Personal Jurisdiction' (2000) 32 *Conn LR* 653.

Roebuck, Will, 'Jurisdiction and E-Commerce' (2002) *CTLR* 29.

Rothchild, John, 'Protecting the Digital Consumer: The Limits of Cyberspace Utopianism' (1999) *Ind LJ* 74, 893.

Rowe, Heather, 'Electronic Commerce and Consumers' (1998) *IBL* 165.

Russell, Michael L., 'Back to Basics: Resisting Novel and Extreme Approaches to the Law of Personal Jurisdiction and the Internet' (1999) 30 *U.Mem.L.Rev* 157.

Salvado, Carlos J.R. 'An Effective Personal Jurisdiction Doctrine For The Internet' (2003) 12 *U. Balt. Intell. Prop. L.J.* 12, 75.

Schu, Reinhard, 'The Applicable Law to Consumer Contracts Made Over the Internet: Consumer Protection Through Private International Law?' (1997) 5:2 *Int J Law and Tech* 192.

Scottish Executive Justice Department, 'Jurisdiction, recognition and enforcement of judgments in civil and commercial matters' (2002) 47 *JLSS* 46.

Scottish Executive Justice Department, 'New Rules on Civil Jurisdiction' (2002) SLT (News) 39.

Siddiqi, Asaad, 'Welcome to the City of Bytes? An Assessment of the Traditional Methods Employes in the International Application of Jurisdiction Over Internet Activities – Including A Critique of Suggested Approaches' (2001) 14 *N.Y. Int'l L. Rev.* 43.

Silberman, Linda J., and Lowenfeld, Andreas F., 'A Different Challenge for the ALI: Herein of Foreign Country Judgments, an International Treaty, and on American Statute' (1998) 74 *Indiana LJ* 1, 635.

Smale, Trevor and Upton, Jack, 'E-Commerce Untangling the International Web' (2000) 5 *EU Counsel* 6, 43.

Sookman, Barry B., 'Electronic Commerce, Internet and the Law – A Survey of the Legal Issues' (1999) *CTLR* 52.

Stevenson, Andrew, 'Businesses as "Consumers"; Jurisdiction Within Scotland' (2000) 33 *Civ P.B*, 4.

Stone, Peter, 'Internet Consumer Contracts and European Private International Law' (2000) 9:1 *Information and Communications Technology Law* 5.

Stone, Peter, 'The Treatment of Electronic Contracts and Torts in Private International Law under European Community Legislation' (2002) 11:2 *Information and Communications Technology Law* 121.

Stott, David L., 'Personal Jurisdiction in Cyberspace: The Constitutional Boundary of Minimum Contacts Limited to a Web Site' (1997) 15 *Marshall J Computer and Info L* 819.

Stuyck, Jules, 'European Consumer Law After The Treaty of Amsterdam: Consumer Policy In Or Beyond The Internal Market?' (2000) 37 *CMLR* 367.

Svantesson, Dan, 'Jurisdiction Issue in Cyberspace What Should Article 7 – Consumer Contracts, of the Proposed Hague Convention, Aim to Accomplish in Relation to E-Commerce?' (2001) 5 *CLSR* 318.

Tamayo, Yvonne A., 'Who? What? When? Where? Personal Jurisdiction and the World Wide Web' (Spring 1998) 4:3 *Rich J L & Tech* 7.

Tang, Z., 'Parties' Choice of Law in E-Consumer Contracts' (2007) 3:1 *Journal of Private International Law* 113.

Tellini, D.E., 'Applicable Law and Electronic Consumer Contracts: A European Perspective' (2005) 16:1 *International Company and Commercial Law Review* 1.

Tillman, Christopher, 'The Relationship Between Party Autonomy and the Mandatory Rules in the Rome Convention' (2002) *JBL* 45.

Tridimas, Takis, and Eeckhaut, Piet, 'The External Competence of the Community and the case-law of the Court of Justice: Principle versus Pragmatism' (1994) 14 *YEL* 143.

Trout-McIntyre, Tammy S., 'Personal Jurisdiction and the Internet: Does the Shoe Fit?' (1997) 21 *Hamline L Rev* 223.

Turner, Mark, and Traynor, Mary, 'Electronic Commerce (EC Directive) Regulations 2002 – Worth the Wait?' (2002) 18 *CLSR* 396.

Van Der Hof, Simone, 'European Conflict Rules Concerning International Online Consumer Contracts' (2003) 12:2 *Information and Telecommunications Law* 165.

Van Loon, Hans, 'Globalisation and The Hague Conference on Private International Law' (2000) 2:4 *International Law Forum du droit international* 230.

Von Mehren, Arthur T., 'Recognition and Enforcement of Foreign Judgments: A New Approach for the Hague Conference?' (1994) 57 *L and Contemp Probs* 271.

Von Mehren, Arthur T., 'Drafting A Convention on International Jurisdiction and the Effects of Foreign Judgments Acceptable Worldwide: Can the Hague Conference Project Succeed?' (2001) 49 *Am J Comp L* 191.

Westermeier, J.T., 'Personal jurisdiction: Today's Hot Issue in E-Commerce,' JILT, <http://www2.warwick.ac.uk/fac/soc/law/elj/jilt/1998_3/westermeier>.

Whittaker, Simon, 'Judicial Interventionism and Consumer Contracts' (2001) 117 *LQR* 215.

Wild, C, Weinstein, .S, and Riefa, C, 'Council Regulation (EC) 44/2001 and Internet Consumer Contracts: Some Thoughts on Article 156 and the Futility of Applying 'In the Box; Conflict of Law Rules to the "Out of the Box" Borderless World' (2005) 19:1 *International Review of Law, Computers and Technology* 13.

Willingham, J., Barrett, 'Electronic Commerce and the Free Trade Area of the Americas' (2000) 6 *NAFTA: Law and Business Review of the Americas* 483.

Withers, Christopher, 'Jurisdiction Clauses and the Unfair Terms in Consumer Contract Regulations' (2002) 1 *LMCLQ* 56.

Yagura, Ryan, 'Does Cyberspace Expand the Boundaries of Personal Jurisdiction?' (1998) 38 *IDEA* 301.

Yeo, Matthews and Berliri, Marco, 'Conflict Looms Over Choice of Law in Internet Transactions' (1999) 4:4 *Electronic Commerce and Law Report* 85.

Zain, Saami, 'Regulation of E-Commerce: Is It Fair To Consumers?' (2000) 31 *UWLA Law Review* 163.

Zaphiriou, G.A., 'The EEC Convention on Jurisdiction and Enforcement of Judgments' (1969) *JBL* 74.

Zaphiriou, George A., 'Basis of the Conflict of Laws: Fairness and Effectiveness' (1988) 10 *Geo Mason UL Rev* 301.

Zembek, Richard, 'Jurisdiction and the Internet: Fundamental Fairness in the Networked World of Cyberspace' (1996) 6 *Albany Journal of Science and Technology* 339.

Books and Chapters in Books

Anton, A. E., *Private International Law*, 2nd ed, W. Green, Edinburgh, 1990.

Arnull, Anthony, Dashwood, Alan, Ross, Malcolm and Wyatt, Derrick, *Wyatt and Dashwood's European Union Law*, 4th ed, Sweet and Maxwell, London, 2000.

Atiyah, P.S., Adams, John S. and MacQueen, Hector, *The Sale of Goods*, 10th ed, Longman, Harlow, 2001.

Barth, Richard C. and Smith, Clint N., 'International Regulation of Enctyption: Technology Will Drive Policy,' in Kahin, Brian and Nesson, Charles (eds), *Borders in Cyberspace Information Policy and the Global Information Infrastructure*, The Mit Press, Cambridge, Massachusetts, 1997.

Basedow, Jurgen, 'The Effects of Globalization on Private International Law,' in Basedow, Jurgen and Kono, Toshiyuki (eds), *Legal Aspects of Globalization Conflict of Laws, Internet, Capital Markets and Insolvency in a Global Economy*, Kluwer Law International, The Hague, 2000.

Basedow, Jurgen and Kono, Toshiyuki (eds), *Legal Aspects of Globalization Conflict of Laws, Internet, Capital Markets and Insolvency in a Global Economy*, Kluwer Law International, The Hague, 2000.

Beaumont, Paul R., *Anton and Beaumont's Civil Jurisdiction in Scotland*, 2nd ed, W. Green, Edinburgh, 1995.

Bieber, Roland, and Monar, Joerg (eds), *Justice and Home Affairs in the European Union The Development of the Third Pillar*, European University Press, Brussels, 1995.

Black, Vaughan, 'Consumer Protection in the Conflict of Laws: Canada, the United States and Europe,' in Ramsay, Iain (ed), *Consumer Law in the Global Economy, National and International Dimensions*, Dartmouth, Aldershot, 1997.

Born, Gary B., *International Civil Litigation in Unites Stated Courts*, 3rd ed, Kluwer Law International, The Hague, 1996.

Bowett, D.W., 'Jurisdiction: Changing Patterns of Authority over Activities and Resources,' in MacDonald, R. St. J., and Johnston, D.M., *The Structure and Process of International Law*, Martinus Nijhoff Publishers, Dordrecht, 1986.

Briggs, Adrian and Rees, Peter, *Civil Jurisdiction and Judgments*, 2nd ed, LLP, London, 1997.

Briggs, Adrian, *The Conflict of Laws*, Oxford University Press, Oxford, 2002.

Burnstein, Matthew, 'A Global Network in a Compartmentalised Legal Environment,' in Boele-Woelki, Katharina and Kessedjian, Catherine (eds), *Internet Law Which Court Decides? Which Law Applies?*, Kluwer Law International, The Hague 1998.

Campbell, Dennis (ed), *Enforcement of Foreign Judgments*, LLP, London, 1997.

Campbell, Dennis (ed), *Law of International Online Business*, Sweet and Maxwell, London, 1998.

Capelletti, Mauro, Seccombe, Monica, and Weiler, Joseph (eds), *Integration Through Law*, Volume 1, Book 2, Walter de Gruyter, New York, 1986.

Cavers, David F., *The Choice of Law Process*, University of Michigan Press, Michigan, 1965.

Chissick, Michael and Kelman, Alistair, *Electronic Commerce Law and Practice*, 2nd ed, Sweet and Maxwell, London, 2000.

Chissick, Michael and Kelman, Alistair, *Electronic Commerce Law and Practice*, 3rd ed, Sweet and Maxwell, London, 2001.

Clarkson, C.M.V. and Hill, Jonathan, *Jaffey on the Conflict of Laws*, 1st ed, Butterworths, 1997.

Clarkson, C.M.V. and Hill, Jonathan, *Jaffey on the Conflict of Laws*, 2nd ed, Butterworths, 2002.

Clarkson, C.M.V. and Hill, Jonathan, *Jaffey on the Conflict of Laws*, 3rd ed, Butterworths, 2006.

Coteanu, Cristina, *Cyber Consumer Law and Unfair Trading Practices* (Aldershot, 2005).

Collins, Lawrence, *The Civil Jurisdiction and Judgments Act 1982*, Butterworths, London, 1983.

Dashwood, Alan, Hacon, Richard, J., and White, Robin C.A., *A Guide to the Civil Jurisdiction and Judgments Convention*, Kluwer Law and Taxation Publishers, Deventer, 1987.

De Boer, T.M., *Forty Years On: The Evolution of Post War Private International Law in Europe, Symposium in Celebration of the 40th Anniversary of the Centre of Foreign Law and Private International Law, University of Amsterdam, on 27 October 1989*, Kluwer, Deventer, 1990.

De Boer, T.M., and Kotting, R., 'Private International Law,' in Chorus, Jemen M., J., Gerver, Piet-Hein M., Hondius, Edwould H., and Koeekkoek, Alis K. (eds), *Introduction to Dutch Law For Foreign Lawyers*, 2nd revised ed, Kluwer, Deventer, 1993.

De Boer, T.M., 'The Relation between Uniform Substantive Law and Private International Law,' in Hartkamp, A.S., Hesselink, M.W., Hondius, E.H., Du Perron, C.E. and Vranken, J.B.M. (eds), *Towards a European Civil Code*, Martinus Nijhoff Publishers / Kluwer Academic Publishers Group, 1994.

Edwards, Lillian and Waelde, Charlotte (eds), *Law and the Internet Regulating Cyberspace*, Hart Publishing, Oxford, 1997.

Edwards, Lillian and Waelde, Charlotte (eds), *Law and the Internet A Framework for Electronic Commerce*, 2nd ed, Hart Publishing, Oxford, 2000.

Fentiman, Richard 'English Private International Law at the end of the 20th Century: Progress or Regress?' in Symeonides, Symeon, C. (ed), *Private International Law at the End of the 20th Century: Progress or Regress?*, Kluwer Law International, London, 2000.

Fletcher, Ian F., *Conflict of Laws and European Community Law*, North Holland Publishing Company, Amsterdam, 1982.

Froomkin, A. Michael, 'The Internet as a Source of Regulatory Arbitrage,' in Kahin, Brian and Nesson, Charles (eds), *Borders in Cyberspace Information Policy and the Global Information Infrastructure*, The MIT Press, Cambridge, Massachusetts, 1997.

Gaja, Giorgio, Hay, Peter and Rotunda, Ronald, D., 'Instruments for Legal Integration in the European Community – A Review,' in Capelletti, Mauro, Seccombe, Monica, and Weiler, Joseph (eds), *Integration Through Law*, Volume 1, Book 2, Walter de Gruyter, New York, 1986.

Gillies, Lorna, E., 'Adapting International Private Law Rules for Electronic Consumer Contracts,' in Rickett, Charles E.F., and Telfer, Thomas G.W. (eds), *International Perspectives on Consumers' Access to Justice*, Cambridge University Press, 2003.

Gillies, Lorna E., 'Legal Regulation of Risk in B2C Electronic Commerce – From Top-Down Regulation to Promoting Consumer Trust' in Ramsay, Iain, Salloum, John Horrox, Naomi, Mowatt, Geoff (eds), *Risk and Choice in Consumer Society*, Ant. Sakkoulas, Athens, 2007.

Goldring, John, 'Netting the Cybershark: Consumer Protection, Cyberspace, the Nation-State, and Democracy,' in Kahin, Brian and Nesson, Charles (eds), *Borders in Cyberspace Information Policy and the Global Information Infrastructure*, The MIT Press, Cambridge, Massachusetts, 1997.

Gottwald, Peter, 'Recognition and Enforcement of Foreign Judgments under the Brussels Convention,' in Carey-Miller, D.L., and Beaumont, Paul R. (eds), *The Option of Litigating in Europe*, The United Kingdom National Committee of Comparative Law, London, 1993.

Grewlich, Klaus W., *Governance in 'Cyberspace' Access and Public Interest in Global Communications*, Kluwer Law International, The Hague, 1999.

Halfmeier, Axel, 'Waving Goodbye to Conflict of Laws?' in Rickett, Charles E.F., and Telfer, Thomas G.W. (eds), *International Perspectives on Consumers' Access to Justice*, Cambridge University Press, 2003.

Hartley, T.C., 'Consumer Protection Provisions in the E.E.C Convention,' in North, P.M. (ed), *Contract Conflicts The EEC convention on the Law Applicable to Contractual Obligations: A Comparative Study*, North Holland Publishing Company, Amsterdam, 1982.

Hay, Peter, Lando, Ole, and Rotunda, Ronald, D., 'Conflict of Laws as a Technique for Legal Integration,' in Capelletti, Mauro, Seccombe, Monica, and Weiler, Joseph (eds), *Integration Through Law*, Volume 1, Book 2, Walter de Gruyter, New York, 1986.

Hay, Peter, *An Introduction to US Law*, 2nd ed, Butterworths, New Hampshire, USA, 1991.

Howells, Geraint and Wetherill, Stephen, *Consumer Protection and Law*, Ashgate, Aldershot, 2005.

Jaffey, A.J.E., *Topics in Choice of Law*, The British Institute of International and Comparative Law, London, 1996.

Joerges, Christian, and Gerstenberg, Oliver (eds), 'Private governance, democratic constitutionalism and supranationalism,' Proceedings of the COST A7 Seminar, Florence, 22 to 24 May 1997.

Johnson, David R., and Post, David G., 'The Rise of Law on the Global Network,' in Kahin, Brian and Nesson, Charles (eds), *Borders in Cyberspace Information Policy and the Global Information Infrastructure*, The MIT Press, Cambridge, Massachusetts, 1997.

Juenger, Friedrich K., 'Jurisdiction, Choice of Law and the Elusive Goal of Decisional Harmony,' in Sumampouw, Mathilde, Barnhoorn, L.A.N.M., Freedberg- Swartzburg, Judith A., Tromm, J.J.M., and Wade, J.A. (eds), *Law and Reality, Essays on National and International Procedural Law in Honour of Cornelis Carel Albert Voskuil*, Martinus Nijhoff Publishers, London, 1992.

Juenger, Friedrich K., *Choice of Law and Multistate Justice*, Dordrecht, 1993.

Kahin, Brian and Nesson, Charles (eds), *Borders in Cyberspace Information Policy and the Global Information Infrastructure*, The MIT Press, Cambridge, Massachusetts, 1997.

Kotting, Roelof, 'The Vicious Circle of Forum Law,' in De Boer, T.M., *Forty Years On: The Evolution of Post War Private International Law in Europe, Symposium in Celebration of the 40th Anniversary of the Centre of Foreign Law and Private International Law, University of Amsterdam, on 27 October 1989*, Kluwer, Deventer, 1990.

Kronke, Herbert, 'Applicable Law in Torts and Contracts in Cyberspace,' in Boele-Woelki, Katharina and Kessedjian, Catherine (eds), *Internet Which Court Decides? Which Law Applies?,* Kluwer Law International, The Hague, 1998.

Lessig,Lawrence, *Code and Other Laws of Cyberspace*, Basic Books, New York, 1999.

Mahoney, Ieuan G., 'United States,' in Campbell, Dennis (ed), *Law of International Online Business*, Sweet and Maxwell, London, 1998.

Millstein, Julian S., Nueburger, Jeffrey D., Weingart, Jeffrey P., *Doing Business on the Internet Forms and Analysis*, Law Journal Seminar – Press, New York, 1997.

Meeusen, Johan Pertegás Marta and Straetmans, Gert (eds), *Enforcement of International Contracts in the European Union: Convergence and Divergence between Brussels I and Rome I* (Antwerp, 2004).

Murray, Andrew D., 'Entering Into Contracts Electronically: The Real WWW,' in Edwards, Lillian and Waelde, Charlotte (eds), *Law and the Internet A Framework for Electronic Commerce*, 2nd ed, Hart Publishing, Oxford, 2000.

MacDonald, R.St.J., and Johnston, Douglas M., 'International Legal Theory: New Frontiers of the Discipline,' in MacDonald, R.St.J., and Johnston, D.M., *The Strucure and Process of International Law*, Martinus Nijhoff Publishers, Dordrecht, 1986.

MacDonald, R.St.J., and Johnston, D.M., *The Strucure and Process of International Law*, Martinus Nijhoff Publishers, Dordrecht, 1986.

McBryde, William W., *The Law of Contract in Scotland*, 2nd ed, W. Green, Edinburgh, 2001.

Nanz, Klaus-Peter, 'The Schengen Agreement: Preparing The Free Movement of Persons in the European Union,' in Bieber, Roland, and Monar, Joerg (eds), *Justice and Home Affairs in the European Union The Development of the Third Pillar*, European University Press, Brussels, 1995.

North, P.M. (ed), *Contract Conflicts The EEC convention on the Law Applicable to Contractual Obligations: A Comparative Study*, North Holland Publishing Company, Amsterdam, 1982.

North, P.M., 'The E.E.C Convention on the Law Applicable to Contractual Obligations (1980): Its History and Main Features,' in North, P.M. (ed), *Contract Conflicts The EEC convention on the Law Applicable to Contractual Obligations: A Comparative Study*, North Holland Publishing Company, Amsterdam, 1982.

North, P.M., 'Is European Harmonisation of Private International Law a Myth or Reality? A British Perspective,' in De Boer, T. M., *Forty Years On: The Evolution of Post War Private International Law in Europe, Symposium in Celebration of the 40th Anniversary of the Centre of Foreign Law and Private International Law, University of Amsterdam, on 27 October 1989*, Kluwer, Deventer, 1990.

North, P.M., and Fawcett, J.J., *Cheshire and North's Private International Law*, 12th ed, Butterworths, London, 1992.

North, P. M., 'The Draft UK / US Judgments Convention: A British Viewpoint,' in North, P. M., *Essays in Private International Law*, Oxford University Press, 1993.

North, P.M., and Fawcett, J.J., *Cheshire and North's Private International Law*, 13th ed, Butterworths, London, 1999.

North, P.M., 'Preface,' in Symeonides, Symeon, C. (ed), *Private International Law at the End of the 20th Century: Progress or Regress?*, Kluwer Law International, London, 2000.

Peers, Steve, *EU Justice and Home Affairs Law*, Pearson Education Limited, Harlow, Essex, 2000.

Perritt, Henry H., Jr., 'Jurisdiction in Cyberspace: The Role of Intermediaries,' in Kahin, Brian and Nesson, Charles (eds), *Borders in Cyberspace Information Policy and the Global Information Infrastructure*, The Mit Press, Cambridge, Massachusetts, 1997.

Peterson, Courtland H., 'American Private International Law at the End of the 20th Century: Progress or Regress?' in Symoenides, Symeon C. (ed), *Private International Law at the End of the 20th Century: Progress or Regress?*, Kluwer Law International, London, 2000.

Ramsay, Iain (ed), *Consumer Protection, Text and Materials*, London, 1989.

Ramsay, Iain (ed), *Consumer Law in the Global Economy, National and International Dimensions*, Dartmouth, Aldershot, 1997.

Ramsay, Iain, Salloum, John, Horrox, Naomi, Mowatt, Geoff (eds), *Risk and Choice in Consumer Society*, Ant. Sakkoulas, Athens, 2007.

Reed, Alan, 'Jurisdiction and Choice of Law in a borderless electronic environment,' in Akdeniz, Yaman, Walker, Clive and Wall, David (eds), *The Internet, Law and Society*, Pearson Education, Harlow, 2000.

Reed, Chris, *Internet Law, Text and Materials*, Butterworths, London, 2000.

Reed, Chris, *Internet Law, Text and Materials*, CUP, 2004.

Reimann Mathias, *Conflict of Laws In Western Europe A Guide Through The Jungle*, Transnational Publishers, Inc., New York, 1995.

Rickett, Charles E.F., and Telfer, Thomas G.W. (eds), *International Perspectives on Consumers' Access to Justice*, Cambridge University Press, 2003.

Scoles, Eugene F., and Hay, Peter, *Conflict of Laws*, 2nd ed, West Publishing Co., St Pauls Minnesota, 1992 together with 1995 packet.

Scoles, Eugene F., Hay, Peter, Borchers, Patrick J., and Symeonides, Symeon C., *Conflict of Laws*, 3rd ed, West Group, St Pauls Minnesota, 2000.

Stone, Peter, *The Conflict of Laws*, Longman, London, 1995.

Stone, Peter, *Civil Jurisdiction and Judgments in Europe*, Longman, London, 1998.

Stone, Peter, *EU Private International Law Harmonisation of Laws*, Elgar European Law, Cheltenham, 2006.

Storme, Marcel, 'Procedural Consequences for a Common Private Law for Europe,' in Hartkamp, A.S., Hesselink, M.W., Hondius, E.H., du Perron, C.E., and Vranken, J.B.M., *Towards a European Civil Code*, Martinus Nijhoff Publishers, London, 1994.

Straetmans, G., 'The Consumer Concept in EC Law,' in Meeusen, Johan Pertegás, Marta and Straetmans, Gert (eds), *Enforcement of International Contracts in the European Union : Convergence and Divergence between Brussels I and Rome I* (Antwerp, 2004).

Symeonides, Symeon, C. (ed), *Private International Law at the End of the 20th Century: Progress or Regress?*, Kluwer Law International, London, 2000.

Van Loon, J.H.A., 'The Increasing Significance of International Co-operation for the Unification of Private International Law,' in T. M. De Boer, *Forty Years On: The Evolution of Post War Private International Law in Europe, Symposium in Celebration of the 40th Anniversary of the Centre of Foreign Law and Private International Law, University of Amsterdam, on 27 October 1989*, Kluwer, Deventer, 1990.

Volkmer, Ingrid, 'Universalism and Particularism: The Problem of Cultural Sovereignty and Global Information Flow,' in Kahin, Brian and Nesson, Charles (eds), *Borders in Cyberspace Information Policy and the Global Information Infrastructure*, The MIT Press, Cambridge, Massachusetts, 1997.

Vonken, A.P.M.J., 'Balancing Processes in International Family Law, On the determination and weighing of interests in the conflicts of laws and the 'openness' of the choice of law system,' in T.M. De Boer, *Forty Years On: The Evolution of Post War Private International Law in Europe, Symposium in Celebration of the 40th Anniversary of the Centre of Foreign Law and Private International Law, University of Amsterdam, on 27 October 1989*, Kluwer, Deventer, 1990.

Waelde, Charlotte, 'International Private Law, Consumer and the Net: A Confusing Maze or a Smooth Path Towards a Single European Market?' in Lilian Edwards (eds), *The New Legal Framework For E-Commerce In Europe*, Oxford, 2005.

Weintraub, Russell, J., *Commentary on the Conflict of Laws*, 3rd ed, The Foundation Press, New York, 1986.

Weintraub, Russell, J., *Commentary on the Conflict of Laws*, 4th ed, The Foundation Press, New York, 2001.

Westenberg, Johan, W., 'The Quest for Unification,' in De Boer, T.M., *Forty Years On: The Evolution of Post War Private International Law in Europe, Symposium in Celebration of the 40th Anniversary of the Centre of Foreign Law and Private International Law, University of Amsterdam, on 27 October 1989*, Kluwer, Deventer, 1990.

Web sites

American Bar Association, Section on Business Law, Committee on Cyberspace Law, Subcommittee on International Transactions, 'Achieving Legal and Business Order in Cyberspace: A Report on Global Jurisdiction Issues Created by the Internet' (London Meeting Draft), at <http://www.kentlaw.edu/cyberlaw/docs/drafts/draft.rtf>.

Brand, Ronald A., 'Due Process as a Limitation on Jurisdiction in US Courts and a Limitation on the United States at the Hague Conference on Private International Law,' February 1998, at <http://www.state.gov/www/global/legal_affairs/brand.html>.

Chicago-Kent Project on Internet Jurisdiction, at <http://www.kentlaw.edu/cyberlaw/resources/guide.html>.

Consumer Project on Technology's discussion forum on the Hague Conference's proposed judgments convention with respect to internet jurisdiction and the Hague Conference on Private International Law's worldwide judgment's convention project available at <http://lists.essential.org/pipermail/hague-jur-commercial-law/2003-December/000848.html>; <http://lists.essential.org/pipermail/hague-jur-commercial-law/2003-December/000852.html>; <http://lists.essential.org/pipermail/hague-jur-commercial-law/2003-December/000854.html>.

E-Commerce Survey by Businesses, 13 October 2006, at <http://www.statistics.gov.uk/pdfdir/ecom1006.pdf>.

European Commission, Communication from the Commission to the European Parliament, the Council, the Economic and Social Committee and the Committee of the Regions, 'Consumer Policy Strategy 2002-2006,' COM 2002 (208) FINAL, 7 May 2002, <http://europa.eu.int/eur-lex/lex/LexUriServ/site/en/com/2002/com2002_0208en01.pdf>.

European Commission, 'Communication From the Commission to the European Parliament, The Council, The Economic and Social Committee and The Committee of the Regions, Consumer Policy Strategy 2002–2006,' Brussels COM (2002) 208, <http://eur-lex.europa.eu/pri/en/oj/dat/2002/c_137/c_13720020608en00020023.pdf>.

European Commission, 'Procedural law: The Commission advocates more efficiency in obtaining and enforcing judgments in the European Union,' in 'Update on the Single Market,' previously available at <http://www.europa.eu.int/comm/dg15/en/update/general/1038.html>.

European Commission, Justice and Home Affairs DG, 'Statement on Articles 15 and 73,' previously at <http://ec.europa.eu/civiljustice/homepage/homepage_ec_en_declaration.pdf>.

EU Commission, 'Proposal for a Decision establishing a programme of Community action in the field of Health and Consumer Protection 2007–2013' (COM(2005) 115 final 2005/0042 (COD)), available at <http://europa.eu.int/comm/consumers/overview/programme_2007-2013_en.htm>.

EU Commission, 'Regulation establishing a European Small Claims Procedure,' COM 2005 87 final, 2005/0220 (COD), 15 March 2005, <http://europa.eu.int/comm/justice_home/fsj/civil/recognition/fsj_civil_recognition_general_en.htm>.

EU Commission, 'Directive on Certain Aspects of Mediation in Civil and Commercial Matters,' COM 2004/0718 final, 2004/0251 (COD) <http://ec.europa.eu/civiljustice/adr/adr_ec_en.htm>.

European Small Claims Procedure, COM 2005 87 final, 2005/0220 (COD), 15 March 2005, <http://europa.eu.int/comm/justice_home/fsj/civil/recognition/fsj_civil_recognition_general_en.htm>.

EU Parliament, 'Opinion of the European Economic and Social Committee on the Proposal for a Regulation of the European Parliament and of the Council on the law applicable to contractual obligations (Rome I),' COM(2005) 650 final – 2005/0261 (COD), 13 September 2006, available at <http://eescopinions.eesc.europa.eu/eescopiniondocument.aspx?language=en&docnr=1153&year=2006>.

Federal Trade Commission, <http://www.ftc.gov/bcp/index.shtml>.

Geist, Michael, 'Is There a There? Towards Greater Certainty for Internet Jurisdiction' (2001) 16 *Berkeley Tech Law Journal* 1345 available at <http://www.law.berkeley.edu/journals/btlj/articles/vol16/geist/geist.pdf>.

Gillies, Lorna, E., 'A Review of the New Jurisdiction Rules for Electronic Consumer Contracts within the European Union,' Commentary, 2001 (1) *The Journal of Information, Law and Technology (JILT)* <http://elj.warwick.ac.uk/jilt/01-1/gillies.html> 28 February 2001.

Hörnle, Julia, 'The European Union Takes Initiative in the Field of E-Commerce,' Commentary 3 *The Journal of Information, Law and Technology (JILT)* (2000), <http://www2.warwick.ac.uk/fac/soc/law/elj/jilt/2000_3/hornle>.

IMRG, 'Internet Shopping Hits £3 Billion in November,' 14 December 2006, available at <http://www.imrg.org/ItemDetail.aspx?clg=News&cid=nws&pid=News_IMRG_Index&language=en-GB>.

Internet Society, The, 'All About the Internet' <http://www.isoc.org/internet/history/> and 'A Brief History of the Internet' <http://www.isoc.org/internet/history/brief.shtml>.

Neligan, Myles, 'Ten Years of Selling in Cyberspace,' BBC News, 25th October 2004, <http://news.bbc.co.uk/1/hi/business/3945775.stm>.

OECD, 'Measuring the Information Economy,' Chapter IV, Electronic Commerce, <http://www.oecd.org/dataoecd/34/35/2771139.pdf>. Copyright OECD.

OECD, 'Consumers in the Online Marketplace: The OECD Guidelines Three Years Later,' Report by the Committee on Consumer Policy on the Guidelines for Consumer Protection in the Context of Electronic Commerce," DSTI/CP(2002)4/FINAL, 3 February 2003, <http://www.oecd.org>. Copyright OECD.

Organisation of American States' Seventh Inter-American Specialised Conference on Private International Law (CIDIP-VII); <http://www.oas.org/dil/Report_Session_January_18_2007.pdf> and <http://www.oas.org/dil/esp/Choice_of_Law_Rules_for_Consumer_Contracts%20_nov_2006.pdf>.

Out-law.com, 'Christmas Figures Reveal Massive Rise in E-Commerce,' 20 January 2006, <http://www.out-law.com/default.aspx?page=6554>.

Peach, Randall J., 'Dot-com's Host Server in N.J. Isn't a Foothold for Jurisdiction,' New Jersey Law Journal, Law.com, August 29, 2000, <http://www.law.com>.

Perritt, Henry J., 'Electronic Commerce: Issues In Private International Law And The Role Of Alternative Dispute Resolution,' at <http://www.wipo.int/edocs/mdocs/mdocs/en/wipo_pil_01/wipo_pil_01_6.doc>.

Perry *et al*, 'Personal Jurisdiction in Cyberspace Where Can you be Sued, And Whose Laws Apply?' New York Law School Communications Media Centre, Volume VII, No.1, Fall 1998, previously available at <http://www.cmcnyls.edu/public/MLP/perryf98.htm>.

Steiner, Peter, 'On the Internet, nobody knows you're a dog,' *The New Yorker*, 5th July 1993, <http://www.cartoonbank.com>.

Trans-Atlantic Consumer Dialogue, <http://www.tacd.org>.

Trans Atlantic Consumer Dialogue, 'Resolution on the Proposed Hague Convention on Jurisdiction and Foreign Judgments in Civil and Commercial Matters,' Ecom-22-01, May 2001, <http://www.tacd.org>.

UK European Consumer Centre and EEJ-Net, Interim Report, January – July 2005, previously at <http://www.euroconsumer.org.uk/index/publications/other_reports/activity_0805_eec_interim_report.htm>.

Vartanian, Thomas P., 'Whose Internet is it Anyway? The Law of Jurisdiction in Cyberspace: Achieving Legal Order Among the World's Nations,' American Bar Association, Section on Business Law, Committee on Cyberspace Law, Subcommittee on Transnational Issues, 2000 Global Internet Summit, 13–14 March 2000, <http://www.kentlaw.edu/cyberlaw/resources/globalsummit.rtf>.

Westermeier, J.T., 'Personal jurisdiction: Today's Hot Issue in E-Commerce,' JILT, <http://www2.warwick.ac.uk/fac/soc/law/elj/jilt/98-3/westermeier.html>.

Wilske, Stephan and Schiller, Teresa 'International Jurisdiction in Cyberspace: Which States May Regulate the Internet?' <http://www.law.indiana.edu/fclj/pubs/v50/no1/wilske.html>.

WTO, 'Work Programme on Electronic Commerce,' Adopted by the General Council, 25 September 1998, <http://www.wto.org/english/tratop_e/ecom_e/wkprog_e.htm>.

Index